Organization and Administration in Higher Education

Second Edition

Situating strategic planning and budgeting within the organization and administration of higher education institutions, this text provides effective and proven strategies for today's change-oriented leaders. Bringing together distinguished administrators from two-year, four-year, public, and private colleges and universities, this volume provides both practical and effective guidance on the intricacies of the institutional structure, its functional activities, and contingency planning. *Organization and Administration in Higher Education* orients future administrators to the major areas of an academic institution and will assist higher education administrators in leading their institutions to excellence.

New in this Second Edition:

- New chapters on the impact of Title IX and social media on higher education.
- Updated coverage throughout on politics, technology, budgeting, program planning, and institutional changes.
- New end-of-chapter discussion prompts.

Kristina Powers is Associate Vice President of Institutional Research Services at Bridgepoint Education, USA.

Patrick J. Schloss is former President of Valdosta State University, USA.

Organization and Administration in Higher Education

Second Edition

Edited by
Kristina Powers and Patrick J. Schloss

Routledge
Taylor & Francis Group

NEW YORK AND LONDON

Second edition published 2017
by Routledge
711 Third Avenue, New York, NY 10017

and by Routledge
2 Park Square, Milton Park, Abingdon, Oxon OX14 4RN

Routledge is an imprint of the Taylor & Francis Group, an informa business

© 2017 Taylor & Francis

First edition published by Routledge 2013

Library of Congress Cataloging in Publication Data
A catalog record for this book has been requested

ISBN: 978-1-138-64119-8 (hbk)
ISBN: 978-1-138-64120-4 (pbk)
ISBN: 978-1-315-63065-6 (ebk)

Typeset in Minion
by Book Now Ltd, London

Dedication

To Tim Powers—your love, support, friendship, and kindness has made me a better person, professional, and researcher. I am forever grateful that we found each other and you are my husband.

—Kristina Powers

CONTENTS

FIGURES

TABLES

PREFACE

SECOND EDITION CHANGES

Often with a second edition, a reader wonders, "what has changed from the first edition?" or "is the second edition materially different from the first edition such that it is worth a new purchase and the time to read?" Of course, you, the reader are the ultimate judge; however, we wanted to share our methodological approach to the second edition so that you could quickly get these questions answered within the first few pages—and hopefully be encouraged to read the second edition, regardless of whether or not you read the first. The second edition includes the following significant changes:

- **Two new chapters**—Given the importance and current events in the areas of Title IX and social media, two new chapters have been added on these topics: Title IX and the Impact on Colleges and Universities Today and Over the Next Decade, and Purpose, Value, and Unintended Consequences of Social Media in Higher Education.
- **Two revamped chapters**—Based on feedback, the chapter on strategic planning has significantly changed to focus on Innovative Strategic Planning for the Institution. Additionally, the chapter on accreditation has been expanded to provide greater emphasis to an Overview of Accreditation.
- **Restructuring chapters**—Given the addition of the two new and two revamped chapters, compared to the first edition the book has been divided into three different sections that better align with the issues and challenges facing higher education administrators. This edition still begins with a focus on people within in higher education—students, faculty and staff—and how they interact with each other in five chapters. As higher education leaders are faced not only with managing resources efficiently, but also effectively and creatively, the second section has focused on covering precisely that aspect in four chapters. Finally, whereas the first edition focused on contingency planning, the third section has been broadened to focus on events and issues that shape higher education today throughout four chapters.
- **Current updates and developments for all chapters**—Each chapter includes relevant developments, including higher education politics, technology, budgeting, program planning, and institutional changes, where applicable.
- **Discussion prompts at the end of every chapter**—Based on discussions with course adopters of the book from the first edition, this addition was recommended for the second edition. Therefore, each chapter concludes with ten discussion prompts.

OVERVIEW OF THE BOOK

Successful technical schools, community colleges, liberal arts colleges, and comprehensive universities can be defined by the quality of their leadership teams. Effective planning and administration, regardless of strategic advantages, can elevate a school beyond its peers in a vast array of critical dimensions. All can enhance recruitment and retention, strengthen student life opportunities, increase extramural support and private giving, and advance the institution's reputation for excellence.

Irrespective of level, leaders who effectively utilize governance groups, planning tools, and budgeting techniques make a difference in the prospects of the institution. More important, they make a difference in the prospects of graduates and other stakeholders. Our primary goal in writing the second edition of *Organization and Administration in Higher Education* was to offer guidance to change-oriented higher education leaders—and to update the content throughout each chapter as well as adding new chapters. The book's contents are also valuable to pre-service administrators taking courses in higher education administration and finance. The book seeks to provide guidance in the best and worst of times, though it is during the hard times that outstanding leadership is most desperately needed.

We refer liberally to "postsecondary" and "higher education" institutions. These terms apply to any institution that builds upon a high school education, including technical schools, liberal arts colleges, specialty institutions, community colleges, and comprehensive universities. Relevant institutions may be private, requiring substantial tuition income, or public, receiving governmental support. They may be operated for profit or not for profit. We also reference institutions that provide Web-based programs or other distance learning options.

This book may be useful to anyone working at or toward the "cabinet" or "senior leadership" level. These individuals may be currently employed in a leadership position, using the contents to expand their perspective and skill, or they may be preparing for advancement into such a position, as would be the case with students in graduate leadership programs.

The contents cut across a wide range of disciplines and areas of expertise. Resource management, finance, law, human capital, and political action all form the basis of effective administration. No single author is likely to be as capable of addressing all these subjects as a team of specialized individuals. For this reason, we called upon a number of chapter authors. Each is a recognized expert in a critical area of higher education administration. These authors followed a common format and style so that, while the expertise underlying the text is diverse, the voice is relatively uniform. We appreciate the authors' flexibility in working within a preset template. While challenging for the authors, this consistency will benefit the reader.

The book is structured around functional themes in the management of postsecondary institutions. Not intended to be a "cookbook" or operations manual, the content strikes a balance between philosophical underpinnings and basic operations. The goal was to make the philosophical foundation clear to the reader while fully developing approaches consistent with that foundation.

The first broad theme is the structure of higher education. Related chapters range from a broad overview of institutions by style and a characterization, key leadership positions, managing human resources, to discussions of institutional and student governance. The second broad theme examines the efficient and effective management of resources. We combine the complex areas of strategic planning and budgeting within the context of organization and academic curriculum as well as managing accreditation. The final theme includes events and issues that shape higher education today, with chapters addressing key legal aspects, Title IX, social media, and crisis management for decision-making. The approach described in the text is comprehensive, including all levels of decision-makers and a full range of objectives. Similarly, the planning and budgeting constructs are applied to all typical postsecondary institutions.

Regardless of the specific focus of a chapter, certain content is woven throughout the text. Special attention is given to the importance of directing institutional resources to areas of strategic advantage, diminishing spending in areas of marginal distinction, cultivating alternative revenue sources, obtaining broad-based support for strategic decisions, and creating a culture of accountability and excellence. Traditional challenges of crisis management, communication, curriculum development, and institutional communication are also addressed.

We often focus on the challenge of declining state appropriations for state institutions and diminishing discretionary dollars from families for private institutions. Efficiency, focus, and accountability have become the defining standards for contemporary educational leaders in all sectors. Regardless of the chapter, there is continual reference to approaches that allow institutions to do more with less.

Legal issues, such as Title IX, social media, and crisis management, have become an increasing part of the landscape in higher education, particularly with respect to personnel issues. For this reason, we have devoted a chapter to each of these topics.

Best practices that have been reported in the literature and for which certain institutions have become renowned serve as a foundation for concepts and techniques described in the text. The content is also shaped by "lessons learned" by the authors, most of whom have held high-level administrative positions in postsecondary institutions. We believe these lessons, combined with the authors' deep knowledge of the professional literature, will make this work both practical and authoritative for current and future administrators.

ACKNOWLEDGMENTS

We would like to express our heartfelt appreciation to those who have made this book possible. First, we would like to acknowledge all of the chapter authors. We are grateful to the chapter authors who returned for the second edition—updating their chapters and being bold enough to join us for a second exciting publishing adventure. We are pleased to have added new chapter authors, who all graciously agreed to contribute their expertise to the project. The authors' collective expertise resulted in a resource of breadth and depth for current and future administrators.

Julia Carpenter-Hubin and Lydia Snover extend their thanks to Greg McDonough of the Massachusetts Institute of Technology for his work to provide updated administrative salaries for the chapter, Key Leadership Positions and Performance Expectations.

It is with great gratitude that we thank Routledge, especially our editor—Heather Jarrow—who has been with us through both editions. It was with delight that we read Heather's email in August 2015, inviting us to submit a second edition. She helped bring this book to completion in the first edition and kindly invited us to create a second edition, providing valuable feedback for enhancements. We are privileged to work with the dedicated and experienced team at Routledge.

We would like to thank the anonymous individuals who took the time to respond to Routledge's survey questionnaire regarding the first edition so that we could make valuable enhancements to the second edition. We have incorporated much of the feedback and comments that consistently emerged. Your early contributions have led to an improved and robust second edition.

We deeply admire the editing expertise of Tracy Kendrick. Her attention to detail—on both the first and second editions—combined with passion for her profession, was the patina on this collective effort. We are thrilled that Tracy was willing to apply her exceptional editing skills to both editions.

Finally, an honorable mention goes to the family and friends of all contributors to this book; it is with their support that we are able to complete the research about which we are so passionate.

Part I

Higher Education Institutions
and the People in Them

1

UNDERSTANDING THE RANGE OF POSTSECONDARY INSTITUTIONS AND PROGRAMS

Angela E. Henderson and Kristina Powers

INTRODUCTION

When traveling, be it for business or for pleasure, we tend to compare and contrast our new location with more familiar surroundings. The new location may be bigger or smaller, more or less diverse, or warmer or colder than our current home. Having a common set of criteria for evaluation allows us to make comparisons and get acclimated. The same is true for higher education institutions and, thanks to a national database with a common set of definitions and variables, it possible to compare more than 7,000 postsecondary schools that submit federal data to the National Center for Education Statistics (NCES) each year.

Current and future administrators seeking to better understand the higher education landscape will benefit from this chapter's detailed descriptions of types of institutions and quality indicators that key external stakeholders such as parents, prospective students, legislators, and media focus on when evaluating an institution. Key internal stakeholders such as presidents, vice presidents, deans, and directors also focus on quality indicators, but do so with unique management challenges described herein.

PRIVATE, PUBLIC, AND PROPRIETARY

Within the general structure of higher education, there are two main categories of postsecondary institutions: public and private. Private institutions are further divided into two types: not-for-profit and for-profit (proprietary).

Public Institutions

The National Center for Education Statistics defines a public institution as "an educational institution whose programs and activities are operated by publicly elected or appointed school officials and which is supported primarily by public funds" (IPEDS, n.d.b, para. 44).

Public institutions include a variety of levels and program offerings, from two-year community colleges to doctorate-granting research-level universities. In 2014–15, public institutions constituted 35% of the degree-granting postsecondary institutions in the United States that submitted data to NCES, with a total enrollment of over 14.6 million students (IPEDS, n.d.a). The key commonality among these institutions is that they all receive some form of public funding.

The number of public institutions in the United States has increased in the last 30 years. In fall 1980, there were fewer than 1,500 public degree-granting institutions, the majority of which were two-year colleges (NCES, 2014). Public four-year degree-granting institutions were less plentiful, comprising less than 40% of all public degree-granting institutions (NCES, 2014). Enrollment at degree-granting public institutions totaled nearly 9.5 million, which represented more than three-quarters (78%) of all students attending postsecondary institutions in 1980 (NCES, 2014). By fall 2014, the number of public degree-granting institutions had risen to just over 1,700, a 14% increase from 1980 (NCES, 2014). As the number of public degree-granting institutions has grown, so too has their total enrollment, to over 14.6 million in fall 2014, a 54% increase from 1980 (NCES, 2014).

Private Institutions

While public institutions receive some public funding, private institutions are "usually supported primarily by other than public funds, and operated by other than publicly elected or appointed officials" (IPEDS, n.d.b, para. 33). They must therefore fund all costs through private means, such as tuition. Private institutions utilize one of two financial structures: not-for-profit or for-profit (or proprietary). Not-for-profit institutions operate similarly to non-profit organizations in that surplus revenue must be directed to institutional goals. For-profit institutions have no restrictions on surplus revenue, but are arguably subject to greater accountability than their counterparts.

Because private institutions do not receive public funding, they have the flexibility to provide educational experiences not available at public institutions, such as faith-based programs. Like their public counterparts, private institutions include two- and four-year postsecondary schools with various degree programs and specialties. In 2014–15, private institutions constituted 65% of the degree-granting postsecondary institutions in the United States that submitted data to NCES, with a total enrollment of nearly 5.6 million, or 28% of all students enrolled (IPEDS, n.d.a). The 35% of private institutions classified as private not-for-profit enrolled 4 million students, and the 30% classified as private for-profit enrolled over 1.5 million (IPEDS, n.d.a). Similar to the trend shown by public institutions, the number of private institutions rose between 1980 and 2014; however, the increase was much greater—84% during that timeframe (NCES, 2014).

Private Not-for-Profit Institutions

Despite the overall growth in private institutions, the total number of degree-granting private not-for-profit institutions increased by only 10% from 1980 to 2014. Figure 1.1 illustrates the distribution of private not-for-profit degree-granting institutions by type as of 2014 (NCES, 2014). With the gain in the number of four-year private not-for-profit degree-granting institutions, total enrollment grew to more than 4 million students, an increase of 60% over fall 1980 (NCES, 2014). Enrollment at private not-for-profit degree-granting institutions grew by 66% at four-year institutions; however, enrollment at the two-year institutions dropped by nearly 73% during the same time (NCES, 2014).

Private For-Profit Institutions

The slight growth in private not-for-profit degree-granting institutions was overshadowed by the considerable growth in private for-profit institutions. While only 165 private for-profit degree-granting institutions existed in fall 1980, by fall 2014 there were 1,457; a nearly 800% increase (NCES, 2014). The number of four-year institutions rose most dramatically, from 20 to 784, an increase of over 3,800% (NCES, 2014). The number of two-year institutions also grew, from 147 to 673, or 358% (NCES, 2014). As illustrated in Figure 1.1, the distribution of two- and four-year private for-profit degree-granting institutions was nearly even, at 46% and 54% respectively, by fall 2014 (NCES, 2014).

As would be expected with such a substantial increase in the number of institutions, enrollment at private for-profit degree-granting institutions rose sharply. In fall 1980, just over 110,000 students were enrolled at private for-profit degree-granting institutions—less than 1% of all students attending postsecondary schools (NCES, 2014). By fall 2014, that number had increased by nearly 1,300% to 1.5 million students, or nearly 8% of all postsecondary students (NCES, 2014). Four-year degree-granting institutions accounted for much of this overall growth; their enrollment totaled nearly 1.3 million students in fall 2014, an increase of 4,400% from 1980 (NCES, 2014). While two-year degree-granting institutions also experienced enrollment growth, the gain (244%) was not as dramatic (NCES, 2014).

Overall Geographical Distribution of Institutions and Enrollment

In 2014, over 4,800 degree-granting colleges and universities in the United States with a collective enrollment of over 20 million students provided data to the National Center for Education Statistics (NCES), a division of the U.S. Department of Education responsible for collecting and analyzing data related to education (IPEDS, n.d.a). Public degree-granting institutions represented 35% of the respondents and enrolled nearly

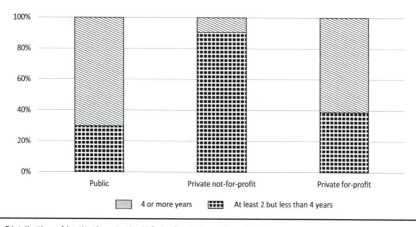

Figure 1.1 Distribution of Institutions in the U.S. by Control and Type, 2014

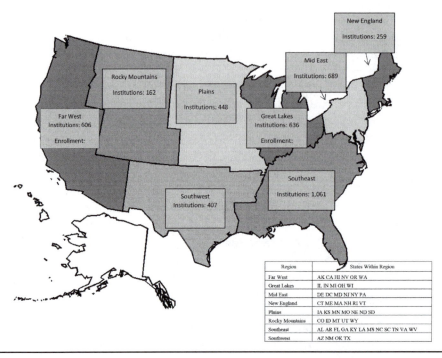

Figure 1.2 Distribution of Carnegie Classified, Degree-Granting, U.S. Institutions and Enrollment by Region, 2014

three-quarters of all students (approximately 15 million), while private degree-granting institutions enrolled nearly 5.6 million students (IPEDS, n.d.a).

Figure 1.2 shows the total number of degree-granting institutions and students enrolled in each of eight regions (as defined by NCES) of the United States as of 2014 (IPEDS, n.d.a). The Southeast region, which includes 12 states (Alabama, Arkansas, Florida, Georgia, Kentucky, Louisiana, Mississippi, North Carolina, South Carolina, Tennessee, Virginia, and West Virginia), accounts for the largest percentage of institutions and student enrollment: 27% of all institutions and 23% of total enrollment. More institutions lie within the Southeast region than in the New England, Rocky Mountains, and Southwest regions combined. Overall, the Southeast region contains the highest number of public and private for-profit institutions, while the Mid East region contains the highest number of private not-for-profit institutions.

CLASSIFICATION OF INSTITUTIONS

Since the 1970s, degree-granting postsecondary institutions in the United States that have attained accreditation and that report data to NCES have been classified using the Carnegie Classification system (Carnegie, n.d.a). The Carnegie Commission's efforts to organize "a classification of colleges and universities to support its program of research and policy analysis" prompted the development and implementation of the categorization process (Carnegie, n.d.a, para. 1). The classifications include all U.S. Title IV eligible, degree-granting colleges and universities that must report data to the National Center for Education Statistics and that conferred degrees in the year prior to the classification update (Carnegie, n.d.c). Of the 4,888 institutions that reported data to NCES in 2014–15, 4,275 (87%) received Carnegie Classifications (IPEDS, n.d.a).

Since its implementation in 1973, and under subsequent revisions and enhancements, the system has become the definitive source of institutional comparison categorization data. This has become increasingly important, as more than 4,000 institutions are classified within the Carnegie Classification system. The Carnegie Classifications allow institutions and researchers to make informed decisions regarding the selection of peer institutions based on analytical groupings of institutions using consistent standards.

The Carnegie Classifications have been revised periodically to reflect changes in higher education, most recently in 2015 (Carnegie, n.d.a). Institutions are categorized based upon data they submit to the Department of Education, the College Board, and the National Science Foundation (McCormick & Zhao, 2005). Carnegie researchers compile the data and classify the institutions based on location, enrollment, programs, and degrees conferred (McCormick & Zhao, 2005). The latest update to the system retained the organizational structure based on the six classifications of institutions implemented in 2005 (discussed in detail in the following paragraphs) but significantly revised the methodology used to classify institutions.

Prior to 2015, the most substantial update to the Carnegie Classification system occurred in 2005, when the structure was revised and the number of categories expanded to make it easier for institutions to identify potential peer institutions (Carnegie, n.d.c). The 2005 classifications (and subsequent updates) were structured around the core aspects of institutions: programs offered, students enrolled, degrees conferred, and size and setting (Carnegie, n.d.a). They were thus designed to allow researchers to "represent and control for institutional differences, and ... to ensure adequate representation of sampled institutions, students, or faculty" (Carnegie, n.d.a, para. 1).

Reflecting the need to select appropriate comparison institutions, the 2005 update offered more specificity than its predecessors, with 33 classifications—15 more than the 2000 version (Carnegie, 2001; Carnegie, n.d.d). The classification of Associate's Colleges experienced the most substantial shift, from a single classification in 2000 to 14 distinct classifications in the 2005 system (Carnegie, 2001; Carnegie, n.d.d). Doctoral and Master's institutions each gained one additional classification level in the 2005 structure (Carnegie, 2001; Carnegie, n.d.d).

In addition to providing a more granular structure, the 2005 system reflected a change in methodology, drawing on the most recent data provided by institutions to NCES "to maximize the timeliness of the classifications" (Carnegie, n.d.c, para. 18). This approach categorized institutions based on "time-specific snapshots of institutional attributes and behavior" (Carnegie, n.d.b, para. 1) rather than on three-year averages of variables, as in previous Carnegie Classification systems. The structure and methodology established with the 2005 revisions formed the basis for the current Carnegie Classifications, which incorporate timely data points and changing demographics to inform current methodologies and classifications. Since 2005, the Carnegie structure has included six areas of classification, with the addition of a seventh in 2015, as shown in Table 1.1.

Table 1.1 Carnegie Classifications and Descriptions, 2015

Classification	Description
Basic Classification	Traditional classification framework developed by the Carnegie Commission on Higher Education in 1970
Size and Setting Classification	Based on institutional size and residential character
Undergraduate Instructional Program Classification	Based on the level of undergraduate degrees awarded, the proportion of bachelor's degree majors in the arts and sciences, in professional fields, in career and technical fields (two-year institutions), and the extent to which an institution awards graduate degrees in the same fields in which it awards undergraduate degrees
Graduate Instructional Program Classification	Based on the level of graduate degrees awarded, the number of fields represented by the degrees awarded, and the mix or concentration of degrees by broad disciplinary domain
Enrollment Profile Classification	Based on the mix of students enrolled at the undergraduate and graduate/professional levels
Undergraduate Profile Classifications	Based on the proportion of undergraduate students who attend part- or full-time; academic achievement characteristics of first-year, first-time students; and the proportion of entering students who transfer in from another institution

Source: Carnegie (n.d.d, n.d.e, n.d.f, n.d.g, n.d.h, n.d.i).

As of 2015, the most commonly used Carnegie Classification system, the Basic Classification, categorizes institutions into seven areas: Doctoral Universities, Master's Colleges and Universities, Baccalaureate Colleges, Baccalaureate/Associate's Colleges, Associate's Colleges, Special Focus Institutions (theological, medical, law, etc.), and Tribal Colleges. The descriptions for each level are shown in Table 1.2 and addressed in detail in the following section.

Table 1.2 Basic Carnegie Classification and Descriptions, 2015

Classification	Description
Doctoral Universities	Award at least 20 research/scholarship doctoral degrees annually (excluding professional doctorates)
Master's Colleges and Universities	Award at least 50 master's degrees and fewer than 20 doctoral degrees annually
Baccalaureate Colleges	Award at least 50% of all degrees as baccalaureate degrees or higher and fewer than 50 master's degrees or 20 doctoral degrees awarded annually
Baccalaureate/Associate's Colleges	Four-year institutions that award fewer than 50% of degrees at the associate's level
Associate's Colleges	Award only associate's degrees
Special Focus Institutions	Award degrees in a single field or set of related fields
Tribal Colleges	All colleges and universities within the American Indian Higher Education Consortium

Source: Carnegie (n.d.d).

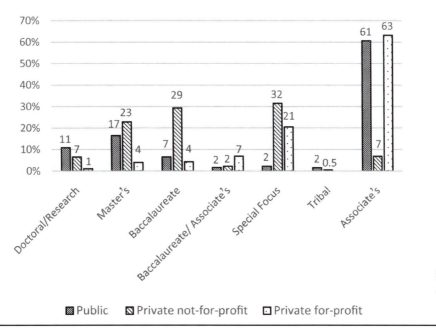

Figure 1.3 Distribution of Institutions in the U.S. by Control and Carnegie Classification, 2014–15

Source: IPEDS (n.d.a).

Table 1.3 shows the total number of institutions and students enrolled at each type of institution by Carnegie Classification as of 2014–15; Figure 1.3, the distribution of institutions by control and Carnegie Classification. Note that although new classifications were released in February 2016, institutional and enrollment data will not be available from NCES for these classifications until 2017–18.

Doctoral/Research Universities

Doctoral Universities have been referred to in prior incarnations of the Carnegie Classification system as Doctorate-Granting, Doctoral/Research I, Doctoral/Research II, Doctoral/Research Extensive, and Doctoral/Research Intensive institutions. In fall 2014, 295 institutions—just under 7% of the total number of institutions—were classified under one of the three Carnegie Doctoral University categories (IPEDS, n.d.a). Nearly 40% were classified as Research Universities: very high research activity; 33% as Research Universities: high research activity; and 30% as Doctoral/Research universities (IPEDS, n.d.a). The majority of Doctoral Universities (60%) were public; over a third (37%) were private not-for-profit; and the remaining 3% were private for-profit (IPEDS, n.d.a). Enrollment at Doctoral Universities totaled over 5.6 million in fall 2014, with over 76% of these students attending public institutions (IPEDS, n.d.a). Despite accounting for only 2% of the Doctoral/Research total enrollment, private for-profit institutions enrolled 13% of all students attending institutions classified as Doctoral/Research Universities (IPEDS, n.d.a).

The 2005 version first separated these institutions into three distinct categories based on their level of research activity (very high research activity, high research activity,

Table 1.3 Distribution of U.S. Carnegie Institutions and Students by Institution Control and Carnegie Classification, 2014–15

Classification Level	Total Number of Institutions	Total Number of Students	Public Institutions				Private Not-for-Profit Institutions				Private for-Profit Institutions			
			Number of Institutions	Percent of Institutions	Number of Students	Percent of Students	Number of Institutions	Percent of Institutions	Number of Students	Percent of Students	Number of Institutions	Percent of Institutions	Number of Students	Percent of Students
RU/VH: Research Universities (Very high research activity)	108	2,963,714	73	68%	2,398,724	81%	35	32%	564,990	19%	0	0%	0	0%
RU/H: Research Universities (high research activity)	98	1,823,151	74	76%	1,517,672	83%	24	24%	305,479	17%	0	0%	0	0%
DRU: Doctoral/Research Universities	89	882,774	30	34%	416,975	47%	49	55%	354,767	40%	10	11%	111,032	13%
Master's/L: Master's Colleges and Universities (larger programs)	392	3,504,595	169	43%	2,048,526	58%	209	53%	1,148,423	33%	14	4%	307,646	9%
Master's/M: Master's Colleges and Universities (medium programs)	176	766,865	61	35%	390,891	51%	106	60%	362,032	47%	9	5%	13,942	2%

Master's/S: Master's Colleges and Universities (smaller programs)	117	355,701	39	33%	194,440	55%	61	52%	124,011	35%	17	15%	37,250	10%
Bac/A&S: Baccalaureate Colleges—Arts & Sciences	261	456,264	33	13%	92,743	20%	222	85%	350,615	77%	6	2%	12,906	3%
Bac/Divers: Baccalaureate Colleges—Diverse Fields	372	697,931	74	20%	263,963	38%	261	70%	404,972	58%	37	10%	28,996	4%
Bac/Assoc: Baccalaureate/Associate's Colleges	133	276,441	27	20%	127,681	46%	37	28%	69,421	25%	69	52%	79,339	29%
Assoc: Associate's Colleges (all)	1,729	7,469,607	988	57%	7,069,867	95%	113	7%	60,169	1%	628	36%	339,571	5%
Special Focus Institutions (all)	760	615,031	37	5%	70,646	11%	519	68%	367,617	60%	204	27%	176,768	29%
Tribal: Tribal Colleges	33	17,691	25	76%	13,986	79%	8	24%	3,705	21%	0	0%	0	0%
Total	4,268	19,829,765	1,630		14,606,114		1,644		4,116,201		994		1,107,450	

Source: IPEDS (n.d.a).

and all other research activity) (Carnegie, n.d.c, para. 5). This level was determined through analysis of research and development expenditures, number of research staff, and number of doctoral degrees awarded (Carnegie, n.d.b, sec. 2). A pair of indices were created "based on aggregate level of research activity and per-capita research activity" to examine institutional variation on the index measures; an institution's "distance from a common reference point" determined its placement into one of the three classifications (Carnegie, n.d.b, sec. 2). As the two indices were considered equal, institutions rating very high or high on either index range were classified as very high research activity or high research activity Research Universities respectively (Carnegie, n.d.b, sec. 2). Institutions not meeting the very high or high criteria for either index (or not included in the data) were assigned to the Doctoral Universities moderate research activity classification (Carnegie, n.d.b, sec. 2).

Table 1.4 illustrates the types of institutions within the doctorate-granting category and provides examples of each.

Master's Colleges and Universities

As of fall 2014, 685 institutions in the United States, or 16% of the total number of institutions classified, were categorized as Master's Colleges and Universities (IPEDS, n.d.a). Of these, 57% were Master's Colleges and Universities (larger programs) and 55% were private not-for-profit institutions (IPEDS, n.d.a). Enrollment in Master's Colleges and Universities totaled over 4.6 million, with the majority (57%) of students attending public institutions (IPEDS, n.d.a).

Table 1.4 Examples of Doctorate-Granting Universities by Carnegie Classification 2010 and 2015

Classification 2010	Classification 2015	Example Institutions
RU/VH: Research Universities (very high research activity)	R1: Doctoral Universities (very high research activity)	Public: University of Virginia, Washington State University, Georgia Institute of Technology
		Private not-for-profit: Cornell University, Duke University, University of Notre Dame
RU/H: Research Universities (high research activity)	R2: Doctoral Universities (high research activity)	Public: Clemson University, Rutgers University, Texas Tech University
		Private not-for-profit: Baylor University, Nova Southeastern University, Wake Forest University
DRU: Doctoral/Research Universities	R3: Doctoral Universities (moderate research activity)	Public: Bowie State University, Florida A&M University, South Carolina State University
		Private not-for-profit: Brigham Young University, Pepperdine University, St. John's University
		Private for-profit: Argosy University, Capella University, University of Phoenix

Source: Carnegie (n.d.j).

Designation as a Master's College or University is dependent upon the number of master's degrees an institution awards per year. In general, institutions classified as Master's-level must award a minimum of 50 master's degrees per year and fewer than 20 research doctoral degrees (Carnegie, n.d.b). Colleges and universities awarding fewer than 50 master's degrees per year are eligible for inclusion in the Master's category if their Enrollment Profile classification indicates they are "Exclusively Graduate/Professional" or "Majority Graduate/Professional" institutions that award more graduate/professional degrees than undergraduate degrees (Carnegie, n.d.b, sec. 3). The three categories of Master's Colleges and Universities are shown in Table 1.5. Table 1.6 provides examples of Master's institutions for each of the Carnegie Classification categories.

Baccalaureate Colleges

As of fall 2014, Baccalaureate Colleges totaled 715 in number, representing nearly 18% of all institutions considered (IPEDS, n.d.a). Over 70% of Baccalaureate Colleges were private not-for-profit institutions (IPEDS, n.d.a). Enrollment at Baccalaureate Colleges totaled nearly 1.6 million students, with over half attending private not-for-profit institutions (IPEDS, n.d.a). Of students enrolled at Baccalaureate Colleges, 39% attended institutions classified as Bac/Diverse: Baccalaureate Colleges—Diverse Fields (IPEDS, n.d.a).

Similar to the classification methodology used for the Master's Colleges and Universities, Baccalaureate Colleges are categorized into three groups based on the number of baccalaureate degrees awarded per year (shown in Table 1.7). Institutions that award a majority of their degrees at the Associate's level but have at least one Baccalaureate degree program are classified as Baccalaureate/Associate's Colleges. Table 1.8 shows examples of Baccalaureate Colleges for each of the 2010 and 2015 Carnegie Classification categories.

Associate's Colleges

Totaling 1,729 in number as of 2014, Associate's Colleges represented over 40% of all Carnegie institutions (IPEDS, n.d.a). While the majority (57%) were public, over a third (36%) were private for-profit institutions (IPEDS, n.d.a). Enrollment at

Table 1.5 Carnegie Master's Colleges and Universities Classifications 2015

Carnegie Classification	Description
Master's Colleges and Universities: Larger programs	Awards 200 or more master's degrees
Master's Colleges and Universities: Medium programs	Awards 100 to 199 master's degrees
Master's Colleges and Universities: Smaller programs	Awards 50–99 master's degrees or fewer than 50 master's degrees with an Enrollment Profile of Exclusively Graduate/Professional or Majority Graduate/Professional with more graduate degrees awarded than undergraduate

Source: Carnegie (n.d.b, sec. 3).

Table 1.6 Examples of Master's Colleges and Universities by Carnegie Classification 2010 and 2015

Classification 2010	Classification 2015	Example Institutions
Master's/L: Master's Colleges and Universities (larger programs)	M1: Master's Colleges and Universities (larger programs)	Public: Alabama State University, Marshall University, University of North Florida Private not-for-profit: Concordia University, Liberty University, Mercer University Private for-profit: DeVry University—California, Full Sail University, University of Phoenix—Atlanta Campus
Master's/M: Master's Colleges and Universities (medium programs)	M2: Master's Colleges and Universities (medium programs)	Public: College of Charleston, SUNY at Fredonia, Western Oregon University Private not-for-profit: Bethel University, Excelsior College, Park University Private for-profit: American InterContinental University, Aspen University, Western International University
Master's/S: Master's Colleges and Universities (smaller programs)	M3: Master's Colleges and Universities (smaller programs)	Public: Coastal Carolina University, University of Guam, Virginia State University Private not-for-profit: Elon University, Lourdes College, Warner University Private for-profit: Argosy University—Tampa, ITT Technical Institute—Indianapolis, University of Phoenix—Tulsa Campus

Source: Carnegie (n.d.j).

Table 1.7 Baccalaureate Colleges Classifications, 2015

Classification	Description
Bac/A&S: Baccalaureate Colleges—Arts & Sciences	Of institutions that award at least half of their undergraduate degrees as bachelor's degrees—those with at least half of bachelor's degree majors in arts and sciences fields
Bac/Diverse: Baccalaureate Colleges—Diverse Fields	Of institutions that award at least half of their undergraduate degrees as bachelor's degrees—those not included in the Arts & Sciences group
Bac/Assoc: Baccalaureate/ Associate's Colleges	Bachelor's degrees represent at least 10%, but less than half, of undergraduate degrees

Source: Carnegie (n.d.b, sec. 4).

Table 1.8 Examples of Baccalaureate Colleges by Carnegie Classification 2010 and 2015

Classification 2010	Classification 2015	Example Institutions
Bac/A&S: Baccalaureate Colleges—Arts & Sciences	Baccalaureate Colleges: Arts & Sciences Focus	Public: Kentucky State University, New College of Florida, Virginia Military Institute
		Private not-for-profit: Beloit College, Furman University, Occidental College, Thomas Aquinas College
		Private for-profit: Argosy University—Denver, Argosy University—Los Angeles, Argosy University—Phoenix Online Division
Bac/Diverse: Baccalaureate Colleges—Diverse Fields	Baccalaureate Colleges: Diverse Fields	Public: California Maritime Academy, Nevada State College, University of South Carolina—Aiken
		Private not-for-profit: Atlanta Christian College, Huntingdon College, Texas Lutheran University
		Private for-profit: Daniel Webster College, Post University, University of Phoenix—Louisville Campus
Bac/Assoc: Baccalaureate/Associate's Colleges	Baccalaureate/Associate's Colleges (broken out into a separate classification with two categories: 1) Baccalaureate/Associate's Colleges: Mixed Baccalaureate/Associate's Colleges 2) Baccalaureate/Associate's Colleges: Associate's Dominant)	Public: Great Basin College, St. Petersburg College, Vermont Technical College
		Private not-for-profit: Arkansas Baptist College, Lincoln College, New England Institute of Technology
		Private for-profit: DeVry University—Michigan, Platt College—Los Angeles

Source: Carnegie (n.d.j).

Associate's Colleges totaled just under 7.5 million, with 95% of students attending public Associate's Colleges (IPEDS, n.d.a).

The most substantial revisions in the 2015 Carnegie Classification update were changes in the methodology for classifying Associate's Colleges. Prior to 2015, institutions were classified as Associate's Colleges if they awarded less than 10% of all undergraduate degrees as bachelor's degrees or awarded no higher degree than the associate's degree (Carnegie, n.d.b.). These institutions were then divided into 14 categories based on institutional control, location, size, and structure (Carnegie, n.d.b). Specifically, Associate's Colleges were classified according to control of institution (public, private, or proprietary), size (small, medium, or large), location (rural-serving, suburban-serving, or urban-serving), and number of campuses (single or multi-campus) (Carnegie, n.d.b, sec. 1).

For the 2015 revised methodology, institutions were divided into two preliminary groups for additional classification: Associate's Colleges and Two-Year Special Focus Institutions. Institutions not meeting the Special Focus criteria (discussed in the following section) received additional analysis based on program and student mix to ensure appropriate classification in the Associate's Colleges categories. Program mix was determined by distribution of awards within three broad field categories (arts & sciences, professional, and career & technical). The percentage of degrees/certificates awarded in each of these areas was used to determine an institution's classification as high transfer, mixed transfer/career & technical, or high career & technical. Associate's Colleges awarding 75% of their degrees/certificates in career & technical fields were classified as having a high career & technical program mix; those with 30–49% of awards in career & technical fields were classified as mixed transfer/career & technical program mix, and those with less than 30% of awards in career & technical fields were classified as high transfer program mix.

The other half of the equation, student mix, was based on "proportion of total enrollment accounted for by 'degree-seeking' students (as opposed to 'non-degree' students), and the ratio of fall headcount to annual unduplicated headcount" (Carnegie Classification of Institutions of Higher Education, 2015). To determine the final classification of an institution, the ratios of degree-seeking students and fall headcount were multiplied and colleges were designated as high traditional, high non-traditional, or mixed traditional/non-traditional based on the resulting figure (Carnegie Classification of Institutions of Higher Education, 2015). Through this methodology, the 2015 Classification system for Associate's Colleges places institutions into one of nine categories, reflecting an intentional shift towards an emphasis on program and student makeup. Categorizing Associate's Colleges based on distribution of degrees/certificates awarded and student type presents a more holistic perspective of an institution than did prior incarnations of the classification system.

Special Focus Institutions and Tribal Colleges

Special Focus Institutions offer specialized degree programs, such as a "concentration of degrees in a single field or set of related fields, at both the undergraduate and graduate levels" (Carnegie, n.d.b, sec. 5). In 2014, 760 institutions received the Special Focus designation; nearly 70% were private not-for-profit institutions (IPEDS, n.d.a). Enrollment at Special Focus Institutions totaled over 615,000, representing 3% of all students attending Carnegie institutions (IPEDS, n.d.a).

In the 2015 update, classification as a Special Focus institution was determined based on distribution of degrees awarded; institutions that awarded a large percentage of degrees/certificates in a single field were classified into a subset of Special Focus groups. Placement into Special Focus groupings occurred if institutions met any of the following criteria: (1) awarding 75% or more of degrees/certificates in a single field (excluding general studies/humanities), (2) providing 70–74% of awards in a single field and awards in two or fewer other fields, or (3) providing 60–69% of awards in a single field and awards in only one other field (Carnegie Classification of Institutions of Higher Education, 2015). Exceptions to the 75% cutoff may be made if an institution has declared "a special focus on the College Board's Annual Survey of Colleges, or if an institution's only recognized accreditation was from an accrediting body related to the special focus categories" (Carnegie, n.d.b, sec. 5).

The inclusion of two-year institutions in the Special Focus classification in the 2015 update represented a major change to the system; a number of institutions previously classified as Associate's Colleges were shifted to the Special Focus category. In prior years, the Special Focus Institution category included only schools that awarded degrees at the baccalaureate level or higher. The addition of the two-year institution category reflects an effort to ensure more appropriate classification and alignment between Associate's and Baccalaureate institutions.

Tribal Colleges constitute less than 1% of all Carnegie institutions and are classified based on institutional reporting status as a Tribal College to NCES and membership in the American Indian Higher Education Consortium (Carnegie, n.d.b, sec. 6). In 2014, there were 33 Tribal Colleges with a total enrollment of just under 20,000, representing 0.1% of all students attending Carnegie institutions (IPEDS, n.d.a).

Carnegie Overall

The detailed descriptions above illustrate just one facet of the Carnegie system: the Basic Classification. The other classifications, while not as commonly employed, provide consistent means for grouping and comparing institutions based on an array of variables. As the definitive system of institutional classification in the United States, Carnegie Classifications are used by administrators, education researchers, educational systems, and a host of other organizations and individuals

KEY INSTITUTIONAL QUALITY INDICATORS

Despite the numerous categories of indicators that theoretically enable key stakeholders (prospective students, parents, administrators, researchers, legislators, media, etc.) to compare institutions, there is variation within each category. The remainder of this chapter focuses on quality indicators that key stakeholders can use to better understand institutions, as well as on unique management challenges related to improving those indicators.

Each year, more than 20 million students attend college (NCES, 2014) after exploring a variety of options to select the institution that best meets their academic and personal needs. There are common institutional quality indicators that influence prospective students and their families in this search. Also utilized by local, state, and federal governments, boards of regents/trustees, independent watch organizations, think-tanks, and others, these indicators include academic selectivity (e.g., high-school grade point average, SAT/ACT test scores), retention and graduation rates, and employment and job placement rates. An additional indicator, less often used by prospective students and parents but tracked by other aforementioned constituent groups, is the alumni giving rate. Each of these indicators is discussed below with regard to the various types of institutions.

College Entry Indicators

Many colleges and universities utilize specific admissions criteria to determine if a prospective student has the potential to be successful at the institution. Typical quantitative entry criteria include high-school grade point average (HS GPA) and standardized test scores (i.e., SAT or ACT). Qualitative indicators such as high-school curriculum rigor and quality may also factor into admissions decisions. Each of these admission entry indicators has an administrative and financial impact on higher education institutions. Research (Braxton, 2000; Camara & Kimmel, 2005;

Heller, 2002) has shown that students who are more academically qualified are more likely to achieve academic success.

Institutions without admissions criteria are referred to as open-access colleges and universities. As the term suggests, these institutions permit access to all students who show a willingness to enroll in college and have the ability to pay for it through financial aid and/or other funding means. Open-access institutions do not review prior academic history or standardized test scores for admissions purposes but often utilize that information when advising students on course selection.

In the fall 2014 IPEDS Institutional Characteristics Survey, 4,642 institutions reported having an open admissions policy for all or most entering first-time undergraduate-level students. Of those institutions, 42% were less than two-year (below associate), 41% were at least two- but less than four-year, and 17% were four- or more year institutions (Integrated Postsecondary Education Data System., n.d.c). When viewed by control type, 64% of open-access institutions were private for-profit, 28% were public, and 7% were private not-for-profit institutions (Integrated Postsecondary Education Data System, n.d.c). Between 2004 and 2014, the number of open-access institutions increased by 1,443. The majority of these were private for-profit institutions, which is consistent with earlier stated findings that enrollment increased the most at for-profit institutions.

Administrative and Financial Impact

While the number of applications for admission is an indicator of interest, even more so is the number of accepted students, as it reflects how many interested students have met an institution's admissions requirements. Another key figure, and arguably the only one that matters, is the actual enrollment of students in the institution. The more precise that an institution can be in enrolling students who are likely to graduate, the fewer administrative and financial resources that the institution expends unnecessarily. Concentrating their financial and administrative resources on assisting students in obtaining a degree allows institutions to invest in student success rather than in replacing students who have transferred or dropped out.

Retention and Graduation Rates and Outcome Measures

Retention and graduation rates are corollaries of college entry indicators. According to federal definitions, retention is defined as:

> A measure of the rate at which students persist in their educational program at an institution, expressed as a percentage. For four-year institutions, this is the percentage of first-time bachelor's (or equivalent) degree-seeking undergraduates from the previous fall who are again enrolled in the current fall. For all other institutions this is the percentage of first-time degree/certificate-seeking students from the previous fall who either re-enrolled or successfully completed their program by the current fall.
>
> (IPEDS, n.d.b)

Graduation rates are calculated from "the number of full-time first-time degree-seeking students in a particular year (cohort) and their status after six years at four-year institutions or after three years at less than four-year institutions" (NCES, 1997, p. II-1). The "rate is calculated as the total number of completers within 150% of normal time divided by the revised cohort minus any allowable exclusions" (IPEDS, n.d., para. 14).

Since spring 2016, Outcome Measures (OM)—a new IPEDS survey—has been required of institutions. OM is different than other IPEDS surveys in that it collects award and enrollment data from degree-granting institutions on awards made to all students within a six- and eight-year period, employing a broader definition than traditional success measures that include only first-time, full-time students. The survey collects award data on a wider swath of students including part-time, first-time; full-time, non-first-time (e.g., transfer students); and part-time, non-first-time, as well as first-time, full-time students. The collection of data for these additional student groups addressed a common complaint among higher educational professionals that IPEDS data only counted outcomes of first-time, full-time student cohorts, excluding the increasingly substantial population of non-traditional students.

While more than 40 years of research (Braxton, 2000; Heller, 2002; Tinto, 1993) have established links between college entry indictors, retention rates, and graduation rates, those links were based on data drawn exclusively from first-time, full-time students. The American Institutes for Research estimated in a 2016 report that "51.2% of entering students were ignored by the IPEDS graduation rate from 2004 to 2013 (approximately 24,500,000 students)" (Soldner, Smither, Parsons, & Peek, 2016, p. 11).

As retention and graduation rates are measures of institutional efficiency and effectiveness, they are often monitored by prospective students and their parents, boards of regents/trustees, state legislators, federal legislators, think-tanks, and interest groups. However, there has been more and more interest among these groups to broaden the scope of students counted in graduation rates. The Student Achievement Measure (SAM) responded to that demand in 2013 by:

> tracking student movement across postsecondary institutions to provide a more complete picture of undergraduate student progress and completion within the higher education system. SAM is an alternative to the federal graduation rate, which is limited to tracking the completion of first-time, full-time students at one institution
> (Student Achievement Measure, 2016, p. 1)

As evidenced by national efforts such as SAM in 2013, the addition of the IPEDS OM survey in 2016, and the American Institutes for Research's study in 2016 (Soldner et al., 2016), there is growing momentum to report on all students. This trend will likely continue, generating more data for research and thus allowing for a greater understanding of the factors that influence student success in all students.

Administrative and Financial Impact

Colleges and universities are held accountable for offering students an opportunity to complete a quality program of study that prepares them for the job market in a timely manner. The question remains whether retention and graduation rates are valid measures of gauging an institution's success in providing students with a quality education and preparing them for employment, since these rates do not count or reflect the success of all students. Per federal definitions, retention and graduation rates are based solely on the success of entering traditional freshmen. This can present a challenge for institutions where this cohort accounts for only a small percentage of the students. However, for institutions where a large proportion (75%+) of enrollment is comprised of first-time, full-time students, these rates are a good measure of quality. As many as "20 percent of the bachelor's degree recipients who start in a four-year school earn the degree from a different four-year school" (Adelman, 2007, para. 7) and are not included in institutional retention and graduation rates. According to the Department of Education, "roughly half of traditional-age undergraduates are excluded from the Education Department's calculation of graduation rates" (Adelman, 2006, p. 57), which is consistent with the findings of the American Institutes for Research (Soldner et al., 2016).

With such variance among institutions, it is unlikely that retention and graduation rates are universally appropriate measures of efficiency and effectiveness. Institutions that have higher retention and graduation rates, which are highly correlated with more academically qualified students, are viewed as being more efficient and effective than community colleges that educate students who would not qualify for admission to a selective institution. As a result, administrators at lower-tiered institutions who focus on increasing retention and graduation rates may be working against stacked odds, and may be better off channeling efforts and resources toward other student progression metrics, such as course completion or certificate completion.

Impact on Doctoral Institutions

Doctorate-granting universities, the most selective of all postsecondary institutions, are large institutions that offer a wide array of degree programs and extracurricular opportunities that appeal to prospective students. As a result, these institutions tend to receive considerably more applications for admission than they can accommodate. This allows them to be selective and offer admission only to the most academically qualified applicants, who tend to graduate at higher rates than students at lower-tiered institutions.

Administrative and Financial Impact on Doctoral Institutions

Not only do doctoral institutions typically enjoy above-average retention and graduation rates because they attract and recruit the most academically qualified students, but their ability to predict, and in some cases cap, the number of entering students enables them to select the best applicants for the slots available. On its face, this ability to select a limited number of the most highly qualified applicants may seem ideal; however, if the number of students entering the institution is restricted, so too is the revenue stream generated by tuition, and in the case of state institutions, state appropriations.

Impact on Master's and Bachelor's Institutions

While master's and bachelor's institutions are often less selective than doctoral institutions, they often offer degree programs in specific areas such as education, liberal arts, or nursing, as well as clubs, sports, and other non-academic activities, albeit on a more limited scale than at doctoral universities. Since these institutions tend to focus their recruitment efforts on a specific region, they generally receive fewer applications than doctoral institutions; however, their acceptance rates are usually higher due to lower admissions requirements.

Administrative and Financial Impact on Master's and Bachelor's Institutions

Master's and bachelor's institutions face a different set of administrative and financial impacts than doctoral universities. One issue unique to these institutions is the challenge of retaining students who enroll with the intention of transferring to a doctoral university. Students unable to meet the admissions criteria at a doctoral university will enroll at a master's or bachelor's institution with the goal of transferring to their first-choice school. This has a domino effect on the institution's indicators of success, as a student who transfers is not included in its retention and graduation rates. Additionally, there is a financial impact on the institution, which must increase its recruiting efforts. For an institution to realize an increase in the incoming cohort, it must replace the number of students lost to transfer and increase enrollment beyond that number.

Impact on Community Colleges and Technical Institutions

Community colleges and technical institutions educate students in liberal arts and technical/trade areas. They are often referred to as "access institutions" because their graduates gain access to bachelor's (or higher) degree-granting institutions that they would not have been able to attend otherwise. Admission and entry indicators are virtually non-existent for these colleges, which do not require standardized test scores and generally have an open admissions policy. Additionally, many of their students do not fit the cohort definition and thus are not counted in retention and graduation rates. Community colleges and technical institutions measure their success by focusing on the rate at which students transfer to a four-year institution and obtain a bachelor's degree.

Administrative and Financial Impact on Community Colleges and Technical Institutions

While individual student entry indicators are not evaluated for admissions due to the open admissions policy, community colleges and technical institutions are still accountable for their retention and graduation rates. Typically, these rates capture approximately 20% of their student population (Adelman, 2007), making it difficult to measure institutional and student success accurately. While community colleges receive "credit for students who transfer … the four-year colleges to which they transfer get no credit when these transfer students earn a bachelor's degree, as 60 percent of traditional-age community college transfers do" (Adelman, 2007, para. 7).

UNIQUE MANAGEMENT CHALLENGES

While the various types of institutions have much in common, each has its own unique management challenges. The remainder of this chapter focuses on these challenges, some of which are discussed in greater detail throughout the book.

Variation in Tuition-Setting Policies

Public and private institutions that rely on tuition and fees as a primary source of revenue suffered a new low in 2010. According to the State Higher Education Executive

Table 1.9 Entity with Primary Authority for Establishing Public Tuition, by State

State	Governor	Legislature	Statewide Coordinating or Governing Agency for Multiple Systems	Coordinating or Governing Board(s) for Individual Systems	Local District Governing Board(s)	Individual Institutions
Alabama						X
Alaska				X		
Arizona				X		
Arkansas						X
California		X				
Colorado			X			
Connecticut				X		
Delaware						X
Florida		X				
Georgia				X		
Hawaii			X			
Idaho			X			
Illinois				X		
Indiana						X
Iowa			X			
Kansas				X		
Kentucky			X			
Louisiana		X				
Maine				X		
Maryland				X		
Massachusetts						X
Minnesota				X		
Mississippi				X		
Missouri						X
Montana			X			
Nebraska				X		
New Hampshire				X		
New Mexico					X	
New York				X		
North Carolina			X			
North Dakota			X			
Ohio						X
Oklahoma			X			
Oregon					X	
Pennsylvania				X		
South Carolina						X
South Dakota			X			
Tennessee				X		
Texas				X		
Utah			X			
Vermont				X		
Virginia						X
West Virginia				X		
Wisconsin				X		
Wyoming						X
Total	0	3	11	19	2	10

Source: SHEEO (2011).

Officers, "educational appropriations per FTE [full-time equivalent student] (defined to include state and local support for general higher education operations) fell to $6,454 in 2010, a 25-year low in inflation-adjusted terms" (SHEEO, 2011, p. 9).

Typically, boards of trustees are primarily responsible for setting tuition and fees at private institutions. The authority for increasing tuition and fees at public institutions varies by state, such that SHEEO has conducted *The Survey of State Tuition, Fees, and Financial Assistance Policies* six times since 1988. Table 1.9 shows the 2010–2011 survey results of the entity with the primary authority for establishing public tuition by state.

The group most commonly responsible for establishing tuition costs for public institutions is the coordinating or governing board(s) for individual systems, followed by state coordinating or governing agencies for multiple systems, individual institutions, the legislature, and the local district governing board(s). Contrary to popular belief, the governor of a state does not set tuition. With the exception of the ten states that allow individual institutions to determine tuition (shown in Table 1.9), all states appoint individuals indirectly connected to higher education to determine the price of tuition. Awareness of the authority that sets tuition, as well as the procedures for determining tuition rates, is vital to institutional administrators, as these factors play a significant role in balancing the institutional budget.

Unionized vs. Non-Unionized Institutions

Unions and the role they play in higher education vary from state to state. In some states, institutions are heavily influenced by unions, which may have an important hand in their administration and internal and external financing; in other states, unions do not even exist. Unions can include faculty as well as staff (e.g., police, physical plant employees). This section outlines the advantages and disadvantages of unionization. One advantage is that unions adhere to a thoroughly vetted set of rules and policies, which university administrators can utilize to govern the institution. In the absence of unions, university administrators must negotiate policy changes and implementation with faculty and staff, spending a substantial amount of time obtaining their input and meeting with leaders to discuss options.

Alternatively, the rules and policies governing unions may be inflexible and minimize an institution's ability to quickly take advantage of, or respond to, economic or environmental changes. While a non-unionized institution that allows for quick action may sound appealing, flexibility brings its own challenges. Administrators who implement changes too quickly are often criticized for not fully vetting the consequences and may be asked to step down (e.g., Carlson, 2011; Fain, 2008a, 2008b, 2010; Stripling, 2011).

Location

Institutional location has significant administrative and financial implications. Colleges and universities in poorer, rural, low-technical areas may lack the philanthropic resources that many other institutions rely on. An urban campus can quickly become landlocked, requiring the purchase of new property and buildings. It is important to note that institutions located within smaller cities can also be landlocked.

In this context, being "landlocked" means that the institution faces challenges in obtaining land contiguous to its campus at fair market value.

Student Body Composition

The composition of the student body greatly impacts the administration and financing of institutional operations. Colleges and universities with high retention and graduation rates typically have a relatively stable and predictable freshman cohort. These institutions are thus able to plan for the number of courses and seats freshmen will need, increasing or decreasing programs and services based on the size of the incoming class.

Many institutions admit transfer students, which complicates administrative and financial operations. For example, as transfer students often have completed some general education courses toward their degrees, they require upper-division courses, which tend to be more expensive because of the need for smaller classes and require a greater investment on the part of the institution.

Housing and Students Living on Campus

Residential housing presents unique financial challenges, be they related to new construction in response to increased demand or the need to ensure sufficient facilities for the existing student body. There is a positive correlation between on-campus living and higher retention and graduation rates (Pascarella & Terenzini, 2005). With the increased enrollment experienced by many institutions, it should come as no surprise that on-campus housing capacity has risen from nearly 2.6 million to 3.1 million (20%) over a 10-year period from fall 2004 to 2014 (IPEDS, n.d.a). The Carnegie size and setting classification includes three residential classifications:

- *Primarily residential:* "25–49 percent of degree-seeking undergraduates live on campus and at least 50 percent attend full time" (Carnegie, n.d.k).
- *Highly residential:* "At least half of degree-seeking undergraduates live on campus and at least 80 percent attend full time" (Carnegie, n.d.k).
- *Primarily non-residential:* "Fewer than 25 percent of degree-seeking undergraduates live on campus and/or fewer than 50 percent attend full time (includes exclusively distance education institutions)" (Carnegie, n.d.k).

While retention and graduation rates may be increased through on-campus housing, so too are liability and administrative challenges. Campuses without housing facilities close each day when the last class concludes, whereas residential campuses remain open throughout the year and around the clock.

CONCLUSION

The large number of colleges and universities necessitates the collection of multiple variables, hence the creation of classifications for comparison purposes. Analysis of annual data allows us to identify patterns and trends at higher education institutions and among the students they serve. As when traveling to a location for the second or third time, we find that the destination is familiar but never exactly the same.

DISCUSSION PROMPTS

1. In terms of classification, which type of institution appeals to you most as an administrator, faculty member, staff member, undergraduate student, or graduate student? Does your choice vary based on the role you consider? Why?

2. Institutions are grouped by characteristics so as to better understand the sets of institutions. While the Carnegie Classification system provides a comprehensive set of categories, are there other grouping categories that might be beneficial?

3. Identify three opportunities and threats for each institutional sector: public, private not-for-profit, and private for-profit.

4. In what ways do key quality indicators influence the institutional mission? What quality indicators does your institution use to measure progress?

5. What are two ways in which institution location might influence institutional operations?

6. Identify innovative opportunities for responding to financial challenges and improving student completion.

7. As an administrator, how would you determine the appropriate level of housing (primarily residential, highly residential, or primarily non-residential) for your institution? What would you base your decision on?

8. What are the advantages and disadvantages for each institution type in setting tuition policies? Do advantages and disadvantages change depending on perspective (i.e., administrator, faculty, staff, or student)?

9. What are some potential challenges for moving from one classification type (e.g., Carnegie Classification, sector) to another?

10. What institutional types make the most financial and administrative sense for partnerships? Why? What potential challenges could arise from collaboration?

REFERENCES

Adelman, C. (2006). The propaganda of numbers. *Chronicle of Higher Education, 53*(8), 57.

Adelman, C. (2007). Making graduation rates matter. *Inside Higher Ed.* Retrieved March 30, 2011 from http://www.insidehighered.com/views/2007/03/12/adelman

Braxton, J. M. (Ed.). (2000). *Reworking the student departure puzzle.* Nashville, Tennessee: Vanderbilt University Press.

Camara, W. J., & Kimmel, E. W. (Eds.). (2005). *Choosing students: Higher education admissions tools for the 21st century.* Mahwah, New Jersey: Lawrence Erlbaum Associates.

Carlson, S. (2011). Provost at Southern Illinois U. at Carbondale resigns after just a month. [Electronic version]. *The Chronicle of Higher Education.* Retrieved March 17, 2011 from http://chronicle.com

Carnegie Classification of Institutions of Higher Education. (2015). *The 2015 update.* Retrieved February 2016 from http://carnegieclassifications.iu.edu/

Carnegie Foundation for the Advancement of Teaching. (2001). *The Carnegie classification of institutions of higher education: 2000 edition.* Retrieved March 3, 2016 from http://carnegieclassifications.iu.edu/downloads/2000_edition_data.xls

Carnegie Foundation for the Advancement of Teaching. (2016). *2015 update facts & figures.* Retrieved February 15, 2016 from http://carnegieclassifications.iu.edu/downloads/CCIHE2015-FactsFigures-01Feb16.pdf

Carnegie Foundation for the Advancement of Teaching. (n.d.a). *About the Carnegie classifications.* Retrieved February 15, 2016 from http://carnegieclassifications.iu.edu/

Carnegie Foundation for the Advancement of Teaching. (n.d.b). *Basic classification methodology.* Retrieved February 17, 2016 from http://carnegieclassifications.iu.edu/methodology/basic.php

Carnegie Foundation for the Advancement of Teaching. (n.d.c). *Definitions*. Retrieved March 2, 2016 from http://carnegieclassifications.iu.edu/definitions.php

Carnegie Foundation for the Advancement of Teaching. (n.d.d). *Classification description: Basic classification*. Retrieved February 18, 2016 from http://carnegieclassifications.iu.edu/classification_descriptions/basic.php

Carnegie Foundation for the Advancement of Teaching. (n.d.e). *Classification description: Enrollment profile classification*. Retrieved February 18, 2016 from http://carnegieclassifications.iu.edu/classification_descriptions/enrollment_profile.php

Carnegie Foundation for the Advancement of Teaching. (n.d.f). *Classification description: Graduate instructional program classification*. Retrieved February 18, 2016 from http://carnegieclassifications.iu.edu/classification_descriptions/grad_program.php

Carnegie Foundation for the Advancement of Teaching. (n.d.g). *Classification description: Size and setting classification*. Retrieved February 18, 2016 from http://carnegieclassifications.iu.edu/classification_descriptions/size_setting.php

Carnegie Foundation for the Advancement of Teaching. (n.d.h). *Classification description: Undergraduate instructional program classification*. Retrieved February 18, 2016 from http://carnegieclassifications.iu.edu/classification_descriptions/ugrad_program.php

Carnegie Foundation for the Advancement of Teaching. (n.d.i). *Classification description: Undergraduate profile classification*. Retrieved February 18, 2016 from http://carnegieclassifications.iu.edu/classification_descriptions/undergraduate_profile.php

Carnegie Foundation for the Advancement of Teaching. (n.d.j). *Lookup and listings*. Retrieved February 18, 2016 from http://carnegieclassifications.iu.edu/lookup/standard.php

Carnegie Foundation for the Advancement of Teaching. (n.d.k). *Size and setting classification methodology*. Retrieved May 20, 2016 from http://carnegieclassifications.iu.edu/methodology/size_setting.php

Fain, P. (2008a). Baylor U. fires president, citing failure to unite campus. [Electronic version]. *The Chronicle of Higher Education*. Retrieved March 17, 2011 from http://chronicle.com

Fain, P. (2008b). President of Southwestern Oregon Community College resigns hastily. [Electronic version]. *The Chronicle of Higher Education*. Retrieved March 17, 2011 from http://chronicle.com

Fain, P. (2010). Birmingham-Southern's president resigns while trustees explain college's financial meltdown. [Electronic version]. *The Chronicle of Higher Education*. Retrieved March 17, 2011 from http://chronicle.com

Heller, D. E. (Ed.). (2002). *Condition of access: Higher education for lower income students*. Westport, Connecticut: Praeger.

Integrated Postsecondary Education Data System. (n.d.a). *IPEDS data center*. [Data file]. Retrieved February 16, 2016 from http://nces.ed.gov/ipeds/datacenter/

Integrated Postsecondary Education Data System. (n.d.b). *IPEDS glossary*. Retrieved May 20, 2016 from http://nces.ed.gov/IPEDS/glossary

Integrated Postsecondary Education Data System. (n.d.c). *IPEDS data center*. [Data file]. Retrieved May 20, 2016 from http://nces.ed.gov/ipeds/datacenter/

McCormick, A. C., & Zhao, C. (2005). Rethinking and reframing the Carnegie classification. *Change,* September/October, 50–57.

National Center for Education Statistics. (1997). *IPEDS graduation rate survey guidelines for survey respondents*. Retrieved from http://nces.ed.gov/ipeds/surveys/1997/pdf/grsguide.pdf

National Center for Education Statistics. (2014). *Digest of education statistics*. [Data files]. Retrieved May 20, 2016 from https://nces.ed.gov/programs/digest/d15/tables/dt15_303.10.asp?current=yes

Pascarella, E. T., & Terenzini, P. T. (2005). *How college affects students*. San Francisco: Jossey-Bass.

Soldner, M., Smither, C., Parsons, K., & Peek, A. (2016, May). *Toward improved measurements of student persistence and completion*. Retrieved from American Institutes for Research: http://www.air.org/sites/default/files/downloads/report/Toward-Improved-Measurement-Persistance-and-Completion-May-2016.pdf

State Higher Education Executive Officers (SHEEO) (2011). *State higher education finance FY 2010*. Retrieved from http://www.sheeo.org/finance/shef/SHEF_FY10.pdf

Stripling, J. (2011). Resigning chief of Huntsville campus had turbulent relations with faculty. [Electronic version]. *The Chronicle of Higher Education*. Retrieved March 17, 2011 from http://chronicle.com

Student Achievement Measure. (2016, May). *About*. Retrieved from Student Achievement Measure: http://www.studentachievementmeasure.org/about

Tinto, V. (1993). *Leaving college: Rethinking the cause and cures of student attrition* (2nd ed.). Chicago: The University of Chicago Press.

2

KEY LEADERSHIP POSITIONS AND PERFORMANCE EXPECTATIONS

Julie Carpenter-Hubin and Lydia Snover

INTRODUCTION

American colleges and universities are like snowflakes, with structures that appear similar to the casual observer though in fact no two have been found to be exactly alike. Degree-granting institutions can be tiny; the Yeshiva Toras Chaim Talmudical Seminary enrolled 15 students and the Central Texas Commercial College reported a total enrollment of 11 for fall 2014. At the upper end of the scale is The Ohio State University; with over 58,000 students on its main campus alone, the school is larger than 38 of Ohio's 50 largest cities (www.ohio-demographics.com/cities_by_population). Research universities, technical and community colleges, religious institutes, liberal arts colleges, and trade schools all have unique facets that require different organizations of administrators and leaders. Even within a particular sector and among institutions of similar sizes, administrative authority may be maintained centrally or decentralized to the academic units. Higher education institutions are complex structures that branch and connect, each forming a distinctive administrative pattern. This chapter examines these unique structures that make up the landscape of American higher education.

GOVERNING BOARDS

The enormous diversity among American colleges and universities is reflected in their disparate governance structures and functions. Although the culture and process of governance varies widely among institutions, the presence of lay citizen governing boards distinguishes American higher education from most of the rest of the world, where universities ultimately are dependencies of the state.

(Association of Governing Boards of
Universities and Colleges, 2010, Foreword)

Institutions of higher education are led by independent governing boards using a variety of names (e.g., board of trustees, corporation board, or board of overseers). The New England Association of Schools and Colleges Commission on Institutions of Higher Education Standards for Accreditation clearly outlines the role of governing boards:

3.3 The governing board is the legally constituted body ultimately responsible for the institution's quality and integrity.

3.4 The board demonstrates sufficient independence to ensure it can act in the institution's best interest. The board assures representation of the public interest in its composition and reflects the areas of competence needed to fulfill its responsibilities. Two-thirds or more of the board members, including the chair, are free of any personal or immediate familial financial interest in the institution, including as employee, stock-holder or shareholder, corporate director, or contractor.

3.5 Members of the governing board understand, accept, and fulfill their responsibilities as fiduciaries to act honestly and in good faith in the best interest of the institution toward the achievement of its educational purposes in a manner free from conflicts of interest.

(New England Association of Schools
and Colleges, n.d., Standard 3)

Governing boards of public institutions are often appointed by public officials such as governors, while boards of private institutions are self-perpetuating. Governing boards of private institutions recruit members using a variety of criteria. Depending upon the mission of the institution, members might represent alumni, the local community, business, or academic disciplines.

In a private college or university, the governing board has fiduciary responsibility for preserving the long-term viability and health of the institution and adhering to the purposes for which the institution was established. It is generally the responsibility of the board to select the president or chief operating officer of the institution. The board must work closely with the senior officers of the institution to ensure that operating practices are consistent with long-term goals and the mission of the college or university. Boards of trustees are often required to approve changes in degree offerings, investment policies, budget and expenditure policies, and appointment of faculty. The following are examples of responsibilities with which various private institutions charge their governing boards.

- Massachusetts Institute of Technology:

  The Corporation—the board of trustees of the Massachusetts Institute of Technology—holds a public trust: to see that the Institute adheres to the purposes for which it was chartered and that its integrity and financial resources are preserved for future generations as well as for current purposes. The Corporation and its committees have responsibility for reviewing and providing guidance on strategic directions, approving annual budgets, exercising long-term fiduciary responsibility, approving the establishment of new degree programs or courses of study, approving degrees, electing the President (as well as the other Corporation officers), and being available (individually as well as collectively) to advise the President on issues that he/she may wish to raise with them.

It is also understood that trustees are expected to represent the interests of MIT to outside constituencies as appropriate and help provide financial support for the Institute.

(http://web.mit.edu/corporation/about.html)

- Reed College:

Legal authority for the operation of the college, under the charter granted by the State of Oregon, rests with the board of trustees .... In practice, it is generally recognized as a chief responsibility of the board of trustees to select the president of the college .... The board also approves faculty appointments, which are recommended by the president and approved by an academic affairs committee of the board. Other specific and important responsibilities of the board include approval of the college budget, including the general salary schedules; management of investment and other financial and property considerations, with the assistance of an investment counsel; approval of new buildings and general planning and upkeep of the campus; and assistance in fund raising.

(http://web.reed.edu/academic/gbook/coll_org/governance.html)

- Washington University in St. Louis:

Washington University's Board of Trustees is the chief governing body of Washington University in St. Louis.

The board is legally responsible for the institution, whose assets it holds in trust. Trustees must assure themselves that the institution is heading in the right direction and is well managed.

The Board of Trustees is made up of men and women from the corporate, professional, educational, governmental and volunteer sectors of the St. Louis community, nationwide and abroad. In addition, emeritus trustees are invited to attend meetings and serve on committees of the board.

The trustees of Washington University:

- o Appoint the chancellor
- o Review and approve or disapprove annual budgets
- o Review and approve or disapprove major capital expenditures
- o Make final decisions on awards of tenure and degrees, and on new degree programs
- o Oversee the management of the endowment
- o Oversee and participate in developmental programs
- o Take an interest in and support the university's people and programs

Trustees exercise a policy and oversight role in contrast to the implementation and operational role of the administration, faculty and staff.

(http://boardoftrustees.wustl.edu/Pages/Home.aspx)

- Emory University:

  The Board of Trustees governs the University by establishing policy and exercising fiduciary responsibility for the long-term well-being of the institution. The board and its Executive Committee act on recommendations from board committees, university officers, and the University Senate.

  (http://secretary.emory.edu/board_of_trustees/index.html)

- New York University:

  As directors of a nonprofit and as leaders of an institution responsible for educating the next generation of world leaders and for creating new knowledge, trustees are the keepers of the mission of NYU: Educating qualified individuals from all walks of life to become the leaders of the local, national, and, now, international community. They must pay particularly close attention to the mission and the obligations to society that are unique to the academic enterprise. NYU's Board of Trustees is the overall fiduciaries for the University. As such it is responsible for, among other things, creating policy, setting mission and purpose, strategic planning, reviewing programs, and relating campus to community and community to campus. Chief among its roles is fund-raising for the University, as well as engaging our alumni, parent, and student communities.

  (http://www.nyu.edu/about/leadership-university-administration/
  board-of-trustees.html)

Adherence to mission, fiduciary responsibility, setting policy, strategic planning, advising, selecting the senior officer, and fund-raising are themes that run through most such statements. The need to balance longer-term issues with day-to-day operations creates tension between governing boards and senior administration. While the board provides oversight, it is not responsible for running the institution.

States have developed multiple approaches to the governance of public colleges and universities, with state boards of postsecondary education following three principal models:

1. *Governing boards*, with governing or line responsibility for institutions. This responsibility may include strategic planning and allocating resources among institutions within their jurisdiction; developing institutional and faculty/personnel policies; appointing, setting the compensation for, and evaluating system and institutional chief executives; awarding degrees; advocating for the institutions to the legislature and governor.
2. *Coordinating boards*, with coordinating responsibility for institutions. This responsibility does not include appointing, determining compensation for, or evaluating institutional chief executives, nor does it include developing institutional and personnel policies. The focus of coordinating boards is more on state and system needs and priorities, and planning efforts may include both public and private institutions, and in some states extend to for-profits as well.
3. *Planning, regulatory, and/or service agency* with either limited or no formal governing nor coordinating authority, and which carry out regulatory and service functions.

(McGuinness, 2003)

In addition to the state boards, public colleges and universities may also have their own institutional boards of trustees. For example, the Board of Regents of the Ohio Department of Higher Education advises the department's chancellor on issues of state-wide importance that affect higher education. In addition, each of Ohio's public colleges and universities is governed by its own board of trustees. These institutional boards of trustees focus on issues of immediate concern to their particular college or university— the salary of the president, the strategic plan, development campaigns, and the like.

State boards may have quite a large staff, with several senior-level administrators. Boards of trustees are often supported by a secretary, with median compensation for this position ranging from $104,000 for the two-year sector to $195,000 for doctoral universities. Members of governing boards usually receive no compensation for their time and are often called upon to provide financial support to the institution through gifts and bequests.

SYSTEM LEADERSHIP

Public colleges and universities may be grouped together as a system led by a chief executive officer (CEO). Some states, such as Ohio, have a single system that oversees all public institutions, including universities, community colleges, and technical colleges. The chancellor of Ohio's Department of Higher Education also serves as the chancellor of the University System of Ohio. Other states group postsecondary institutions by sector, with separate systems for technical colleges, community colleges, and universities. The Texas Higher Education Coordinating Board serves as a coordinating board for Texas's eight higher education systems (Alamo Colleges, Texas A&M University System, Texas State Technical College System, Texas State University System, Texas Tech University System, The University of Texas System, University of Houston System, and University of North Texas System), each of which is headed by its own chancellor. Nearly every variation between these two extremes can be found as well.

Much of the system CEO's time is spent demonstrating higher education's value to the state legislature, advocating for resources, and creating fair, equitable strategies for distributing those resources to advance the missions of the various system institutions. Institutions may well resist subjugating their own goals for the good of their system, and system CEOs must work to demonstrate the value in collective action. This may take a very practical form; in many states, systems have encouraged greater collaboration between member institutions with regard to business practices, including sharing services such as payroll and instituting collective purchasing programs. Collective planning processes can ensure that students can easily transfer from one state institution to another, that institutions do not unnecessarily duplicate academic programs, and that information about effective and efficient practices at one institution can be made known to other member institutions.

Depending upon the structure of the governing board, a system CEO may well have the authority to mandate such policies. Yet even when this is the case, persuasion is often a more effective means to achieving desired ends. Successful system CEOs demonstrate moral authority; they understand that intelligent leaders act in the best interest of their organization, and they persuade their college and university presidents that the shared goals of the system will best serve the individual institutions. Successful system CEOs help their institutions to garner necessary resources, assure the quality of the academic programs, and provide greater access to higher education.

The CEO of a system, whatever his or her title, earns a median salary of between $299,000 and $500,000, depending on the sector to which institutions in the system belong.

ACADEMIC LEADERSHIP

The academic leadership structures of colleges and universities are fairly standard across all types of institutions, though institutional size and mission play a significant role in the number and scope of positions involved. The organization charts in Figures 2.1 and 2.2 show two very different types of institutions. As is typical, both have a provost who reports to the president, and deans who report to the provost. Other reporting lines are less standard. The organization chart for Columbia State Community College reflects the critical role of economic and workforce development in the mission of community colleges, while the chart for Massachusetts Institute of Technology highlights the importance of research and graduate and professional studies.

Presidents

College and university presidents are the public faces of their institutions, and good presidents interact regularly and often with students, parents, and alumni; with boards of trustees, faculty, and staff; with representatives of the media and with legislators; and with donors and prospective donors. Presidents are properly seen as accountable to all of these constituents through their boards of trustees and other governing bodies, and they are accountable for achieving institutional goals in accordance with institutional values.

The scope of topics that constituent groups expect presidents to address ranges from the very narrow to the broadest possible—from individual student concerns to institutional policy matters, from individual cases of employee or student misconduct to larger questions about institutional accountability, from the value of a particular degree program to the value of higher education in general. Because presidents cannot themselves have firsthand knowledge and understanding of every issue and activity on their campuses, their most important role is to assemble and guide the senior leadership team for their institution. Fundamental to this role are the abilities to appropriately interpret constituent goals and to create a vision, potentially transformational for long-term goals, to achieve them; to build support for that vision among the senior leadership, throughout the organization, and among constituents; and to hold senior leaders accountable for fulfilling the vision in accordance with institutional values. Presidents who have mastered these abilities can confidently address the full scope of their constituents' concerns.

Presidents do not, of course, envision the path forward in solitude, nor is there but a single path that will advance their institutions. Colleges and universities are made up of academic and administrative units, each of which has specific interests that it hopes to promote, and that it sees as contributing to the goals of the institution. Within those units are subunits, and within those subunits are individual faculty, students, and staff;

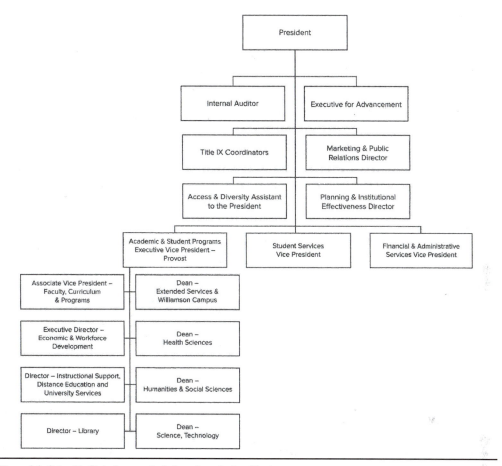

Figure 2.1 Columbia State Community College Organization Chart

Source: Columbia State Community College website.

each level reveals competing ideas and interests, many of which could reasonably be seen as furthering the institution's goals and values. External constituents as well advocate on behalf of aspects of higher education ranging from career training to basic research, and their support for a president's vision may be largely shaped by their own values. Presidents are thus challenged to hear the voices of individuals and small groups, to move those voices from cacophony to conversation, and to lead, informed by the multiple perspectives represented in the conversation.

The median salary for a president of a doctoral university is $450,000; for a president of a two-year institution, $188,000.

Provosts

Provosts serve as the chief academic officers of their institutions and are often given the additional title of Vice President for Academic Affairs. At most institutions, they are considered first among equals with regard to other vice presidents, as they oversee those activities at the very core of higher education: teaching, learning, research,

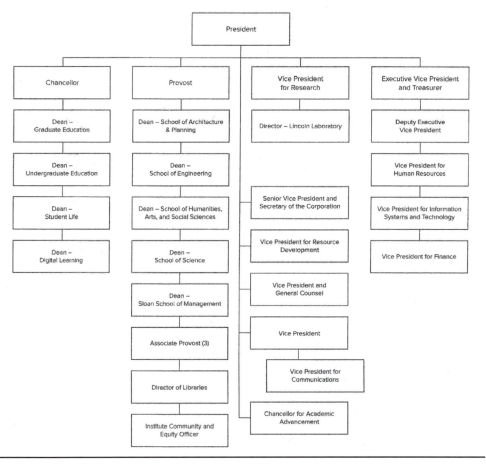

Figure 2.2 Massachusetts Institute of Technology Organization Chart

Source: Massachusetts Institute of Technology website.

and innovation. Provosts report to the president of their institution, but typically interact as well with trustees and other governing bodies. Depending on the size of their college or university, provosts may delegate high levels of authority to vice provosts or associate provosts.

The level of authority vested in a provost and his or her senior staff varies in accordance with the level of centralization or decentralization of the academic structure of the institution. Some institutions devolve nearly all of the academic decision-making to college deans, with the provost serving primarily to coordinate and promote the work of the colleges. More typically, however, deans of colleges report to the provost, and the provost, along with his or her senior staff, ensures that resources are distributed to academic units in accordance with the goals and values of the institution; that qualified faculty are hired, promoted, tenured, and compensated through processes that are fair and equitable; and that students receive a quality education through exposure to a challenging and vibrant curriculum. Provosts play a central role in strategic planning for their institutions.

Like presidents, provosts face the difficulty of competing interests and limited resources. It is incumbent upon the provost to encourage and support creativity and innovation throughout the academic community; it is essential as well that the institution live within its means. The challenge for today's provosts goes beyond making difficult resource allocation decisions, however. Provosts must engage the campus community in developing new models of teaching and learning that use resources more efficiently, fostering innovation not only among individuals, but also collectively as an organization. And they must ensure that their institutions demonstrate value, effectiveness, and efficiency, for without this evidence, resources will be ever more difficult to garner.

A provost's success is best judged by the success of the students and the faculty. Successful provosts are those who recruit and retain students and faculty whose own goals are well supported by the mission of the institution and whose endeavors in turn advance institutional priorities; who enable students to complete their desired programs of study in a reasonable time frame and serve their communities as educated citizens; and who support and honor faculty success as outstanding teachers and innovators.

Median salaries for provosts range from $131,000 in the two-year sector to $337,000 at doctoral universities. The range of median salaries for assistant provosts, associate provosts, and vice provosts extends from $101,000 for an assistant provost at a two-year college to $212,000 for a vice provost at a doctoral university.

Academic Dean/Associate Deans

Large colleges and universities group similar academic departments into colleges or schools headed by academic deans. Academic deans typically report to the provost and are expected to provide active leadership in the promotion, direction, and support of the educational and research activities of the institution (The Ohio State University, 2015). The deans are thus, in a very real sense, the chief academic officers of the academic colleges or schools they oversee.

While the array of responsibilities delegated to deans varies by institution, academic deans and their staff usually have oversight of the curricula and instruction offered by their departments and centers, and they are often responsible for student academic advising and career services. They ensure support for faculty teaching and research, which may include sabbatical leave, computer and technical asistance, and provision of administrative services. In many institutions, academic deans and their staff decide which departments may hire faculty and also review hiring, tenure, and promotion decisions regarding faculty in their colleges and schools, primarily to ensure fair and equitable processes. These are their official responsibilities, but the overarching job of an academic dean is to develop a community of scholars, to facilitate collaborations between teachers and researchers with similar interests, to promote the intellectual experience of their faculty and students, and to further knowledge in the disciplines of their organization.

Salaries for academic deans and associate deans depend both on the sector of the institution in which they work and on their discipline. Deans of colleges of medicine earn the highest median salary, at $526,000. They are followed by deans of dentistry, public health, and law, whose median salaries range from $272,000 to $339,000 in the doctoral university sector. Deans of business schools at two-year institutions earn a median salary of $100,000, and those at doctoral universities $200,000. Deans who oversee colleges made up of some or all of the arts and sciences disciplines draw median salaries of between $94,000 and $250,000, depending on the disciplines under their jurisdiction.

Salaries for associate and assistant deans follow the same pattern, with medicine heading the median salary list at $215,000. Associate and assistant deans of arts and sciences have median salaries ranging between $77,000 and $133,000.

Department Chairs

Academic departments are the unit of the institution most directly responsible for teaching, research, and outreach, and they are led by department chairs. At most institutions, these chairs are appointed by academic deans in consultation with members of the department, and they generally serve for an agreed-upon number of years. Department chairs have two main spheres of responsibility; they are both the business manager and the academic leader of their units.

As few department chairs (outside of colleges of business!) have backgrounds in accounting or other business practices, most delegate the associated tasks to professional staff. Nonetheless, department chairs are accountable to their deans for accomplishing the expected teaching, research, and service within their allotted budgets, and for assuring that their department's business practices conform to the rules of the institution.

As the academic leaders of their departments, chairs are accountable both to their faculty and to their deans for allocating resources to best support departmental missions. Thus, the department chair has multiple "bosses," serving both the dean and, collectively, the members of the department faculty. Chairs are in no way, however, subordinate to individual faculty members. They make decisions about such issues as which courses faculty will teach, the salary increases they will receive, and whether or not research leaves may be granted.

The nature of this position is all the more complicated because the chair does not leave the faculty to become an administrator, but remains a teacher and scholar, and so a peer of his or her faculty. The best chairs develop good relationships with their colleagues and make decisions through consensus building. The wise chair keeps in mind that the next department chair will surely be chosen from among the colleagues affected by his or her decisions, and sets fairness and the good of the department as a whole as the standard.

In general, department chairs receive some pay in addition to their faculty salary, but practices for determining the additional compensation are not standardized across institutions and may vary even within a single college or university.

Academic Library Directors

Academic library directors commonly report to the provost. Depending on the size of the college or university library, its director may be considered a peer of the deans or of the department chairs. Academic librarians, including the library director, often have faculty status, and the Association of College and Research Libraries has promulgated guidelines for the promotion and tenure of library faculty (Association, 2011).

Higher education's transition from print on paper to digital and electronic technologies is transforming instruction, scholarly communication, and the storage and preservation of knowledge. The library will need to become the institutional provider of scholarly tools in all forms—books, databases, and means of manipulating the scholarly record, such as statistical and graphics packages or concordance programs. Academic librarians are challenged by constituents who expect ever increasing ease of use and institutions that expect cost containment (Lewis, 2015). Median salaries for directors of academic libraries range from $88,000 to $180,000.

Other Academic Unit/Department Heads

Many institutions have created interdisciplinary centers to bring together faculty from different departments to collaborate on scholarship that benefits from multiple perspectives. These centers are generally headed by faculty members appointed as directors. Much of the description of the department chair position holds true for center directors, but the center director may find it still more challenging to build consensus and collegiality among faculty with different disciplinary backgrounds. The development of innovative courses and scholarship that integrate methods and ideas across disciplinary boundaries is the hallmark of a successful center and center director.

As is the case for department chairs, other academic unit heads may receive pay in addition to their faculty salary, but here too, practices for determining the additional compensation are not standardized across institutions and may vary even within a single college or university.

Faculty

While they do not appear on most administrative organization charts, faculty are the core of every higher education institution. Members of the faculty have multiple responsibilities, including teaching, scholarship and research, public service, and administration. Many institutions operate using a model of shared governance between the faculty, the governing board, and the senior administration. Faculty participation in administration includes service on institutional and departmental committees, as well as development of junior faculty, staff, and students.

Higher education administration traditionally draws from the ranks of the faculty for many important positions, including president, provost, deans, and department heads. In the case of deans and department heads, these positions are usually for a defined term, after which individuals often return to the regular faculty to teach and do scholarly research. One of the challenges for faculty assuming these roles is a lack of preparation and administrative training when they are thrust into positions of authority above their once and future colleagues.

Regardless of whether the institution is a community college, private liberal arts college, public university, or research university, its faculty are responsible for turning its educational mission into an appropriate curriculum and pedagogy. These educational duties include student advising and institutional and departmental service. Members of the faculty at research universities must secure funding for research and supervise how that money is spent (pre- and post-award management). At research-intensive universities, the administrative responsibilities of the faculty, comprising fiscal management, compliance with government regulations, and supervision of research and clerical staff, may dwarf other obligations. No clear division between administrative and educational responsibilities exists with regard to the supervision of graduate students; faculty supervise both their educational and their funded research, which, in the best of all worlds, are highly related.

There are myriad complexities in the interaction of faculty with administration. Because members of the faculty perceive that they have the overall responsibility for the educational mission, they often regard management changes as challenges to that role. For example, budget constraints often result in changes in class sizes or the hiring of non-tenure-track faculty to supplement the regular faculty. In large research universities, the ever-present need for resources (people, money, and space) creates constant strain between faculty and administration.

In some universities, each member of the faculty is able to negotiate with the administration with regard to compensation, workload, and resources. In others, the faculty are represented by a union. Each of these models presents its own challenges. In the former case, individual faculty negotiations can be inordinately time-consuming for the administration (department chairs, academic deans, and chief academic administrators). In the latter, negotiations with faculty unions may inhibit rapid response to economic pressures or changes in pedagogical requirements.

Evaluation of faculty performance is very much dependent upon the type of educational institution and the specific academic discipline. In large research universities, faculty productivity metrics include the number and quality of publications, citations, and honors and awards; the amount of research funding; and successful graduation of doctoral students. Other types of institutions rely more heavily on metrics such as teaching evaluations, number of courses taught, and advising performance.

Faculty salaries vary widely by institution and discipline. The American Association of University Professors' annual survey of faculty compensation is a useful guide (http://www.aaup.org/aaup).

STUDENT LIFE LEADERSHIP

Students' higher education experiences extend beyond the classroom. Whether they live on a residential campus, commute to their schools, or connect primarily online, students are supported in their success and development by a network of student life professionals. Figure 2.3 provides an overview of the complex organization overseen by the Vice President of Student Life at The Ohio State University, illustrating the myriad activities for which student life leadership may be responsible.

Vice President/Dean

Vice presidents or deans of student life promote student success and enrich the student experience through a multitude of services that address all aspects of the students' lives outside the classroom. Depending on the degree to which student life is viewed as being aligned with and supporting the academic side of the institution, the vice president may report to the provost or to the president. Regardless of where student life lands on the organization chart, the vice president must connect with every major organization of the institution, because each one touches the lives of students.

Perhaps the best way to understand the responsibilities of vice presidents of student life is to examine the various functions over which they preside. As with most college and university senior administrative positions, responsibilities vary depending on the size and type of institution. As one might expect, technical colleges that primarily serve adult learners offer services very different from those provided by universities that serve a large, traditional-aged undergraduate population, especially those with a large number of students who reside on campus.

The residence and dining halls unit is one of the largest within student life on most residential campuses, and is overseen by an associate or assistant vice president or director, depending in part upon the size of the operation. The director of residence and dining halls is usually responsible for residential management, social and educational programming in the residence halls, facilities improvements, leases and assignments, fiscal management, building services, and campus dining services. Today's director of residence and dining halls faces many of the same challenges directors have always faced—providing safe and enriching environments in which young adults living away from home for the first time can grow and mature.

Student life's programming to enhance student learning and enrich student lives reaches far beyond the residence halls. Student life staff develop opportunities for students to engage in community service, to participate in clubs and student organizations, and to experience leadership opportunities. Spirituality and religious life are supported by a student life office on many campuses, and most student life organizations have staff devoted to meeting the needs of particular groups, including commuter students, minority students, students with disabilities, and lesbian, gay, bisexual, and transgender (LGBT) students. Student life staff are also responsible for developing and upholding the institution's code of student conduct.

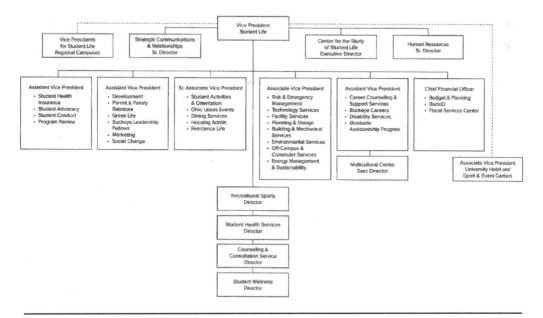

Figure 2.3 The Ohio State University Organization Chart for the Division of Student Life

Source: The Ohio State University website.

Student life offices address the health and well-being of students in multiple ways, reducing the barriers to student success. At some institutions, student health centers are part of the student life organization, and many student life offices offer psychological counseling services. Recreational sports programs support students' fitness goals, providing social opportunities at the same time.

Student life vice presidents operate multi-million dollar organizations and must be adept managers of people and other resources. In addition to the student life offices that most directly touch the lives of students, vice presidents of student life in large institutions rely upon a cadre of senior staff who manage their unit's administration, human resources, communications and marketing, strategic planning, development, and information technology operations. Student life offices of research and assessment support functions throughout the organization through their analysis of current practices and methods.

At some colleges and universities, admissions, financial aid, and registration are part of the student life organization. These units will be discussed later in this chapter, as part of the portfolio of the chief enrollment management officer. Some vice presidents of student life have responsibility for athletics as well (athletics will be discussed as a separate unit headed by the athletic director).

The chief student affairs officer earns a median salary of between $110,000 and $213,000, depending on the size of the institution and the complexity of the position. Median compensation for associate and assistant vice presidents ranges from $90,000 at baccalaureate institutions to $131,000 at doctoral universities. Directors of student affairs organizations, including minority affairs, student activities, campus recreation, and student housing, earn median salaries of between $52,000 and $111,000.

ADMINISTRATIVE LEADERSHIP

Colleges and universities organize their administrative units in some ways that are fairly predictable and in others that are less so. Most colleges and universities, including some community colleges, have a vice president for research, a position that at research universities may be combined with that of dean of the graduate school. In the main, colleges and universities have a high-level person, often a vice president, in charge of human resources. The chief information officer is generally a position equivalent to vice president. In recent years, the position of director of enrollment management has at many institutions been elevated to the vice presidential level. Colleges and universities may have one or more vice presidents devoted to administrative, financial, and other business affairs. Vice presidents of communications, government relations, and development, along with the chief legal counsel, a vice presidential-level position, round out the list of usual vice presidents in higher education. The following sections briefly describe the positions mentioned above and note the major director positions that report to each.

Vice President for Research

The position of vice president for research is typically found in research universities. In most institutions, the vice president for research is a member of the senior officer cabinet or team. Duties will vary according to the breadth and depth of research activities, but typically include responsibilities related to government relationships, compliance, conflict of interest, negation of employee benefits, and indirect cost recovery rates. Vice presidents for research have ultimate responsibility for the pre- and post-award activities of the institution, and they are often involved in negotiating a wide range of research grants and contracts. Some have responsibility for the negotiation and implementation of affiliation agreements when there is a relationship between the institution and an independent entity.

Some vice presidents for research are responsible for supervising interdepartmental or interdisciplinary laboratories, i.e., laboratories or centers that include faculty and research from more than one school. A few universities have taken on the supervision of Federally Funded Research and Development Centers such as SLAC at Stanford or Lincoln Laboratory at MIT. The oversight of these entities often falls to the vice president for research.

Technology transfer is usually part of the portfolio of this position. It is through the licensing of technology that discoveries made at universities are transferred to the public sector and move to applied uses. Technology transfer includes disclosure of research results, applying for patents and copyrights, and licensing. The U.S. government, which provides the bulk of external funding for research at universities and colleges, promotes commercialization of the results of research for the public good. Licensing also provides needed revenue to institutions and the inventors.

Most vice presidents for research spend a large amount of their time working with government agencies, either independently or in concert with organizations such as the Association of Public and Land-grant Universities (www.aplu.org), Association of American Universities (www.aau.edu), National Council of University Research Administrators (www.ncura.edu), or Association of University Technology Managers (www.autm.net), as well as state and local agencies.

Evaluation of the performance of the vice president for research ultimately includes the success of an institution at attracting and sustaining externally sponsored research and minimizing issues related to the conduct of that research. Among these responsibilities are the provision of oversight for animals in university research activities, and the assurance that adequate protections are in place before human subjects participate in research projects. The median salary for the vice president for research ranges from $87,000 at baccalaureate institutions to $278,000 at doctoral universities.

At many master's and doctoral institutions, the vice president for research is supported by one or more associate or assistant vice presidents, who may or may not be members of the faculty. Associate and assistant vice presidents for research earn median salaries of $96,000 at master's institutions and $131,000 at doctoral institutions. Chief technology transfer and senior technology licensing officers may also report to the vice president for research. Such positions are found almost exclusively at doctoral institutions. The median salary for chief technology officers is $182,000; for senior technology licensing officers, $104,000. Directors of sponsored research and programs are found in all sectors, with median salaries ranging from $85,000 to $129,000.

Vice President for Human Resources

The vice president for human resources is responsible for supporting the recruitment and hiring of faculty and staff, ensuring quality compensation and benefits programs for employees, and providing education and training to further faculty and staff development. In addition, this vice president attends to the climate and quality of work life.

Because the hiring of faculty is primarily conducted by search committees, human resources staff generally play the smallest of roles in that process. Nonetheless, the human resources vice president is responsible for developing and promulgating policies that ensure fair and equitable hiring practices for faculty and staff alike. Directors of affirmative action and equal employment, disability services, and labor relations are among the human resources staff who support the vice president in developing and implementing such policies. At smaller institutions, these functions may be clustered under an employment services director.

Determining and providing appropriate compensation and benefits for both faculty and staff are among the responsibilities of human resources vice presidents. College and university offices of human resources exchange information about salaries through their professional associations, and institutions draw on this information as they compete for talent. At large colleges and universities, this responsibility is often delegated to a director or assistant vice president.

Human resources staff offer new employee orientations, ongoing professional development, support for performance management, and organizational development training—vital services for a high-performance organization. Human resources information systems staff provide data and analysis to inform the entire campus about staffing-related trends and outcomes.

Vice presidents of human resources clearly demonstrate success through high levels of employee retention and satisfaction. The capacity to control the cost of employee benefits while ensuring access to quality health care is another hallmark of an outstanding human resources leader.

Median salaries for vice presidents of human resources range from $91,000 to $172,000, depending on the sector. Median salaries for assistant vice presidents and directors range from $74,000 to $118,500.

Vice Presidents for Business, Administration, and Finance

Ivory towers are neither cost-free nor maintenance-free, and the business of higher education is complex. Every college and university has one or more senior officers who are responsible for its business, administrative, and financial operations. Where these roles are split among multiple senior officers, institutions—even those similar in size and belonging to the same sector—have developed different reporting schemas. At some institutions, the chief financial officer and the chief business or administration officer both report to the president. At others, the chief business officer reports to the chief administration officer—or vice versa. Still another model has the chief budget officer or the chief administration officer reporting to the chief financial officer. While no organizational pattern emerges as typical, what is clear is that numerous operations support, but are quite distinct from, the academic enterprise. These operations include facilities planning, operation, maintenance, and development; parking and transportation; campus security; accounting and budgeting; risk management; purchasing; and printing and mail services.

One might argue that colleges and universities are no different from any other large organization with regard to business, administrative, and financial services. That similar services are needed in both non-academic and academic organizations is certainly true; the culture of academia, however, requires a different approach to business decision-making. For example, at most colleges and universities, governance structures give faculty a significant voice in determining institutional priorities, and this affects all aspects of planning and budgeting. Faculty committees do not generally make final decisions, but wise administrators take their advice and recommendations seriously. Furthermore, faculty at most institutions act with a great deal of autonomy. As experts in their fields, they know best the types of equipment and facilities they need to accomplish their teaching and research. It may be necessary for faculty to deviate from a preferred vendor list to purchase the equipment and materials that best suit their needs; they may have a better understanding of laboratory design than facility planners. The challenge for vice presidents with responsibility for business and administrative operations is to involve faculty in decision-making in a way that harnesses and respects their expertise while helping them understand the fiscal, political, and legal constraints within which the institution must operate.

Median salaries for vice presidents for business, administrative, financial, planning, and budget operations range from $128,000 to $277,000, depending upon the individual's portfolio, the reporting line, and the sector and size of the institution. Salaries for staff reporting to these vice presidents vary along similar lines, and also with regard to educational requirements. University architects' median compensation ranges between $102,000 and $137,000, and directors of real estate and space management receive similar remuneration, ranging between $105,000 and $126,000. Median salaries are somewhat lower for directors of accounting and purchasing, at $68,000 to $103,000 and $74,000 to $113,000 respectively.

Chief Investment Officer

The chief investment officer is responsible for managing the institution's investment pool, which includes selecting investment managers, developing and implementing investment policy, and providing leadership on asset allocation. Chief investment officers often report both to the board of trustees' investment committee and to the institution's president or chief financial officer. Return on the investment pool is the clear performance metric for this position, and chief investment officers are often rewarded for success with bonuses. According to College and University Personnel Association data, 15% of chief investment officers at reporting institutions received bonuses for performance, and the average payment exceeded the median salary for these positions. Depending on the size and sector of the institution, median salaries, not including bonuses, range between $109,000 and $306,000 for chief investment officers.

Chief Legal Officer

Not surprisingly, the National Association of College and University Attorneys (NACUA) provides the best description of the college and university chief legal officer position. The organization's website (www.nacua.org) explains that these attorneys are:

> involved with issues such as governance, employment and human resources, student affairs, campus security, athletics, financial and business affairs, risk management, compliance, government and community relations, contracts, intellectual property, and various forms of dispute resolution. Attorneys who practice higher education

law may be involved with virtually every part of the institution since legal matters that affect colleges and universities can arise from almost everything a college or university or its employees and students do.

The NACUA website further explains the structure of higher education legal offices:

Some colleges employ a single attorney or rely solely on outside counsel for their institutional representation. Other institutions have multiple attorneys serving as in-house counsel. In-house counsel are often supplemented with external counsel who have particular expertise or who are asked to provide advice or representation on specific matters. Higher education attorneys must help their institutions manage compliance with federal, state, and local laws to address important policy matters and to manage potential legal liability. By practicing preventive law, they enable those on campus to apply legal principles and to respond to difficult situations having potential legal implications.

Median salaries for chief legal affairs officers range from $148,000 to $232,000.

Chief Information Officer

The chief information officer at a college or university provides services to help faculty, students, and staff use technologies in learning, teaching, research, and administrative settings. The CIO does not, however, simply provide the services requested, but rather seeks to innovate, inform, and lead the campus community toward new and better ways of accomplishing their work supported by technology. Criteria listed for the Chief Information Officer Innovation Leadership Award, given annually at the Massachusetts Institute of Technology Sloan CIO Symposium, describe the key characteristics of great CIOs:

- Exceptional Communicator—Articulates a vision for strategic business value from IT and works across the organization to build partnership around this vision. Focuses communications on value and innovation, not technology. Helps all IT staff to understand the business and speak the language of business leaders.
- Recognized IT Leader ("Cheap Information Officer")—Clearly demonstrates value-for-money in the management of core IT services—providing the right services at the right price and the right level of quality. Recognized among peers as an effective leader of the IT unit.
- Driver of Business Value ("Chief Improvement Officer")—Understands the business and needs of the CEO, CFO, Line-of-Business heads and other senior executives. Ensures clear focus on potential and realized value in all IT initiatives. Incorporates IT into business decision-making by participating in key strategic conversations, suggesting innovative uses of IT, and for managing risk.
- Trusted Partner ("CIO-Plus")—Exercises authority beyond IT itself. Considered a trusted member of the senior executive team, not just a technology leader. Suggests innovative uses of IT to transform the business—and successfully executes the changes. May receive additional non-IT responsibilities such as Chief Operating Officer or VP of Strategy, or strategic temporary roles such as Head of M&A integration.

(MIT Sloan Boston Alumni Association, n.d.)

Median salaries for chief information officers range between $111,000 and $230,000. Senior-level staff reporting to the chief information officer include directors of academic computing, enterprise information systems, instructional technology, and telecommunications and networking. Salaries for these professionals range from $66,000 to $137,000.

Chief External Affairs Officer

External affairs may comprise governmental and legislative relations, as well as communications and marketing. A single vice president may be charged with both of these components, as at Duke University (Duke University Office of Public Affairs & Government Relations, 2016), or each component may be led by a separate vice president, as at the University of Michigan (University of Michigan, 2016).

Vice presidents whose portfolios include government relations pursue policy outcomes that benefit their institutions and higher education more broadly. They and their staff monitor legislation of interest to universities, identifying emerging federal and state issues affecting students, faculty, and staff. Large institutions may have offices in Washington, D.C., enabling government relations staff to facilitate meetings between senior personnel and legislators and policy makers. At both the state and federal levels, government relations staff endeavor to build and maintain good working relationships with public officials. In addition, government relations staff respond to public officials' requests for data and information about the institution.

Not all government relations are federal or state. Most institutions, both small and large, have to deal with local communities. Sometimes it is just one city or town, but it is not unusual for there to be two or more communities involved, especially for universities with large campuses. Local governments issue permits, provide services, including fire and policing, and maintain infrastructure. Many institutions have negotiated PILOTs (payments in lieu of taxes) and submit yearly town-gown reports. There is always the issue of off-campus students whose need for local housing or youthful exuberance can cause rifts in otherwise excellent relationships.

Not every college and university has staff devoted to government relations, but it is inconceivable that an institution of higher education would not have communications and marketing staff. Vice presidents of communications and marketing may be responsible for media relations, advertising, and public relations for the institution as a whole, or, especially at smaller institutions, for units within the university. Their portfolio may or may not include media relations for their athletic department and sports teams, or production of marketing materials for admissions and recruitment. Where communications responsibilities are distributed, with academic units, athletics, and other departments responsible for their own marketing and media relations, successful vice presidents develop ways to collaborate with their campus colleagues.

Communications offices have found innovative ways to take advantage of new media, and even the smallest institutions have links to Twitter, Facebook, and YouTube on their home pages. With today's volume of information and the multiple delivery channels, the challenge for communications offices is to be heard—to provide timely information in a way that captures the attention of the intended audience.

Median salaries for chief external affairs officers range between $139,000 and $221,000, depending on the sector of the institution and the scope of the position. Directors of federal relations, positions primarily found at doctoral universities, have a median salary of $156,000, and directors of state government relations at doctoral universities earn slightly less, with a median income of $142,000. Salaries for directors of marketing, publications, and news services range between $68,000 and $100,000.

Vice President for Development

The goal of the vice president for development is to attain private philanthropic funding from alumni, friends, corporations, and foundations. The vice president typically reports to the college or university president. Development offices and foundations organize and coordinate fundraising programs for colleges and universities to support the academic missions and objectives determined by the academic leadership of the institution. Many schools have adopted structures for development that include both a centralized office that coordinates efforts across the institution and decentralized development staff who work closely with specific units, such as the office of student life or the school of social work.

The vice president of development at a public institution may also serve as the president or executive director of a separate college or university foundation, organized as a not-for-profit 501(c)(3) corporation. Governed by a board of directors, these fundraising foundations allow for confidentiality of donors' personal documents, greater flexibility with regard to expenditures, and opportunities for higher investment returns than can be attained under the low-risk, low-return strategies required by many states.

Vice presidents for development at large institutions are usually supported by associate/assistant vice presidents or directors with responsibility for annual giving, planned giving, and corporate and foundation relations. Median salaries for vice presidents for development range between $108,000 and $282,000; associate/assistant vice presidents and directors earn median salaries of between $97,000 and $193,000.

Vice President for Enrollment Management

Chief enrollment management officers most commonly report to the president, provost, or vice president of student life. The vice president for enrollment management brings together the offices that recruit, fund, track, and retain students, facilitating the coordination of staff, flow of information, and integration of decisions to coordinate and improve the following processes (Kurz and Scannell, 2006):

- research, planning, recruitment, and communication;
- admissions marketing that attracts appropriate students in sufficient numbers;
- implementing pricing and financial aid strategies that optimize the institution's ability to generate net tuition revenue and attract and retain the desired mix of students;
- anticipating immediate and long-term student demand and improving the institution's ability to respond to these interests; and
- identifying reasons for attrition, minimizing it to the extent desirable, and enrolling qualified transfer students as replacements.

Offices of enrollment management evolved to help institutions better target the shrinking population of traditional-age college students and, at many colleges and universities, to attract more highly qualified students. These challenges persist, and those involved with enrollment management must continually create new strategies to meet the goals of their institution. Chief enrollment management officers earn median salaries of between $99,000 and $186,000, depending on the sector in which they are employed and the size of their institution. Among the senior staff who report to vice presidents for enrollment management are registrars, with median salary ranges of $72,000 to $119,000, and directors of admissions and financial aid, with median salary ranges of $73,000 to $115,000.

Chief Diversity Officer

Over the last decade, increasing numbers of colleges and universities have appointed a chief diversity officer to develop and drive their diversity agenda. While many institutions have historically had senior staff responsible for promoting access to higher education for minority students and to employment opportunities for minority faculty and staff, Damon A. Williams and Katrina C. Wade-Golden argue for a "C"-level executive role, with the following definition:

> The [CDO] position designates an individual who serves in a senior administrative role working toward diversity-themed organizational change as a top priority at the highest levels of leadership and governance. The role is integrative, spans administrative and institutional boundaries, and reflects the CDO's capacity to lead, coordinate, facilitate, enhance, and at times supervise the formal diversity capabilities of the institution in an effort to create an inclusive and academically rewarding environment for all. Within this context, diversity is not merely a demographic goal but a strategic priority that is fundamental to creating a dynamic educational and work environment that fulfills the teaching, learning, research, and service mission of the institution.
>
> (Williams & Wade-Golden, 2013)

Most college and university strategic plans for diversity emphasize recruitment and retention of diverse students, faculty, and staff not only as an issue of fairness and equity, but also in recognition of the benefit of diverse perspectives for the growth and learning of the entire community. Effective chief diversity officers promote a campus climate that embraces and celebrates diversity and inclusion throughout their institution, and this is reflected not only in the size and success of the minority population, but also in the enhanced cultural competencies of the entire campus community.

The chief diversity officer may report to the president, to the provost or an associate provost, or to the vice president for student life, depending upon the focus of the position. Median salaries for this position range from $90,000 to $163,000, depending upon the size and sector of the institution.

STUDENT LEADERSHIP

Student leaders provide colleges and universities with valuable perspectives and insights. Undergraduate and graduate students serve at various levels throughout their colleges and universities, and their opportunities for leadership and input are as varied as the institutions they attend. The most visible role is as a member or officer of a student government or other official student body. Members and officers of these organizations are usually elected by their peers, and at most institutions there is a process to ensure that those elected are representative of the student body in terms of major or discipline. Generally, at master's and doctoral institutions, there are separate such organizations for undergraduate and graduate students. These organizations advocate on behalf of students with regard to issues as diverse as the information institutions should provide on diplomas to expenditures of student fees. In recent years, student leadership organizations have campaigned for more affordable textbooks and against college and university apparel manufactured in sweatshops. Undergraduate and graduate student organizations have joined forces both within and across institutions to support sustainability efforts at colleges and universities.

Students may also serve on their institution's board of trustees, and in leadership roles within their college, school, or department. In this capacity, students can provide reflections on their academic experience that can be invaluable in the shaping of curricula and advising. It can be tempting for those outside of the academy to describe such feedback as "customer input." This temptation to think of students as "customers" of the faculty with whom they study must be resisted. The student–faculty relationship, in which both parties commit to the student's learning and development, is time-honored, and is diminished rather than enhanced by the "customer" designation. Nonetheless, the student perspective on the quality and benefits of the student–faculty relationship within a particular department is immensely valuable for improving the educational experience.

A particular challenge for student leaders is time management. David Bowers, president of The Ohio State University's Council of Graduate Students for 2015–16, notes that constituents raise more issues than can be addressed. Student leaders are required to determine how they can effect the greatest good with the resources available, and these triage skills may not come naturally to student activists who care deeply about each of their constituent groups. He adds that "Learning to accept a degree of imperfection in oneself and in those on whom one depends as a leader is important. Some emails won't be sent, some meetings will be missed. Student leaders, who tend to be perfectionists, must learn to accept this and move on" (Bowers, 2016).

Assuring a sustainable and well-connected student organization is a further challenge. Bowers sees discussions of succession planning as critical, with conversations about potential members and officers occurring early and often. Student leaders must also learn the organizational structure and maintain an awareness of the cross-institutional working relationships. He explains,

> An administrator I'm meeting with may not be able to change whatever I've come in to speak with her about, but she might be heading to a committee meeting with another administrator who can. Remembering to ask "who might be able to help us out, and can you help me get to that person" can be vital to achieving the organization's goals.
>
> (Bowers, 2016)

Members of student government organizations, and especially officers, may receive a stipend for their services. Most, however, serve without financial compensation.

CONCLUSION

It should be clear from this review of higher education leadership positions that there is no single administrative pattern for colleges and universities, nor is there even a best pattern. Administrative configurations within colleges and universities evolve over time, according to the needs of the institution, and, in part, according to the competencies of talented institutional leaders. The higher education world is a learning community, and academic leaders learn about the administrative structures of units with goals similar to their own through professional organizations and networks. Many structures can be successful, and institutions striving to become more effective have multiple models to examine and evaluate.

DISCUSSION PROMPTS

1. How does the role of an institution's governing board differ from that of the institution's senior leadership, including the president and provost?
2. Describe the structure and responsibilities of the governing body that has oversight of the institution at which you are a student.
3. Find or create a high level organization chart for the institution at which you are a student. How do the reporting lines compare with those provided in Figures 2.1 and 2.2?
4. Discuss the different challenges presented by leading an academic unit as a dean, associate dean, or department chair versus leading a non-academic unit as a vice president.
5. While there may be some few exceptions, academic departments are, as a general rule, led by faculty department chairs. Given that these department chairs are tasked with managing the day-to-day operations of their unit, what are the advantages of this structure as opposed to appointing fiscal/human resources experts to lead academic departments?
6. Why do most colleges and universities consider it important for faculty not serving in administrative roles to have a significant voice in determining institutional priorities?
7. Several senior leadership positions, such as the Chief Investment Officer or the Chief Financial Officer, might be assumed to have little day-to-day contact with faculty and students. How can leaders assure that they are getting the input they need without creating an undue burden for themselves and their constituents?
8. While each of the senior leaders has a portfolio of work for which they are responsible, much of their work affects and is affected by the work of other senior leaders. Select two of the senior leadership positions described in this chapter and discuss the impact of the performance of the two on each other's work.
9. Discuss specific ways in which student leaders can support the work of student affairs and other administrative leaders.
10. The criteria listed for the Chief Information Officer Innovation Leadership Award given annually by MIT are provided earlier in the chapter. How would you revise and broaden those criteria so that they would be applicable to all senior leadership positions?

REFERENCES

Association of College and Research Libraries. (2011). Retrieved December 2015, from http://www.ala.org/acrl/standards/promotiontenure

Association of Governing Boards of Universities and Colleges. (2010). Statement on board responsibility for institutional governance, http://www.agb.org/news/2010-03/statement-board-responsibility-institutional-governance

Bowers, D. (2016) Interview. February, 10.

Columbia State Community College organization chart. Retrieved February 2016, from http://www.columbiastate.edu/docs/default-source/policies-procedures/01-01-00_appendix_a_cscc_organizational_chart

Duke University Office of Public Affairs & Government Relations. (2016). Retrieved February 2016, from http://publicaffairs.duke.edu/staff

Kurz, K. A., & Scannell, J. (2006). *Enrollment management grows up*. Retrieved February 2016, from University Business: http://www.universitybusiness.com/article/enrollment-management-grows

Lewis, D. W. (2015). Inventing the electronic university. *College & Research Libraries, 76* (3), 296–309.

McGuinness, A. C. (2003). *Models of postsecondary education coordination and governance in the States*. Denver, CO: Education Commission of the States.

MIT Organization Chart. Retrieved February 2016, from http://orgchart.mit.edu

MIT Sloan Alumni Club of Boston. (n.d.). *MIT Sloan CIO Symposium Award; © 2003–2011 All Rights Reserved.* Retrieved February 2016, from http://www.mitcio.com/award/award-application/

New England Association of Schools and Colleges. (n.d.). Standards for Accreditation, Section 3.3, 3.4, 3.5. Retrieved February 2016, from https://cihe.neasc.org/sites/cihe.neasc.org/files/downloads/Standards/CIHEofNEASC_Standards_July_1_2016.pdf

The Ohio State University. (2015). *Bylaws of the Board of Trustees of The Ohio State University*, April 3. Columbus, OH.

University of Michigan. (2016). *University of Michigan Standard Practice Guide*. Retrieved February 2016, from http://spg.umich.edu/org-charts/organizational-structure

Williams, D. A., & Wade-Golden, K. C. (2013). What is a Chief Diversity Officer. *Inside Higher Ed.*, April 18. Retrieved February 2016, from https://www.uc.edu/content/dam/uc/diversity/docs/What_is_a_Chief_Diversity_Officer.pdf

3

THE ROLE OF INTERNAL GOVERNANCE, COMMITTEES, AND ADVISORY GROUPS

Kerry Brian Melear

INTRODUCTION

While institutions of higher education must operate by integrating the directives articulated by many external constituents, including state legislatures, boards of trustees, and various accrediting agencies, they also function through a system of shared governance on the internal institutional level, which has "significant consequences for the health of institutions" (Minor, 2004b, p. 361). The American system of higher education, at all types of institutions, is largely characterized by this participatory governance model in both the public and private sectors, through which operations are facilitated by a central administration in concert with input from faculty, staff, and students. A myriad of committees, advisory groups, task forces, and panels form the threads that are woven into the tapestry of internal governance, from community colleges to liberal arts colleges to research universities to online institutions. Concerning campus-level operations, Salter and Tapper (2002) posit:

> The internal governance of universities is shaped by a political environment which encourages, chastises or is indifferent to the various forms that governance may take. To the extent that institutions adopt a form of governance which can readily engage with the pressures generated by their environment, they are then able to compete effectively in the political game for resources. To the extent that they do not, they will fall behind and, ultimately, succumb.
>
> (p. 245)

While different types and sectors of higher education institutions operate differently, they all largely have similar structures with senior leadership, both academic and non-academic, managing decisions through governance. Institutional decision-making is deliberate and largely flows from executive authority. The results of these decisions are typically implemented quickly at institutions that are more nimble and innovative, which tend to have an organizational structure that can easily adapt to change (e.g., continuous enrollment). Indeed, Gayle, Tewarie, and White (2003) reason that "the extent to which campus stakeholders perceive institutional governance to be shared can enhance or constrain the role of a college or university as a vehicle for teaching and learning" (p. 73).

This chapter explores the role of some of the basic advisory bodies inherent in most colleges and universities, as well as the influence of campus-wide forums and university foundations in internal governance questions. Specifically, the chapter addresses the faculty's role in shared governance through the lens of the faculty senate and the curriculum committees, and then transitions into a discussion of other functional groups, such as space and facilities committees, planning and budget committees, and athletics committees, along with the impact of personal and professional decision processes within those contexts. The chapter then examines the internal role played by external university foundations, legally separate entities, yet integral to internal operations, and briefly discusses the benefit of campus-wide forums in terms of the dissemination of information to the campus community and the opportunity for robust discourse and discussion. Because of the variance in institutional types and internal governance models across the broad range of higher education institutions, these functions are addressed in generally applicable terms.

FACULTY SENATE

The faculty senate is a primary vehicle through which members of the professorate exercise the shared governance that characterizes higher education. Such bodies provide a forum for faculty and administrators to deliberate a range of issues associated with academic administration (Pope & Miller, 2005). As noted by Bess and Dee (2008), a faculty senate bears primary responsibility for academic concerns, "but it shares responsibility with the administrative structure for others. The responsibilities of and relationships between these two entities are inherently somewhat ambiguous, and important institutional policy decisions must often be negotiated" (p. 176). Faculty senates exist at institutions across the spectrum of higher education, from the community college to the university—including online institutions—although some scholars contend that faculty governance issues are less problematic at the community college level because of more clearly articulated faculty expectations (Miller, 2003; Miller & Miles, 2008). While the challenges for faculty senates at online institutions share similarities with their non-online counterparts, online institutions have the added task of engaging faculty throughout the United States or even the world, spanning multiple time zones.

The role of the faculty in sharing academic governance was emphasized when the American Association of University Professors (AAUP), founded in 1915, promoted the concept in one of its early committees. The AAUP urged that faculties should share in the process of administration and should be the controlling voice concerning academic matters. This philosophy did not manifest until after World War II, when faculties began to enjoy a more powerful role, controlling appointments, academic calendars, and work schedules, either by delegation of authority from governing boards or approval of trustees (Brubacher & Rudy, 1976). The AAUP affirmed its position in 1966 in its

Statement on Government of Colleges and Universities, which calls for faculty primacy over the curriculum and faculty involvement with internal administrative matters (AAUP, 1966). By the 1970s, senates of the faculty "had evolved into influential policy-making bodies on many campuses" (Brubacher & Rudy, 1976, p. 375), thus formalizing increased faculty power and input on campus (Kezar & Eckel, 2004).

It has been long recognized, however, that the faculty senate is but one participant in shared campus governance, along with administration and students (Lizzio & Wilson, 2009). Faculty senates on campuses that permit faculty unionization share governance over faculty-related matters, with senates focusing on academic concerns and faculty unions working on employment-related matters such as salaries and benefits (Aronowitz, 2006). In 1973, Bornheimer, Burns, and Dumke noted:

> Thus, while we feel that the faculty should have primacy in curricular matters, it should be no means be exclusive. When other responsible voices are heard along with the faculty, in determining the courses that shall be taught, the final product is well balanced and even the faculty is better served than if it alone made all the decisions in this sensitive area.
>
> (p. 83)

For the most part, contemporary faculty senates do not wield great power beyond their advisory capacities, particularly with regard to non-academic matters. Since the 1960s and 1970s, their relative power on campuses has waxed and waned according to economic pressures and accountability initiatives emanating from state legislatures (Lee, 1979). Further, faculty senates face new internal governance challenges as higher education continues to rely on external funding sources, such as curricular regulation of special-interest centers funded by outside parties (Burgan, 2009). Barbara Lee's 1979 assessment rings true today: "The faculty role in academic governance at institutions of higher education remains a topic of controversy, ambiguity, and misunderstanding among faculty themselves, administrators and, more recently, state legislators" (p. 565).

Indeed, faculty senates have faced criticism for being weak and exerting little influence beyond their advisory roles (Birnbaum, 1989). With regard to budget matters, for example, Sufka (2009) found that senates are challenged by lack of understanding of budget processes, short response times required by state-level leadership, apathy on the part of some faculty members about financial issues and their role in addressing them, and inability to respond quickly because of internal structures and processes. He suggested senates could play a positive role in budget matters if they improved response times, identified strong leaders, and developed a statement of values to follow during times of fiscal crisis. Through survey research, Minor (2004a) found that faculty senates are challenged because they are understudied, exist in multiple governance environments, and suffer from a lack of faculty interest and the incongruence between the philosophy of shared governance and its function.

Although faculty governance bodies such as senates are quite common in higher education, research into their efficacy is scant (Kezar & Eckel, 2004). Miller and Pope (2003) note the ambiguity surrounding faculty senates and their roles on campuses, recognizing that multiple factors affect the influence of senates, which makes it difficult to generalize about them:

> The push and pull environment that has arisen in faculty governance is often one of adversarial relationships that either produce hostility or inhibit effective decision-making. In other instances, the converse is true, as senates serve as healthy instruments of communication between and among faculty and administrators.
>
> (p. 121)

Miller and Pope did state, however, that consistent themes demonstrated the ambiguous nature of faculty senates. The structure of senates has not been fundamentally altered, but respect afforded senates and perceptions of their usefulness on campus has been eroded by delays in decision making and lack of internal cooperation. For example, the governing board of Rensselaer Polytechnic University suspended the faculty senate in 2007 for refusing to include non-tenure track faculty in membership. The administration cited the senate's interference in the review of faculty governance as one part of the rationale for its suspension and created an interim faculty governance structure in its place (Olson, 2011).

Minor (2004b) proposes four useful and distinct models of faculty senate composition: functional, influential, ceremonial, and subverted (Figure 3.1). In the functional model, the most traditional rendering of the structure of faculty senates, a senate primarily represents and protects the faculty interest in academic decisions. Members are elected from the faculty, the group is led by a chair or president, and various committees undertake the duties of the senate. By-laws or other governing documents guide the work, and advisory statements are issued through deliberation and formalized voting processes.

An influential faculty senate has status within a college or university as a legitimate governing body; rather than focusing solely on curricular matters, it makes significant contributions to decisions across a broader cross-section of the institution. Such senates are powerful, and Minor underscores that they traditionally exist on campuses where "the power center shifts between constituencies as the contextual circumstances change" (Minor, 2004b, p. 350). Administrators recognize their legitimacy as a viable governing body on campus.

Ceremonial faculty senates "exist in name only and operate as symbolic artifacts" (Minor, 2004b, p. 351), meeting infrequently and contributing little to campus governance. Presidential and administrative power in institutions with such a faculty senate is strong, and decision-making with regard to academic issues is delegated to individual colleges and departments. While not powerful, such senates can serve useful latent functions (Birnbaum, 1989). "By providing opportunities for socialization,

> • Functional: Powerful and elected
> • Influential: Significant contribution
> • Ceremonial: Symbolic
> • Subverted: Not recognized as contributory

Figure 3.1 Minor's Faculty Senate Governance Model

congregation, discussion, professional screening, and the like, senates can contribute to institutional stability in the potentially contentious, volatile environment of higher education" (Helms, 2005, p. 35).

Finally, a subverted faculty senate's role in institutional governance is diminished by alternative methods of faculty input. Administrators consider such bodies to be obstacles rather than viable sources of assistance. Minor notes that subverted senates "usually suffer from negative cultural and communicative aspects that affect their role in campus decision-making" (Minor, 2004b, p. 353), and campus leaders and other members of the community lack confidence in decisions rendered by such groups. As a result, these senates are avoided in the decision-making process.

CURRICULUM COMMITTEE

The centrality of the curriculum committee on college campuses clearly illustrates the primary role that the faculty plays in academic governance. The primary function of curriculum committees is to maintain an institution's curricular offerings through approval of proposals for new courses of study, oversight of current offerings, course discontinuances, program reviews, determination of course articulation, and recommendations about the curriculum to the appropriate governing body, provost, or faculty. Such committees have long been integral to faculty oversight of academics in liberal arts colleges and universities, but their importance at other types of institutions is also now greatly emphasized because of the increasing role that faculty members play in governance (Miller & Miles, 2008). Additionally, accrediting bodies have become more explicit in their standards for accreditation regarding the material role that faculty are expected to play in curriculum development and oversight of new and existing programs.

Institutions commonly employ numerous curriculum committees, particularly on campuses with both undergraduate and graduate programs. Because of the diversity of institutional types, governance models, and programs, curriculum committees operate at numerous levels on college and university campuses. Individual colleges and schools may house a curriculum committee composed of members of the faculty and responsible for overseeing the academic programs offered within that unit. Administrators such as provosts, deans, and registrars are often ex-officio members. A campus might be home to both an undergraduate curriculum committee that oversees the institution's baccalaureate courses of study and a graduate curriculum committee responsible for a graduate school's academic programs. The process of marshaling a particular institution's curriculum is specific and appropriate to a given campus and its programs, and Muffo (2001) cautions that curriculum committees should not lose sight of the general education, or core curriculum, by focusing attention on other functions, such as new course approvals.

Curriculum committees must be responsive to the evolution of the collegiate course of study over time. As noted by Clark Kerr (1977, as cited in Rudolph, 1977):

> In the final analysis, the curriculum is nothing less than the statement a college makes about what, out of the totality of man's constantly growing knowledge and experience, is considered useful, appropriate, or relevant to the lives of educated men and women at a certain point of time.
>
> (p. xxi)

Curriculum committees are:

- Broadly constructed or related to specific programs, majors, departments, or fields
- Composed of faculty and some administrators, such as provosts and deans
- Focused on general requirements on the undergraduate and graduate levels
- Sensitive to field-specific and accreditation concerns, such as law and medicine

Figure 3.2 Curriculum Committees

"In a college-wide curriculum committee, differences in academic values and norms can create tensions that may not lead to participant learning and changed unless specifically acknowledged and dealt with" (Lattuca & Stark, 2011, p. 325). The curriculum in American higher education has changed dramatically since the inception of our system of higher learning, and now reflects an amazing spectrum of courses of study ranging from the liberal arts to professional preparation programs, for which curriculum committees bear primary responsibility. "The specific needs of the students, society, and the sector should be addressed in the curriculum" (Collins, 2006, p. 53).

Not only must members of curriculum committees remain responsive to the curriculum itself, they must also be mindful of accreditation, particularly for professional programs for which outside bodies set standards that must be met to maintain programmatic recognition. Accrediting bodies are influential and play a critical role in the administration of an institution's curriculum. Loss of accreditation, particularly regional accreditation, can lead to severe penalties that can adversely affect a college or university's function or even solvency.

Increasingly, external funding sources have also begun to exert influence on collegiate curricula in the United States. As noted by Burgan (2009), special-interest research and teaching centers sponsored by outside parties have proliferated in recent years, and those sponsoring benefactors often "expect to be involved in the content and management of programs they pay for" (p. 15). She further argues that while such centers may provide tangible benefits and enrich a campus environment, they can also distort the priorities associated with regulation of the curriculum. Curriculum committees must remain flexible and responsive to the needs of external constituents, but mindful of protecting academic integrity. Figure 3.2 highlights key characteristics of curriculum committees.

SPACE AND FACILITIES COMMITTEE

Allocation of space and facilities on postsecondary campuses is a function of balancing needs across various constituencies, and is a process that is becoming increasingly complex as colleges and universities evolve, the demand for available space grows, and the workforce morphs to use more technology to accomplish their jobs. One major challenge involves the unique requirements of Millennial college students, born between 1982 and 2002, who "influence space planning, design, and construction and will continue to transform higher education as they return to campus as faculty and staff" (Rickes, 2009, p. 7). These students are inveterate users of technology and have different spatial needs than their predecessors, necessitating careful space administration and planning.

As Romano and Hanish (2003) note, meeting the needs of a diverse and consistently shifting student population is becoming more complex an endeavor for many reasons, "not the least of which is financial" (p. 3).

Administrators have been grappling with limited space while trying to contain costs and retaining talented staff. One strategy utilized by many institutions that is a win–win for space and costs is allowing employees to work from home or advertising for difficult to recruit for positions (e.g., technology) as work from home positions, for those positions where it is feasible. When employees work from home either full- or part-time, the institution can save on space as well as retain and attract the best talent for the most affordable cost.

Issues surrounding sustainability are now also at the forefront of administrative discussion. However, in Wright and Wilton's (2012) survey of facilities management managers, they found that while the majority had an interest in seeing their institutions become sustainable, not all had a clear conception of the portrait of a sustainable university. This is an issue that will continue to face space and facilities management committees as institutions embrace important green initiatives on college campuses.

In addition to accommodating students, institutions must also be sensitive to the needs of faculty, staff, and external constituencies who all compete for a finite pool of spatial resources based on their particular needs; faculty members, for example, may require substantial research space. A college or university must therefore develop space management methods that coalesce with its research missions, priorities, and culture (Fink, 2004). Classroom space is always at a premium, especially as enrollments increase.

Colleges and universities establish space and facilities committees to evaluate and allocate space; these committees are known by various names on different campuses. It is also not uncommon for institutions to establish committees that are responsible for campus planning as well as space allocation, but planning committees will be discussed in the following section.

The primary function of space and facilities committees is to facilitate the equitable and most efficient, cost-effective allocation of campus space in order to maximize the learning environment for students, faculty, staff, and external constituents. These committees must evaluate requests for use of space or reallocation of unused space. If they do not also embody a planning component, they must work in concert with university planning committees to reduce redundancy and marshal resources effectively while allowing for future needs or challenges.

Membership on space and facilities committees is institutional-specific, but is typically composed of senior administrators, such as provosts; vice presidents for finance, administration, student affairs, and planning; various deans; representatives from the faculty; physical plant directors; and occasionally students. The committees typically report in an advisory capacity to the institution's president or to a vice president charged with campus facilities, or they issue decisions about space requests to the campus community at large. These committees meet regularly, usually monthly and on an ad hoc basis to respond to the constantly changing space requests on campuses.

Some institutions have adopted guiding principles to facilitate the distribution of campus space. For example, the University of California has adopted a set of "Space Management Principles" that establish seven goals for allocating facilities

---

Campus Space Planning

"The Space Planning Advisory Group (SPAG) has been formed to assist University officers in making sound judgments regarding the allocation and utilization of space. (NOTE: The SPAG Policy, which authorizes this document, can be found in the University Policy Manual.) SPAG members represent the needs of their various constituencies and are expected to consult with deans and other administrators within their program centers regarding their specific space needs and concerns. This group will be involved in all major space use considerations as well as those addressed in this document. The group will also assist in more routine matters such as adjudicating controversial use requests, space change requests that impact capacity, function, or physical configuration, and developing policy and procedure for space use" (California State University, Sacramento, 2011, p. 1).

Responsibilities

"The Space Planning Advisory Group's activities will typically address such questions as: Who should occupy new or vacated space? What types of space should be emphasized in facilities planning? The group will address such policy and procedural issues as: How should faculty and staff offices be allocated? How should space use priorities be set? What rules should govern the use of space for noninstructional purposes? In addition, all space issues that are anticipated to result in an expenditure > \$25K will be forwarded to the University Budget Committee for financial consideration, prior to submission to the Vice President and Chief Financial Officer. The work of SPAG is in the form of recommendations to the Vice President and Chief Financial Officer, who will consult with the affected vice presidents and/or the Provost prior to submission to the President for consideration and decision" (California State University, Sacramento, 2011, p. 1).

Figure 3.3 California State University, Sacramento Space Planning Policy

and space: functionality (meets functional requirements), equity (fair distribution across all divisions), consistency (all practices are identifiable and user-friendly), efficiency (space is utilized to the greatest extent possible), flexibility (current needs are met while being mindful of the future), cost-effectiveness (fiscally responsible allocations), and proximity (facilitates coordination of university business matters) (University of California, 2010, p. 3).

Likewise, California State University, Sacramento, has established guidelines to assist its "Space Planning Advisory Group." As shown in Figure 3.3, these guidelines contain detailed information regarding the types of decisions that may face the committee, as well as regulations to provide a framework for decision-making, in order to address growth and "the changing needs of the University and those whom it serves" (California State University, Sacramento, 2011, p. 1). The University of Dayton has also adopted space management guidelines that provide guiding principles for space allocation decisions, outline operating procedures, detailed information about the space and facilities allocation process on that campus in order to "facilitate an effective and efficient utilization of University space resources resulting in a quality learning and working environment for students, faculty, and staff" (University of Dayton, 2011, p. 3).

PLANNING AND BUDGET COMMITTEE

Planning and budget committees on college and university campuses are critical elements of internal governance. Where space and facilities committees focus on maximizing available resources, planning and budget committees seek to maximize future resources including facilities and beyond. These committees are charged with a broad, complex, and difficult task that requires environmental scanning and predictions of future resource availability, or lack thereof, in a constantly changing world:

> Every day, college and university campuses change—usually imperceptibly and occasionally dramatically. Programs change, people change, financial resources change, buildings change, land and landscapes change, environs change. The way campuses look today is the result of all the minor and significant, casual and formal, rational and irrational decisions that are made in the day-to-day dynamic interaction of a living institution responding to such changes.
>
> (Lidsky, 2002, p. 69)

Strategic planning has become increasingly prominent in higher education as a more nuanced approach to long-term planning. In general terms, Bess and Dee (2008) find the concept of aligning organizational resources and goals to be congruent with the organization's environment. Dooris, Kelley, and Trainer (2004) define strategic planning in the postsecondary context as follows:

> In higher education, bettering one's condition includes hiring better faculty, recruiting stronger students, upgrading facilities, strengthening academic programs and student services, and acquiring the resources needed to accomplish these things. Since most institutions of higher education share a similar mission and compete for these same objectives, an essential part of strategic planning involves shaping the institution in ways that ensure mission attainment by capturing and maintaining a market niche in the quest for resources, faculty, and students. Thus, strategic planning has both external and internal faces.
>
> (p. 6)

Planning and budget exist in a state of symbiosis; one concept remains dependent upon the other as they cycle together, and problems associated with one will certainly affect the other. For this reason, planning and budget committees are integral to the overall health of a college or university, as the decisions they reach and recommend to upper administration can have far-reaching consequences. This requires deliberate and judicious planning processes that are "woven tightly into the day-to-day operations and interactions of the institution, whatever its type" (Lidsky, 2002, p. 70). Sound planning is essential to good budgetary practices, particularly because higher education faces "increasingly complex facilities, shortening time lines, proliferating code and regulatory requirements, emerging technologies, and growing concerns for indoor air quality and environmental sustainability" (Guckert & King, 2003–2004, p. 24).

Planning and budget committees are thus typically designed to provide an institution's chief executive officer with guidance and input regarding the evolution of the environs and the effect of that evolution on the academic experience and institutional tenets. They often work in concert with other committees, such as long-range planning committees or academic planning committees. The institution's budgetary and academic priorities are considered, as well as the context of institutional mission.

Faculty senates may have planning and budget subcommittees, but these are composed and governed only by members of the faculty. Broader administrative planning and budget committees also include faculty representation, as well as upper-level administrators such as provosts; vice presidents for finance, administration, and student affairs; deans; staff representatives; and students.

It is noteworthy that some institutions have expanded the role of the planning committee into separate planning departments with staff members responsible for numerous facets of institutional forecasting, master planning, or space allocation. Such campuses include Carnegie Mellon University; the University of California, Los Angeles; and Massachusetts Institute of Technology (Fink, 2004). This trend will likely continue, as institutions recognize the importance of judicious planning and the volume of effort associated with that endeavor.

ATHLETICS COMMITTEE

The intent of intercollegiate athletics is to provide an extracurricular developmental outlet for college students to enrich their learning experience and campus life on the whole. Athletics, while certainly not without its criticisms, provides this experience for students and affords institutions a valuable framework to increase alumni connections and philanthropy. The financial impact of college athletics is tremendous and undeniable across the spectrum of higher education, as the revenue generated through intercollegiate athletics reaches new levels. According to the National Collegiate Athletic Association (NCAA), the Division I Football Bowl Subdivision alone reported median revenues of $62,275,000, with the largest reported revenue at $196,030,000 (NCAA, 2015).

Intercollegiate athletics has long been under the lens of scrutiny for many reasons, including questions of academic quality and student engagement with campus life. Athletics committees must police these issues on college campuses. For example, one study indicated that many faculty members felt disconnected from campus athletics, found the salaries paid to coaches excessive, and felt that decisions regarding campus sports were driven by external entities without regard to academic mission (Sander, 2007). This perceived tension between commercial values and institutional mission was addressed by a 2010 report by the Knight Commission on Intercollegiate Athletics, which urged institutions to bring athletics and academics back into balance through greater transparency of financial reporting, placing incentives on prioritizing student-athlete academics, and emphasizing the notion that student athletes are students, not professional athletes (Knight Commission on Intercollegiate Athletics, 2010).

As with the committees previously discussed, the structure of the athletics committee as a form of internal governance will vary according to the institution in which it is housed, and will reflect the nature of that college or university's athletic program. The NCAA permits institutions to participate as members of one of three divisions, each with differing requirements regarding the number of sports offered. Regardless of divisional association, the NCAA regulates intercollegiate athletics, and postsecondary institutions must comply with these regulations closely or risk costly sanctions. Assisting with that compliance process is one of the key roles of the athletics committee.

Athletics committees have numerous duties, according to the size and extent of an institutional athletics program. In general, athletics committees are responsible for overseeing the athletics programs, with particular regard to compliance with NCAA regulations, as mentioned above. Such committees also typically render recommendations for practice regarding athletic policy and programming on campus, as well as regulate academic requirements for student athletes.

As with the committees previously discussed, the composition of the athletics committee on most campuses illustrates key principles of shared governance. Membership of postsecondary athletics committees is typically drawn from a broad cross-section of the campus community, with representation from upper-level administration, the faculty, the student body, and the institution's athletic foundation, a separate legal entity that supports campus athletic programs through philanthropy and development.

RESPONSIBILITY FOR COMMITTEE DECISION-MAKING

Service on various departmental and institutional committees sometimes requires a balance of personal responsibility with responsibility to committee function. Committees formed within individual colleges housing multiple departments may find that individual department perspectives dominate the discussion. Bright and Richards (2001) argue that "departmental barriers frequently seem insurmountable to those inside them. This silo mentality impedes progress both internal and external" (p. 84). Likewise, Buller (2006) encourages administrators, particularly department chairs, to cultivate relationships outside of the department, arguing that to meet with success, "you will need to know how you can best serve these external constituents, where to draw the line with them, under which circumstances to turn to them as allies, and when it is desirable to maintain a distance" (p. 237).

Service may also require a balance of what is best for an individual against the collective interest of the academic department. Wheeler et al. (2008) refer to this phenomenon, particularly among faculty members, as "distributed loyalties," and caution that administrators must find the delicate balance that satisfies both personal aspiration and the needs of a department or unit (p. 38). The concept of distributed loyalty is woven into the fabric of higher education for faculty members, who are not only individual scholars requiring autonomy but also members of programs, departments, colleges, and ultimately, the college or university, as well as outside professional and personal associations. Wheeler et al. suggest charting individual progress toward shared goals as a method to overcome the effect of distributed loyalties. Figure 3.4 highlights key components of committee service.

Service on committees requires:

- Balance of self-interest with department or programmatic concerns
- Significant investment of time and intellectual resources
- Cultivation of relationships and shared decision processes

Figure 3.4 Committee Service

FOUNDATIONS

Although college and university foundations are separate legal entities and not part of the system of shared governance that typifies higher education, they play an integral role in campus operations that bears discussion in this context. Publicly funded as well as private not-for-profit colleges and universities are typically supported by foundations responsible for developing private gifts to the institution and maintaining those gifts in endowments. While this has long been true for universities, community colleges have only recently begun to establish separate foundations for their support (Gose, 2006). The role of private giving for all of public higher education continues to increase in importance as state funding steadily decreases (Kelderman, 2011).

Foundations are not operational units of a college or university. Rather, they are separate, not-for-profit educational corporations under Section 501(c)(3) of the United States Internal Revenue Code and established to support institutions of higher learning under the laws of each respective state. The intent of establishing a separate legal entity to seek private external funding and manage these funds once they are endowed is the removal of the endowment and other private funds from direct control and influence of college and university administration (Mississippi Legislature, 2007). Also, public funds can remain under the purview of state legislatures, so removing private gifts from the public domain insulates the institution's endowments from governmental intrusion and provides more privacy for the donor. A foundation is directed by a chief executive officer who is advised by a board of trustees, and a college or university is associated with a foundation through a contractual affiliation agreement.

Because foundations are separate entities, they are more insulated from state open-meetings and open-records laws than the public institution itself. However, while foundations are separate legal entities, the very rationale for their existence is to support the college or university with which they are affiliated. As a result, foundations do come to bear in a discussion of various forms of internal governance because institutional administration influences how foundations go about the business of supporting a college or university. Foundations raise money in various ways, including through annual giving programs, planned giving, and major fund-raising campaigns. Institutional administration can play a very influential role in major fund-raising initiatives by providing direction for how a campaign should proceed and what areas of campus it is intended to benefit. This position was clearly articulated by the University of Iowa Foundation:

> Because the UI Foundation was established to facilitate the University's mission, the Foundation's major initiatives, such as large capital campaigns, are set the by University's President, Provost, and central administration with concurrence of the Foundation's management group and board of directors.
>
> (University of Iowa Foundation, n.d.)

In this way, presidents and other upper-level administrators provide guidance to the foundation as it seeks to support the institution's mission, and an external entity becomes critical to internal operations. Figure 3.5 highlights key features of foundations.

College and University Foundations are:

- Separate legal entities
- Integral to operation via fundraising
- Sometimes subject to open records requests
- Supportive through small gift programs, annual giving initiatives, and major fundraising programs

---

Figure 3.5 Foundations

CAMPUS-WIDE FORUMS

The campus-wide forum is a hallmark of higher education and can be a useful tool for promoting shared governance on campus and providing the campus community with information and opportunity for input. Campus-wide forums are called to address numerous issues—from social to political to financial—at the forefront of discussion at a college or university.

During periods of financial exigency, it can be useful and effective to hold a campus-wide forum to discuss budget procedures or explain methodologies for making budget reductions, thus providing transparency to the campus community. For example, the president of Western Carolina University called a campus-wide forum in January 2011 to address the impact of North Carolina's nearly $4 billion state revenue shortfall on university operations (Holcombe, 2011).

Forums are also useful to provide a framework for public discussion of campus-specific issues that may have caused acute controversy, such as the campus-wide smoking ban instituted at Texas State University. At two forums held in 2010, one for students and one for faculty and staff, the director of University Health Services discussed his review of the institution's smoking policy and his recommendations (Venable, 2010). Likewise, in 2016, Western Michigan University held a campus-wide forum to discuss mental health concerns, including suicide prevention (Puca, 2016). Such forums also give members of the campus community an opportunity to express their feelings about decisions that can be used to guide good practice.

CONCLUSION

Shared governance colleges or universities is an integral tenet of internal institutional operation. Postsecondary institutions are unusual in that, as corporate bodies, they seek input directly from so many constituents to effect operations, but this is a defining factor of higher education that has long been advocated, especially by the faculty. Faculty senates variously yield great power over institutional decisions or no power at all, depending on the context of the institution. They remain, however, a powerful voice through which faculty members can exert influence or, at a minimum, state a position on an issue of import to a particular campus.

Curriculum committees also provide a window for faculty input, as well as student and staff perspectives. Curriculum committees will continue to face challenges as they navigate an ever-changing set of demands from students, parents, and the public to respond to contemporary professional educational concerns, while seeking to remain true to traditional educational philosophies relative to the liberal arts curriculum and its role in the general curriculum. Likewise, facilities and space committees will remain challenged as enrollments increase without a corollary increase in physical space or campus facilities. The work performed by such committees requires a careful balance of the needs of several constituency groups, including faculty, staff, students, and members of the external community. These committees must be sensitive to the needs of all of these groups while working within the context of a finite physical environment.

Planning and budget committees are similarly challenged to balance the needs of a variety of constituencies, but must further consider those needs projected into the future in relation to forecasts of available resources. These committees work in concert with other campus committees to achieve campus academic and cultural missions within the framework of changing financial and physical resources.

Athletics committees are composed of a broad campus cross-section, and are responsible for overseeing athletics programs, protecting the academic and physical interests of student athletes, and ensuring compliance with NCAA regulations specific to a particular campus. Such committees have been challenged in the past by questions of academic integrity, scandals, and costly sanctions, but are charged with the important duty of marshaling the student athlete's experience and providing alumni and other members of the campus community a valuable outlet to express institutional loyalty.

Service to institutions on committees, advisory groups, or task forces compels members of the campus community to balance individual needs with the collective needs of departments or the institution. This delicate balance requires a judicious inquiry into what is best for the professional health of all parties involved, and must be reached in order to maximize benefit to a particular campus's internal governance.

Foundations, although separate legal entities, are integral to the internal operations of publicly funded colleges and universities. They are charged with developing private funding to support a college's or university's mission while maintaining separation from direct internal administration. However, because foundations exist specifically to support an affiliated institution, their development activities are strongly influenced by members of central administration, thus yielding an external entity central to internal campus operations.

Finally, campus-wide forums provide a window of opportunity for members of the campus community to express opinions and receive information. Such forums can provide transparency into institutional administrative decisions across a range of issues, such as budgetary concerns or acute campus controversies. They are also used to address broader social issues and invite a robust discussion of concepts and events that help shape the contours of the marketplace of ideas that is the American college or university.

DISCUSSION PROMPTS

1. Of the governance groups that were discussed in this chapter, which is the most important for student success?
2. Which group would you like to serve on and why? What would be your top two goals when serving on the committee and how would you go about accomplishing the goals?

3. Which group would be the most challenging to manage and/or work with as an administrator? What strategies would you employ with the group to be effective in advancing the institution?

4. Select a governance group. Discuss how the group membership, mission, and goals would be different for at least three different types of institutions (e.g., public, private not-for-profit, for-profit, online, predominately adults, remote, urban, etc.)

5. Find the most recent meeting minutes and informational documents (e.g., charge, mission, goals, principles, etc.) for a governance group at your institution. Based on a review of the documents, what role does the governance group play at the institution? Provide support for your statement.

6. What innovative ideas has and/or should your institution use with regard to governance? How do and/or should they vary by governance group?

7. How has your institution utilized campus-wide forums to communicate and share information? What strategies were effective and ineffective?

8. Using three governance groups, identify the role that faculty, staff, and students should play.

9. Relationship building with governance leaders is key to effective management. What strategies would you use to establish and encourage a positive relationship with governance leaders at your institution?

10. What are the advantages and disadvantages to appointing vs electing committee members? Discuss this with specific reference to two governance groups.

REFERENCES

American Association of University Professors. *1966 Statement of Government of Colleges and Universities.* Washington, DC: American Association of University Professors.

Aronowitz, S. (2006). Should academic unions get involved in governance? *Liberal Education, 92*(4), 22–27.

Bess, J. L., & Dee, J. R. (2008). *Understanding college and university organization: Theories for effective policy and practice.* Sterling, Virginia: Stylus.

Birnbaum, R. (1989). The latent organizational functions of the academic senate: Why senates do not work but will not go away. *Journal of Higher Education, 60*(4), 423–443.

Bornheimer, D. G., Burns, G. P., & Dumke, G. S. (1973). *The faculty in higher education.* Danville, Illinois: The Interstate Printers and Publishers.

Bright, D. F., & Richards, M. P. (2001). *The academic deanship: Individual careers and institutional roles.* San Francisco: Jossey-Bass.

Brubacher, J. S., & Rudy, W. (1976). *Higher education in transition: A history of American colleges and universities, 1636–1976.* New York: Harper & Row.

Buller, J. L. (2006). *The essential department chair: A practical guide to college administration.* Bolton, Massachusetts: Anker Publishers.

Burgan, M. (2009). Faculty governance and special-interest centers. *Academe, 95*(6), 15–19.

California State University, Sacramento. (2011). *Space planning guidelines and criteria for the assignment of university space.* Retrieved July 16, 2016, from http://www.csus.edu/aba/space/documents/spag_procedures_070111.pdf

Collins, A. B. (2006). Adding a course to the curriculum? Dilemmas and problems. *Journal of Travel and Tourism, 6*(4), 51–71.

Dooris, M. J., Kelley, J. M., & Trainer, J. F. (2004). Strategic planning in higher education. *New Directions for Higher Education, 2004*(123), 5–11.

Fink, I. (2004). Research space: Who needs it, who gets it, who pays for it? *Planning for Higher Education, 33*(1), 5–17.

Gayle, D. J., Tewarie, B., & White, Q. (2003). *Governance in the twenty-first century university: Approaches to effective leadership and strategic management* (ASHE-ERIC Higher Education Report *30*(1)). San Francisco: Jossey-Bass.

Gose, B. (2006). At a growing number of community colleges, fund raising is no longer optional. *Chronicle of Higher Education.* Retrieved from http://chronicle.com/article/At-a-Growing-Number-of/26509/

Guckert, D. J., & King, J. R. (2003–2004). The high cost of building a better university. *Planning for Higher Education, 32*(3), 24–29.

Helms, R. M. (2005). Who needs a faculty senate? *Academe, 91*(6), 34–36.

Holcombe, R. (2011). WCU chancellor to host campus-wide budget forum Monday. *Tuckasegree Reader.* Retrieved from http://www.tuckreader.com/wcu-chancellor-to-host-campus-wide-budget-forum-monday/

Kelderman, E. (2011). State spending on higher education edges down, as deficits loom. *Chronicle of Higher Education.* Retrieved from http://chronicle.com/article/State-Spending-on-Colleges/126020/

Kezar, A., & Eckel, P. (2004). Meeting today's governance challenges: A synthesis of the literature and examination of a future research agenda for scholarship. *Journal of Higher Education, 75*(4), 371–399.

Knight Commission on Intercollegiate Athletics. (2010). *Restoring the balance: Dollars, value, and the future of college sports.* Retrieved from http://www.knightcommission.org/images/restoringbalance/KCIA_Report_F.pdf

Lattuca, L. R., & Stark, J. S. (2011). *Shaping the college curriculum: Academic plans in context* (2nd ed.). San Francisco: Jossey Bass.

Lee, B. A. (1979). Governance at unionized four-year colleges: Effect on decision-making structures. *Journal of Higher Education, 50*(5), 565–585.

Lidsky, A. J. (2002). A perspective on campus planning. *New Directions for Higher Education, 119,* 69–76.

Lizzio, A., & Wilson, K. (2009). Student participation in university governance: The role conceptions and sense of efficacy of student representatives on departmental committees. *Studies in Higher Education, 34*(1), 69–84.

Miller, M. T. (2003). The status of faculty senates in community colleges. *Community College Journal of Research and Practice, 27,* 419–428. doi:10.1080/10668920390129022

Miller, M. T., & Miles, J. M. (2008). Internal governance in the community college: Models and quilts. *New Directions for Community Colleges, 41,* 35–44. doi:10.1002/cc313

Miller, M. T., & Pope, M. L. (2003). Faculty senate leadership as a presidential pathway: Clear passage or caught in a maze? *Community College Journal of Research and Practice, 27,* 119–129. doi:10.1080/10668920390128762

Minor, J. T. (2004a). Four challenges facing faculty senates. *Thought and Action: The NEA Higher Education Journal, 19,* 125–140.

Minor, J. T. (2004b). Understanding faculty senates: Moving from mystery to models. *The Review of Higher Education, 27*(3), 343–363. doi:10.1353/rhe.2004.0004

Mississippi Legislature, Joint Legislative Committee on Performance Evaluation and Expenditure. (2007). *An analysis of the legal status of university foundations, their oversight, and the authority of the PEER committee to review university foundations.* Retrieved from http://www.peer.state.ms.us/reports/rpt500.pdf

Muffo, J. A. (2001). Involving the faculty in assessing the core curriculum. *Assessment Update, 13*(2), 4–5.

National Collegiate Athletic Association. (2015). 2004–2014 NCAA Division I Intercollegiate Athletics Programs Report. Retrieved from http://www.ncaa.org/sites/default/files/2015%20Division%20I%20RE%20report.pdf

Olson, G. A. (2011). When to dissolve a faculty senate. *Chronicle of Higher Education.* Retrieved from http://www.chronicle.com/article/When-to-Dissolve-a-Faculty/126827/

Pope, M. L., & Miller, M. T. (2005). Leading from the inside out: Learned respect for academic culture through shared governance. *Community College Journal of Research and Practice, 29,* 745–757. doi:10.1080/10668920591006610

Puca, D. (2016). Campus wide forum explores student health concerns. *WMU News.* Retrieved from https://wmich.edu/news/2016/02/30388

Rickes, P. C. (2009). Make way for the Millennials! How today's students are shaping higher education space. *Planning for Higher Education, 37*(2), 7–17.

Romano, C. R., & Hanish, J. (2003). Balancing multiple needs through innovative facility design. *New Directions for Student Services, 101,* 3–15.

Rudolph, F. (1977). *Curriculum: A history of the American undergraduate course of study since 1636.* San Francisco: Jossey-Bass.

Salter, B., & Tapper, T. (2002). The external pressures on the internal governance of universities. *Higher Education Quarterly, 56*(3), 245–256.

Sander, L. (2007). Report: Faculty feel "disconnected" from college sports, think some coaches' salaries are excessive. *Chronicle of Higher Education*. Retrieved from http://chronicle.com/article/Faculty-Feel-Disconnected-From/68/

Sufka, K. J. (2009). How to make faculty senates more effective. *Academe, 95*(6), 20–21.

University of California. (2010). *UCOP space management principles*. Retrieved July 16, 2016 from http://www.ucop.edu/building-administrative-services/_files/documents/space-principles.pdf

University of Dayton. (2011). *Space management guidelines*. Retrieved July 16, 2016, from https://www.udayton.edu/finadmin/_resources/docs/campusplanning/documents/Space_Management_Guidelines_-January__2011.pdf

University of Iowa Foundation. (n.d.). *Frequently asked questions*. Retrieved March 30, 2011, from http://www.uifoundation.org/about/faq/

Venable, A. (2010). Smoking ban: Public forum tonight. *The University Star*. Retrieved from http://star.txstate.edu/node/2087

Wheeler, D. W., Seagren, A. T., Becker, L. W., Kinley, E. R., Mlinek, D. D., & Robson, K. J. (2008). *The academic chair's handbook* (2nd ed.). San Francisco: Jossey-Bass.

Wright, T. S. A., & Wilton, H. (2012). Facilities management directors' conceptualizations of sustainability in higher education. *Journal of Cleaner Production, 31*, 118–125.

4

EFFECTIVELY MANAGING HUMAN RESOURCES IN COLLEGES AND UNIVERSITIES

Valerie Martin Conley, Kristina Powers, and Kent J. Smith, Jr.

INTRODUCTION

At any given postsecondary institution, there are several different categories of employees. Most institutions categorize full-time employees as faculty or staff. The latter may be administrative, professional, or support staff. Regardless of their category, all employees are expected to contribute in some way to student success as well as to the overall mission of the institution. Additionally, many institutions utilize part-time employees, including faculty, staff, and students. As a result, effectively managing human resources in colleges and universities is a challenging and complex endeavor.

Consider the following new employees at a given institution:

- Assistant Professor of English;
- Assistant Director of Student Activities;
- Director of Buildings and Grounds; and
- Instructional Technology (IT) Specialist.

It is their first day on the job, and they are all required to attend the same new employee orientation. While this is not a requirement at all universities and colleges, most institutions have some type of new employee orientation, which often places all categories of employees together.

While this may not seem like an important event in the life of a university or college employee, it is actually fascinating as it may be the only time during that person's career at the institution that he or she will be intentionally partnered with personnel from all other employee groups for the same training. Colleges and universities depend on people in order to fulfill their institutional missions. Students, staff, faculty, and administrators are all necessary participants in the effective operation of postsecondary schools. The complex interplay of roles, responsibilities, and authority on college and university campuses makes human resources management in higher education a challenging undertaking! For example, student employees have dual roles. They are simultaneously students and employees of the institution, making them both customers and service providers.

The 1940 Statement on Academic Freedom and Tenure highlights the importance of freedom and economic security as "indispensable to the success of an institution in fulfilling its obligations to its students and to society" (AAUP, 1940). Tenure protects academic freedom. Yet the percentage of tenured faculty members has decreased relative to other types of instructional employees in higher education, and recent legislative proposals have sought to eliminate or curtail tenure, raising questions about the best way to ensure academic freedom.

However, many argue that the tenure debate centers not on academic freedom, but instead on productivity and performance. Numerous articles, book chapters, and monographs describe ways to enhance the productivity and performance of tenured faculty members. Universities and colleges nationwide have implemented post-tenure review processes with varying levels of success.

As the tenure debate rages on, Leslie (2007) concludes that the American academic workforce is being dramatically reshaped by "tectonic" forces (p. 3). Tectonics is a branch of geology that focuses on the structure of the crust of planets or moons, and in particular on the fault lines that produce jagged effects that are not uniformly distributed. Are colleges and universities appropriately staffed to deliver high-quality, affordable (i.e., effective) postsecondary education, research, and outreach? Do jagged staffing patterns denote a strength of postsecondary education or a cause for concern?

Below, a description of the types of personnel employed in colleges and universities provides context for this discussion. Next, the chapter outlines strategies for selecting and developing full- and part-time faculty and staff, approaches for improving performance, and ways to accommodate the short- and long-term budget reductions necessary to enhance productivity and efficiency. It concludes with a discussion of the need to engage in purposeful, mission-driven, data-informed human resources planning and decision-making that takes into consideration the complexity of employment relationships at colleges and universities.

PERSONNEL

The U.S. Department of Education's National Center for Education Statistics (NCES) collects data from institutions on human resources through its Integrated Postsecondary Education Data System (IPEDS) Human Resources (HR) Survey. All institutional employees are classified by full- or part-time status, faculty status, and occupational category. When applicable, institutions also provide additional data on faculty, such as tenure status, contract length, and academic rank. In fall 2013, the IPEDS HR survey reflected multiple data collection changes, one of the largest being the categorization of employees according to the 2010 Standard Occupational Classification (SOC) system as defined by the Bureau of Labor Statistics (BLS).

Institutions use the following 14 categories to classify each employee's primary responsibility:

1. Instruction;
2. Research;
3. Public Service;
4. Library and Student and Academic Affairs and Other Education Services Occupations;
5. Management Occupations;
6. Business and Financial Operations Occupations;
7. Computer, Engineering, and Science Occupations;
8. Community, Social Service, Legal, Arts, Design, Entertainment, Sports, and Media Occupations;
9. Healthcare Practitioners and Technical Occupations;
10. Service Occupations;
11. Sales and Related Occupations;
12. Office and Administrative Support Occupations;
13. Natural Resources, Construction, and Maintenance Occupations; and
14. Production, Transportation, and Material Moving Occupations.

The extent to which these categories adequately reflect staffing practices of postsecondary institutions varies. Categorizing employees by "primary" responsibility is an attempt to normalize the variability.

Employee Composition Over Time and by Institutional Type

The composition of the 3.9 million employees at degree-granting postsecondary institutions (as of fall 2013) has been morphing, particularly for faculty, who represent a little less than half (1.5 million) of the total. While the percentage of faculty increased overall during this time, the largest gain was seen in part-time faculty. The *Digest for Education Statistics* reports that:

> between 2003 and 2013, the number of full-time staff increased by 19 percent, compared to an increase of 29 percent in the number of part-time staff. Most of the increase in part-time staff was due to the increase in the number of part-time faculty (38 percent) and graduate assistants (23 percent) during this time period
> (National Center for Education Statistics, 2014, para 15)

The percentage of full-time employees varies across sectors and institutional types (as shown in Table 4.1). The percentage of full-time staff ranges from 44 to 69, while faculty has a larger range—15 to 67 (National Center for Education Statistics, 2014).

It is an understatement to say that the distribution of employees in higher education by primary functional area or occupational activity looks vastly different in fall 2013 (latest national data available) than it did just 25 years ago. Figure 4.1 illustrates the change in the number of full- and part-time employees by primary responsibility for selected years from fall 1991 through fall 2013. Due to primary occupations being reclassified as of fall 2013, executive, administrative, and managerial are included in "Other" to show

Table 4.1 Percentage of Full-Time Employees by Staff and Faculty by Sector and Institutional Type

Sector	Institutional Type	% Full-Time Employees	
		% of Staff	% of Faculty
Public	2-year colleges	47	30
	4-year colleges and universities	68	67
Private Not-for-Profit	2-year colleges	60	43
	4-year colleges and universities	69	57
Private For-Profit	2-year colleges	63	42
	4-year colleges and universities	44	15

Source: Author analysis of data in the 2014 Digest of Education Statistics (National Center for Education Statistics, 2016).

historical data. While the number of employees grew across the board, faculty positions increased more rapidly than did graduate assistant and other positions between 1991 and 2013. The number of faculty rose by 32%, graduate assistants by 23%, and other positions by 16%.

Figure 4.2 shows the change in the number of employees by primary responsibility for part-time employees only for selected years from fall 1991 through fall 2013. Among part-time professional employees, there was a 38% increase in faculty, a 23% increase in graduate assistants, and a 14% increase in other professionals. The shift to a part-time faculty workforce is characterized by modest growth in full-time faculty positions coupled with rapid growth in part-time faculty and graduate assistant positions (Figure 4.3). An informed discussion requires an understanding of faculty and instructional staff, who they are, and what they do, which will be addressed further in the next section.

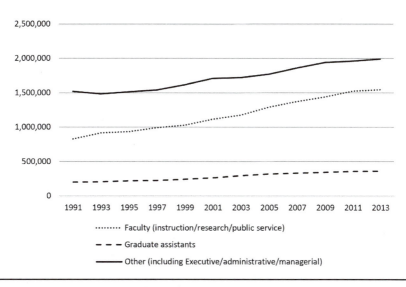

Figure 4.1 Full- and Part-Time Employees in Degree-Granting Institutions, by Primary Occupation: Selected Years, Fall 1991 Through Fall 2013

Source: Author analysis of Table 314.20, *Digest of Education Statistics*, 2014.

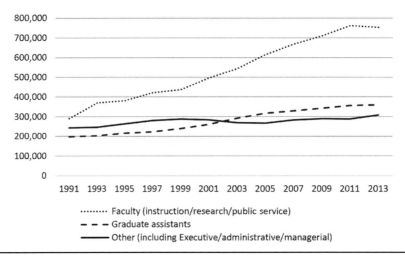

Figure 4.2 Part-Time Professional Employees in Degree-Granting Institutions, by Primary Occupation: Selected Years, Fall 1991 Through Fall 2013

Source: Author analysis of Table 314.20, *Digest of Education Statistics*, 2014.

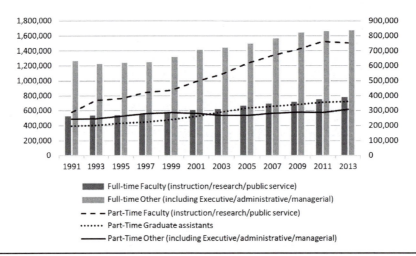

Figure 4.3 Comparison of Full- and Part-Time Professional Employees in Degree-Granting Institutions, by Primary Occupation: Selected Years, Fall 1991 Through Fall 2013

Source: Author analysis of Table 314.20, *Digest of Education Statistics*, 2014.

Faculty

IPEDS defines instructional staff as:

> an occupational category that is comprised of staff who are either: 1) primarily instruction or 2) instruction combined with research and/or public service. The intent of the instructional staff category is to include all individuals whose primary occupation includes instruction at the institution.

(IPEDS, n.d.)

In addition to collecting data through IPEDS, NCES manages the National Study of Postsecondary Faculty (NSOPF), a sample survey of faculty and instructional staff. This survey has been conducted four times since 1987–88, most recently in 2003–04. The target population included full-time and part-time employees with faculty status, regardless of whether or not they taught for credit, and anyone else with instructional responsibilities, regardless of whether or not they held faculty status. By casting a wide net, the NSOPF sample included a broad cross-section of professionals responsible for the instructional and research missions of colleges and universities at that point in time. The data, which offer a glimpse into the lives of some of these individuals, have been used in numerous studies.

In *Teaching Without Tenure*, for example, Baldwin and Chronister (2001) used NSOPF data to trace the growth of full-time non-tenure-track appointments and describe their characteristics. Their findings coalesced around five key themes:

1. The traditional full-time tenure-track faculty model is no longer adequately meeting the educational needs of a complex, dynamic society.
2. A two-class faculty system has emerged in American higher education.
3. At present, many institutions with long-term needs are treating full-time non-tenure-track faculty as short-term solutions who are expendable and easily replaced.
4. No consensus has yet emerged within higher education on the terms and conditions of employment of full-time non-tenure-track faculty.
5. The quality of students' educational experience and the overall health of our higher education system depend on a vigorous academic profession—including faculty in non-tenure-track positions (Baldwin & Chronister, 2001, pp. 7–8).

These themes still resonate today. From their extensive research, including analyses of data from NSOPF; a survey of institutions about their use of full-time non-tenure-track faculty and policies in place to govern such appointments; a review of available institutional policies; and interviews with faculty, department chairs, faculty leaders, and administrators at 12 institutions, Baldwin and Chronister (2001) identified 11 components of a good practice model:

1. A defined probationary period (p. 147)
2. Explicit evaluation criteria (p. 149)
3. Multi-year contracts following a probationary period (p. 150)
4. Defined dates for contract renewal or termination (p. 151)
5. An equitable salary system (p. 153)
6. An equitable fringe benefit program (p. 154)
7. A system of sequential ranks (p. 155)
8. Support for professional development (p. 156)
9. Meaningful involvement in governance and curriculum development (p. 159)
10. Recognition of and reward for contributions (p. 160)
11. Procedures for protecting academic freedom (p. 161).

To aid institutions in meeting these goals, the authors developed a framework for self-assessment that guides users through a series of questions designed to determine the extent to which the institution is engaging in good practices regarding personnel policies and full-time non-tenure-track faculty. The self-assessment covers four areas: the purpose and procedures for hiring, contractual arrangements, integration into the campus community, and oversight and monitoring (Baldwin & Chronister, 2001, pp. 206–210).

Examples of the types of questions in the first section include: "Does the institution have a comprehensive faculty staffing plan?" (p. 206) and "Has the institution clearly articulated the reasons for hiring non-track faculty?" (p. 207). In the section on contractual agreements, questions include: "Has a clearly defined position description been articulated for each non-track position?" (p. 207). One of the questions in the section on integration into the campus community asks: "Is there a formal orientation program for new full-time non-tenure-track faculty?" (p. 209). The final section poses questions such as: "What type of monitoring is conducted to ascertain that the policies and procedures governing the employment of full-time non-tenure-track faculty are consistently and equitably implemented?" (p. 210).

While the self-assessment guide was developed with full-time non-tenure-track faculty in mind, it could be modified to focus on each specific employee type to determine how well policies and practices in place are meeting the needs of the institution and the individuals. An important element is developing clear and reasonable expectations for each employee group.

Davis (2003) discusses managing people and encouraging development, as well as the key role of leaders in maintaining a positive work environment. He cites the dimensions of healthy work environments: (a) open communication, (b) employee involvement, (c) learning and renewal, (d) valued diversity, (e) institutional fairness, (f) equitable rewards and recognition, (g) economic security, (h) people-centered technology, (i) health-enhancing environments, (j) meaningful work, (k) family/work/life balance, (l) community responsibility, and (m) environmental protection (p. 178).

As postsecondary work environments become more complex and the roles of employees more ambiguous, it will become even more critical to focus attention on the policies and procedures that delineate management of personnel functions. Effective human resource management practices in business and industry do have relevant application in postsecondary education settings. Davis (2003) emphasizes the importance of "a commitment to core values such as respect for all, lifelong learning, and celebrating diversity" in promoting healthy work environments (p. 178).

Professional Staff (A.K.A. Non-Faculty)

It is becoming more difficult to distinguish when, where, and how instruction takes place as programming related to the first-year experience, retention, and learning communities has become commonplace outside of the physical or online classroom. A philosophy that focuses the mission of the entire institution on student learning further blurs academic vs. non-academic lines. The Student Personnel Point of View (SPPV) emphasizes development of the whole student, inside and outside of the classroom. The emergence of student affairs as a field within higher education and commensurate growth in the number of professional staff employed in related positions are indicators that institutions are embracing this philosophy. To date, however, IPEDS does not collect separate data on individuals whose primary occupation is student affairs.

In *Improving Staffing Practices in Student Affairs* (1997), Winston and Creamer present the synergistic supervision model, which provides guidance for ensuring quality in the profession. The components of the model include staff recruitment and selection, orientation, supervision and management, development, and performance appraisal. Conley (2001) adds "separation," noting that it is an integral aspect of the staffing process. While focused on student affairs, Winston and Creamer's model is applicable to other employee groups in higher education institutions. Given the complexity of employment relationships in colleges and universities today, effective staffing practices that incorporate strategies for selecting and developing traditional and non-traditional faculty and staff are critical.

STAFFING PRACTICES

In any staffing practices model, recruitment and selection, orientation, supervision, performance evaluation, professional development, turnover, and retirement must be considered. Yet colleges and universities occupy a unique position within our society that requires them to go beyond effective human resources practices. As learning organizations, they must transcend the tenets of business and industry. This is particularly challenging given the fiscal constraints facing many institutions, prompting some to question the priorities of those responsible for hiring decisions. Davis (2003) recommends a four-step process:

1. Describe the job,
2. Identify skills, knowledge, and personal characteristics required to do the job,
3. Establish selection criteria, and
4. Develop an assessment procedure to guide the selection.

The last step is critical to ensure consistency and fairness. Even so, "Vigilant efforts need to be maintained to see that the process is fair, that discrimination is absent, and that adequate records of the process are kept" (Davis, 2003, p. 182). Attention to process contributes to vigilance, a positive workplace environment, and compliance with state and federal workplace laws.

By way of example, Table 4.2 presents an excerpt from Ohio University's *Hiring Processes Overview*.

Table 4.2 Example Hiring Process Overview: Excerpt from Ohio University's *Hiring Processes Overview*

Step	Procedure
Job description	Complete a job description and submit to UHR compensation for proper classification if it is a new position, the job description is more than 3 years old, or the primary duties and responsibilities have changed more than 50%.
Essential position review	Complete and submit the EPR form www.ohio.edu/hr/forms.cfm to Rebecca Watts in the Office of the President for approval to post. NOTE: The following employment categories are exempt from the EPR process—positions fully (100%) supported through grant funding, student employment requests, internal postings of existing bargaining unit positions, and non-benefits-eligible term appointments.

(Continued)

Table 4.2 (Continued)

Step	Procedure
Posting	Concurrent with Step 2, the hiring manager creates an electronic requisition to post via the University's employment website: www.ohiouniversityjobs.com/hr. University Human Resources (UHR) will complete the posting process and contact the hiring manager to coordinate posting and advertising dates.
Recruitment and advertising	HR will post all benefits eligible vacancies to the University website as well as OhioMeansJobs.com and HigherEdJobs.com. Additionally, UHR will place all advertisements for classified positions. The hiring department is responsible for all recruitment activities including ad placement for administrative, faculty and student employment opportunities.
Screening and interviewing process	HR will pre-screen to identify classified candidates that meet the minimum qualifications for classified positions. For all other employment types, departments are responsible for conducting screening processes to determine finalist candidates.
Selection process	The hiring department is responsible for checking references for potential offerees. Once the department has identified the candidate(s) that are potential hires, the hiring manager must complete the online hiring forms and make their selections via the University's employment website to submit to either UHR or the Office of Institutional Equity (depending on employment type) prior to any offer or negotiation with the candidate.
Negotiation	HR will extend the official offer of employment as well as negotiate compensation and starting date for classified positions. For all other employment types, the hiring department is responsible for these negotiations. As part of the negotiation process, being familiar with the University's benefits.
Complete the hire	HR will process all new hire information for classified employees and will prepare and submit the official offer letter. Unsuccessful classified candidates will receive a regret email notification from UHR. UHR will schedule new hire orientation for classified employees. The hiring department is responsible for completing the on-line appointment form, offer letter, letters of regret, and scheduling new employee orientation for faculty and administrative hires. NOTE: I-9 forms MUST be completed within 48 hours of employment start date. If the employee is not scheduled for orientation until a later date, please ensure the employee comes to UHR within the first two days of employment to complete the I-9 in order to be in compliance with this important Federal Regulation UHR will process all new hire information for classified employees and will prepare and submit the official offer letter. Unsuccessful classified candidates will receive a regret email notification from UHR. UHR will schedule new hire orientation for classified employees. The hiring department is responsible for completing the on-line appointment form, offer letter, letters of regret, and scheduling new employee orientation for faculty and administrative hires. NOTE: I-9 forms MUST be completed within 48 hours of employment start date. If the employee is not scheduled for orientation until a later date, please ensure the employee comes to UHR within the first two days of employment to complete the I-9 in order to be in compliance with this important Federal Regulation.
On-boarding	The first few weeks of the new employee's experience will shape their lasting impression of Ohio University. Please be sure to make the new employee feel welcome in their new environment. Checking in with them regularly, assigning a mentor, providing departmental handbooks, are all good ways to help ease their transition. You might also consider a "welcome" package that includes helpful information about the department and planning unit. Some useful information might include where to find basic office supplies and departmental housekeeping information such as where to get coffee, where are the restrooms, etc.

Source: http://www.ohio.edu/hr/employment/upload/hiring_processes_overview.pdf

Vacancies

Employees leave, or separate from, their positions for many reasons—some voluntary, others involuntary. An individual may leave a position for professional reasons (e.g., to accept a promotion or for a higher salary) or personal reasons (e.g., to relocate closer to family). As the age of the population increases, more people are retiring from postsecondary institutions than ever before. Vacancies create losses but also opportunities. Winston and Creamer (1997) recommend conducting a thorough job analysis as a prerequisite to filling a vacancy. However, their case data reveal "that such practice is nowhere near universal or consistent" (p. 125). Davis (2003) also recommends conducting a careful job analysis: "Ask the person currently in the job, superiors, subordinates, and colleagues to describe the job. Examine existing job descriptions. Consider what exemplary performers of this job or similar jobs do and set reasonable performance standards" (p. 181).

The resulting data can be used to prepare exemplary job descriptions, the basic elements of which required are described below.

Job Descriptions

Job descriptions help articulate the most important outcomes needed from an employee performing a particular job. The basic elements of a job description include the position title, the name of the unit in which the position is located, responsibilities, and qualifications. Job descriptions for faculty positions may include other elements as well. Winston and Creamer (1997) call the position description "a crucial outcome of position analysis" and note, "A position description normally is thought of as the formal statement of duties that defines a position" (p. 130). These descriptions may be posted in a number of ways; potential avenues include the institution's human resources website, external employment websites, email, and social media. Typically, multiple methods of posting are used.

Job Posting Best Practices

The hiring department is typically responsible for all recruitment activities, including ad placement for administrative, faculty, and student employment opportunities (Ohio University *Hiring Processes Overview*, November 2009, Step 4, p. 1). Davis (2003) summarizes:

> Developing a job description, statement of qualifications, and a job posting that is distributed widely, avoids the tendency to "build a job around a promising person" or to become attracted to people "close at hand." Not only are such practices risky from a legal standpoint, they do not serve the institution well in the long run in locating the very best talent.
>
> (p. 182)

It is often a challenge to coordinate these activities in higher education because most vacancies are filled based on the recommendation of an ad hoc search committee convened for the purpose of completing the search.

Search Committees

Most searches in postsecondary institutions are filled with the assistance of a search committee. It is imperative that the roles and responsibilities of the search committee be clear from the outset. This can be accomplished through written invitations to serve on the committee and a charge from the supervisor or individual vested with hiring authority. Generally, research on what makes a search committee successful suggests that clarity throughout the process is a critical factor. Clarification up front can ensure a smoother process later. For example, a key question to consider before the search begins is whether the committee should forward a ranked or unranked list of qualified candidates to the hiring authority. Knowing the expectations from the outset can reduce tensions at the conclusion of the search.

One of the most critical steps in the hiring process is conducting interviews, of which there are several types. Denham (2009) lists (a) informational interviews, (b) screening or telephone interviews, (c) individual interviews, (d) small group or committee interviews, (e) the second or on-site interview, (f) behavioral-based interviews, (g) task-oriented or testing interviews, and (h) stress interviews.

In higher education, most of these interview types are utilized. The typical flow begins with the telephone interview (some institutions are now conducting video interviews during this phase), followed by the individual (on-site) interview, which can last one to two days and include group meetings and possibly a presentation on a given topic.

Reference checks are also interviews. A reference check is an interview of an applicant's former employer, former supervisor, current supervisor, or colleague. In higher education, a member of the search committee, the hiring supervisor, or a search firm hired by the institution usually conducts reference checks. The timing of the reference check varies by institution and by search committee; for instance, some choose to conduct reference checks prior to campus visits, while others wait until finalists are named for the vacant position.

Background checks go beyond reference checks to include criminal records and credit reports. Such checks are commonplace for administrative positions and are being utilized more and more in faculty searches.

Candidates should also be aware that search committees, search firms, and hiring authorities usually conduct Internet searches as a means of better understanding a candidate's background and breadth of experience. Increasingly, institutions are using social media sites such as Facebook, LinkedIn, and Twitter to obtain information about the prospective employee. Yet there is growing concern about the legalities associated with using information from cyberspace to make hiring and firing decisions.

Once the search process has concluded and a candidate has been identified for the position, a salary offer is made. Salary offers are handled differently in different institutions. The next section provides a general overview.

Salary Offer

The salary offer can occur in a variety of ways, the most common being by telephone call from the hiring supervisor. Many institutions are beginning to adopt standard human resources policies to ensure consistency when making salary offers, conducting salary negotiations, and answering new employees' questions about benefits, which are probably not the hiring manager's area of expertise.

In part, institutional culture determines where the hiring decision and responsibility for making salary offers reside. For faculty positions, department chairs may have authority to hire adjunct, temporary, or part-time faculty. Deans may reserve the right to negotiate offers with full-time tenure-track or non-tenure-track faculty. Hiring decisions for staff in administrative units are typically made at the director level or above.

Budget constraints create justifiable pressures and may tempt those responsible for hiring decisions to bring individuals into the organization at the lowest possible salary. Women, on average, still earn less than men in similar positions. In academia, the wage gap has narrowed in recent years but is still between 4% and 6% even after controlling for factors that are generally accepted as impacting faculty salaries (e.g., publications and grants) (Toutkoushian & Conley, 2005). One reason for the persistent gap may be that women do not negotiate as well as men (Miller & Miller, 2002). Starting salary has implications for future earnings, with a lower starting figure being compounded over time. Salary information is widely available today, especially for public institutions. Making this information transparent during the hiring process is one strategy for safeguarding against salary equity issues.

Hiring is an expensive process. Given the amount of time and effort that goes into such decisions, it is no wonder that recruitment and retention are seen as critical human resource issues in higher education. As discussed below, an effective orientation process will help to ensure a return on the investment.

Orientation

There is no shortage of resources on designing effective orientation programs for new higher education employees. For example, *The Missing Professor: An Academic Mystery* (Jones, 2005) takes a lighthearted approach by providing informal case studies and discussion stories that can be used as part of new faculty orientation, faculty development, and campus conversations. Winston and Creamer (1997) offer a comprehensive resource on staffing practices in student affairs, including new employee orientation.

These excellent resources notwithstanding, orientation is often defined by a planned event or series of events organized at the beginning of each academic year for a cohort of newly hired employees. These events are important because they introduce new employees to the institution and its culture and provide an opportunity to process necessary paperwork for health insurance, retirement plans, and, of course, parking.

Effective orientation is associated with processes that integrate the employee (faculty or staff) into the institution on an ongoing basis. As individuals take on new responsibilities and institutions take on new initiatives, orientation and professional development have the potential to become seamless synergistic processes that incorporate new and existing staff. Issues important to consider for existing staff are highlighted below.

Existing Staff

The number of new employees hired at an institution in a given year is small compared to the number of continuing employees. It goes without saying that highly effective organizations depend upon the productivity of the latter group. Effective management of human resources in higher education requires institutions to concentrate their attention on existing staff. Bolman and Deal (1997) describe one useful tool for doing so—the human resources framework. The simple constructs of this theoretical framework are a reminder that organizations and people need each other. Organizations need the talent, skills, and abilities that individuals bring to positions. Individuals need the jobs and resources provided by the organization.

Highly effective human resource managers understand the importance of professional development in helping employees achieve continued personal and professional growth. College and university faculty and staff are experts on student development and the importance of nurturing the whole student. The same constructs should be applied to understanding employee development.

However, separation is also a natural part of the staffing process. Individuals leave organizations for many reasons. Accepting a position at another institution and retirement are two of the most common. As the age of the population increases, retirements in higher education are becoming more commonplace. As the economy continues to recover, there will be opportunities for advancement. Understanding employees' strengths, opportunities for improvement, and aspirations will better position highly effective institutions to respond to demands for innovative strategies for delivering higher education to learners. Approaches for improving performance are essential to success; these include conducting honest and accurate evaluations appropriate for the type of employee, using progressive discipline techniques, providing recognition and incentives, and identifying and empowering change agents.

Evaluations

Evaluations are key to understanding employees. Organizations perform evaluations in an effort to assess employee performance accurately. While evaluations serve a similar purpose for all types of employees, the process involved differs from group to group even within the same institution. For example, Winston and Creamer (1997) focus on supervision as the central mechanism for achieving effective staffing practices in student affairs. Evaluations are the primary tool supervisors use to provide feedback.

Evaluations are equally critical for faculty, but the processes involved are typically different than those for administrative and other staff members at an institution. Faculty members value autonomy; where they are concerned, then, supervision is not the primary mechanism for achieving effective staffing practices. Faculty performance evaluation is a continuous, multifaceted process including input from students, peers, department chairs, and deans.

Indeed, faculty members are evaluated in a variety of ways, one being based on the courses that they teach. Course evaluations provide instructors with feedback on students' perceptions of the course overall and the effectiveness of instructional methods used. Their primary purpose is to enable instructors to make informed decisions about improving the course. In addition, institutions use course evaluations to assess the instructor's teaching abilities.

Faculty members are also evaluated through peer review, which is typically conducted annually by a committee made up of colleagues at the same or higher rank within an academic department. The committee makes recommendations to the department chair and the dean regarding the performance of each faculty member within the department. The process for determining merit increases and the decision-making authority for allocating such increases varies from institution to institution. In their role as supervisor, department chairs are typically required to conduct their own evaluations of the faculty within their department.

When a faculty member goes up for tenure and/or promotion, that individual's accomplishments to date are reviewed more thoroughly. Evaluations of his or her portfolio are solicited from faculty in the discipline outside of the institution. Other forms of faculty peer review include proposal processes for conferences, publications, and grants. It is important to note that administrators are increasingly being evaluated through peer review. The extent to which research and creative activity are expected or considered part of the normal duties of the position varies from institution to institution.

All individuals involved in evaluation processes at an institution should be provided with information regarding expectations for the position and their role in performance review.

Progressive Discipline

Progressive discipline is a process for dealing with job-related behavior that does not meet expected and communicated performance standards. Its primary purpose is to assist the employee in understanding that a performance problem or opportunity for improvement exists. Many colleges and universities have a defined progressive discipline protocol. While progressive discipline processes may vary by institution, most include a verbal warning or reprimand. Should the performance problem continue, the discipline progresses to a written reprimand, suspension, and ultimately termination if the issue is not resolved.

Progressive discipline is typically applied differently with different employee groups. For example, a progressive discipline policy for addressing job-related behavior of student employees usually involves four basic steps: a documented verbal warning, a written warning, a suspension, and termination. Similar protocols are usually followed for non-faculty employees. Table 4.3 provides an example progressive discipline policy.

Table 4.3 Example Progressive Discipline Policy: Excerpt From The University of Alabama's Progressive Discipline Policy

Sections Included	Example Excerpted Wording
Purpose	The purpose of the procedure listed here is to encourage and help employees work together harmoniously according to the standards of The University of Alabama.
Policy statement	Progressive steps will be followed in employee disciplinary matters except in matters the University, its representatives, or its management determine need to be addressed outside of the progressive system.
Types of disciplinary action	*Verbal Counseling:* Verbal counseling sessions may take place between employees and supervisors in situations that are deemed less serious in nature. Every effort to determine and resolve the cause of the problem should be made. At the same time, however, it should be specifically stated that the employee is receiving a formal warning. Documentation of the verbal counseling should be made and maintained in departmental files for verbal counseling sessions. *Written Counseling:* Written counseling sessions take place between a supervisor and an employee when the behavior of the employee: is a repeated violation and verbal counseling has been administered; hinders the progress of the department in which the employee works; or hampers the progress of the University. Copies of all written warnings should be distributed as follows: one copy to the employee, one copy to the University's Department of Human Resources for inclusion in the employee's file, and one copy maintained in departmental files under lock and key.

(Continued)

Table 4.3 (Continued)

Sections Included	Example Excerpted Wording
Types of disciplinary action *(continued)*	*Suspension:* Suspension, or release from duty, is a more severe action that may be used to continue investigations and/or for constructive improvement. Suspensions are issued when it is determined that a second warning would not suffice or that an initial incident is too severe for a warning yet not sufficiently severe for dismissal. Suspensions may vary in length, according to the severity of the offense or deficiency. Where a suspension has failed to produce the proper results, consideration should be given for a more lengthy suspension or the dismissal of the employee.
	Suspension notices should indicate the following: a. the reason(s) for the discipline, b. the inclusive dates of the suspension, and c. the employee's right of appeal.
	Dismissals: An employee's employment may be terminated after other disciplinary measures have failed or when a first time incident occurs that is extremely serious.
Behaviors that may result in disciplinary action	• Displaying a disrespectful and/or inappropriate behaviors toward a student, employee or supervisor; • Refusing to do assigned work or failing to carry out the reasonable assignment of a manager, supervisor or department head; • Falsifying a time card or other University record or giving false information to anyone whose duty is to make such record; • Being repeatedly or continuously absent or late, being absent without notice or reason satisfactory to the University or leaving one's work assignment without appropriate authorization; • Smoking within no-smoking areas or no-smoking operations or any area of the University that must be entered for the conduct of University business; • Conducting oneself in any manner which is offensive, abusive or contrary to common decency or morality; carrying out any form of harassment including sexual harassment; • Operating state-owned vehicles, equipment or private vehicles on state business without proper license or operating any vehicle on University property or on University business in an unsafe or improper manner; • Having an unauthorized weapon, firearm or explosive on University property; • Appropriating state or student equipment, time or resources for personal use or gain; • Computer abuse, including but not limited to, plagiarism or programs, misuse of computer accounts, unauthorized destruction of files, creating illegal accounts, possession of unauthorized passwords, disruptive or annoying behavior on the computer and non-work related utilization of computer software or hardware; • Conviction of a felony; • Unlawfully distributing, selling, possessing, using or being under the influence of alcohol or drugs when on the job or subject to duty; • Interfering in any way with the work of others; • Stealing or possessing without authority any equipment, tools, materials or other property of the University or attempting to remove them from the premises without approval or permission from the appropriate authority; • Willful violation of safety rules or University policies.

Source: http://hr.ua.edu/empl_rel/policy-manual/counseling-discipline.htm

Different protocols are followed for faculty members—especially those with tenure, which is earned through an extensive review process after a probationary period. Afforded a high level of autonomy in their work, tenured faculty members have a responsibility to their subject—to seek and to state the truth as they see it—and devote their energies to developing and improving their scholarly competence. Tenured faculty members are guided by ethical principles of the profession and accept the obligation to exercise self-discipline and judgment in using, extending, and transmitting knowledge. Termination for cause of a tenured faculty member is a serious matter. The faculty handbook of an institution outlines the process. For example, the *Ohio University Faculty Handbook* states:

> Termination for cause of a continuous appointment, or the dismissal for cause of a teacher previous to the expiration of a term appointment should, if possible, be considered by both a faculty committee and the governing board of the institution. In all cases where the facts are in dispute, accused teachers should be informed before the hearing in writing of the charges against them and should have the opportunity to be heard in their own defense by all bodies that pass judgment upon their case. They should be permitted to have with them an advisor of their own choosing who may act as counsel. There should be a full stenographic record of the hearing available to the parties concerned. In the hearing of charges of incompetence, the testimony should include that of teachers and other scholars, either from their own or from other institutions. Teachers on continuous appointment who are dismissed for reasons not involving moral turpitude should receive their salaries for at least a year from the date of notification of dismissal whether or not they are continued in their duties at the institution.
>
> (Section I.4.A.d)

Care should be taken to distinguish between human resources management issues and breaches of ethics. If they are to enhance individual and institutional productivity, mechanisms for handling performance problems or opportunities for improvement among faculty must be based on clearly articulated expectations, and acceptable and trustworthy evidence (Braskamp & Ory, 1994).

An important provision for faculty is the ability to appeal a decision. "Faculty have the right to question a decision and be given an opportunity without threat of retaliation, to question the fairness of the assessment process" (Braskamp & Ory, 1994, p. 162). Disciplinary action cases for faculty should be handled with sensitivity given the nature of the tenured faculty member's position in the institution and within his or her academic field of expertise; these cases have the potential to affect an individual's status and the institution's reputation (Braskmap & Ory, 1994).

In addition to applying discipline fairly, effective human resources management also emphasizes recognition and incentives. The next section explores strategies that can be used to acknowledge the value of higher education employees, something particularly important in today's economy.

Recognition and Incentives

In a difficult economy, supervisors are always searching for ways to recognize dynamic employee efforts and simultaneously create a motivational environment where employees work at optimal levels to accomplish agreed-upon objectives. The term "incentives" most often calls to mind monetary rewards. It is important to keep in mind, particularly given the tough economic climate, that incentives take a variety of forms. Perhaps one of the most effective incentives an institution can provide is a positive work environment and campus climate or the possibility of working from home a few days a week.

Workplace motivators include both monetary and non-monetary incentives and should vary based on the career stage and generation of the employee. It should be noted that not all employees are solely motivated by monetary incentives. Although the use of positive reinforcements is good practice in the workplace, it must be done correctly. A balance between monetary and non-monetary incentives should be used to satisfy the diverse needs and interests of employees.

Evidence suggests that different incentives are important to employees from different generations. Generational non-monetary incentive differences are linked to career stage and proximity to retirement: the older the individual, the greater the focus on retirement or supplementing retirement income with part-time or temporary jobs; the younger the individual, the greater the focus on job satisfaction and work environment. The bottom line is that organizations must tailor incentives to the needs of employees rather than using a "one-size-fits-all" approach, which is impersonal and sometimes ineffective.

Budget Reductions

In most colleges and universities, budget reductions are a regular occurrence. Regardless of whether the budget reduction is short-term or long-term, it is not an easy task because it will affect something or someone adversely. In order to develop a strategy for combating reductions, one must understand why the cuts are being implemented, how much of a reduction is needed, how the reduction can be distributed across departments, and in what time frame the reduction will have to be absorbed.

It is important to know whether the reduction is happening because of occurrences, or trigger events, within the college or university (e.g., low enrollment, reduction in investment income, increased expenses, need for infrastructure improvements) or as a result of external factors (e.g., reduction in state subsidy or federal grants, down economy, or legislative changes). Once the reason for the reduction is known, the institution can plan accordingly to prevent future cuts, finding alternative methods of replacing the lost income and/or finding ways to absorb the reduction. Because higher education relies heavily on human resources, many budget reductions impact personnel.

Some strategies that can be employed to assist in combating short-term and long-term budget reductions include: (a) increasing revenue, (b) implementing hiring freezes and/or reductions in staff, (c) conducting environmental scans, (d) making tough decisions, and (e) involving faculty, staff, and students in the process.

CONCLUSION

This chapter began by examining trends in the distribution of higher education employees. The discussion continued with a review of recommended strategies for selecting and developing faculty and staff, and then explored approaches for improving performance and ideas for accommodating the short- and long-term budget reductions necessary to enhance productivity and efficiency in today's postsecondary education environment.

The chapter now concludes with an overarching recommendation to engage in purposeful, mission-driven, data-informed human resources planning and decision-making that takes into consideration the complex employment relationships found in colleges and universities. Specific advice focused at the institutional level and at individuals responsible for managing human resources is intended to provide guidance on how to create and maintain highly effective organizations composed of highly effective employees.

First, clarify, simplify, and streamline processes while respecting the autonomy of units engaged in searches. Even small institutions often have multiple job searches going on at the same time. Leverage mechanisms to make the most of the institutional resources available to support these searches. For example, provide a template for job descriptions; delineate the key steps in the process from approval of the search to making an offer; and organize and make widely available tips on key questions to ask (and not to ask).

Attending to basic structural issues and clarifying policies and procedures will go a long way in ensuring organizational effectiveness. Of course, the culture of the institution influences the structure and the extent to which processes are centralized or decentralized. While structure matters, there should be a degree of flexibility inherent in human resources processes, particularly given the increasing complexity of employment relationships in colleges and universities today. Instead of thinking about processes as centralized or decentralized, highly effective organizations will strike an appropriate balance between the two.

Second, use a human resources framework and synergistic supervision to guide decision-making to improve performance. Review language in accrediting bodies' guidelines related to human resources. Mission-driven staffing practices that align with these guidelines will be most effective.

Third, budgets are value statements for colleges and universities, and unfortunately budget reductions are a harsh reality. Institutions must have a great understanding of what they are trying to accomplish and why. In combating short-term and long-term budget reductions, several options can be deployed. These include increasing revenue, implementing a hiring freeze or reduction in staff, conducting an environmental scan, doing less with less, and involving faculty and students in the entire conversation.

Finally, it should be clear from the complex employment relationships that exist on college and university campuses that effective human resources management requires multiple processes and structures. Winston and Creamer (1997), among others, emphasize that at its core human resources involves people. It is possible to take this a step further by suggesting that everyone in higher education is involved in human resources. This approach requires constant, consistent communication; knowledge of institutional policies; and budget training.

DISCUSSION PROMPTS

1. Do the changes in employee composition reflect a change in the way higher education accomplishes its mission? Do they demonstrate that colleges and universities have been under-resourced and/or do they denote a purposeful redirecting of resources away from the academic mission of institutions?

2. In what ways has your institution changed its hiring policies and procedures over the last three to five years? Are there differences for faculty vs. staff and part-time vs. full-time?

3. What innovative ideas does and/or should your institution use to retain employees? How do and/or should they vary by employee type?

4. What are three strategies administrators with direct and indirect reports should focus on to bolster employee success?

5. Based on the significant change in use of part-time employees, identify three unintended consequences and three benefits of a having a higher percentage of part-time employees.

6. What value do search committees bring to the process? Under what circumstances should a search committee be formed instead of allowing the hiring manager to conduct the search alone?

7. How can managers improve the value of employee evaluations? What elements are missing from employee evaluations at your institution?

8. What is progressive discipline and when should it be employed? Identify the section on progressive discipline (may use different wording) in your employee handbook. As a supervisor, what questions or concerns do you have about the process? In what ways are your concerns similar to or different from those of an employee in a non-supervisory position?

9. What information should be included in an institution-wide orientation? What are three pros and cons of an institution-wide orientation and why?

10. What creative (and legal) job recruiting practices would you use to find the best candidates?

REFERENCES

American Association of University Professors (AAUP) (1940). *1940 statement of principles on academic freedom and tenure*. Retrieved July 7, 2011 from the AAUP website: http://www.aaup.org/AAUP/pubsres/policydocs/contents/1940statement.htm

Baldwin, R. G., & Chronister, J. L. (2001). *Teaching without tenure: Policies and practices for a new era*. Baltimore, Maryland: The Johns Hopkins University Press.

Bolman, L. G., & Deal, T. E. (1997). *Reframing organizations: Artistry, choice, and leadership* (2nd ed.). San Francisco: Jossey-Bass.

Braskamp, L. A., & Ory, J. C. (1994). *Assessing faculty work: Enhancing individual and institutional performance*. San Francisco: Jossey-Bass.

Conley, V. M. (2001). Separation: An integral aspect of the staffing process. *The College Student Affairs Journal, 21*(1), 57–63.

Davis, J. R. (2003). *Learning to lead: A handbook for postsecondary administrators*. ACE/Praeger Series on Higher Education. New York: Rowman & Littlefield.

Denham, T. J. (2009). *The 8 major types of interviews*. Retrieved July 7, 2011 from the Career Center Toolbox website: http://www.careercentertoolbox.com/interviews/the-8-major-types-of-interviews

Integrated Postsecondary Education Data System. (n.d.). *IPEDS glossary*. Retrieved June 2016 from the National Center for Education Statistics website http://nces.ed.gov/IPEDS/glossary

Jones, T. (2005). *The missing professor: An academic mystery*. Sterling, Virginia: Stylus Publishing.

Leslie, D. W. (2007). The reshaping of America's academic workforce. TIAA-CREF institute. *Research Dialogue, 87*, 1–23.

Miller, L. E., & Miller, J. (2002). *A woman's guide to successful negotiating: How to convince, collaborate, and create your way to agreement*. New York: McGraw-Hill.

National Center for Education Statistics. (2014). *Digest of Education Statistics: 2014*. Retrieved June 2016, from Chapter 3: Postsecondary Education: http://nces.ed.gov/programs/digest/d14/ch_3.asp

Ohio University Faculty Handbook (n.d.). Retrieved July 7, 2011 from the Ohio University Faculty Senate website: http://www.ohio.edu/facultysenate/handbook/index.cfm

Toutkoushian, R. K., & Conley, V. M. (2005). Progress for women in academe, yet inequities persist: Evidence from NSOPF:99. *Research in Higher Education*, 46(1), 1–28.

Winston, Jr., R. B., & Creamer, D. G. (1997). *Improving staffing practices in student affairs*. San Francisco: Jossey-Bass.

5

STUDENT GOVERNANCE AND INVOLVEMENT IN INSTITUTIONAL LEADERSHIP

Shouping Hu, Danielle Morgan Acosta,
Carrie E. Henderson, and Jennifer Iacino

INTRODUCTION

In 2015, a heightened, broad-based activism swept college campuses across the country, with students voicing their concerns both about the stark inequality in American society and about issues directly related to their own lives. The #BlackLivesMatter movement continued to spread to college campuses, where student activists began expanding its scope to include not only injustice felt nationally, but on their own campuses as well. Demonstrations at the University of Missouri and coalitions across campuses began to mobilize more frequently than had been seen in recent history, most notably through the "Occupy Colleges" movement. Student activism of such breadth and intensity hadn't been seen since the 1960s and 1970s. Often, student activism and participation stem from national movements; other times, movements begin on campus and move more gradually. Given what has been happening in colleges and universities, understanding student governance structures and the roles they can play in institutional leadership and policy-making is critical for effective higher education administration.

This chapter briefly documents the historical evolution of student governance in U.S. higher education, discusses the various functions of student governance in institutional leadership, describes the diverse venues in which students can play a role in institutional leadership and related issues, and presents examples of notable practices in higher education.

American higher education has undergone drastic transformations since the establishment of Harvard College in 1636, successfully evolving from an elite to a mass system, and then to universal access. Student populations have also changed drastically, adding an incredibly diverse population and new sets of needs and voices to the campus community. The attention on students and their expectation of instantaneous change has evolved along with the environments within and beyond higher education.

When "in loco parentis" doctrine permeated American colleges and universities, students were treated as somewhat passive participants in higher education under the care and supervision of college administrators. As Horowitz (1987) documents in her historical analysis, campus life was defined by battles between the administration and students. Initially, student clubs and organizations were a way for students to enjoy campus life and deal with college administrators when frustrations surfaced. Eventually, college administrators introduced formal student governance structures as a way to work with students and better manage campus life (Laosebikan-Buggs, 2006).

As higher education has transformed, so has the relationship between students and the institutions they attend. In particular, the rise of consumerism has led to students' increasing demand to participate in the decision-making process that impacts their education. Student governance is a widely implemented customary practice for most institutions of higher education in the United States, and is mandated by state law in many states, including Wisconsin, Florida, and California.

Jones (1974) acknowledges "governance" is a nebulous term requiring further explanation. The definition of student governance varies by scholar. Schenkel (1971) says governance is the process of direct control by different individuals within an institution. Love and Miller (2003) describe how student governance has evolved to mean student involvement in traditional areas of academic oversight, such as student activities and student organization funding. Miller and Nadler (2006) describe student governance as the involvement of students in institutional management, either through formal or informal organizations. Friedson and Shuchman (1955) characterize student governance through student governments: "a type of organization which by virtue of its composition and constitution is entitled to represent the student community as a whole" (p. 6). Finally, May (2009) links student governance to American democratic ideals:

> The earliest student bodies desired to establish representative governments mirroring those of the emerging young nation. The evolution of student self-governance continues its healthy course on today's colleges and universities campuses, and it is truly a mark of this nation's democratic principles and standards. As higher education in the United States has matured and expanded, so has student self-governance, sustaining the argument that student governance is a key component to this growth. Student self-governance will continue to evolve and expand, particularly as a means to reach students where administration and faculty cannot—by engaging students in the campus community and by giving students a voice.
>
> (p. 486)

Birnbaum (1988) notes there is no one common definition of campus governance; "a governance system is an institution's answer—at least temporarily—to the enduring question that became a plaintive cry during the campus crisis of the late 1960s and early 1970s: 'Who's in charge here?'" (p. 4). Accordingly, institutions have wide discretionary range to shape and cultivate student governance opportunities in terms of scope, level of involvement, and impact. Their leaders must weigh pressures from students and other constituents against institutional values to ensure that increased student involvement will enhance the administrative decision-making process and provide opportunities for both student and institutional growth.

IMPORTANCE OF STUDENT GOVERNANCE AND ENGAGEMENT

Student involvement in institutional leadership has the unique capacity to meet two major institutional purposes simultaneously: the development of students and the improvement of institutional effectiveness. The higher education literature has unequivocally confirmed that the more students are engaged in college activities, the more they will gain and learn from their college experience (Astin, 1993; Hu & Kuh, 2003; National Survey of Student Engagement, 2004, 2005; Pascarella & Terenzini, 1991, 2005). Research specifically on student governance experiences also shows desirable effects on student development (Komivies, Wagner, & Associates, 2009; Kuh & Lund, 1994), especially in the areas of leadership development and civic engagement. Due to current demographic changes and social transformation, many pressing issues such as inequality in educational and economic attainment are posing challenges to American society as a whole (Smith, Altbach, & Lomotey, 2002; St. John, 2003). When reflecting on these challenges, Astin and Astin (2000) comment that "the problems that plague American society are, in many respects, problems of leadership" (p. 2). They argue American colleges and universities have a responsibility to develop college students into future leaders able to effect social change. Student participation in governance and institutional leadership can be an effective means of fulfilling that responsibility.

Higher education institutions are constantly criticized for not meeting the needs of students and the broader society, as students graduate disillusioned by the current job market and the amount of their student loan debt. The general public, and families footing the bill, perceive colleges and universities as organizations lacking in effectiveness and efficiency. With public funds being invested in higher education, the discontent about student learning outcomes has never been higher (Arum & Roksa, 2011; National Commission on the Future of Higher Education, 2006). Students on campus, focused on jobs and listening to the rhetoric of national criticisms, may serve as participants and often partners to the institution through student governance structures. Such involvement serves not only as a vehicle for providing students with soft skills necessary in the workplace, but also requires institutional leaders to understand the messages students are bringing with them to the table.

Student involvement in institutional leadership has the potential to improve the quality of institutional decisions and enhance student satisfaction on campus. The multiple potential benefits to the institution include improved implementation of decisions, evaluation of curricula and teaching practices, and the promotion of an atmosphere of openness, community, solidarity, and trust (Menon, 2003). While some scholars argue that students have relatively little impact on campus policy, others have shown the involvement of students to be an important aspect of campus decision-making (Jones, 1974; Miller & Nadler, 2006). Such participation varies by institution, but often takes the form of student government associations. Student governance:

can placate the need to speak out, it can improve the level of acceptance of a decision on campus, and it can allow students the opportunity to openly challenge administrators and faculty. In a broad sense, student involvement in institutional governance provides a system of checks and balances with administrators and faculty.

(Love & Miller, 2003, p. 522)

Institutions of higher education have not changed radically over time, but students have. Digital natives from diverse racial, ethnic, socioeconomic, and educational backgrounds can support and engage the institution by providing voice and forward momentum to a positive collegiate experience. It is important to note that student governance is not only beneficial to the student, but can be beneficial to the institution as a whole.

STRUCTURE AND PROCESS OF STUDENT GOVERNANCE

Institutional culture and organization play an important role in the structure and process of student governance opportunities. Kuh and Whitt (1988) define culture as:

persistent patterns of norms, values, practices, beliefs, and assumptions that share the behavior of individuals and groups in a college or university and provide a frame of reference within which to interpret the meaning of events and actions on and off campus.

(p. iv)

Cultural norms for individual campuses invisibly establish boundaries for student governance that fit the overall customs of the institution. These boundaries are not fixed, but instead are malleable and stretch or contract as specific players transition into and out of the institution. A specific administrator may ask for student opinion on a particular issue, or students who advocate on behalf of a problem they see on campus may become a sounding board for another staff member as they move forward with a charge. Listening to student voice is an important aspect of the college experience, but less structured systems may be personality or issue based and change rapidly as administrators or students leave.

Within formal structures, an officially chartered student government association, student senate, or student assembly is common, though the purpose of these bodies can vary widely. Students, often elected by their peers, have the authority to represent wider groups of students on the campus (by academic year or program of study, for example), and may cast official votes in the governance process. Laosebikan-Buggs (2006) describes the primary functions of formal student government associations as follows:

- official voice of students to the administration (representation);
- participation in the decision-making processes of university governance (voice);
- ethical and responsible collection and dissemination of student fees; and
- recognition of student organizations as well as the coordination of the activities clubs and organizations on campus (advocacy) (p. 3).

This description is clearly reflected in the constitution of Florida State University's student body, which states that:

> the mission of the Student Government Association (SGA), is to provide FSU students with representation, services and advocacy within the university structure. The Student Government Association provides quality leadership for, and accountability to its constituency by recognizing that strength arises from diversity, engagement, and dialogue.
>
> (2009)

This statement not only highlights the role of student governance in student "representation services and advocacy" within the university community, but also indicates its ability to provide opportunities for and accountability to its constituents.

Students are also often included in more informal processes of governance through invitation by faculty and administrators to join committees and special project work groups. Students are typically a small minority on these committees but frequently have a powerful voice in the discussion; faculty and staff with somewhat limited exposure to student opinions on governance topics are often quite interested to know students' perspectives on critical issues. The inclusion of students in decisions, however marginal, is beneficial: students gain power through access to institutional leaders and a forum to voice student opinions, with or without voting rights.

ROLES AND FUNCTION OF STUDENT GOVERNANCE

Significant differences exist among institutions with regard to the role and function of student governance, such as which issues are available or "on the table" for students to address. Some public and private institutions may have a relatively consistent history of meaningful student participation in institutional governance, including a vibrantly elected SGA, student involvement in fee allocation processes, and an assortment of campus committees or student conduct boards. Others may have periods marked by student activism for greater levels of involvement, such as meetings with the university president on controversial issues or a student vote on the institution's board of trustees. Still others (typically young and/or private institutions) may have limited experience with student governance and hesitate to include students in decision-making processes. Community colleges and regional commuter campuses may provide student governance opportunities, such as student programming councils responsible for campus events, but face apathy and limited engagement from the student body.

Braskamp, Trautvetter, and Ward (2006) discuss the centrality of shared governance on collaborative campuses, based on their study of ten faith-based liberal arts colleges:

> Creating community—a community where faculty involvement in student development is supported—calls for collective responsibility. Faculty and staff mentioned that being part of a community means stepping outside oneself ... We also learned that students play central roles in maintaining the campus community. Students are empowered and often provide input on the direction of the campus.

This merits comment on two fronts: The students interviewed were highly involved in the campus community, and this involvement connects them with faculty. Faculty, students, and administrators work side by side as part of shared governance.

(p. 164)

Institutional leaders have the opportunity to involve students at many governance levels and in a wide variety of issues. Search committees allow for students to have a say in selecting new administrators or faculty, or in selecting large campus vendors through a competitive bid process (such as the food service contract, which has a major impact on student quality of life), while also providing candidates and companies with information about student culture. For example, at Florida State University, two students nominated by the student body president serve on each university presidential search committee, communicating information to other students and voicing current student concerns during the selection process in active and meaningful ways.

Student funding committees through SGA can be a significant and highly valued responsibility assigned to student leaders; public institutions often collect "activity" fees through tuition payments, and SGAs or committees may have discretion to allocate those funds within established parameters and guidelines (the senior student affairs officer typically has veto power over these student decisions). As institutions face budgeting challenges as well as mounting criticism for increasing tuition, working with students to shape the co-curricular experience and allocate funds becomes even more important, particularly as these funds shape not only student activities, but auxiliary services or whole departments on campus.

There are few limits to student participation. Strategic planning and accreditation committees, diversity or homecoming week initiatives, appellate decisions for transportation violations, and academic policy appeals are among the many ways an institution can engage students in its structures and policies. Participation on these types of committees might be seen at institutions with a long-standing tradition of high student integration at all levels of governance.

Finding meaningful ways to enrich student engagement experiences also provides decision-makers with critical feedback about student perspectives, while students gain insight into larger campus issues and can thus become partners in supporting institutional initiatives. In these partnerships, decisions are often made by the chair or deferred to the consensus of the group, and it can be valuable to have the enthusiasm and creativity of students to energize what may be routine tasks.

Table 5.1 provides further information about these broad categories of student involvement in institutional leadership processes, including some desirable characteristics of students serving these groups, expectations for participation, and special challenges to consider. Each institution should expand these categories in consideration of its unique circumstances, purpose, values, and culture.

Many institutions have both undergraduate and graduate enrollment, so there is a need to consider the most suitable structure for involving different student populations in institutional leadership. Love and Miller (2003) find the needs of undergraduates involved in student government differ from those of graduate students.

It is increasingly important that similarities and differences between undergraduates and graduate students be identified and clarified in an effort to build a more cohesive and potentially powerful force that advocates for students on campus, particularly in light of the encroaching corporate model of institutional management.

(p. 534)

Although most institutions still combine graduate student representation with broader student government, some research universities have graduate student government associations that serve and advocate on behalf of the graduate student population more effectively.

Graduate students employed by universities have also sought representation through collective bargaining agreements and unions. For public institutions, collective bargaining and unionization falls under state law, so some states encourage collective bargaining, while others restrict it. For private institutions, collective bargaining and unionization fall under the federal Taft–Hartley Act. Overall, graduate student employees at public and private institutions have exercised their rights and attempted to influence institutional governance through unions (Berquist & Pawlak, 2007).

Table 5.1 Examples of Student Governance and Involvement in Institutional Leadership

Categories of Student Governance	Common Examples	Desirable Student Characteristics	Participation Expectations	Special Challenges
Search Committees	Food service vendor; university president; various levels of administrators or faculty	Process-oriented; represent particular campus constituencies	Gather information and communicate to other students; provide critical feedback to those responsible for selection	Creating "meaningful" experiences for students when the ultimate decision does not rest with the committee
Funding Committees	SGA activity fees; building projects; student scholarships	Fiscally oriented; engaged in campus politics or formal governance structures; appointed or elected to committee	Follow established policies; make critical decisions; exercise responsible discretion	Holding students accountable to policies and guidelines without overturning funding decisions
Strategic Planning and Accreditation Committees	Mission revision; Quality Enhancement Plans; re-branding initiatives	Values-oriented; interested in aligning policy and practice or setting high standards	Focus on broad issues; bring student voice to the discussion	Communicating broader vision and context to students for their meaningful participation
Institutional Administration and Special Topic Committees	Academic program review; honor code/ civility board; homecoming week	Task-oriented; able to take on projects as part of the group; able to communicate ideas and plans to other students	Contribute ideas; volunteer time to advance new initiatives; consistently participate for duration of committee	Setting reasonable limits on student ideas without discouraging creativity or enthusiasm

FACILITATING STUDENT GOVERNANCE IN INSTITUTIONAL LEADERSHIP

Student governance emphasizes the role and voice of students, but campus administrators can effectively facilitate student participation in institutional leadership by following the steps described below.

Orienting Student Leaders to Governance Processes

Communicating expectations to students and orienting them to specific roles and customs are vitally important to their successful engagement in meaningful governance opportunities. It is beneficial to guide and develop in students the knowledge and skills that will support their participation so they are prepared to interact with administrators, faculty, and other constituents.

Students often perceive participation in governance to be a privilege and seek to exercise professionalism. Their mentors and advisors have a valuable opportunity to help them gain further appreciation for the importance of professional conduct and customs, hone their leadership skills, and increase their job marketability after graduation.

Additionally, students must understand the charge of the committee, as well as any relevant work history or background of individuals on the committee or connected to the project. Taking time to properly orient students to the governance process and cultivate their ability to positively contribute can ensure maximum benefit both for the students and for the committee.

Including Students

Where there are no state mandates for student governance, institutional leaders often have the authority to facilitate and authorize student participation in governance processes. When this does not occur, students may request or demand more responsibility than leaders are willing to allow. For example, students may become dissatisfied with a particular employee working in an area funded by student fees and demand authority to terminate his or her employment, or students may become opposed to a particular corporate sponsor of university athletics or other prominent program and want the discretion to terminate a partnership lucrative for the institution. While there are no "one size fits all" solutions, effectively communicating and engaging with students proactively can make it easier for the institution to navigate such complex and tumultuous situations.

Important questions for institutional leaders to ask themselves include:

- Am I building collaborative relationships with student leaders so we can work together to effectively address issues?
- Am I facilitating adequate opportunities for student voices to be heard, recognized, and considered around this issue?
- Are we challenging students to engage in deeper issues and to help generate solutions and/or options to consider?
- Are there important legal limitations or other legitimate reasons students should not be included in the decision-making process on this issue, and are these being communicated effectively and clearly?

- What precedents are being established by inclusion or exclusion of student voices on this issue? Who is not at the table?
- Am I truly open to hearing the concerns students have on this issue and following up with students accordingly?

Birnbaum (1988) notes that the culture of an institution may place high value on symbolic action or the appearance of meaningful response to student concerns without the intention or desire for true interaction and inclusion. Institutional leaders must ensure that efforts to include students in important decisions or to respond to their concerns are not shallow, symbolic gestures, but, to the extent practical, meaningful opportunities for mutual learning and community building.

INSTITUTIONAL DIFFERENCES REGARDING STUDENT GOVERNANCE IN INSTITUTIONAL LEADERSHIP

Higher education in the United States is diverse and complex, with more than 4,000 institutions nationwide. Different types of colleges and universities have different missions, student populations, campus cultures, and institutional contexts, and student governance structures and engagement vary accordingly.

For example, at community colleges, which account for more than half of undergraduate enrollment overall, involving student governance in institutional leadership can be a challenging task because of the large number of part-time and working commuter students. With limited time and competing outside commitments, community college student governments can be "up and down" in their level of effectiveness: they might have a few strong leaders for a while, but then slip badly after those officers graduate. Due to the transient student population, many of these student bodies start over from scratch annually (ASGA, 2011).

Despite the challenges, some community colleges manage to have student governance in institutional leadership. Grand Rapids Community College has a student congress whose purpose:

> shall be to represent the students at Grand Rapids Community College and promote their interests and welfare in the college decision-making process. The Student Congress is thereby the voice of the Student Body. The Student Congress will also be responsible for the allocation of funds for recognized student organizations and campus life.
>
> (GRCC Student Congress Constitution, 2011)

One specific way Grand Rapids students are involved in institutional governance is through Student Congress, the body that governs and manages campus activities fees. Members serve alongside college officials on the budget, campus elections, communication and technology, recognition and involvement, and rules committees.

For example, private institutions can also face challenges in engaging student governance in institutional leadership, mainly because of how they are funded, run, and structured. Private schools are not required to provide public records, and their governing boards are appointed by the schools themselves rather than by the state or governor, which can lead to a lack of information in the eyes of students. Often the cost of such institutions encourages students' expectations, and in some cases, demands, to increase as well.

Despite these challenges, a number of private institutions have sought to include students in their decision-making processes. Columbia College Chicago (CCC) is a private liberal arts college. The American Student Government Association recognized CCC for making great strides in student governance:

> SGA now sits on several campus-wide committees that had been closed to students in the past. It has a representative on CCC's board of trustees—a position that even many long-established SGs do not possess. Members work together with administrators on issues facing students, such as coming up with alternatives to expensive textbooks.
>
> (Campitelli, 2007)

A number of activities demonstrate how students at CCC are engaged in institutional leadership. The SGA holds student forums, puts out a student-driven agenda, conducts student polls, reaches out to participating students, sends representatives to every college-wide event, finds common ground between faculty and administrators, provides tangible benefits and funding to students, and takes on long-term projects in the community.

Similarly, Middlebury College has a student government association that serves as the main channel for student involvement in institutional governance:

> The Student Government Association is the vehicle through which students can participate in the formulation of institutional policy affecting academic and student affairs and collectively express their views on matters of general interest to the student body. The SGA makes student appointments to student, joint student/faculty, and trustee councils and committees. The SGA also allocates student activities fees and authorizes student activities for their eligibility to receive funds. The SGA provides services to the student body as deemed necessary.
>
> (Middlebury Student Government Association, 2012)

Public universities, particularly big research universities, have actively engaged student governance in institutional leadership. The University of California, San Diego, has a policy for student participation in institutional governance in its student conduct regulations. Purdue University boasts separate undergraduate and graduate student governments. Purdue Graduate Student Government has worked on a number of university governance initiatives, including a smoking ban policy, travel grants, and negotiated health care costs. Florida State University, a research university known as the "Berkeley of the South," has a long tradition of involving students in many avenues of governance and institutional leadership (Marshall, 2006); most notably, the student body president is a voting member of the Board of Trustees and the Student Senate allocating the activity and service fee budget of $13 million.

Private research universities can also successfully engage student governance in institutional leadership. Students at Duke University developed a general statement of rights and freedoms (Duke Student Government, 2011). Designed to guide future university actions to ensure that students were not only represented but also had a voice in the decision-making process, this statement signaled a fundamental change in the Duke community.

ENABLING FACTORS AND BARRIERS FOR STUDENT GOVERNANCE IN INSTITUTIONAL LEADERSHIP

A number of factors determine the extent to which students participate in institutional governance. However, there are ways in which institutions can encourage fruitful student involvement in leadership and decision-making. First, statutory requirements, when available, or formal university policies, seem to promote student inclusion. Student congresses, student government associations, and student conduct processes represent good practices of shared governance among students and across a variety of institutions. The primary means for student involvement appears to be student government associations, which vary at large research universities based on undergraduate and graduate student participation. Additionally, graduate students employed by public and private institutions can seek representation through collective bargaining and unionization, when legal.

Campuses where student governance involvement is effective generally share many of the following characteristics: (1) institutional culture that supports collaboration; (2) student-focused mission; (3) clear definitions of the rights of student government; (4) active advising; and (5) involvement from senior administrators. Love and Miller (2003) and Laosebikan-Buggs (2006) describe the importance of a campus culture that supports collaboration among students, faculty, staff, and administrators.

For student involvement in governance to work, the campus must inherently support the students. Miller and Nadler (2006) assert that a student-focused mission is paramount to effective student governance, as it suggests that the institution is dedicated to the students and will be more receptive to student involvement. Brunfield (2006) claims campuses should clearly define students' role in campus governance. Finally, Miller and Nadler (2006) maintain that active campus advising and involvement from senior administrators will support student involvement in institutional governance.

Student governance in institutional leadership can be very effective when supported by an institution that values student government and student input, particularly when clearly defined goals, expectations, and training have been established. Active advising and involvement from senior-level administrators reflect on institutional culture and values, and could help foster effective student involvement. A good example is Florida State University, where SGA has dedicated professional staff advisors who support student initiatives, direct communication with senior-level officials, and encourage campus-wide collaboration. These relationships support institutional missions while including students in the decision-making process.

There are also barriers to student participation in institutional governance, including: (1) lack of trust between students, faculty, and administrators; (2) internal and political strife within the student body organization; (3) a belief among student leaders that student government power is limited, which translates to apathy; and (4) student government that is not representative of the campus population.

Miller and Nadler (2006) explain that if students, faculty, and administrators do not trust each other, then creating a working relationship becomes difficult. Both Miller and Nadler (2006) and Laosebikan-Buggs (2006) see dangers in internal strife within student government associations or similar bodies. If these organizations do not function internally, then working collectively to advance the institution is nearly impossible.

Miller and Nadler (2006) also describe how the mentality of students must be positive in order to impact institutional policies. Specifically, students must believe they can influence campus governance in order to do so. Finally, Miller and Nadler (2006) and Laosebikan-Buggs (2006) argue that SGAs, or any student body, must be representative of the general student body in terms of demographics and opinions of campus policy. If the representative body is not actually representative, then effective student governance may be threatened.

CONCLUSION

Student governance is a very important feature of American higher education. Constantly in the limelight of criticism, institutional administrators are under pressure to hear students' voices and attend to their concerns. Student movements focusing on social justice and equality serve as a reminder to university administrations across the country of the urgent need to address this issue. Administrators can effectively utilize student governance structures, formally or informally, to actively engage students in institutional leadership and other decision-making processes. Administrators should realize that student participation in governance can have strong impacts on student learning and personal development, as well as lasting effects on individual students, the institution, and society as a whole.

Student governance can be a valuable channel for communication and dialogue, allowing for an effective partnership between institutional administrators and students to explore, design, adopt, and evaluate campus policies, programs, and practices, regardless of institutional type. Opportunities for student governance to be a part of institutional leadership are abundant. All those concerned about institutional effectiveness and student outcomes from college should seek to eliminate the barriers and create favorable environments to facilitate and engage student governance in institutional leadership and decision-making processes. In particular, higher education leaders and administrators can intentionally design the structures needed for successful student participation; foster campus cultures that value collaboration between administrators, faculty, and students; and promote student involvement in institutional leadership. Building and maintaining collaborative and respectful relationships between administrators, faculty, and students is critical for success in institutional leadership and ultimately leads to benefits for all involved.

DISCUSSION PROMPTS

1. Scholars have various definitions of student governance. What does it look like at your institution?
2. How do students define governance on your campus?

3. What do you see as the potential opportunities and challenges of strong student governance structures on college campuses?
4. What are some potential barriers to student governance on your campus? Which ones can you remove and how?
5. How does your institutional culture support or inhibit student governance opportunities?
6. What current student governance opportunities exist at your institution? What are some additional opportunities you can implement?
7. Who are key constituents at your institution that can foster student governance development?
8. What differences or similarities exist, if any, between undergraduate and graduate student governance at your institution?
9. What are creative ways to engage students in governance and leadership at institutions that may struggle due to a transient student population?
10. How could you go about building strong relationships with student governance on your campus? What are the characteristics or examples of positive relationships between students, faculty, and administrators on college campuses?

REFERENCES

American Student Government Association. (2011). *For every college*. Retrieved January 31, 2011 from http://www.asgaonline.com/ME2/Default.asp

Arum, R., & Roksa, J. (2011). *Academically adrift: Limited learning on college campuses*. Chicago, Illinois: University of Chicago Press.

Astin, A. W. (1993). *What matters in college: Four critical years revisited*. San Francisco: Jossey-Bass.

Astin, A. W., & Astin, H. S. (Eds.). (2000). *Leadership reconsidered: Engaging higher education in social change*. Battle Creek, Michigan: W. K. Kellogg Foundation.

Berquist, W. H., & Pawlak, K. (2007). *Engaging the six cultures of the academy*. San Francisco: Jossey-Bass.

Birnbaum, R. (1988). *How colleges work: The cybernetics of academic organization and leadership*. San Francisco: Jossey-Bass.

Braskamp, L. A., Trautvetter, L. C., & Ward, K. (2006). *Putting students first: How colleges develop students purposefully*. San Francisco: Jossey-Bass.

Brunfield, R. (2006). A case of student governance. In M. Miller, & D. Nadler (Eds.), *Student governance and institutional policy: Formation and implementation* (pp. 43–59). Charlotte, North Carolina: Information Age Publishing.

Campitelli, A. (2007). *A solid foundation: Building blocks for SGA growth*. Retrieved on July 2, 2012 from http://www.asgaonline.com/Media/PublicationsArticle/SLSpring2007_A-Solid-Foundation.pdf

Duke Student Government. (2011). *Your rights*. Retrieved March 25, 2011 from http://dsg.dukegroups.duke.edu/your-rights/

Florida State University Student Body. (2009). *Constitution of the student body*. Retrieved on December 12, 2011 from http://sga.fsu.edu/PDF/CONSTITUTION_OF_THE_STUDENT_BODY.pdf

Freidson, E., & Shuchman, H. L. (1955). Student government in American colleges. In E. Freidson (Ed.), *Student government, student leaders, and the American college* (pp. 3–28). Philadelphia: United States National Student Association.

GRCC Student Congress Constitution (2011). Retrieved on July 2, 2012 from http://web.grcc.edu/Pr/student life/2007/sc_constitution_1.22.07.pdf

Horowitz, H. L. (1987). *Campus life: Undergraduate cultures from the end of the eighteenth century to the present*. New York: Knopf.

Hu, S., & Kuh, G. D. (2003). Maximizing what students get out of college: Testing a learning productivity model. *Journal of College Student Development, 44*, 185–203.

Jones, D. H. (1974). *An analysis of students' perception of their role in governance at Gaston College*. Fort Lauderdale, Florida: Nova University.

Komives, S. R., Wagner, W., & Associates. (2009). *Leadership for a better world: Understanding the social change model of leadership development*. San Francisco: Jossey-Bass.

Kuh, G. D., & Lund, J. P. (1994). What students gain from participating in student government? In M. C. Terell, & M. J. Cuyjet (Eds.), *New directions for student services: Developing student government leadership* (pp. 5–17). San Francisco: Jossey-Bass.

Kuh, G. D., & Whitt, E. J. (1988). *The invisible tapestry: Culture in American colleges and universities*. ASHE-ERIC Higher Education Report No. 1. Washington, DC: Association for the Study of Higher Education.

Laosebikan-Buggs, M. O. (2006). The role of student government. In M. Miller, & D. Nadler (Eds.), *Student governance and institutional policy: Formation and implementation* (pp. 1–8). Charlotte, North Carolina: Information Age Publishing.

Love, R., & Miller, M. (2003). Increasing student participation in self governance: A comparison of graduate and undergraduate student perceptions. *College Student Journal, 37*, 533.

Marshall, S. J. (2006). *The tumultuous sixties: Campus unrest and student life at a southern university*. Tallahassee, Florida: Sentry Press.

May, W. P. (2009). Student governance: A qualitative study of leadership in student government association. Educational Policy Studies Dissertation. Retrieved from http://digitalarchive.gsu.edu/eps_diss/36

Menon, M. E. (2003). Student involvement in university governance: A need for negotiated education aims? *Tertiary Education and Management, 9*, 233–246.

Middlebury Student Government Association. (2012). College governance. Retrieved on July 2, 2012 from http://www.middlebury.edu/about/handbook/governance/SGA

Miller, M. T., & Nadler, D. P. (2006). Student involvement in governance: Rationale, problems, and opportunities. In M. Miller, & D. Nadler (Eds.), *Student governance and institutional policy: Formation and implementation* (pp. 9–18). Charlotte, North Carolina: Information Age Publishing.

National Commission on the Future of Higher Education (2006). *A test of leadership: Charting the future of U.S. higher education*. Washington, DC: U.S. Department of Education.

National Survey of Student Engagement (2004). *Student engagement: Pathways to collegiate success*. Bloomington: Indiana University Center for Postsecondary Research.

National Survey of Student Engagement (2005). *Student engagement: Exploring different dimensions of student engagement*. Bloomington: Indiana University Center for Postsecondary Research.

Pascarella, E. T., & Terenzini, P. T. (1991). *How college affects students: Findings and insights from twenty years of research*. San Francisco: Jossey-Bass.

Pascarella, E. T., & Terenzini, P. T. (2005). *How college affects students: A third decade of research*. San Francisco: Jossey-Bass.

Schenkel, W. (1971). Who has been in power? In Hodgkinson, H. L., & Meeth, L. R. (Eds.), *Power and authority*. San Francisco: Jossey-Bass.

Smith, W. A., Altbach, P. G., & Lomotey, K. (Eds.) (2002). *The racial crisis in American higher education: Continuing challenges for the twenty-first century*. Albany, New York: State University of New York Press.

St. John, E. P. (2003). *Refinancing the college dream: Access, equal opportunity, and justice for taxpayers*. Baltimore, Maryland: Johns Hopkins University Press.

Part II

Efficient and Effective Management
of Resources

6

INNOVATIVE STRATEGIC PLANNING
FOR THE INSTITUTION

Charles Mathies and Christopher Ferland

INTRODUCTION

When Hurricane Katrina hit New Orleans in late August of 2005, it wrought destruction on a scale unseen before or since in the United States. More than 1,800 people lost their lives, and damages totaled over $108 billion (Knabb, Rhome & Brown, 2011). In the immediate aftermath of the storm, medical workers and local hospitals were overwhelmed with patients and struggled to provide care (Fink, 2009). One of the more publicized situations occurred at Memorial Medical Center. With the hospital's power supply fading, doctors had to make life and death decisions while treating many ill and injured patients without evacuation assistance (Fink, 2009). The story of Memorial Medical Center brought to light questions about who gets care in a crisis, when they receive it, and how these decisions are made.

Memorial Medical Center had developed triage protocols as part of its strategic planning for disaster preparedness. However, the protocols provided little guidance during this crisis, as most of the staff were not adequately familiar with them and a number of situations transpired that the protocols did not even address (Fink, 2009; Sweeney, 2014). Ultimately, decisions were made under the guise of doing "the most good with the limited pool of resources" (Fink, 2009). Put another way, attending doctors' professional opinions determined who got treatment at the expense of another. Some doctors based their decisions on the number of lives that could be saved, while others used the number of years of life that could be saved, thus focusing on the healthiest and youngest patients. Analyses of the decisions made at Memorial Medical Center in the aftermath of Katrina, including the euthanizing of some patients (Fink, 2009; Sweeney, 2014), makes it clear that better planning, training, and communication could have enhanced staff's management of triage and, in turn, possibly saved more lives (Sweeney, 2014).

Higher education institutions rarely face life or death situations, but the story above highlights the importance of strategic planning and its execution: a strategic plan is of little use without a means of implementation. However, while implementation is one of the more difficult aspects of strategic planning, it is certainly not the only challenge. The literature on strategic planning has, to date, been primarily grounded within the disciplines of business and economics. Some of the classic publications include Alfred Chandler's *Strategy and Structure* (1962), H. Igor Ansoff's *Corporate Strategy* (1965) and *Strategic Management* (1979), and Michael Porter's *Competitive Strategy* (1980). The classic business components of strategic planning include the formation of a plan, consideration of various viewpoints and constraints both inside and outside of the organization, and integration of the plan and its principles into all functional areas of the organization (Freeman, 2010).

Modern business literature expands the classic definition of strategic planning to include its dynamic nature. Strategic planning is now seen as a process that details how an organization will execute a deliberate strategy; i.e., where an organization intends to position itself in the future and how it will get there (Macintosh & Maclean, 2015; McClean, 2015). Strategic planning is still seen as a fundamentally cyclical process, but one where the cycles, or phases, are shorter due to an environmental context of globalization and instant communication. The literature often makes a distinction between strategic planning and strategic management. Strategic management encompasses more than just planning because it links strategy formulation and implementation with evaluation, adoption, and achievement (Dooris & Rackoff, 2012). A key concept of this approach is that intentionality lies at the heart of both strategic planning and its management (Dooris & Rackoff, 2012).

Within higher education, strategic planning has been conceived and defined in similar ways as in the business literature. However, if one can generalize, more attention is paid to external stakeholders (government and accountability measures) and environmental influences (diminishing availability of resources and increasing competition) (see Chaffee, 1984; Dooris, Kelley, & Trainer, 2004; Dooris & Rackoff, 2012; Hinton, 2012; Keller, 1983; Servier, 2000; Tolmie, 2005; Welsh, Nunez, & Petrosko, 2006; and Yeager, El-Ghali, & Kumar, 2013). George Keller's (1983) *Academic Strategy: The Management Revolution in American Higher Education* is recognized as perhaps the first book on strategic planning in higher education, and has been highly influential (Dooris et al., 2004; Dooris & Rackoff, 2012; Hinton, 2012). Keller (1983) wrote that while strategic planning requires buy-in from all areas of the institutional community, there is no secret formula that can be applied to every institution and every situation. What works at one college or university will not necessarily work at another, as the history, available resources, leadership, and, perhaps most importantly, culture varies from institution to institution.

Peter Drucker, one of the most famous thinkers on organizational management, is famously attributed to the quote, "culture eats strategy for breakfast" (McGregor, 2015). If organizational strategy is breakfast, then its structure is often lunch, since institutions typically link their structure to their strategy. No matter how well conceived a strategy may be, it will never come to fruition if it does not recognize the prevailing institutional culture. A strategy that ignores institutional culture may not attract the attention and buy-in of those intended to implement it (Hinton, 2012). There is often a tension between an institution's strategy and its culture; a new organizational structure or strategy will not necessarily create a new culture. Institutional culture is a messy blend of attitudes, beliefs, and norms, while organizational structure and strategies are more clearly defined. Culture is the environment in which an institutional strategy either thrives or dies. Successful administrators improve their units by addressing the shortcomings within the existing institutional culture.

In practical terms, strategic planning should be more concerned with "doing the right things" than with "doing things right" (McClean, 2015). "Doing things right" occurs at the operational and tactical planning level. Put another way, strategic planning focuses on "what we do"; operational and tactical planning focuses on "how we do it" (Hinton, 2012, McClean, 2015). In higher education, operational planning often takes place within departments or colleges, while tactical planning involves institution-wide policies and procedures necessary for budgeting, assessment, and overall institutional management (Hinton, 2012).

At its best, strategic planning is visionary and proactive, as organizations should anticipate change rather than adapt after the fact (McClean, 2015). This chapter, while covering the purpose and components of strategic planning in higher education, focuses on the application of the strategic plan. However, a strategic plan cannot be successfully implemented without acknowledging, understanding, and working with the dominant institutional culture.

PURPOSE OF STRATEGIC PLANNING

Strategic planning is a set of concepts, procedures, methodologies, tools, techniques, and actions that can help organizations become more successful in defining and achieving their mission, vision, and guiding principles (McClean, 2015). In the past few decades, higher education has faced many changes, such as reduced public funding, evolving student demographics, credential inflation, and new instructional delivery methods (massive open online courses, or MOOCs, for example). It is argued that the best way to manage these changes is through a formalized strategic plan (Swenk, 1999).

Some scholars (Alexander, 2000; Keller, 1983; Shirley, 1988) frame the importance of strategic planning as a compass for navigating continuously changing economic and political conditions. Additionally, there are those who feel that higher education is inefficient and thus requires a formal strategic planning process to assist in maintaining the public's trust. In some states, governing bodies require a strategic planning process in an attempt to please legislative authorities (Watson, 1995). Welsh, Nunez, and Petrosko (2006) stress that strategic planning in higher education has intensified over time due to the changing economic and political conditions and the increased accountability imposed by external agencies from both the state and federal (Integrated Postsecondary Education Data System—IPEDS) government and invested third parties (e.g., Lumina Foundation, Gates Foundation, Complete College America).

Chaffee (1984) argues that there are two models of strategic planning in higher education: adaptive and interpretive. The adaptive model treats the institution as an individual entity with its own direction and goals, while the interpretive model acts as a network of participants pursuing similar goals. Institutions using the adaptive approach follow market trends and will often change academic programs in response to supply and demand in the environment. Examples include the current moves toward more health professional programs and online graduate programs. Institutions applying the interpretive model rely on symbolic interactionism, collective realities, and a sense of identity. This model often involves selling the institutional story, e.g., Georgia College is the state of Georgia's designated public liberal arts university. The administrators and faculty believe this story but also act out of self-interest, to some degree, to pursue their own goals. Chaffee (1984) showed that the adaptive approach alone is less effective than a combined or interpretive approach.

Others approach strategic planning differently, believing that an institution can never accurately predict the future. From that perspective, the primary purpose of strategic planning is to cope with and manage change (Baker & Martin, 1994). The planning process involves periodic evaluations of the college or university's missions, programs, and goals set against changing internal and external environments in an effort to improve institutional effectiveness (Baker & Martin, 1994; Schmidtelin & Milton, 1990; Swenk, 1999). Many accreditation agencies include strategic planning in their recommendations and reviews for affirmation and reaffirmation. Reviewing goals annually ensures that institutions will deliver quality education and services, enabling them to be more fluid in their planning and to adjust quickly to changes in the environment. Additionally, these reviews allow for accomplished goals or new priorities to be dropped, modified, or added into the strategic plan. However, annual reviews are often reactionary and not strategic in nature. The future rarely looks just like the past. If it did then reviews and straight-line projections from the past would work perfectly for future planning (McClean, 2015). Therefore, strategic planning needs to be more than annual reviews and for making minor adjustments to the institution's operations.

Colleges and universities should avoid narrowly focusing on measuring efficiency when the real emphasis should be on measuring effectiveness (Swenk, 1999). Institutions face scrutiny for everything from student achievement and student learning outcomes to financial efficiency. To meet the needs of statutory, constitutional, and legislative reporting, they increasingly rely on institutional data and analysis (Clagett, 2004). These external reporting requests correlate with what administrators usually wish to improve: retention and graduation rates, alumni giving, space utilization, low-producing programs (credits and degrees), and faculty tenure and promotion information (scholarship, teaching, and public service). However, the financial environment and reduction in spending on higher education in many states has caused many administrators to focus only on efficiency. A well-structured strategic plan though makes it possible to track and measure quality, improving overall institutional effectiveness.

KEY STAKEHOLDERS

The strategic planning process requires commitment and participation from the entire institutional community. Welsh, Nunez, and Petrosko (2006) argue that for a strategic plan to be successful, campus-wide buy-in from administration, faculty, staff, and students is essential. In particular, faculty require transparency, communication, and planning activities with senior administrators; without faculty support, senior administrators find that most of their strategic plans never reach the desired level of success (Garmon, 1984; Rhoades, 2000; Welsh et al., 2006). When contemplating a strategic plan, administrators should invite all community members (faculty, staff, and students) to participate in every step of the process through open dialogue and written documentation. While it would be naive to believe that all participants will agree on how to proceed (Delprino, 2013), a transparent means of gathering input from the campus community creates a sense of openness and shows that administrators are listening to concerns even when it is not possible to incorporate all ideas into the plan.

It is important to establish a relatively small steering committee to oversee the development and assessment of the plan. In most institutions, the faculty and/or staff senate should be involved in selecting individuals to serve on the various planning committees. Without the participation of members of these two key groups, the strategic plan will have limited success. Administrators provide a comprehensive view of the institution that faculty and staff do not possess because of their specific departmental or program responsibilities (Delprino, 2013). This said, administrators should not lead the planning process but rather help manage it from a distance while a selected faculty member has direct charge (Delprino, 2013). This approach often creates buy-in from faculty, thus enhancing the chances of a successful implementation.

When evaluating people to serve on the steering committee, it is necessary to consider a variety of stakeholders, all of whom are important to the institution in some fashion. These stakeholders may include student representatives, alumni, development officers, finance personnel, facilities staff, student affairs professionals, institutional research staff, faculty, and administrators. Depending on its governance structure, an institution may wish to invite representatives from unions, governing boards, and even accreditation bodies (Delprino, 2013). Inclusion of student representatives means balancing their expectations with those of the administrators, faculty, and staff. Students deserve the opportunity to provide input and share in the process, though they should not be allowed to bog down the conversation with an undue focus on common student complaints (regardless of their validity), such as dining service quality, parking, course availability, and increased costs.

Finding the right size of steering committee requires a delicate balance. A group that is too large can be unruly, yet a group that is too small can be deemed controversial and handpicked. Many authors feel that a committee of 15 to 20 people works well, with each member sitting on a subcommittee in their area. One frequent concern is individual agendas and priorities. Awareness that committee members are pushing an agenda requires an astute chair or co-chairs. If an agenda is identified, it should be addressed with sensitivity while keeping the strategic process flowing.

Examples of such agendas include reducing the teaching workload, asking for more tenure-track versus limited-term adjunct lines, and seeking increased compensation for service work. Finally, the steering committee should remain intact for the duration of the strategic planning process.

Clagett (2004) contends that decision-support units, such as institutional research and institutional assessment (or effectiveness) offices, can contribute to strategic planning in a variety of ways. There are many institutions where institutional research and institutional assessment offices operate under the same umbrella. The professionals in these areas have ready access to institutional data and skills to provide useable information. Clagett (2004) uses enrollment forecasting, trend analysis, and institutional assessments as examples of this. If such individuals are not formally a part of the strategic planning committee, they should be in constant contact with the committee and serve in a support function.

DEVELOPING, IMPLEMENTING, AND MANAGING THE STRATEGIC PLAN

The literature on strategic planning both in business (see Freeman, 2010; Macintosh & Maclean, 2015; McClean, 2015 as examples) and in higher education (see Dooris & Rackoff, 2012; Hinton, 2012; Welsh et al., 2006; and Yeager et al., 2013 as examples) describes a range of phases or stages. For some authors, strategic planning has as few as two stages; others have detailed five, six, or more. In our view, there are three distinct phases of strategic planning in higher education: development, implementation, and management. While each phase is unique, they are all interconnected and build on one another. If there is a failure in one, then the entire process is likely to fail, as all three phases are essential (and need to be completed) for strategic planning to be successful.

During the first phase, strategic plan development, three main questions must be answered:

1. What is our current state?
2. Where do we (as an institution) want to be?
3. How do we get there?

These three questions are "strategic" in nature and focus on "doing the right things" as opposed to "doing things right" (McClean, 2015). "Doing things right" is a more appropriate focus in the operational or tactical stages of planning, as these address what the institution "does" (Hinton, 2012). These questions are the foundation from which everything in the strategic planning process should derive.

As indicated by the first question, strategic planning begins with examining the institution's current situation. An in-depth analysis needs to occur to determine the present status of all aspects of the institution, from facilities, faculty and staff, and finance to undergraduate and graduate curriculum, admissions, and student affairs. The list of areas included in the analysis will differ by institution, but a holistic review must take place so the plan is not limited to just one area, which in most institutions tends to be academic affairs.

Additionally, the mission statement, values (or principles), and vision must be thoroughly reviewed, as these items inform the development of the plan (Hinton, 2012). The mission statement indicates the purposes and operation of the institution. Over time, mission statements have become shorter and more direct (Hinton, 2012). Hinton (2012) claims that comprehensive mission statements create limitations in planning due to their breadth, complexity, mission creep, and focus on institutional culture. We argue that a concise statement that targets specific areas or goals in one page or less works well when planning. A good value statement relays the culture and beliefs of the institution to the reader, while the vision statement outlines where the strategic plan should take the institution. The planning process begins upon reviewing, reframing, and gaining consensus on these items across all stakeholders.

The next step is to understand where institutional leadership wants to go in the future. The senior administrators and/or board typically provide targets for the next five to ten years. These ideas will usually be very specific, requiring the steering committee to broaden them with underlying objectives. It should be noted that chasing rankings is an inappropriate approach. The rankings themselves are often problematic, and pursuing them can have negative impacts (see Hazelkorn, 2015a, and 2015b for details).

Once an institution has determined its present state and desired future, it must plan how to reach its goals. This may be the most time-consuming part of developing the strategic plan. Multiple approaches exist, with some institutions forming steering subcommittees to address specific topics, such as student success. In other cases, the work may be performed by the whole steering committee, operating with transparency through open forums or drafts placed on a website. Either approach works, but the key is to create a map detailing how to achieve the larger goals through smaller objectives. For example, an institution wishing to increase retention and graduation rates by ten percentage points may attempt to achieve this goal through such varied means such as enhanced advising strategies, earlier identification of D/F/W grades, increased faculty mentoring, expansion of undergraduate research, and modified residential living requirements.

While the higher education literature presents many examples and concepts from which institutions can draw (see Cowburn, 2005; Dooris & Rackoff, 2012; Hinton, 2012; Keller, 1983; Yeager et al., 2013), we argue that there are three tangible elements or "tasks" in this phase. First, a strategic planning document needs to be produced. This document should be visionary and comprehensive, yet simple and easily understood. In particular, the terminology and word choices need to be clear and be aligned with the institution's culture and context. Successful strategic planning documents typically contain four to six goals with approximately a dozen initiatives (Hanover Research, 2013). Goals can address themes common among the constituents and are often suggested by the steering committee.

It is important for the strategic planning document to maintain a mission focus, rather than a flexible plan, for consistent improvement over time (Aloi, 2005). A successful process of constant improvement stems from sound, measurable goals and objectives aligned with a periodic assessment plan (Aloi, 2005). When drafting the plan, the steering committee should ensure that the periodic assessments will make it possible to determine whether a particular goal has been met (Hanover Research, 2013). The flexibility provided by periodic assessment offers greater utility to the institution than long-term plans measured only at five- or ten-year intervals. This is especially true in today's fast-changing policy and social media world, where information moves so much more quickly than in the 1970s and 1980s.

The second task is to clearly communicate the strategic vision to the entire institutional community. For a strategic plan to be successful, everyone at every level must understand the strategic vision and disconnect in communication among organizational levels is the number one reason why strategic plans fail (McClean, 2015). Within higher education, this includes senior institutional leadership, trustees, faculty, staff, and students. As shown in the Memorial Medical Center example, neglecting to communicate the strategic vision and goals throughout the organization dooms a plan to failure. In contrast, a good strategic plan is a "living document" and becomes ingrained in the institutional culture (McClean, 2015).

The third and final task is to create an implementation plan that includes actionable tasks, measurements, and objectives complete with target dates for implementation and milestone checkpoints (McClean, 2015). Above all else, the implementation plan needs to be directive, clear, and comprehensive (Hinton, 2012).

During the second phase, implementation, four core questions must be answered:

1. How much will it cost?
2. What is our institutional mission and culture, and how does our planning connect to them and to the needs of the state and our stakeholders?
3. What are our target dates for measurements and completion?
4. Who is responsible for getting us there?

These four questions are excellent guides for institutions as they implement their strategic plan (Hinton, 2012; McClean, 2015; Wells 2015). These questions are more operational and tactical than strategic, as they look to "do things right" rather than "doing the right things" (Hinton, 2012; McClean, 2015). While there are distinct differences between operational and tactical planning, both are outcome focused and are needed to achieve an institution's goals and vision (Hinton, 2012; McClean, 2015). These questions are often embedded in the implementation plan, and the answers to them will evolve over time as people change positions, new information becomes available, or new policies are enacted by the state or institution.

The financial costs of executing a strategic plan and achieving its goals require that the plan be directly linked to the budgetary process (Hinton, 2012). Starting new or altering current programs to meet strategic objectives takes financial resources and often involves multiyear commitments. Sufficient dedicated financial resources are thus required to effectively meet institutional strategic objectives (Hanover Research, 2013). Including projected costs in the strategic plan is a simple and clear way to help ensure that strategic goals become a reality.

The impact of the institution's mission, history, and culture on strategic planning cannot be overestimated (Hinton, 2012). As few colleges and universities have similar missions and histories, each exhibits its own unique culture (environment and context). When institutions respond to external forces, it is referred to in the literature as an adaptation; when they implement a new program or practice it is called innovation; when they mimic or "borrow" from others, it is called isomorphism (Kezar, 2013). Institutions often "borrow" ideas and practices from other institutions and try to incorporate these into their strategies and policies.

Implementing a strategic plan and measuring progress towards its goals requires an understanding of the institutional culture (James 2012; Mathies 2015). Challenging and changing institutional culture is a difficult and complex process; it takes time, evaluation of available options, and planning (Farkas, 2013; Hinton, 2012; Kezar, 2013; Kezar & Eckel, 2002). Consequently, what works for one institution to meet strategic objectives will not necessarily work for another. An institution's strategic initiatives need to be linked to its unique mission and structures and fit within its culture and norms.

Target dates in the implementation plan serve as checkpoints and provide a specific timetable for the completion of various actions, such as the development of programs or policies. The measures or data that will be used to assess the implementation of the strategic plan should be specified. Many institutions use planning calendars or clocks as a visual tool for remembering key target dates (particularly for reoccurring events or milestones).

While developing, implementing, and managing the strategic planning process involves many people across the institution, usually an individual or small group becomes the "face" of planning as it is beneficial to have a "face" or a "home" to steward the planning process (Hinton, 2012). At the institutional level, it is often the responsibility of an official committee to monitor, recommend changes to, and generally manage the strategic plan (Yeager et al., 2013); however, a small group or an individual performs the bulk of the work (Hinton, 2012). Adding strategic planning tasks ad hoc to someone's duties or addressing the tasks intermittently is never successful in the long term. The synergy created when an individual or a small group is able to provide context and linkages across divisional and departmental silos is invaluable in implementing and managing the strategic plan (Hinton, 2012).

In this third phase, managing the strategic plan, four key questions need to be answered:

1. Are goals being achieved or not?
2. Are the goals and objective still realistic?
3. Are target dates being met? If not, why and is there a need to readjust the targets?
4. Are there adequate resources available to meet the goals?

These four questions are extremely useful guides for institutions measuring their progress towards meeting strategic objectives (McNamara, 2007; Yeager et al., 2013). Sometimes referred to as the monitoring phase, the managing phase is often the longest in duration and can last months and even years. One common development in this phase is the "adaptation to" the current assessment cycle and culture at an institution. An assessment cycle is a regular schedule of assessments and modifications to university initiatives and programs (Hinton, 2012); examples include program review and financial/budget requests and evaluations.

Part of managing the strategic plan is making sure an assessment cycle is functioning, complete with a feedback loop. This is done by reviewing evaluation results and adjusting the strategic plan accordingly. A feedback loop informs institutions how effectively their plans are fulfilling their institutional mission and planning goals (Middaugh, 2009). The feedback loop is "missed" or is "incomplete" when assessments and evaluations are not integrated back into the institution's system of self-regulation and improvement (McClean, 2015; Middaugh, 2009). The success of a strategic planning process requires continual progress monitoring and integration of the results of evaluations back into the plan.

If resources, both financial and human, are being dedicated to fulfill the strategic initiatives, it is important to measure the initiatives' success via data, metrics, and analytics (McClean, 2015). The generation, collection, and use of data, metrics, and analytics should tie directly into the strategic plan. Intentionality and relevance of what is collected and used is key; including peripheral data only adds to the clutter and creates confusion as to the primary goals and purpose of the institution and its strategy (Calderon, 2015a). Decision support units, such as the information technology (IT), institutional research, institutional effectiveness, and assessment are common sources of data, metrics, analytics, and their analysis. These units form the starting point, as they are often the official sources and keepers of an institution's performance analytics (Calderon, 2015a).

While the contents of the strategic plan vary by institution, there are common themes that stretch throughout higher education. Four areas commonly monitored in strategic planning processes are budget (financial resources), human resources, students, and facilities. Budgets at all levels (university, college, and department) can be used as a basis for monitoring how well the plan is being integrated, as they should reflect the strategic goals and priorities of the institution (Hinton, 2012). Sequencing and aligning strategic priorities within the budgetary process allows institutions to check progress towards strategic goals as well as move into a proactive role by anticipating future financial needs and commitments (Breslawski, 2013; Hinton, 2012). The key is the ability to promote budget alignment with strategic goals where appropriate. Showing faculty and staff the importance of prioritizing strategic goals through the funding of academic or non-academic pursuits assists in achieving a campus culture that supports the plan.

The annual personnel review processes should also be linked to the institution's strategic plan. If any part of the plan and its application affects personnel (job security, status, tasks, etc.), the institution and its leaders should pay close attention to their reactions and be prepared to address any issues directly and swiftly (Choban, M., Choban, G., & Choban D., 2008). Once someone, regardless of position, interprets the strategic plan as a threat to their well-being, the entire plan can be jeopardized (Rowley, Jujan, & Dolence, 2001). Personnel reviews can ensure that the institution has enough suitable faculty, support staff, and other employees to meet its short-term and strategic goals. However, managing personnel of a department, let alone an entire institution is usually more complicated in higher education than in the corporate world (Hinton, 2012) due in large part to the uniqueness of faculty positions (tenure, skill requirements, etc.), the culture of academia and, in the case of public institutions, workplace regulations governing public employees.

The most common ways institutions use student data to monitor their progress towards strategic goals is through examining enrollment goals and trends, the impact of new academic initiatives or programs (typically on academic performance and enrollments), and use of services (support, facilities, activities, etc.). The purpose of higher education, while hotly debated over the years, has students at its core (Altbach, Reisberg, & Rumbley, 2009). Whether the goal is to prepare individuals for the labor market, provide a means for personal development, promote an educated citizenry, or produce new research, students are almost always directly impacted.

Facilities are often not fully integrated into the strategic planning process.

Faculty members, in particular, are tempted to stop participating in the process, as many have little or no interest in planning activities not focused on academics (Hinton, 2012). But their input is important as there is a strong need for facilities that are functional while supportive of the institution's academic initiatives (Hinton, 2012). Incorporation of a facilities master plan into the strategic plan aligns the academic plan with the physical space requirements. This provides a blueprint for the long-range allocation of resources and phasing initiatives so they can realistically support the current and anticipated needs of students, staff, and faculty (Hinton, 2012).

The frequency of progress monitoring of various aspects of the strategic plan is highly dependent on the institution's culture and available resources. Colleges and universities use scorecards and dashboards to provide "high-level" monitoring of key indicators for each area (Hanover Research, 2013). The method and frequency of progress measurement should be detailed within the implementation plan to make clear to the entire institutional community when and how the strategic plan will be monitored. In summary, all four of these areas (budget, personnel, students, and facilities) have a direct bearing on the coordination and use of resources and should thus be measured and monitored (Hinton, 2012). In other words, these four areas are the centerpiece of an institution's operations.

APPLYING THE STRATEGIC PLAN: INNOVATIVE CONSIDERATIONS

Colleges and universities have typically been very good at developing strategic plans. There are numerous articles and, books, and other materials that they can use as resources (see Dooris et al., 2004; Dooris & Rackoff, 2012; Hanover Research, 2013; Hinton, 2012; Keller, 1983; Noel-Levitz, 2009; Servier, 2000; Tolmie, 2005; Welsh et al., 2006; and Yeager et al., 2013 as examples). The real challenge is to actually apply the plan and put it into action; particularly in ways that are original and address current as well as future issues. While previous sections focused on what goes into strategic planning and who's involved, we now explore three specific areas where an institution can be innovative in applying its strategic plan.

Digital Strategy

A digital strategy does not have to do with hardware or software; it is a strategy for servicing the "digital consumers" on campuses (Boag, 2014b). Digital consumers are not just students, most of whom are digital natives, but also faculty, staff, senior leadership, and external stakeholders. Digital consumers see and interact differently with the world as they view the virtual and physical as having equal relevance (Boag, 2014b). A key point is that "digital" is more than just the Internet; it is a convergence of the Web, social media, mobile technology, cloud computing, IT security, and information (Boag, 2014a, 2014b; Selingo, 2015). Digital consumers carry their friends and family everywhere they go via apps and mobile phones and have expectations for on-demand service, data, and information (Boag, 2014b).

Most colleges and universities have approached digital strategies by looking inwards, focusing on what *they* want to say (Boag, 2014a). The result has been a proliferation of content on institutional webpages, much of which is seldom visited. Instead, institutions need to think of their digital strategy with their users' needs in mind. While some argue that colleges and universities already have a good idea of how their community is using and engaging with technology, technology's constant development leaves many institutions playing catch-up (Boag, 2014a). A digital strategy needs to consist of clear and practical ways of addressing the problems faced by and interests of digital consumers (Boag, 2014b). Examples of problems range from connectivity and bandwidth issues on campus to not being able to pay for goods and services electronically. Examples of interests range from the breadth of the library's electronic collections and admissions' informational videos to interacting with fellow students, staff, and their faculty through electronic communications and social media platforms. Institutions need to take a step back, investigate, and try to understand how exactly their users expect to engage digitally with the institution and while on the campus (Boag, 2014a).

Mapping the digital user's conception of "campus" is one of the most effective ways to gather information about various touch (interaction) points and user goals (Boag, 2014a). This mapping includes documenting both where and how digital users access the institution's network, including the software or apps used, as well as the integration plans of digital technologies into classrooms and student learning support. Digital strategies should not come from data managers, the IT team, or even decision support units like the institutional research or assessment office. It is the senior leadership's responsibility to develop and integrate a digital strategy guided by the institution's strategic vision. The digital strategy ultimately needs to be more than a set of vague goals about meeting users' technology needs; it should be a detailed plan to integrate the concept of "how technology is used" within an institution's strategic planning, culture, and organizational structures (Boag, 2014b).

When applying strategic planning to institutions with limited physical campuses (i.e. online) one needs to be considerate of student access, convenience, instructional delivery methods, and program development (Xu and Jaggars, 2011). These institutions need long-term strategies to manage the growth of online courses in order to establish quality programs while ensuring student success. Student support services, such as financial aid, registrar services and library, need to exist for full or partially online programs, with an emphasis on convenience and engagement. A reduction in either of these services hiders the overall effectiveness and value of the program.

Distance learning may seem relatively simple to implement; however, the reality is that to be successful an interdisciplinary approach across the campus and IT needs to be followed. This is true for online only as well as multi-campus and "traditional" institutions with an online presence. The relationships between IT, faculty, and student services need to be open and inclusive. Distance learning requires professional development in terms of information technology, instructional delivery, classroom structure, and assessment. Teaching online courses occurs in a fluid environment with continual technological improvements during the term the course is being delivered.

Consideration of Current and Future Student (and Staff) Technology Needs

There is ample evidence that a number of technological innovations are already "disrupting" many of the traditional ways colleges and universities provide teaching, services, and support, such as library services, to their students, faculty, and staff (Calderon, 2015b; Selingo, 2015). These disruptions have created new modes and types of interactions between institutions and their community members (students, staff, and faculty), altering many long-held norms and conventions (Calderon, 2015b). Today's students represent the first generation to grow up with the Internet and mobile technologies (Prensky, 2001, 2010). As such, current and future students are dubbed "digital natives" and expect to interact with institutions, both in and out of the classroom, via technology (Autry & Berge, 2011; Calderon, 2015b; Prensky, 2001, 2010).

However, most faculty and staff are "digital immigrants," those who, while not born into the digital world, have adopted many aspects of technology into their professional and personal lives (Autry & Berge, 2011; Prensky, 2001, 2010). An important distinction between the two groups, digital natives and digital immigrants, is that while some immigrants may adapt to technology better than others, they never attain native fluency and always retain to some degree their "accent" or past way of doing things (Prensky, 2001). An example of this seen in the classroom; immigrants may adopt new technologies into how they teach and interact with their students, but their pedagogical perspective remains rooted in where they were trained, which was based on traditional lectures and face-to-face interactions (Autry & Berge, 2011). In short, the differing needs, abilities, and expectations of digital natives and immigrants have created disconnects between what students want and what institutions provide.

The contrasting communication styles of natives and immigrants are a great example of how the disconnect plays out in the classroom. Digital natives prefer to receive information fast, connecting to and engaging with a "network" of others, all while multitasking with various social media and academic work (Prensky, 2001, 2010). Conversely, most teachers, who are still predominantly digital immigrants, feel more secure delivering traditional lectures and assigning reading materials straight from textbooks and journals (Prensky, 2001).

The literature assessing the positive and negative aspects of the digital native/ immigrant divide in higher education (see Bennett, Maton, & Kervin, 2008; Helsper & Enyon, 2009; Smith, 2012; and Thomas, 2011 as examples) makes clear that teachers, regardless of whether they are digital immigrants or natives, can "speak the same language" as their students if they continually integrate new technologies into their pedagogical and curriculum planning. Institutions should find ways for their teachers and students to "partner" in the teaching/learning process (Prensky, 2010) while at the same time support and encourage faculty (and staff) development in the use of new educational technologies.

The consideration of future technology needs is similar to and often overlaps the digital strategy. However, they are two distinct and separate matters. Digital strategy focuses on "how" and "where" students and staff are using technology, while the consideration of future technology focuses more on "why" or "for what purpose" they are doing so. Both concepts should be addressed in the strategic planning process. This is becoming more critical as time passes, because the expectations of using technology on campuses are increasing. Digital natives are no longer just students, they are also the newest generation of staff and faculty, and more are coming every year.

Student Learning Outcomes

Student learning outcomes "are statements of what a learner is expected to know, understand, and/or be able to demonstrate at the end of a period of learning" (Adams, 2008, p. 4). They have often been linked to assessments of quality of education and are concerned with outcomes of the educational process (Adams, 2008). At the most basic level, these assessments suggest that success occurs when learning goals are identified and corresponding curricula are developed and then competently taught (Breslawski, 2013). Two of the most traditional methods of measuring quality of education have been student-to-teacher ratios and course evaluations (Calderon, 2015a). Despite the fact that both measures are limited and have serious methodological issues (Calderon, 2015a) student learning assessments have become increasingly important in regional and programmatic accreditations (Breslawski, 2013). In fact, many accreditation agencies now require institutions to measure student learning outcomes as part of the accreditation process. However, some of the newer methods introduced have been large-scale national assessments such as the Collegiate Learning Assessment (CLA) and the National Survey of Student Engagement (NSSE), which have their own methodological issues or limitations (Chen & Mathies, 2016). This has left institutions needing to think more holistically and strategically in their approach to assessing student learning outcomes.

It is also quite common for an institution or system to "borrow" novel ideas or best practices from another in an effort to improve student learning. Adopting an external assessment method or tool requires additional work; the institution must first consider the compatibility of its organizational structure and culture (Chen & Mathies, 2016; Mathies, 2015). As discussed previously in this chapter, organizational culture is perhaps the biggest issue to be addressed in developing a successful strategic plan or adopting a policy or program from another institution or department. A student learning assessment tool that is effective in one setting might be totally inadequate in another (Chen & Mathies, 2016).

This leads us back to the strategic planning process and selecting metrics used to measure student learning. While student learning outcome assessments are not new or innovative per se, what is new is adopting a comprehensive approach to assessing student learning and its inclusion in the strategic planning process. Many institutions and state systems struggle to implement "good" assessments of student learning and a large variation exists amongst institutions in their standards, practices, and procedures (Chen & Mathies, 2016). It is not uncommon to find student learning outcome assessments cobbled together piecemeal over time. This often happens as "new" ideas or assessment goals (a recent example is workforce development) gain in popularity and influence. The result is that institutions need to incorporate into their strategic planning process not only how to assess student learning outcomes (assessment tool/practice) but also why (philosophically) they assess.

Assessment of student learning is difficult, and there is no "one size fits all" approach for colleges and universities or even departments, given the significant differences between institutions as well as between disciplines (Breslawski, 2013). Therefore, multiple methods of assessing student learning should be embedded in regular institutional assessments as well as in the strategic planning process. There are two distinct ways in which assessment can be employed to improve student learning and outcomes (Chen & Mathies, 2016). First, personalized learning assistance should be provided to students through assignment and course feedback (grades, pre/posttest evaluations, etc.), while career centers should offer career and psychological tests to help students identify professional interests and align course and degree choices. Second, organizational change should occur where individual results, aggregated from assessment tools such as the CLA and NSSE, present an organizational picture that indicates areas for improvement. In summary, student learning assessments must be proactive in nature and include multiple measures which are embedded in the various stages of the strategic planning process.

CONCLUSION

Strategic planning is a process, not a document (Dooris & Rackoff, 2012). While documents and metrics are certainly developed and used, these should not be the focus. Instead, attention should be centered on developing a vision or goal-based planning model that can help guide an institution into the future. The strategic planning process, though, is a difficult and time-consuming endeavor. It also impacts people, and where people are involved, there are politics (Delprino, 2013). On many levels, strategic planning is a political process; within an institution, the effective use of politics can facilitate change and help the campus community adapt to any accompanying uncertainty, thereby minimizing dissonance (Delprino, 2013). A balance must be struck between a commitment to the strategic planning process and the realities of the institution's situations (Delprino, 2013). In our view, the ultimate success of a strategic plan depends on how well it fits within the institutional culture.

Colleges and universities should identify what they are good at and leverage those strengths into new opportunities. When developing a strategic plan, leadership should be careful not to limit the potential of the institution through overregulation, forcing it to operate as it has in the past or in traditional ways. Rather, the strategic planning process is about introducing and managing change. Changes, especially strategic ones, need to be undertaken with careful consideration not only of the institution's strengths, but also of its traditions, character, and culture (Delprino, 2013). The strategic planning process should change an institution for the better, leading its students, staff, and faculty in a clear, desirable, and engaging direction.

DISCUSSION PROMPTS

1. What are the three key phases of strategic planning? Why are they each important?
2. How are data and its analytics used in strategic planning?
3. Why is understanding the institutional culture important in strategic planning?
4. What are key obstacles in developing a strategic plan?
5. Who are the various stakeholders in strategic planning and how do they fit into the planning process?
6. What is the difference between "strategic" planning and "operational" or "tactical" planning?
7. What is the first step in developing a strategic plan? Why is this important?

8. What should an institution do before implementing an idea or best practice "borrowed" from another institution?
9. How are target dates important and influential in the strategic planning process?
10. How does your institution address (or acknowledge) the three suggested innovative considerations (digital strategy, current and future technology needs, and student learning outcomes) in its strategic planning process?

REFERENCES

Adams, S. (2008). Learning outcomes current development in Europe: Update on the issues and applications of learning outcomes associated with the Bologna Process. *In Bologna seminar: Learning outcomes based higher education: The Scottish experience.* Retrieved from: http://www.ehea.info/uploads/seminars/edinburgh_feb08_adams.pdf

Alexander, F. K. (2000). The changing face of accountability: Monitoring and assessing institutional performance in higher education. *Journal of Higher Education, 71*, 411–431.

Aloi, S. (2005). Best practices in linking assessment and planning. *Assessment Update, 17*(3), 4–6.

Altbach, P., Reisberg, L., & Rumbley, L. (2009). *Trends in global higher education: Tracking an academic revolution.* Report prepared for UNESCO 2009 World Conference on higher education. UNESCO: Paris.

Ansoff, H. I. (1965). *Corporate strategy: An analytic approach to business policy for growth and expansion.* McGraw-Hill: New York.

Ansoff, H. I. (1979). *Strategic management.* Wiley: New York.

Autry, A., & Berge, Z. (2011). Digital natives and digital immigrants: Getting to know each other. *Industrial and Commercial Training, 43*(7), 460–468.

Baker, D., & Martin, R. J. (1994). A framework for strategic planning and change in higher education: The case of a business school. Paper presented at 33rd Annual Forum for Institutional Research, May 16–19, 1993, at Chicago (ERIC Document Reproduction Service No. ED 360918).

Bennett, S., Maton, K., & Kervin, L. (2008). The "digital natives" debate: A critical review of the evidence. *British Journal of Educational Technology, 39*(5), 775–786.

Boag, P. (2014a). *Higher education & digital transformation.* Blog post. Retrieved from: https://boagworld.com/digital-strategy/the-higher-education-needs-to-face-the-digital-reality/

Boag, P. (2014b). *What the heck is "digital" anyway?* Blog post. Retrieved from: https://boagworld.com/digital-strategy/what-the-heck-is-digital-anyway/

Breslawski, S. (2013). Strategic planning when aligning curriculum and resources. In Patrick Schloss & Kristina Cragg (Eds.), *Organization and administration in higher education* (1st ed.). Routledge: New York, pp. 151–176.

Calderon, A. (2015a). In light of globalization, massification, and marketization: Some considerations on the uses of data in higher education. In Karen Webber & Angel Calderon (Eds.), *Institutional research and planning in higher education: Global contexts and themes.* Routledge: New York, pp. 186–196.

Calderon, A. (2015b). Exploring the future global flows of knowledge and mobility: Implications for international education. In Leasa Weimer (Ed.), *A wealth of nations: 2015 conference conversation starter.* EAIE: Amsterdam, pp. 45–52.

Chaffee, E. (1984). Successful strategic management in small private colleges. *The Journal of Higher Education, 55*(2), 212–241.

Chandler, A. (1962). *Strategy and structure: Chapters in history of the industrial enterprise.* The MIT Press: Cambridge, Massachusetts.

Chen, P. D. & Mathies, C. (2016). Assessment, evaluation, and research. In Dennis C. Roberts & Susan R. Komives (Eds.), *Enhancing student learning and development in cross-border higher education: New directions for higher education, No. 75.* John Wiley & Sons Inc.: Hoboken, New Jersey, pp. 85–92.

Choban, M., Choban, G., & Choban D. (2008). Strategic planning and decision-making in higher education: What gets attention and what doesn't. *Assessment Update: Progress, trends, and practices in higher education, 20*(2), 1–2, 13–14.

Clagett, C. (2004). Applying ad hoc institutional research findings to college strategic planning. *New Directions for Institutional Research, 123*, 33–48.

Cowburn, S. (2005). Strategic planning in higher education: Fact or fiction? *Perspectives: Policy and practice in higher education, 9*(4), 103–109.

Delprino, R. (2013). *The human side of the strategic planning process in higher education.* Society for College and University Planning: Ann Arbor, Michigan.

Dooris, M., Kelley, J., & Trainer, J. (2004). Strategic planning in higher education. *New Directions for Institutional Research, 123,* 5–11.

Dooris, M., & Rackoff, J. (2012). Institutional planning and resource management. In R. Howard, G. McLaughlin, & W. Knight (Eds.), *The handbook of institutional research.* Jossey-Bass: San Francisco, pp. 183–202.

Farkas, M. (2013). Building and sustaining a culture of assessment: Best practices for change leadership. *Reference Services Review, 41*(1), 13–31.

Fink, S. (2009). The deadly choices at memorial. *N.Y. Times.* Aug. 25. Retrieved Feb. 2016 from http://www.nytimes.com/2009/08/30/magazine/30doctors.html

Freeman, R. E. (2010). *Strategic management: A stakeholder approach.* Digital printed version. Cambridge University Press: Cambridge.

Garmon, C. (1984). *A comparison of world view among faculty and administration in institutions of higher education.* Vanderbilt University: Nashville, Tennessee. Unpublished doctoral dissertation.

Hanover Research (2013). *Strategic planning in higher education: Best practices and benchmarking.* Author. Retrieved from http://www.hanoverresearch.com/media/Strategic-Planning-in-Higher-Education-%E2%80%93-Best-Practices-and-Benchmarking.pdf

Hazelkorn, E. (2015a). *The obsession with rankings in tertiary education: Implications for public policy.* Presentation to the World Bank. Retrieved from https://hepru.files.wordpress.com/2015/01/the-obsession-with-rankings-in-tertiary-education_wb_0115.pdf

Hazelkorn, E. (2015b). *Rankings and the reshaping of higher education: The battle for world-class excellence* (2nd ed.). Palgrave MacMillan: London.

Helsper, E., & Enyon, R. (2009). Digital natives: Where is the evidence? *British Educational Research Journal, 36*(3), 503–520.

Hinton, K. (2012). *A practical guide to strategic planning in higher education.* Society for College and University Planning: Ann Arbor, Michigan.

James, G. (2012). Developing institutional comparisons. In R. Howard, G. McLaughlin, & W. Knight (Eds.), *The handbook of institutional research.* Jossey-Bass: San Francisco, pp. 644–655.

Keller, G. (1983). *Academic strategy: The management revolution in American higher education.* Johns Hopkins Press: Baltimore, Maryland.

Kezar, A. (2013). *How colleges change: Understanding, leading and enacting change.* Routledge: New York.

Kezar, A., & Eckel, P. (2002). The effect of institutional culture on change strategies in higher education: Universal principles or culturally responsive concepts? *The Journal of Higher Education, 73*(4), 435–460.

Knabb, R., Rhome, J., & Brown, D. (2011). *Tropical cyclone report: Hurricane Katrina: 23–30 August 2005.* National Hurricane Center.

Macintosh, R., & Maclean, D. (2015). *Strategic management: Strategists at work.* Palgrave: London.

Mathies, C. (2015). Transnational IR collaborations. In Karen Webber & Angel Calderon (Eds.), *Institutional Research and Planning in Higher Education: Global contexts and themes.* Routledge: New York, pp. 28–39.

McClean, D. (2015). *Strategic planning: As simple as A, B, C.* Lulu Publishing Services: Raleigh, North Carolina.

McGregor, C. (2015). The man who invented management. *General Counsel.* Spring. Retrieved from http://www.legal500.com/assets/pages/gc/spring-2015/the-man-who-invented-management.html February 2016.

McNamara, C. (2007). *Field guide to non-profit strategic planning and facilitation.* Authenticity Consulting Inc.: Minneapolis.

Middaugh, M. (2009). Closing the loop: Linking planning and assessment. *Planning for Higher Education, 37*(3), 5–14.

Noel-Levitz, Inc. (2009). Six essentials – and six common mistakes – in cabinet-level strategic enrollment planning. *Noel-Levitz executive briefing.* Author: Iowa City. Retrieved from https://www.noellevitz.com/documents/shared/Papers_and_Research/2009/SixEssentialsinCabinetLevelSEP0209.pdf

Porter, M. E. (1980). *Competitive strategy: Techniques for analyzing industries and competitors.* Free Press: New York.

Prensky, M. (2001). Digital natives, digital immigrants. *On the Horizon, 9*(5), 1–6.

Prensky, M. (2010). *Teaching digital natives: Partnering for real learning.* Corwin: Thousand Oaks, California.

Rhoades, G. (2000). Who's doing it right? Strategic activity in public research universities. *The Review of Higher Education, 24*(1), 41–66.

Rowley, D. J., Lujan, H. D., & Dolence, M. G. (2001). *Strategic change in college and universities: Planning to survive and prosper.* San Francisco: Jossey-Bass.

Schmidtelin, F., & Milton, T. (Eds.) (1990). Adopting strategic planning to campus realties. *New Directions for Institutional Research,* No. 67. Jossey-Bass: San Francisco.

Selingo, J. (2015). *College disrupted: Perspectives on how technology is changing the college education model.* The Chronicle of Higher Education: Washington, DC.

Servier, R. (2000). *Strategic planning in higher education.* CASE: Washington, DC.

Shirley, R. C. (1988). Strategic planning: An overview. *New Directions for Higher Education, 16*(4), 5–14.

Smith, E. (2012). The digital native debate in higher education: A comparative analysis of recent literature. *Canadian Journal of Learning and Technology, 38*(3), 1–18.

Sweeney, V. (2014). The story of Hurricane Katrina and Memorial Hospital. *Law School Student Scholarship.* Paper 589.

Swenk, J. (1999). Planning failures: Decision cultural clashes. *The Review of Higher Education, 23.1,* 1–21.

Thomas, M. (Ed.) (2011). *Deconstructing digital natives: Young people, technology, and new literacies.* Routledge: New York.

Tolmie, F. (2005). The HEFCE guide to strategic planning: The need for a new approach. *Perspectives: Policy & practice in higher education, 9*(4), 110–114.

Watson, C. (1995). Strategic planning for higher education. *Journal of Professional Issues in Engineering Education and Practice, 121*(3), 187–190.

Wells, J. (2015). Planning in a global university: Big challenges and practical responses. In Karen Webber & Angel Calderon (Eds.), *Institutional research and planning in higher education: Global contexts and themes.* Routledge: New York, pp. 174–185.

Welsh, J., Nunez, W., & Petrosko, J. (2006). Assessing and cultivating support for strategic planning: Searching for best practices in a reform environment. *Assessment & Evaluation in Higher Education, 12*(3), 693–708.

Xu, Di, and Shanna S. Jaggars. 2011. The effectiveness of distance education across Virginia's Community Colleges: Evidence from introductory college-level Math and English Courses. *Educational Evaluation and Policy Analysis, 33*(3), 360–377.

Yeager, J., El-Ghali, H., & Kumar, S. (2013). A guide to the development of an institutional strategic plan. In Patrick Schloss & Kristina Cragg (Eds.), *Organization and administration in higher education* (1st ed.). Routledge: New York, pp. 127–150.

7

THE NATURE AND ROLE OF BUDGET PROCESSES

Patrick J. Schloss and Kristina Powers

INTRODUCTION

Few issues in higher education have commanded the attention of the media more than mounting student loan debt. The 10th Annual Report from the Institute for College Access & Success, for example, states that student debt has risen over 50% over the course of the last decade. The average student graduating in 2014 was obligated to repay $28,950 (Institute for College Access & Success, 2015). This figure understates the actual liability, as obligations of transfer students are not included in the analysis and many private loans are not reported.

The report's authors emphasize the importance of accountability on the part of university administrations. More important is the challenge to make institutions more affordable through enhanced efficiencies and budget moderation/reduction. The College Board's 2015 report indicates that while nearly all stakeholders embrace these goals, there is little evidence of even marginal success in achieving them. The average educational expenditure per student has substantially outpaced inflation over the past decade, while the share of expenses paid by public revenue has decreased and tuition and fees have increased.

The economic burden that the cost of postsecondary education places on families is alarming. Reducing this burden may be one of the top priorities for administrators. However, cost reduction can never be accomplished without considering institutional priorities—many of which require additional funding. For example, imagine the dilemma of the contemporary budget committee as they attempt to reduce overall expenditures while enhancing technological services, scientific equipment, access for non-traditional students, counseling services, student safety, student life opportunities, and transportation.

Any chance of moderating institutional costs requires a clear understanding of existing revenue and expenditures as well as expectations for the future. Determining future action in the face of these variables must be focused and deliberate. This chapter is intended to equip administrators with resources to meet these objectives. It emphasizes action-oriented administration within the context of diminishing resources and increasing expectations. It also emphasizes a democratization of the planning and budget process to give all participants and stakeholders a voice in critical decisions.

IMPORTANCE OF PLANNING AND BUDGETING

The effective management of postsecondary institutions depends strongly on aligning resources with objectives. The focal point of this activity is the planning and budget process. Possibly no other process is as important to the quality of an institution (Barr & McClellan, 2011; Hinton, 2012; Kezar & Lester, 2009; McKeown-Moak & Mullin, 2014). This may explain why The University of Chicago downgraded athletics to NCAA Division III while mounting one of the world's preeminent nuclear physics programs or why Harvard and Stanford universities do not offer undergraduates a business major yet have one of the strongest master's in business administration programs in the country.

The unique characteristics of postsecondary schools present distinct challenges for budget managers. Primary budget sources can be wide-ranging and include student tuition, state appropriation, auxiliary income (e.g., residence halls, bookstores, food services), foundation income, incidental or targeted income (e.g., athletic receipts, performing arts receipts, parking fines), extramural funds from grants and contracts, and income from intellectual property (e.g., licenses, patents, royalties).

Restrictions on the use of this income can vary within an institution. For example, at a given school, tuition and state appropriations may not be spent on hospitality items and surpluses may not be carried forward from one year to the next. On the other hand, foundation income and endowments can grow indefinitely and be spent on dinners, social travel, and entertainment. Public institutions in one state may be able to accumulate a reserve of tuition money, while those in another may be required to expend all funds by the end of the fiscal year.

Further adding to budget challenges at postsecondary institutions, the relationship between mission and expenditure or cost is not often well defined (Weisbrod, Ballou, & Asch, 2010). In fact, in some cases it is illogical. A technical school may be charged with preparing the workforce for critical shortages in applied vocations, such as nursing and welding. A careful analysis may reveal that these are among the two most costly programs offered. General education, as a transfer curriculum to colleges or universities, may be a peripheral focus offered solely for the convenience of young people in the region. One would expect budget support to follow the mission, with more dollars being allocated to nursing and welding and less to general education. In reality, the very costly welding and nursing curricula that require substantial equipment and staffing levels generate the same income per student as the less costly general education curriculum.

Finally, though they must manage extensive and complex budgets, many postsecondary school administrators have little or no formal preparation in finance. The typical university president first developed expertise as a musician, social scientist, or teacher educator. He or she advanced from faculty member to department chair to dean and eventually to president. Based on this career path, his or her sensitivity to curriculum delivery may be exceptional. Sensitivity to the financing of the curriculum may be lacking.

MONEY FOLLOWS MISSION

No single budget principle is more important than the philosophy characterized by the phrase "Money follows mission." The aforementioned example of nursing and welding is a case of the mission following the money, which most would agree is highly destructive. Carried to the extreme, this approach would cause technical schools to experience "mission creep" until their offerings were weighted heavily toward high-income and low-cost general education. The effect would be the loss of their central mission of workforce development.

Conversely, one would expect liberal arts colleges to use fiscal resources to strengthen opportunities in traditional arts and science fields while maintaining only marginal support for graduate and professional programs. Curiously, Baker, Baldwin, and Makker (2012) report that, in recent decades, there has been a major decline in support for undergraduate arts and science degrees at our nation's liberal arts colleges. At the same time, there has been an increase in other programs. This has led 39% of schools that have traditionally espoused a liberal arts mission to more closely parallel comprehensive institutions with teaching, business, health care, and other professional programs.

"Money follows mission" means that the institution must have a clear and well-vetted mission statement, such as "to provide training in applied disciplines that are essential to meeting the workforce needs of the local region." Figure 7.1 presents additional examples.

Binghamton University, State University of New York

Our mission is to provide an affordable, world-class education to high-caliber students from culturally and economically diverse backgrounds. Our focus is always on the student. Our internationally renowned faculty members produce amazing scholarship and art, and bring their spirit of inquiry and discovery into the classroom.

Bowling Green State University

Bowling Green State University (BGSU) provides educational experiences inside and outside the classroom that enhance the lives of students, faculty and staff. Students are prepared for lifelong career growth, lives of engaged citizenship and leadership in a global society. Within our learning community, we build a welcoming, safe and diverse environment where the creative ideas and achievements of all can benefit others throughout Ohio, the nation and the world.

California Institute of Technology

The mission of the California Institute of Technology is to expand human knowledge and benefit society through research integrated with education. We investigate the most challenging, fundamental problems in science and technology in a singularly collegial, interdisciplinary atmosphere, while educating outstanding students to become creative members of society.

Cornell University

Cornell is a private, Ivy League university and the land-grant University for New York State. Cornell's mission is to discover, preserve, and disseminate knowledge; produce creative work; and promote a culture of broad inquiry throughout and beyond the Cornell community. Cornell also aims, through public service, to enhance the lives and livelihoods of our students, the people of New York, and others around the world. Our faculty, students, alumni, and staff strive toward these objectives in a context of freedom

(Continued)

Figure 7.1 (Continued)

with responsibility. We foster initiative, integrity, and excellence, in an environment of collegiality, civility, and responsible stewardship. As the land-grant University for the State of New York, we apply the results of our endeavors in service to our alumni, the community, the state, the nation, and the world.

Massachusetts Institute of Technology

The mission of MIT is to advance knowledge and educate students in science, technology, and other areas of scholarship that will best serve the nation and the world in the 21st century. The Institute is committed to generating, disseminating, and preserving knowledge, and to working with others to bring this knowledge to bear on the world's great challenges. MIT is dedicated to providing its students with an education that combines rigorous academic study and the excitement of discovery with the support and intellectual stimulation of a diverse campus community. We seek to develop in each member of the MIT community the ability and passion to work wisely, creatively, and effectively for the betterment of humankind.

Notre Dame

The University seeks to cultivate in its students not only an appreciation for the great achievements of human beings, but also a disciplined sensibility to the poverty, injustice, and oppression that burden the lives of so many. The aim is to create a sense of human solidarity and concern for the common good that will bear fruit as learning becomes service to justice.

University of California, Los Angeles

UCLA's primary purpose as a public research university is the creation, dissemination, preservation, and application of knowledge for the betterment of our global society. To fulfill this mission, UCLA is committed to academic freedom in its fullest terms: we value open access to information, free and lively debate conducted with mutual respect for individuals, and freedom from intolerance. In all of our pursuits, we strive at once for excellence and diversity, recognizing that openness and inclusion produce true quality.

University of Illinois

The University of Illinois will transform lives and serve society by educating, creating knowledge and putting knowledge to work on a large scale and with excellence.

University of Michigan

The mission of the University of Michigan is to serve the people of Michigan and the world through preeminence in creating, communicating, preserving and applying knowledge, art, and academic values, and in developing leaders and citizens who will challenge the present and enrich the future.

Vanderbilt University

Vanderbilt University is a center for scholarly research, informed and creative teaching, and service to the community and society at large. Vanderbilt will uphold the highest standards and be a leader in the quest for new knowledge through scholarship, dissemination of knowledge through teaching and outreach, creative experimentation of ideas and concepts. In pursuit of these goals, Vanderbilt values most highly intellectual freedom that supports open inquiry, equality, compassion, and excellence in all endeavors.

Figure 7.1 Sample Mission Statements

Expenditures should be judged against this mission statement. All things being equal at the technical institution mentioned above, welding instruction would maintain priority over college transfer sociology courses. Similarly, a liberal arts university's mission to provide education in the arts, sciences, and humanities leading to a broadly educated student would emphasize support for library holdings, lab equipment, and terminally qualified/student-centered faculty. A premium might also be placed on small class sizes. All things being equal, less support would be given to business programs, engineering programs, and athletics.

Institutions of all types and levels build sufficient flexibility into their mission statement to allow for serious competition among diverse activities. For example, Ezra Cornell founded Cornell University with a commitment to providing for human development in all disciplines and skills that would advance society. The school assigns exceptional resources to many of the country's best programs, including engineering, agriculture, hotel management, and the liberal arts. It is not surprising that assigning resources is far more challenging at Cornell than at a more homogenous institution.

One caveat to the money/mission axiom—introduced here to avoid the appearance of idealism—involves supporting a program or activity that is distinct from yet "enables" the mission. This is exemplified by the "Flutie Effect," or the impact of a successful sports team on university enrollment and reputation. Boston College quarterback Doug Flutie's Hail Mary pass against Miami clinched a win and is said to have increased applications in the following two years by over 25%.

A related exception may be that of the "cash cow." Many institutions offer programs on the fringe of their curriculum to generate revenue for their core mission. For example, many proud "liberal arts" institutions offer professional programs clearly not grounded in the liberal arts tradition. It can easily be demonstrated that business or education majors can be produced at a substantially lower cost than music majors. Removing the professional programs that run with 30 students to the professor would eliminate a revenue stream that offsets the 6:1 student–professor ratios in the performing arts.

Administrators are often tempted to ignore their institution's mission when assigning resources. Sometimes an administrator would like to keep his or her favorite program, even if it's costly. Other times an administrator wants to eliminate a costly or otherwise burdensome program, even if it is central to the institution's mission.

Organizing with a focus on the school's mission, not that of any one individual, is critical to strengthening the core of the institution (d'Ambrosio & Ehrenberg, 2007; Mactaggart, 2010; Manning, 2013; Martin & Samels, 2013). What follows is a description of a number of practices that ensure, to the extent practical, that money finds its way to the mission. These should be read with only a modest level of confidence. As has been said, "There are a number of ways to skin a cat." The practices below are included as they are simple yet effective methods for managing an institution.

IDENTIFY FUNDS AND EXPENDITURES

At the simplest level, the budget process we advocate involves laying all funds on one side of a budget and all potential expenditures on another. This enables leaders to compare the value of the various expenditures within their institution in an effort to reduce costs and put into perspective which items are most "valuable." Since there are invariably more needs than funds, needs must be prioritized. Those most important to the mission should be funded; those least should not. While all of the previous year's expenditures are technically eligible for increase or reduction, some administrators rightly protect certain line items. These may include expenditures required by law, prioritized by the governing board, or essential to public safety. Further, some authors have advocated protecting staff line items over others (Brown & Gamber, 2002).

For the process to have integrity, all available funds and all potential expenditures should be known to budget managers. Projected expenditures are seldom "hidden" from budget managers; a portion of available funds frequently is. As the experienced reader will know, the "hidden" funds are typically used by the less-than-forthcoming manager to support "pet projects" that may not be central to the mission.

As an example, a small southeastern university suffered severe budget reductions. Following the major principle of transparency, all funds were placed on a ledger with fund requests. Because of the reductions, low-priority and unfunded projects included library acquisitions, scientific equipment, and professional travel. Though replacements for four-year-old vehicles were not on the funding request list, new vans appeared on campus. When questions were raised, it was found that a director had not disclosed income from parking fines, room service fees, and other miscellaneous sources. He had independently directed this income to the vehicle purchase without considering the overall budget process.

The problem is that the value of library holdings, equipment, and travel, when judged against the mission, may have been greater than that of new vehicles. Because the income was hidden from the budget authority, this judgment could not be made.

To reemphasize, all available funds and all fund requests should be known to decision makers. Hidden funds will likely be directed to special projects that are not as important as the least important project known to budget managers. Essentially, "a budget doubles as an accountability and control device, against which expenditures can be monitored for compliance" (Lasher & Greene, 2001, p. 475).

Being aware of all funds available is not an easy task for most postsecondary institutions. Below is a description of typical sources.

Tuition Payments

Depending on the governing board, tuition can be collected and retained entirely by the school or remitted to a central agency (e.g., state system office) with a portion being returned to the school. Further, the board may determine that only a portion of the tuition should be returned for institutional expenditures and another be directed to grow the school's endowment or financial reserves. Tuition rates at public institutions are generally established directly or indirectly (with consultation) by a statewide or local governing board. These may include boards of regents, trustees, or school boards. Private school tuitions are generally set by trustees, who, in keeping with general business practices, attempt to strike a balance between student willingness and ability to pay and the funds required to offer a quality education.

The governing board also balances local tuition rates with those of competitors. The goal is to achieve full enrollment while accruing sufficient tuition from each student to provide high-quality instruction in a well-managed physical plant. If tuition is excessive, the school will not achieve full enrollment. The loss of students will result in a loss of revenue, and the quality of instruction and attractiveness of the physical plant will suffer. This may further inhibit the ability to fill seats, leading to a downward spiral. Conversely, if tuition is too low, a school may achieve full enrollment but have insufficient revenue to maintain quality programs.

Tax Appropriations

State governments or local governing bodies may provide tax receipts to postsecondary institutions based on a funding formula or an annual decision. The formula may be as simple as a dollar amount for each credit generated or as complex as assigning a portion of an overall tax pool based on variables such as credits generated, student head counts, physical plant size, or participation in special programs. Appropriations can be earned immediately, with formula results being directed into the current year budget, or can lag, with formula funds generated in a given year being paid out years later.

Public institutions almost always balance appropriated funds with tuition rates. During the post-World War era, when higher education access proliferated, appropriations accounted for the largest portion of institutional budgets. A ratio of 70% appropriations to 30% tuition was common. In recent years, state budget problems, the cost of the "war on drugs," and possibly a loss of cachet for higher education have reversed this ratio, so that many students now pay 70% of the cost of their education. Some state institutions (e.g., Penn State and The University of Virginia) have cynically described themselves as "state-related" or private, as government support has fallen below 20%.

In a manner similar to tax appropriations, private schools must strike a balance between tuition payments and tuition discounts against the published rate. While the institution may announce a cost of $30,000 in tuition and fees, it budgets for a "discounted" cost of $20,000 per student because, on average, students receive a $10,000 "scholarship" package against the full cost of tuition.

Interestingly, a 2015 report by the National Association of College and University Business Officers indicates that the 2014 average tuition discount for first-time freshmen at private schools was 48%. A decade ago, the discount rate was under 38%.

If there is a quick check of the fiscal health of a private or public institution, it is the budget surplus or deficit from year to year. For private schools, this appears as changes in the endowment. For public schools, it appears as funds carried forward from one year to the next. Of course, this increase must be in the context of full enrollment of high-quality students, full staffing, and a well-maintained physical plant.

Auxiliary Income

A majority of colleges and universities generate income outside of the tuition-based cash stream. Typical sources include food service contracts, parking fees, residence hall rents, and health fees. These revenues may be segregated from the overall budget but applied to the purpose for which they were collected. Parking fees may be used exclusively to maintain lots and structures. Residence hall rents may be applied to debt services and maintenance on dormitories. Health fees may be applied to professional salaries, equipment, and pharmaceuticals.

As emphasized earlier, these funds, though segregated, should be known to the overall budget authority. A case in point: At one school that collected one of the highest health service fees in its state, the funds were not disclosed to the general budget manager and so duplicate expenditures were made from auxiliary funds and appropriated funds, with both the auxiliary director and student life director funding and managing very similar health education programs.

Extramural Funds

Postsecondary institutions generally derive income from grants and contracts. At the high end, this income can exceed hundreds of millions of dollars. At the low end, it can be measured in the tens of thousands. In any case, direct costs budgeted in each grant or contract are generally assigned for the purpose of the project and not transferable to other purposes.

A project to train migrant workers may have a substantial budget, but the granting agency expects funds to be directed toward project objectives—travel to migrant worker housing, tuition expenses for migrant workers, staff salaries, telecommunications, and so on. Funds cannot be shifted to non-project expenses such as technology used in the university library, salaries of general departmental secretaries, graduate student stipends for teaching assistants in introductory classes, or student scholarships.

Many federal grants reimburse the institution for "indirect costs" that are incidental but critical to project objectives. These expenses include utilities for project offices, administrative time, and custodial care of program space. Indirect costs are generally figured as a percentage of the direct costs and can provide flexibility in the institution's budget. Because custodial support, administrative salaries, and utilities are already budgeted, grant money frees general operating funds for other institutional practices. Since grants and contracts are often a key part of an institution's mission, it is a common practice to direct money generated by indirect costs to objectives related to grant and contract procurement.

Foundation Funds

Foundations have been established at almost all public institutions. Though they operate independently, their explicit purpose is to support the mission of the institution. Foundation income is generally from private gifts, special projects, and investments. Expenditures are free of state and federal restrictions that constrain the general operating budget.

The effectiveness of a foundation may be measured in several ways. The first method is by determining the amount of funds raised through annual campaigns. This may include routine annual solicitations of alumni and friends via phone, mailings, or personal contacts. Another method is to determine funds gathered through capital campaigns or periodic fundraising efforts.

These activities generally focus on special projects important to the development of the school. A campaign may occur over several years, procuring major gifts and pledges for an athletic complex, library, or scholarships. Funds may be raised through special projects such as sales of intellectual property generated through foundation assets, admissions receipts from foundation events, and sponsorships from university performing arts and athletic activities.

The success of a foundation may also be measured by the growth of assets from year to year as well as the overall size of the endowment. The endowment is the total liquid and illiquid assets managed at any one time. Finally, the foundation may be judged by the total funds distributed in support of the college or university each year. This may be to all institutional interests, such as endowed chairs, equipment, and facilities, or specifically to scholarship support.

All funds of private institutions are generally free of restrictions imposed by state government. Consequently, foundations are not needed to avoid governmental restrictions. Further, a private school's development office can generate funds equivalent to those accrued through a public school's foundation. The growth may include tuition and fee revenue and the overall value of the private school's endowment not expended in a given year. Finally, while foundations of public institutions operate independently, the equivalent body of a private institution is most often an integral part of the administration.

MATCH FUND SOURCE RESTRICTIONS
WITH FUNDING NEEDS

Unfortunately, the use of funds generated by public postsecondary schools may be restricted based on the fund source. For example, in the state of Georgia, tuition cannot be discounted or used to provide scholarships, and it can be spent by the institution the day it is received. State appropriations carry similar restrictions but may be spent two years after the year in which they are earned. Neither can be used for student scholarships, athletic support, alcohol, or purchases of over $5,000 that have not been bid in the manner prescribed by the State Purchasing Manual. Also, on frequent occasions, the legislature restricts the use of tuition and appropriations for such purchases as vehicles and major equipment.

In Georgia, fee money can be used only for the explicit purpose for which the fee was generated, with athletic fees being used in part to provide athletic scholarships. Fees and appropriations cannot be carried forward from one year to another. Auxiliary funds (generated by dorm rents, food service deposits, parking fees, etc.) can be carried forward indefinitely. Foundation money can be used for nearly any legal purpose, notably hospitality (including alcoholic beverages), student scholarships, athletic support, and major purchases from a single source. Foundation funds can also be carried forward and invested indefinitely in common financial vehicles including stocks, bonds, and bank instruments.

There may be a temptation by university administrators to align the budget authority to the fund source without regard to the funding need. For example, the director of auxiliary services may claim authority over all auxiliary income, including revenue from the bookstore, the residence hall, food services, the print shop, and parking. Allowing this to happen would cost the institution a major source of flexible funds and would deviate from the principle that money follows mission.

An example, based on funding restrictions at a major state system, makes the case. Auxiliary income, while relatively plentiful, is not needed to support mission-related critical needs. Although the bookstore generates substantial income, the expenses are fairly low—a few employees, utilities, modest advertising, and maintenance. It is not uncommon for the operation to accrue tens of thousands of dollars annually. At the same time, appropriation and tuition policy have resulted in the biology faculty not having an adequate vehicle for student work at a field station, and the state has imposed a freeze on the use of tuition and appropriations for vehicle purchases.

Given that there are no unmet needs in the bookstore that rival the need for a vehicle, the institution-wide budget committee should be able to recommend that bookstore revenue be used for the vehicle purchase (even against the objections of the director of auxiliary services). There are a lot of ways to justify this encroachment on the director's "turf"; the most simple is that money follows mission.

PROMOTE TRANSPARENCY OF INCOME AND EXPENDITURES

It has been said that no single factor is more likely to be associated with the failure of an organization than for key decision makers not to understand the budget. No single budget process or principle is as important as the recognition that money follows mission. Knowledge of this principle must be embraced by those concerned about the overall financing of the school as well as those operating at the lowest level. For money to follow mission, personnel at all levels must know the mission and income sources. They must know how to connect the two for the optimum advantage of the mission.

It is noteworthy that "money follows mission" examples exist outside of higher education. For example, top accountants at major public firms do not have offices. Their mission is fiscal support for firms that are distant from the home office. Securing office space in a single building would not be conducive to that mission and would be a drag on the budget. Conversely, because they support firms across the country, much of their time is spent on the road. Obviously, their travel budgets are very large—money follows mission.

To the casual observer, MIT and Cal Tech have very "industrial" physical plants. There are few signature rooms with "picture postcard" architecture. Loading docks and ventilators are often the prominent architectural features. It is clear that institutional resources are directed to a physical plant that is optimal for engineering research and production.

Promoting knowledge of the institution's mission and budget processes should be a core part of institutional culture. One best practice is to view the budget units in the form of a pyramid, as illustrated in Figure 7.2. At the top of the pyramid would be the university budget council; at the bottom, each individual staff or faculty member with discretion over a set pool of funds. The top committee would advise the president and account for the oversight and, with the president, distribution of all fiscal resources. In the case of a moderate-sized state or private university, this could be over $200 million. A small technical school or community college budget might be under $5 million. The very bottom of the pyramid might be occupied by the advisor of the school newspaper, who operates on a budget of several hundred dollars.

All funds at the lower echelons of the pyramid would be included in the upper echelons of the pyramid. Oversight and distribution of funds at the top echelon would be to the second echelon, oversight and distribution of second-echelon funds to the third, and so on.

As an example, the university budget council might assign funds to the academic affairs division or provost and council of deans. It might also distribute funds to the division of finance and administration through the vice president for administrative affairs and directors' council. A portion would also go to the division of student life through the dean of students and council of student affairs directors.

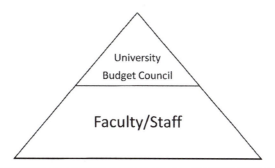

Figure 7.2 University Budget Council Structure

The university budget council, through open sessions and public reporting, would determine the relative needs for each of the second-echelon units. It would also establish regulations on how funds would be expended. These regulations would include whether funds could be shifted from line item to line item (e.g., using operating money to hire personnel). The budget council might also establish budget policy for all levels based on input from those affected.

The university budget council would not direct expenditures for the second echelon or lower. For example, it might provide a line item of $40 million for academic faculty but would not determine how much would be allocated to each department or whom to hire in each department. This authority would rest with the provost and council of deans at the second level.

Similarly, the provost and deans would assign funds to each college and might establish additional regulations beyond those indicated by the university budget council. They might specify the overall amount authorized for personnel in each college. The dean and council of chairs would determine the amount to be assigned to each department and the specific individuals to be employed. Finally, each academic department would receive an allocation for personnel, determine the specialty for each faculty line, and make the actual selection of faculty.

While respect for the authority of each level is important, one cannot overstate the value of communication and consultation between levels. To maximize interaction, there should be substantial overlap between professionals at each level. The university budget council must have representatives from each level. Meetings must be open so that budget managers can understand directly how and why distributions are made at the upper echelons. There must be periodic opportunities to revisit the mission statement and conceptualize strategic plans in order to keep campus leaders focused on activities that support mission and plans alike.

The typical university budget council might include each of the vice presidents, a faculty member from each college, a couple of deans, the director of the physical plant, the human resources officer, the director of auxiliary services, and several members of the plant staff. Though non-voting members, deans and key directors should attend all meetings.

It is advisable that faculty be overrepresented on the council to emphasize that the mission is education and training, and that faculty are closest to the mission. Also, because the vice president for finance and administration has the closest functional knowledge of the budget, he or she may be the most important consultant to the council. The provost and vice president for academic affairs should chair the council—money follows mission.

Of course, the president should attend all meetings. He or she should set the tone for the council through strategic planning, periodic state-of-the-institution addresses, and reports to and from the governing board. He or she should also select and evaluate administrative personnel at the top echelon. Finally, as the council is advisory to the president, he or she should have ultimate budget authority.

INSTITUTION-WIDE FOCUS

The university budget council and each subsequent budget manager in the pyramid must possess all information relevant to the council or individual manager's authority. It is equally important that the information be presented in an easily understood manner. Owing to the complexity of most institutions, the actual budget document may be a 6-inch-thick sheaf of 15-inch-wide green bar sheets. While this level of detail may be needed for an individual budget manager or auditor, it is of little use to the university budget council. In fact, there is no possible way that a chief academic officer, dean, or plant manager will have the inclination, time, or ability to extract or aggregate critical information from all other entries.

It is important to provide budget summaries containing only the level of information needed by the budget manager or advisory group. As shown in Figure 7.3, this can be done in a page or two. The university budget council would generally focus on the overall balance of funds distributed to units, the relationship between income and expenditures (hopefully they balance), and the impact of major expenditures or revenues. It might also be concerned about year-to-day expenditures against revenue but would have little need for details regarding departmental personnel, equipment, or operating expenditures.

Though the council would work from a one- or two-page sheet containing this information (as shown in Figure 7.3), the institutional budget officer would have the green bar reports as back-up. He or she would also have the abstracted reports provided to managers and committees lower in the pyramid. These documents could be used to answer any questions requiring more granular responses.

ADOPT MODIFIED ZERO-BASED BUDGETING

Zero-based budgeting requires that all funds in the annual budget be zeroed out at year's end. Either the fund manager fully depletes the budget line item (i.e., spends all available funds) or the remaining funds are "swept up" at a given date and returned to the central budget, at which point a zero fund balance is indicated in the line item.

Each line item is replenished in the next fiscal year based on an indication of need as it pertains to the mission. In the extreme, all line items go to zero and returning funds in the next fiscal year must be fully defended. One year's budget may bear no relationship to funds assigned in the previous year.

The extreme version of zero-based budgeting is seldom used because few organizations are so dynamic as to require a full overhaul of all line-item distributions. At a technical school, the number of students in welding classes is set by the capacity

	A		B	C	D	E	F
				APPROVED 3-11-11			
	FY12 BUDGET - April 19, 2011	Assumptions: -4 % enrollment	**BASELINE**	9% reduction in state appropriations	4-19-11 - Update from the System Office	4-19-11 - less additional 2%	**NOTES**
1	**REVENUES**						
2	State Appropriation Revenue		48,849,407.00				
3	Less: ERS cost increases				601.00	601.00	
4	Less: Unemployment Insurance				23,766.00	23,766.00	
5	Add: Formula Funding increase		-				
6	Total State Appropriation Revenues		48,849,407.00	45,918,443.00	45,942,810.00	45,942,810.00	42% E&G
7	Reductions from FY11 - 6% total		(2,930,964.00)				
8	REDUCTION TARGETS for FY12			(4,132,659.87)	(1,439,980.00)	(2,297,140.50)	
9	**Tuition/Student Revenues**						
10	Annual tuition projection (Includes: WebMBA, Erate, 12-15 CH, new stu)		47,853,337.92	47,853,337.92	47,853,337.92	47,853,337.92	
11	GOML		2,577,000.00	2,577,000.00	2,577,000.00	2,577,000.00	
12	Institutional Fee per student per semester (annualized)		8,022,246.97	8,022,246.97	8,022,246.97	8,022,246.97	$295 per student per semester
13	Total Tuition Revenues		58,452,584.89	58,452,584.89	58,452,584.89	58,452,584.89	56% E&G
14	Other Revenues		2,568,734.00	2,568,734.00	2,568,734.00	2,568,734.00	
15	Other Estimated Lapse		3,000,000.00	3,000,000.00	5,000,000.00	5,000,000.00	
16	Academic Lapse funding		500,000.00	500,000.00	500,000.00	500,000.00	
17	Tuition Carryover from FY11 (One time funds)		1,543,729.00	1,543,729.00	1,543,729.00	1,543,729.00	
18	Interest and Dividends		175,000.00	175,000.00	175,000.00	175,000.00	
19	MRR Funds			1,400,000.00	1,400,000.00	1,400,000.00	
20	**TOTAL REVENUES**		112,158,490.89	109,425,831.02	114,142,877.89	113,285,717.39	
21	**EXPENDITURES**						
22	Off The Top						
23	FY12 Estimated Expenditures from FY11 original and earlier scenarios		88,217,550.00	88,217,550.00	88,454,952.00	88,454,952.00	
24	ERS cost increases (employer matching)				601.00	601.00	
25	Unemployement Insurance, DOAS				23,766.00	23,766.00	
26	Electricity and Natural Gas Increase				285,651.75	285,651.75	
27	Employee Health Insurance Increase				732,848.54	732,848.54	
28	New Retiree Employer portion of Health Insurance				130,943.52	130,943.52	
29	GOML Expenditures		2,577,000.00	2,577,000.00	2,577,000.00	2,577,000.00	
30	Faculty FY11 from increased enrollment		1,446,229.00	1,446,229.00	1,446,229.00	1,446,229.00	
31	FY11 Academic Personnel Pool Additions		185,298.00	185,298.00	185,298.00	185,298.00	
32	FY11 Staff Personnel Additions - Finance and Admin		243,749.00	243,749.00	243,749.00	243,749.00	131,187 Available
33	FY11 Staff Personnel Additions - Student Affairs		68,373.00	68,373.00	68,373.00	68,373.00	21,420 Available
34	FY11 Staff Personnel Additions - Unaligned		65,284.00	65,284.00	65,284.00	65,284.00	55,284 Available
35	QEP		100,000.00	100,000.00	100,000.00	100,000.00	
36	Strategic Focus Pool		2,000,000.00	2,000,000.00	2,000,000.00	2,000,000.00	
37	Capital Fund (Bailey Addition)		2,700,000.00	1,605,491.00	1,605,491.00	1,605,491.00	
38	Capital Fund (Ashley Hall)			750,000.00	1,687,397.00	1,687,397.00	
39	Capital Fund (Ashley Hall) - MRR Funds			649,416.00	900,000.00	900,000.00	
40	Capital Fund - Remaining MRR Funds			250,584.00	-	-	
41	Restoring Operating Budgets by 10%				500,000.00	500,000.00	
42	Subtotal		97,603,483.00	98,158,974.00	101,007,583.81	101,007,583.81	

	A		B	C	D	E	F
	FY12 BUDGET - April 19, 2011	Assumptions: -4 % enrollment	**BASELINE**	Based upon 9% reduction in state appropriations	4-19-11 - Update from the System Office	4-19-11 - less additional 2%	**NOTES**
43	**Flexibility pools**						
44	University Pool for Deferred Maintenance, Enrollment, Utilities		3,233,995.24	842,956.98	2,373,655.66	2,547,929.95	
45	Capital Projects, unallocated		2,808,182.23	988,608.00	1,978,808.00	947,373.21	Spring Release / Maximum Tuition Carryover
46	Tuition Carryover to FY13 (See Col E for Estimated Maximum Carryover) One Time Funds		1,512,910.14	1,512,910.14	1,512,910.14	1,512,910.14	1,512,910.14
47	Flexibility Pool - (One time funds)		-	-	-	-	
48	**New Personnel**						
49	Academic Affairs for FY12 enrollment		-	-	-	-	$0 allocated due to no anticipated enrollment growth.
50	Academic Affairs Pool remaining for FY12 enrollment, including conversions		-			-	$0 allocated due to no anticipated enrollment growth.
51	Academic Promotions and Tenure		114,400.00	114,400.00	114,400.00	114,400.00	
52	FY12 Other Divisions Personnel additions		-		-	-	$0 allocated due to no anticipated enrollment growth.
53	**Pools for Divisions:**						Fall Release / Spring Release / Pool Manager
54	*Academic Affairs*		-				
55	Graduate Assistant Stipend Pool		500,000.00	700,000.00	500,000.00	500,000.00	500,000.00
56	Academic Equipment/Materials and Maintenance Pool		600,000.00	400,000.00	600,000.00	600,000.00	300,000.00 300,000.00
57	Library Reference/Special Collections		100,000.00	25,000.00	100,000.00	100,000.00	50,000.00 50,000.00
58	Faculty Scholarly Travel		200,000.00	175,000.00	200,000.00	200,000.00	100,000.00 100,000.00
59	Release Time for Research, Reassigned Time		200,000.00	140,000.00	200,000.00	200,000.00	100,000.00 100,000.00
60	Major Scientific Equipment for Research		250,000.00	200,000.00	250,000.00	250,000.00	125,000.00 125,000.00
61	Summer Faculty Pool		3,000,000.00	2,500,000.00	3,000,000.00	3,000,000.00	3,000,000.00
62	Erate Pool		150,000.00	100,000.00	150,000.00	150,000.00	75,000.00 75,000.00
63	Art Pool		50,000.00	50,000.00	50,000.00	50,000.00	50,000.00
64	*Finance and Administration*		-				
65	Instructional Setting Renovation Pool - MRR Funds		500,000.00	300,000.00	500,000.00	500,000.00	250,000.00 250,000.00
66	General Maintenance Pool		428,500.00	200,000.00	428,500.00	428,500.00	200,000.00 228,500.00
67	Vehicle Maintenance and Replacement Pool				170,000.00	170,000.00	85,000.00 85,000.00
68	Equipment Maintenance and Replacement Pool				100,000.00	100,000.00	50,000.00 50,000.00
69	*Student Affairs*		-		-	-	
70	Student Affairs Equipment Pool		50,000.00	50,000.00	50,000.00	50,000.00	50,000.00
71	*Advancement*		-		-	-	
72	Showcase University Events		50,000.00	10,000.00	50,000.00	50,000.00	50,000.00
73	*Unaligned*		-		-	-	
74	Computer Replacement Pool		300,000.00	300,000.00	300,000.00	300,000.00	150,000.00 150,000.00
75	IT Infrastructure		400,000.00	400,000.00	400,000.00	400,000.00	200,000.00 200,000.00
76	**TOTAL EXPENDITURES**		112,051,470.61	107,167,849.12	114,035,857.61	113,178,697.11	########### 4,713,500.00
77	**Estimate of Funds Available / (Further Reduction Needed)**		107,020.28	2,257,981.90	107,020.28	107,020.28	

Figure 7.3 Sample Two-Page University Budget

of the facility. Since enrollment does not change from year to year, the number of instructors does not change. Consequently, there is little need to defend relatively stable personnel costs. The same would apply to materials, utilities, and supervisory expenses. In this case, the only changes would be incremental inflation adjustments and possibly new expenditures required by changing missions or equipment made necessary by technological advancements.

Conversely, an electrical technology program may have a steady decline in enrollment. Without appropriate consideration and defense, the program may be substantially overstaffed. Annual review would result in funds being reduced in the personnel line item proportionate to the loss of students. Similar reductions could occur in supplies. Of course, the funds could be reassigned to programs with growth potential.

Some form of zero-based budgeting is critical to all educational programs. However, as emphasized above, it is seldom rational to expect a full defense of every line item in a budget. In most educational institutions, tenure and employee loyalty create very stable employment patterns. Programs with declining enrollment may be staffed by fully tenured faculty members, making proportionate staff reductions either awkward or impossible. The opportunity to shift personnel funds to other programs occurs only upon the resignation of a faculty member.

The university budget council should identify line items that must be defended annually and others that are static (allowing for inflation adjustments). Alternatively, the council could assign a percentage of a unit's budget to be defended annually. These practices allow funds to be redistributed based on the shifting needs of the institution. They avoid, however, defending funds that cannot or should not be shifted under any circumstance. This hybrid approach also conserves resources, as individual managers and budget committees can rest easy with stable base funding while focusing on strategic plans and marginal budget changes.

Rising enrollment and revenues present a unique opportunity. The budget committee can distribute funds following the same budget used in the past year. New funds resulting from enrollment/income increases can be assigned based on proposals that enhance the mission.

Declining enrollments and revenue present obvious problems. To bring order and avoid destructive concern, it is advisable to assign a budget reduction target proportionate to twice the loss expected in the overall budget. While strains on fiscal resources in the 1980s and 1990s were difficult (Mumper, 2001), the current state of the economy calls for new ways of dealing with reductions, which are unprecedented.

It is important to refer individual units defending an increase back to the institutional budget reduction target or the proposed higher budget reduction. Doing so is politically charged and highly challenging. No budget manager wants to deal with budget reductions. It is not the loss of money that is distressing; it is the loss of valued personnel, promotion opportunities, merit salary increases, and other amenities that enhance morale in challenging times. The recommendation to deduct twice the amount needed to balance the budget and require a defense to earn funds back to the unit would seem to exaggerate the potential trauma.

The justification for following the recommendation lies in the next budget principle, which involves redistributing and investing one's way out of a budget challenge. Put in the form of a simple parable, no matter how bad conditions were for Depression-era farmers, they would always buy seed, even if it meant depriving their families of gifts, clothing, even food. The next year's crop, resulting from this redistribution and investment, was the best chance the family had to break free of the bad economic circumstances.

Similarly, the best chance a school has to overcome challenging economic circumstances is to shift resources and energy from less productive activities that are peripheral to the mission to activities that may be more productive and mission centered. No matter how great the challenge, the budget process must provide an opportunity to shift funds to unfunded or underfunded activities that have a better chance of advancing the mission and returning revenue.

CREATE A STRATEGIC INITIATIVE POOL

Strategic planning and the resulting initiatives are hallmarks of reengineering an institution. Research points to strategic planning as a key first step (Bolman & Deal, 2013; Middaugh, 2010; Morrill, 2010). Once a plan is devised, action is needed; otherwise the plan simply sits on the shelf. Individual departments and colleges may engage in strategic planning and shift funds from existing activities to new programs as indicated by the plan.

In a similar manner, there should be a process that encourages strategic planning among units and facilitates the shifting of funds as appropriate. Since no single unit would have the funds, technical expertise, or interest to support interdepartmental initiatives like living-learning communities that integrate the academic curriculum with residence life, international programs that engage faculty from a number of departments and students from a number of nations, new athletic teams that require additional facilities, scholarships from university relations, and coaches who may be members of the faculty, a university-wide budget council facilitates the discussion and funding of such activities.

It is strongly recommended that the university budget council set aside a pool of money annually for broad-based strategic initiatives that cannot be accomplished with typical departmental allocations. Ideally, the money would come from increased institutional funding resulting from revenue sources discussed previously, such as enrollment growth, tuition increases, gifts to the school, increases in research indirect costs from grants, and so on.

If such funds are not available, there may be an assessment to each budget area that is either "across the board" or based on centrality to the mission and productivity. The latter is the better of the two options, as it is consistent with the overarching principle that money follows mission. Across-the-board reductions are indiscriminate and will adversely affect mission-critical and marginal operations equally. They will also disproportionately affect offices with little discretionary budget. A 3% reduction may not be remarkable for a continuing education program that uses temporary part-time staff in rented class space. A 3% reduction to residence life, where 90% of the budget is spent for bond debt on new buildings and utilities, can be catastrophic.

Once the fund pool is established, the university budget council may request proposals for new funding from all campus constituents. Figure 7.4 shows a sample strategic initiative process. To ensure attention to interdisciplinary and cross-unit proposals, various vice presidents, deans, and directors may cultivate relationships

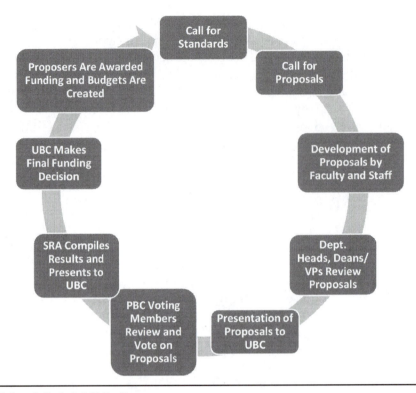

Figure 7.4 Sample Strategic Initiative Process

that result in joint submissions. A proposal for a new athletic team may be fostered by the athletic director but also involve the facilities manager, provost, and vice president for university relations. A proposal for living-learning communities may be prompted by the dean of students but include the provost, dean of arts and sciences, and director of auxiliary services.

This request and the subsequent review of proposals should be consistent with the aforementioned principle of transparency. Specifically, the committee should establish the criteria for proposals and the method of evaluation in open session. All members of the academic community should have the opportunity to provide feedback on the standards. In some form, the standards should ensure that the successful proposals will be those that most directly advance the mission and have the greatest chance of being economically self-sustaining. To ensure that proposals deliver against their promise, it may be prudent to require that each new initiative be reviewed annually for three years. If the program delivers as proposed during that period, the funding will become permanent and an annual defense will no longer be required.

In keeping with the hierarchical budget authority discussed previously, it is desirable for all proposals to be reviewed and approved by higher-level budget managers within the institution. For example, a nursing educator responsible for basic skills instruction may have an idea for increasing lab size that requires funding for simulation units. The cost of the units would easily be covered by an increase in the student–faculty ratio from 6:1 to 10:1. The faculty member would draft the proposal for review and approval by the coordinator of the basic skills center, then the proposal would be reviewed and approved by the dean of health sciences and chief academic officer. Finally, it would be reviewed and approved by the university budget council.

This example further illustrates the importance both of the hierarchical budget authority and of transparency. Acting in isolation, the university budget council would not be likely to assess the impact of the new lab arrangement on nursing accreditation, nor would it be fully sensitive to staffing issues in the nursing program. "However, if all meetings were open and reviews occurred from the department up to the university budget council, issues of pedagogy, staffing, and accreditation would be addressed.

As described, the process for obtaining new funds should be clear and unambiguous. A faculty or staff member should thus be able to anticipate funding simply by judging his or her own proposal against the criteria. This approach is characteristic of the overall budget process.

This chapter has advocated a highly structured budget approach in which all processes are vetted publically, known by all members of the institution with budget authority, and fully consistent with the view that fiscal resources are assigned based on their ability to advance the institutional mission. Sadly, it would only be in higher education fantasy world that one could lay out a spending plan and stick to it. The need to manage unexpected events forms the basis of the next principle.

PROVIDE FOR SUFFICIENT BUDGET FLEXIBILITY TO ADDRESS PROBABLE CONTINGENCIES

As emphasized at the beginning of the chapter, postsecondary institutions are highly complex organizations that include a vast array of fund sources, each with its own restrictions. Their missions are not captured by a single activity like "promoting the most absorbent towel on the market" or "providing the lowest price and outstanding customer service." Postsecondary school missions generally refer to multiple areas of attention, such as "teaching, research, and public service." Teaching is frequently divided among wide-ranging departments, from restaurant management and performing arts to math and physics. Research can range from multimillion-dollar federally funded institutes to a single faculty member evaluating stock selection strategies. Service can be to a myriad of private and public individuals and organizations.

In short, the typical sources of income and diversity of mission in business and industry would be comparable to those of a jewelry store at the mall. The usual income sources are retail purchases and repairs; the mission is to sell high-quality jewelry in a trustworthy and friendly atmosphere. This is comparable in complexity to a single academic department at a postsecondary school. To extend the simile, a postsecondary institution is more like the entire mall, with each college or department resembling a store and a corner hotel, food court, and paid parking included.

The budget process must be sufficiently flexible to accommodate the diverse character of the institution. The wide range of income sources and mission-related activities exposes the school to a wide range of risks and opportunities. Any variable can change without warning, and a school must be able to react to an unexpected threat or unanticipated opportunity.

The "hurricane cone" often used in television weather reports is a good analogy for the planning and budget cycle. Budgets are generally planned three to six months from the start of the year, just as hurricane tracking often begins days or weeks ahead of landfall. Early on, little is known about the final path of the hurricane. The predicted path therefore begins across the breadth of a tropical depression and produces a very wide possible track. As the days pass and the hurricane forms and approaches land, more is known about atmospheric conditions, and the expected path becomes increasingly narrow. A week from landfall, the region predicted to be affected by the storm may cover two or three states; a day from landfall, the range may be a few miles.

Similarly, it is often impossible when budgeting to predict key variables with a high level of certainty. The further out from the first day of class, the less focused and more potentially inaccurate the prediction. As time passes and more accurate data are acquired from budget-related events (e.g., enrollment, fee payment, financial aid applications, residence hall receipts), the budget predictions become increasingly accurate.

Events that occur during the year may also be highly dynamic. Local boards and state legislatures have been known to remove portions of appropriated money mid-year. Utility companies may introduce a rate hike early in the year. Contract settlements may unexpectedly increase staff and faculty costs. The budget must be sufficiently flexible to adapt to these contingencies through reserve holdings or optional expenditures that can be made late in the year.

Early in the formation of a hurricane, forecasters inform the public of "remote" possibilities but encourage very basic planning. Regardless of how far out the eye of the storm is, residents should have an evacuation plan and a plan to secure their structure. In other words, buy a few sheets of plywood and a map—just in case.

Administrators of postsecondary schools may need more than a few sheets of plywood and a map to adjust to the myriad of contingencies that may come their way. Strategies for ensuring flexibility differ from the time budget planning begins to the moment the budget is in force. Many institutions develop the first budget draft six months prior to the start of the fiscal year. Consistent with the earlier discussion of zero-based budgets and the high level of fixed expenses, the first draft appears remarkably similar to the previous year's budget.

Notwithstanding this tendency, there will be changes in circumstances that introduce small modifications. Most likely, there will have been salary increases, utility increases, enrollment changes, initiation of new programs, personnel changes, and so on. Obviously, the first budget scenario will reflect all of these changes. It will also reflect changing events that are anticipated throughout the year.

Like the hurricane prediction, however, that original scenario will only be a rough approximation of what will actually occur. Every couple of weeks until the start of the fiscal year, the institutional finance officer and institutional budget committee will evaluate the current scenario against any relevant new information. Increased applications/expected enrollment, increased appropriations, a major gift, and so on may lead the committee to increase income and expenditures. Approval of a new program may lead to the redistribution of funds during the start-up year.

If the budget officer and committee judge that the changes require a better budget forecast, they may agree on a second budget scenario. Of course, this scenario would replace the original scenario. The process of evaluation and revision continues until the start of the fiscal year, at which time the last of the budget scenarios becomes the operating budget.

Incidentally, as scenarios are approved, the institutional budget director and/or committee may allow the eventual fund recipient to begin operating with the line item (or a portion of the line item) or may require that funds not be encumbered until the budget year begins. Obviously, personnel costs involving contractual staff would be released, while one-time non-essential purchases would be held.

Restrictions on funds and enrollment will determine the best course for maintaining flexibility. Below are several key approaches to engineering flexibility into the budget. Of course, others are possible.

DEFERRED ENROLLMENT AND INCOME

Some schools admit only a portion of available applicants. This practice offers the immediate advantage of ensuring that a budget problem does not result from declining student numbers. The admissions office can always dig deep enough to fill the student ranks and the tuition-driven portion of the budget. If application rates are high, admissions can be increased to offset shortfalls in other budget sectors, such as declining appropriations or declining private gifts.

The process normally involves placing the most qualified students who are not admitted on a waiting list. As budget needs and the admissions yield (number of students admitted who enroll) materialize, the admissions office may accept wait-listed students. Of course, to meet a budget shortfall, students admitted from the wait list must be served at little additional cost over the value of tuition and appropriations (if available). The challenge of this approach is that as the school digs deeper into the wait list and overall applicant pool, the reported selectivity of the institution is diminished. The loss of status associated with reducing selectivity may further erode the institution's reputation and limit future applicant pools. In addition, serving additional students at little additional cost generally means increasing class size and instructional resources available on a per-student basis, which has a similarly negative impact on the reputation of the institution.

HOLDING FINANCIAL RESERVES

The institutional budget committee may establish a "contingency reserve" line item. If all goes well during the year, the fund will not be depleted and will be available for year-end capital projects (e.g., repairing cracked sidewalks, reroofing a building, creating a parkway). Of course, it can be drawn down to address a contingency such as lower than expected enrollment, unexpected damage to the physical plant, or higher salaries. It is important to maintain discipline in the use of this reserve. If the school needs to repair roofs, "roof repair" should be an explicit line item in the budget. Keeping it as a "contingency item" puts the physical plant at risk of deteriorating year after year while less important items are supported.

LOANS FROM OTHER FUND SOURCES

Many institutions have flexible fund sources that exist outside of the annual operating budget. A private school, for example, may have a substantial endowment that can be used for virtually all purposes. Public schools in many states can maintain a reserve that allows for flexible spending when challenging financial circumstances occur. Universities are rightly cautious about reducing their endowments or reserves; once those funds are eliminated, there are few options for handling a financial challenge other than reducing staff or cutting into critical programs. For this reason, a reduction in reserves or endowments is best treated as a short-term loan.

When an institution finds it necessary to draw funds against its reserves or endowment, the university budget council should draw up an explicit payback schedule as well as a budget scenario for the payback period to ensure that the fund will be replenished. Obviously, this means that whatever circumstances caused the shortfall must be corrected and additional income and/or efficiencies identified. It is generally best to use a loan only when an explicit change in circumstances is expected. This may include the start of a new endowed fund, a change in the state funding formula, or an amendment of tuition policy. If these guidelines aren't followed, the problems that necessitated the loan may be magnified by the requirement to replenish the funds.

CONCLUSION

This chapter repeatedly emphasized that planning and budgeting center on one dominant principle: money follows mission. Even the best financial managers can do a disservice to a university if they are unfamiliar with its priorities and thus do not support those priorities in the budget. Since many administrators are not formally trained in finance, it is critical to identify, comprehend, and be able to articulate in a very easy to understand manner the budget process and plan for the institution. It is not enough for the budget plan to be understood by a few; it must be understood at least at a basic level by all institution constituents. This includes everyone from students, to all levels of staff and faculty, and administrators.

Common fund sources for colleges and universities were described in this chapter. Higher education leaders at all levels should learn the different funding sources and expenditure categories at their institution. This enables an administrator to know which "levers" can be pulled. For example, for-profit institutions typically do not have a foundation. Therefore, using foundation account dollars is not an option for administrators in that sector.

Strategies for managing institutional budgets such that they are at least revenue neutral, and perhaps even digging out of the hole for revenue positive, were also discussed. Many public institutions are legally required to return any excess funds to the state at the end of the year. In such cases, revenue-positive funds can be turned into seed money through a strategic funding pool, as described in this chapter.

It is typical for faculty and staff to emphasize that higher education is not a business and should not be bound to strictures associated with commercial enterprise. To the contrary, postsecondary schools have income in the form of tuition and fees, and have expenses in the form of salaries and operating expenditures. The most successful institutions balance these elements, leaving substantial reserves to ensure stability (Prowle & Morgan, 2005). Harvard, for example, carries an endowment exceeding $35 billion. This endowment can fluctuate by as much as $8 billion annually. Without a doubt, administrators at Harvard University are fully aware of dynamics involving income and expenses. In fact, more has been written about the management of a school's endowment relative to enrollment and educational expenditures than just about any other topic in higher education.

Interestingly, large endowments are not the sole province of private institutions. The University of Michigan's endowment approaches $10 billion. Other multi-billion dollar state endowments include those of Ohio State, Wisconsin, and the University of Virginia. Administrators of these institutions must be equally astute. However, they have the added challenge of predicting or influencing state appropriations and mandated tuition restrictions.

One of the most interesting controversies in higher education is the extraordinary growth of the endowment within select institutions. Harvard's mission includes world-class teaching, research, and service. Many have argued that an insufficient amount of endowed funds are being directed to the mission. They would assert that the mission of Harvard University appears to be to grow its endowment. The same criticism may apply to Yale, Michigan, Florida State, or Ohio State. This criticism may be particularly acute when computing the size of a school's endowment per individual student. Princeton, for example, possesses nearly $2 million in its endowment for every tuition-paying student.

A typical technical school, college, or university should have a well-developed mission statement, and there should be a strong connection between the allocation of resources and this statement. A majority of income for technical schools should be directed to facilities, supplies, and faculty that allow for high-quality technical education. The budget of a research university should include major expenditures for scientific equipment, graduate assistantships, and research scholars. Community colleges should focus spending on classroom instruction and facilities.

Regardless of the institution in question, the key takeaway is that "money follows mission." Communicating this to all campus stakeholders and getting them to make budget requests and decisions with this in mind will help the institution achieve its mission.

DISCUSSION PROMPTS

1. Describe how the budget process works at your institution? What two strategies described in this chapter would you recommend leadership employ to improve the financial health and stability of the institution?

2. Who should be involved in the university budgeting process? Why? Why is it important to have each of those individual/positions involved?

3. What does "money follows mission" mean? Is the spirit of this concept used at your institution? Why? Why not? Should it be used? Why? Why not?

4. How can a modified version of zero-based budgeting help an administrator not only balance the budget, but redirect money to those things that are closer to the mission? What challenges may arise from using a modified zero-based budgeting model?

5. From the chapter section on funds and expenditures, identify one item that could be added and one that your institution does not have. Discuss the strengths and weaknesses of each.

6. If you were an administrator during a fiscal crisis at your institution, what financial strategies would you use to mitigate the problem so that students can still progress in their courses and people do not lose their jobs?

7. How does the transparency of the institutional budget through an institution wide council require the vice president for finance to work differently with stakeholders? What are the pros and cons of this model?

8. Identify three creative ways to handle budget challenges. How would you implement them? What challenges and opposition would you face in doing so?

9. What role do system offices, state legislatures, parent companies, boards of trustees, etc., play in the budgeting process?

10. In a budget shortfall one strategy may be to admit all students on the wait list. What are the strengths and weaknesses of using that option? What other enrollment strategies that you could use if your institution does not have a wait list (e.g., lower admissions requirements)?

REFERENCES

Baker, V. L., Baldwin, R. G., & Makker, S. (2012). Where are they now? Revisiting Breneman's study of liberal arts colleges: Shared futures, difficult choices. *Liberal Education, 98*(3), 48–53.

Barr, M. J., & McClellan G. S. (2011). *Budget and financial management in higher education.* Hoboken, New Jersey: Jossey-Bass.

Bolman, L. G., & Deal, T. E. (2013). *Reframing organizations: Artistry, choice and leadership* (3rd ed.). San Francisco: Jossey-Bass.

Brown, W. A., & Gamber, C. (2002). *Cost containment in higher education: Issues and recommendations* (Vol. 28). New York: John Wiley & Sons.

d'Ambrosio, M. B., & Ehrenberg, R. G. (Eds.). (2007). *Transformational change in higher education: Positioning colleges and universities for future success.* Northampton, Massachusetts: Edward Elgar.

Hinton, K. E. (2012). *A practical guide to strategic planning in higher education.* Ann Arbor Michigan: Society for College and University Planning.

Institute for College Access & Success (2015, October). *Student debt and the class of 2014.* Retrieved from http://ticas.org/sites/default/files/pub_files/classof2014.pdf

Kezar, A. J., & Lester, J. (2009). *Organizing for higher education: A guide for campus leaders.* San Francisco: Jossey-Bass.

Lasher, W. F., & Greene, D. L. (2001). College and university budgeting: What do we know? What do we need to know? In J. L. Yeager, G. M. Nelson, E. A. Potter, J. C. Weidman, & T. G. Zullo (Eds.), *ASHE reader on finance in higher education* (2nd ed.). Boston: Pearson Custom Publishing.

Mactaggart, T. (Ed.). (2010). *Academic turnarounds: Restoring vitality to challenged American colleges and universities.* Lanham, Maryland: Rowman & Littlefield.

McKeown-Moak, M. P., & Mullin, C. M. (2014). *Higher education finance research: Policy, politics, and practice.* Charlotte, North Carolina: Information Age Publishing.

Manning, K. (2013). *Organizational theory in higher education.* New York: Routledge.

Martin, J., & Samels, J. E. (2013). *Turnaround: Leading stressed colleges and universities to excellence.* Baltimore, Maryland: Johns Hopkins University Press.

Middaugh, M. F. (2010). *Planning and assessment in higher education: Demonstrating institutional effectiveness*. San Francisco: Jossey-Bass.

Morrill, R. L. (2010). *Strategic leadership: Integrating strategy and leadership in colleges and universities*. Lanham, Maryland: Rowman & Littlefield.

Mumper, M. (2001). State efforts to keep public colleges affordable in the face of fiscal stress. In M. B. Paulsen, & J. C. Smart (Eds.), *The finance of higher education: Theory, research, policy and practice*. New York: Agathon Press.

Prowle, M., & Morgan, E. (2005). *Financial management and control in higher education*. New York: Routledge.

Weisbrod, B. A., Ballou, J. P., & Asch, E. D. (2010). *Mission and money: Understanding the university*. New York: Cambridge University Press.

8

MANAGING ACADEMIC PROGRAM RESOURCES

Steven T. Breslawski

INTRODUCTION

For millennia, man has attributed much importance to celestial alignments, believing them to be harbingers of great events. The location of the planets and stars determined the date on which the Roman emperor Julius Caesar was assassinated. The assassins chose the date and hour when they would strike based upon the alignment of the planet Mars, whose position in the sky suggested that the emperor's protection would be at its weakest.

ALIGNMENT: THE FOUNDATION OF PROGRAM RESOURCE MANAGEMENT

On its face, managing academic program resources includes (1) allocation of resources, (2) ensuring that allocated resources achieve desired outcomes, and (3) scrutiny of program costs and methods so that outcomes are achieved in an efficient manner. However, the success of these endeavors will depend largely on whether certain aspects of the educational institution are well aligned, rather like pieces of a puzzle that must be aligned before they will all fit together.

This chapter considers some organizational "alignments" that, while a bit more down to earth than those considered by the Romans in their decision-making, are fundamental to properly managing academic program resources. Specifically addressed are the issues and challenges associated with three different alignments: (1) curriculum alignment, (2) strategic alignment, and (3) resource alignment. These three constructs have meaning as individual concepts as well as in gestalt, with the cumulative alignment of strategy, curriculum, and resources commonly referred to as having achieved *resource alignment*. The overarching goal of resource alignment, in concert with strategic and curriculum planning, is the effective and efficient allocation of available resources to the delivery of curricula.

Given the difficult budget environment faced by many institutions of higher education, the careful allocation of resources to curricula has never been more important. Done well, resource alignment will ensure a number of positive outcomes. First, resources devoted to delivering curricula will support the strategic goals and priorities of the institution. Second, resources expended will reflect the learning goals and outcomes defined by the institution's curricular units on behalf of its stakeholders. Third, resource alignment will help colleges and universities to be more responsive to calls for improved outcomes in terms of the knowledge and skills possessed by the students that they graduate. Finally, alignment provides a necessary foundation as institutions seek to reduce per-student costs through increased efficiency and enhanced curriculum capacity. This will help educational institutions as they try to do more with less in response to the current funding environment.

Our discussion of managing academic resources within the framework of resource alignment is presented in five sections, the first of which has been this introduction. The next section introduces and defines the concept of alignment as it pertains to curriculum and strategic matters. The third section then considers strategic curriculum planning in more depth, including the strategic roles of curricula and the challenges faced by many educational institutions in this area. We make the case that, despite these challenges, academic program resources are best managed in environments where strategic plans include a curriculum component.

In the fourth section, the focus turns to achieving curriculum alignment, whose relationship to resource alignment is also developed more fully. Matters of personnel, including aptitudes, buy-in, and training, are also considered. Fifth, we address various cost aspects of resource alignment, including the economics and costs of delivering curricula. Cost and non-cost considerations associated with class size are also examined. The chapter concludes with a discussion of business process reengineering (BPR) as a tool for exploring how resources can be applied more efficiently and effectively in the educational environment.

DEFINING ALIGNMENT

In the context of higher education, resource alignment requires the melding of two bodies of thought. The first, referred to as *curriculum alignment*, is a topic frequently encountered in the education literature. The second, referred to as *strategic alignment*, has been advanced by strategic management practitioners and theorists.

Curriculum Alignment

In the lingo of the discipline, curriculum alignment ensures that that which is written (i.e., educational standards/goals), that which is taught, and that which is tested are consistent. As perspectives on assessment have evolved beyond traditional testing, *learning outcomes assessment* now extends the curriculum alignment process to include assurance of learning. The concept of curriculum alignment has been discussed for some time, primarily in the K-12 education literature. English's work (1992) is seminal. Curriculum alignment has received increased attention in the K-12 literature in part due to some of the mandates associated with the No Child Left Behind legislation, Common Core, and the emergence of strong accountability frameworks adopted in many states (Dingman, 2010; Glatthorn, 1999).

More recently, authors have extended the curriculum alignment paradigm to include instructional resources such as media, technology, and library resources (Lowe, 2001). Others have contemplated extension of the basic concept to include better alignment of formal curriculum with informal learning that takes place in classrooms (Glatthorn, 1999). The P-20 literature extends the concept to include preparation of students for success in pursuing education beyond the 12th grade.

While the adoption of formal curriculum alignment processes has found increasing support among practitioners and in the literature, it also has its detractors. The most common derogatory characterization is "teaching to the test." See Wraga (1999) for a discussion of competing perspectives.

As learning outcomes assessment and assurance of learning requirements have found more prominence in the regional and programmatic accreditation standards for higher education organizations, the topic of curriculum alignment has been discussed with increasing frequency in the higher education literature. For many programs, the mandate to devise assessment protocols has dictated the specification of learning outcomes for courses and programs and motivated discussions about how learning outcomes are best achieved. In essence, an almost accidental "reverse engineering" approach to curriculum alignment has taken place on some college campuses.

For the purposes of this chapter, curriculum alignment is defined as the process of ensuring that the subject matter taught in a course, the pedagogy employed for a course, and the assessment protocols assigned to the course are consistent with the learning goals established for that course. Resource alignment extends the curriculum alignment paradigm to include the allocation of resources sufficient to support the aligned curriculum, including resources to support both teaching and assessment. Resource alignment and curriculum alignment are thus closely linked.

Strategic Alignment

The concept of strategic alignment has its roots in the management planning literature. Although much of the work in this area focuses on for-profit business organizations, the associated concepts are just as relevant for institutions of higher education. Strategic alignment proponents espouse the critical importance of aligning functional area or subunit goals and activities with the strategic plan of the organization. Consider, for example, a company whose strategic plan includes internationalizing its operations. The HR strategy has to evolve so that qualified candidates with aptitudes and interests related to international business can be hired or developed. The company's financial strategy has to evolve to include foreign currency transactions and hedges against exchange-rate fluctuations. The logistics strategy has to now consider potential problems associated with inventory crossing international borders, the navigation of customs processes, and the need to rely on international carriers for transport. Finally, the risk management strategy must protect the organization and its agents when an employee inadvertently violates international laws.

In short, strategic alignment is about ensuring that an organization's strategic goals, business processes, and company culture are congruent such that the organization can achieve its purpose with maximal efficiency and effectiveness. For higher education, proper alignment must explicitly consider the portfolio of curricula as well as curriculum planning and development.

Strategic alignment has been a challenge for many organizations. Consequently, various authors have proposed frameworks for achieving strategic alignment in any organization; see, for example, the "balanced scorecard" proposed by Kaplan & Norton (1996) and *One Strategy* (Sinofsky & Iansiti, 2009).

The Relationship Between Strategic, Curriculum, and Resource Alignment

English (1992) supports his discussion of curriculum alignment with a triangular model that places the curriculum at the top, the teacher at the lower left, and the test at the lower right. Curriculum alignment is necessary to ensure that these three elements are consistent with one another, or aligned. Figure 8.1 presents a parallel model to convey the relationship between strategic, curriculum, and resource alignment.

Effective resource alignment depends on both competent curriculum alignment and consideration of curricular priorities within the strategic plan. Specifically, resource alignment and curriculum alignment efforts must be preceded by thoughtful and purposeful strategic curriculum planning (discussed in the next section). Thus, several key processes, required to ensure both a high-quality education and efficiency, are inexorably linked, as shown in Figure 8.2.

This chapter will attempt to make the case that an optimal allocation of resources cannot occur without competent strategic curriculum planning and thoughtful curriculum alignment. An example will help support that assertion.

Consider a hypothetical course, Philosophy 101, taught at hypothetical institution XYZ University. How should resources be allocated to this course? Should the course be taught in a large lecture format or as a seminar? Should it be writing intensive and/or require students to do substantial library research? Should it be staffed by full-time faculty or adjuncts? Do the faculty assigned to this course require Ph.D. credentials? How many sections should be offered? How extensive and intensive should the outcomes assessment process be? What level of resources should be devoted to the assessment process?

These questions cannot be answered without understanding the role of this course in the broader curriculum and within the strategic context of colleges or universities.

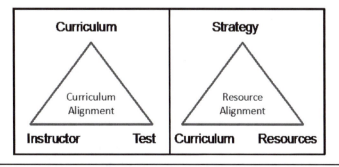

Figure 8.1 Curricula and Resources Applied Must Be Consistent with the Strategic Plan

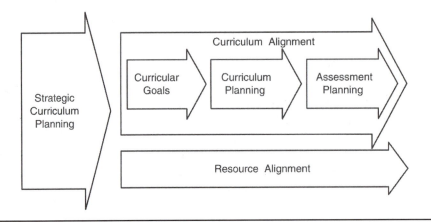

Figure 8.2 Resource Alignment Must Be Preceded by Strategic Curriculum Planning

Institutions offer courses for many reasons, some programmatic, others learning related. These reasons include:

- Developing desired skills (e.g., communication, critical thinking);
- Remediating weak skills (e.g., math skills, reading skills, writing skills);
- Satisfying the requirements of licensure or mandate;
- Providing a foundation of knowledge necessary to succeed in a sequel course;
- Supporting a general education component of an undergraduate degree program;
- Supporting a program major, minor, or certification;
- Providing breadth or depth in subject offerings;
- Providing an integrative, capstone experience;
- Supporting the contemporary interest of some stakeholder group (including faculty); and
- Inertia: The course has been taught for many years and continues to be taught.

The reasons listed above are not intended to be either mutually exclusive or collectively exhaustive, but rather to make the point that it is necessary to understand the role and purpose of a course, as well as the strategic role of the program(s) it supports, in order to properly assign resources to that course.

STRATEGIC CURRICULUM PLANNING

This section addresses the importance of strategic curriculum planning, the planning and alignment challenges faced by institutions of higher education, and the strategic role that curricula play as an institution assembles its competitive portfolio of programs.

The strategic planning process helps determine how an organization will define and fulfill its mission, compete with other organizations, and distinguish itself from competitors. For educational institutions, curriculum planning decisions (including curricula offered, scope, focus, and delivery methods) represent a critical aspect of

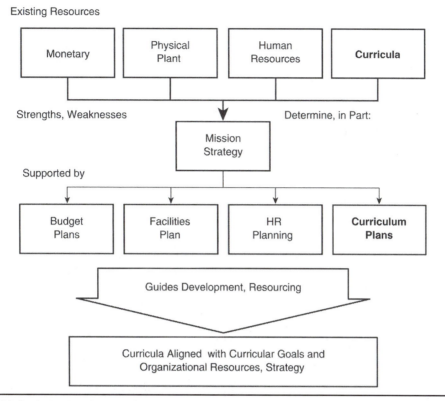

Existing Resources

Figure 8.3 Curriculum Is an Important Component of Strategic Planning

competitive differentiation and are a primary determinant of revenues and costs. For this reason, the importance of strategic curriculum planning as a prerequisite to resource alignment and allocation cannot be overstated. A strategic curriculum plan should be included in the outcome of any strategic planning process (see Figure 8.3).

Challenges to Planning and Alignment

Educational institutions are not the only organizations that find strategic planning and alignment difficult. Even if a stellar plan is produced, implementation presents its own challenges. To draw an analogy, wedding vows are fairly simple to utter; following through on them is the real challenge. The challenges faced by educational institutions can be divided into four groups: (1) challenges faced by all organizations (business and non-business alike), (2) challenges stemming from the unique nature of postsecondary schools and curricula, (3) challenges due to organizational structure, and (4) the expertise and interests of college personnel. Understanding these challenges is prerequisite to addressing them.

Challenges Faced by All Organizations

Studies of organizations with alignment problems (e.g., Miller, 1997) reveal four common underpinnings of misalignment:

1. *The strategic planning process is flawed:* It is impossible to align a bad strategic plan. Therefore, a robust planning process is crucial to avoid strategy misalignment. The vision may be brilliant, but vision and goals must be driven down into the organization through detailed planning and execution. A poor strategic planning process will fail to adequately define goals that are concise and measurable. Strategic planning initiatives often lack detailed operational planning and change management components. Most of all, plans often fail to assign specific responsibility for activities and deliverables. A fundamental tenet of organizational management is that if no one is responsible for a task, the task is unlikely to be completed. The devil is in the details (although a concise executive summary is also nice).

2. *Faulty strategic plan governance:* Plan governance is essentially a form of project management and ensures that the plan is managed through to execution. Plan governance requires that progress towards the plan's goals is periodically measured and that implementation of the plan is brought back in line quickly if the organization heads off course. Without plan governance, strategy misalignment will almost certainly occur.

3. *Poor communication of the strategic plan:* Alignment requires the development of a communications strategy that helps individuals responsible for the plan's success to know what they are expected to do, when they are expected to do it, and what the deliverables are to be. Failure to communicate the plan nearly guarantees strategic misalignment down the road. An important part of communication is periodically reporting progress and success while also acknowledging challenges and shortcomings.

4. *Poor buy-in and motivation:* Especially when an organization has a history of poor strategic planning and plan execution, cynicism can creep into the ranks and the plan can become an administrative charade. If the rewards structure of the organization is not aligned with the plan, it is difficult to generate and maintain buy-in and ownership. It is important for individuals at all ranks to develop the sense that the plan's success will help them thrive in their professional life.

The Nature of Colleges and Curricula

While the pitfalls discussed above are relevant to all organizations, they seem to be particularly germane in the domain of higher education. It is striking to discover the frequency with which a strategic curriculum plan or a curriculum planning process is omitted from a college's or university's strategic plan. References to curriculum in strategic plans are often limited to platitudes such as "strengthen existing programs" or broadly stated goals such as "increase graduate enrollments by 20%." However, there is rarely a serious assessment and articulation of how existing or proposed programs fit into the strategic goals of the institution.

There are a number of reasons that postsecondary institutions fail to consider curricula explicitly in their strategic plans. To begin with, educational institutions are relatively new entrants to the realm of strategic planning and are therefore notoriously bad at developing strategic plans. Strategic planning begins with defining a mission (i.e., a purpose for existence). Many educational institutions were established by mandate and thus, to some, their reason for existence is a matter of franchise rather than contemplation. Similarly, their programs (curricula) exist because they always have; the notion that programs should serve a (sometimes competitive) purpose is a foreign concept. The "not-for-profit" designation ascribed to many colleges and universities may play a factor in diminishing the competitive focus of their strategic plan.

Another reason curriculum is frequently absent from the strategic plans of educational institutions may be that these plans are often developed in a spirit of collaborative, shared governance. While this may assist in developing buy-in to the plan, the resulting mission statement often lacks focus and instead describes an institution that is everything to everyone. The mission statement may describe (or justify) the school as it is rather than as it should be. In the absence of a more dictatorial structure, it may be difficult to identify programs and courses that lack strategic value and should thus be terminated or granted fewer resources. Tenure and seniority rights come into play as well. Educational institutions do not like to retrench programs; it is an ugly business. Strategic curriculum planning may be viewed as a Pandora's box that no one wants to open.

It is important that faculty and staff in each program understand how their curriculum fits into the strategic plan of the institution. This will help them to better understand budget and resource decisions made in support of the strategic plan and to make more informed choices about their continuing professional development, career path, and future with the school.

Impediments Due to Administrative Structures

A final but key reason that strategic curriculum planning is difficult for educational institutions has to do with their often concentric organizational structure, as depicted in Figure 8.4. While colleges and universities vary greatly in their administrative structure, Figure 8.4, in whole or in part, is representative of the organizational context in which many educational institutions operate. This unique context, in which strategies evolve and curricula are typically designed and delivered, presents some very real challenges.

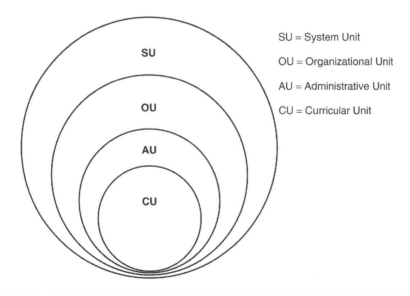

SU = System Unit

OU = Organizational Unit

AU = Administrative Unit

CU = Curricular Unit

Figure 8.4 Alignment and Planning May Be Inconsistent Across Levels of the Organization

In explaining this assertion, it is helpful to begin by defining a few terms:

- *Curricular Unit (CU):* Refers here to the organizational unit that is directly responsible for the design and delivery of a particular curriculum. Typical names include area, program, or department. An individual commonly referred to as a head, director, coordinator, or chair has administrative authority and direct supervisory control over the faculty delivering said curriculum.
- *Administrative Unit (AU):* Refers to a high-level span of (primarily administrative and resource) control that includes one or more CUs. Common names include school, college, or division. The AU may span a set of closely related curricular units (e.g., college of applied sciences, school of medicine) or, alternatively, a set of CUs that have a common purpose (e.g., division of continuing education). An individual such as a dean, director, or assistant provost is charged with administrative and budget oversight for the AU.
- *Organizational Unit (OU):* The aggregate organization in which educational services are delivered (i.e., the educational institution itself). The OU may be a community college, major research institution, liberal arts college, or trade school. An individual with a title such as president, working with a board of directors, is commonly responsible for developing a vision, mission, and brand for the OU and for developing corresponding strategies for achieving the mission.
- *System Unit (SU):* The OU may be part of a broader SU (e.g., state university system) and subject to the policy requirements, political concerns, and resource constraints set forth by that system. While organizational theory would suggest that policy directives at the highest (SU) level of the organization would be highly strategic in nature and, as such, far removed from the curriculum and operational decisions of the CU, the opposite may be true. Liberal course transfer policies or lax transfer student admission policies set forth by the SU may make it difficult for the CU to ensure that certain learning outcomes are achieved and measured. General education mandates set forth by the SU may limit or complicate curriculum design decisions and reduce the OU's control over the assignment of resources. SU policies may limit the degree to which the OU, AU, or CU is able to develop the resources necessary to obtain curricular goals, forcing curriculum and resource decisions (e.g., class size, staffing levels) that conflict with strategic and curricular goals of the lower levels.

Depending on mandates, statutes, tradition, or leadership preferences and skills, strategic curriculum planning may occur, in whole or part, at any level of the organization. A poor plan (or constraints imposed by a plan) at any level will impact the ability of inner levels to align resources and curriculum.

A second impediment to strategic alignment is that, in higher education, strategic planning has traditionally been viewed as something done by administrators at the OU level, while curriculum design and implementation have been viewed as the franchise of the faculty at the CU level. In such environments, a curriculum planning component is likely to be absent from strategic plans. Often, curriculum design and implementation have more to do with the interests and expertise of the faculty than the broader strategic goals of the institution.

However, curriculum decisions can be made at any level of the organization. For example, in secondary education, curricula are often specified (mandated) by an authorized board or committee at the SU level. Curriculum decisions can be made at the SU level in tertiary education as well. For example, at the SU level, the organization may adopt a cost-reduction strategy that limits duplication of programs. Consider a hypothetical state university system consisting of 20 campuses. The SU's plan may dictate that any particular program (e.g., a bachelor of arts in psychology degree) will be offered by, at most, five campuses. This limitation will obviously place constraints on the strategic plans of the 20 campus units in terms of programs offered.

Another example might be a CU accredited by an organization that requires it to develop detailed strategic plans that define its mission and differentiate its programs from other programs. During accreditation review, the CU is judged on the degree to which its curricula, and the resources that support them, are consistent with its stated mission. However, it is very difficult to do meaningful strategic curriculum planning at the CU level if plans are nebulous or absent at the AU and OU levels. The CU cannot develop strategic plans without guidance, authorization, and buy-in at the AU and OU levels. Further, strategic planning at the CU level cannot run counter to plans at the AU and OU level.

Thus, curriculum planning can occur at any level of the organization, but the curriculum planning process may or may not be strategic in nature or related to the institution's strategic plan. However, resource alignment will be most effective if strategic plans at each level contain a curricular component, even if that component is nothing more than a coordinated and purposeful delegation of curriculum decisions to the next lower level of the hierarchy. For example, the SU of a state university system may delegate any and all curriculum decisions to the OU level.

The Expertise and Interests of College Personnel

One strategic planning and alignment problem that is unique to institutions of higher education has to do with the expertise, skills, and abilities of the individuals involved in the planning process. Administrators at universities are often culled from the faculty ranks. Many administrative assignments are temporary in nature. The consequence is that those charged with developing and implementing strategic plans at each level are likely to differ greatly in their understanding of strategic planning, the skill level they bring to the task, and the importance they place on the task. The degree of coordination in planning, between levels, can vary greatly.

Very much like outcomes assessment, strategic curriculum planning does not work well if people are doing it only because they have been told that they should do it or that they have to do it. Benefits are likely to accrue only if the individuals involved embrace the purpose and importance of strategic planning. In another similarity to outcomes assessment, buy-in from the faculty is particularly important if strategic curriculum planning is to be meaningful and if alignment is to occur. As discussed later in this chapter, organizations may need to invest heavily in training and education in order to convey the importance of, and methods for, competent strategic curriculum planning.

Because of these challenges, strategic plans and implementation efforts have the potential to be ineffective. As illustrated in Figure 8.5, multiple agents will be "pulling"

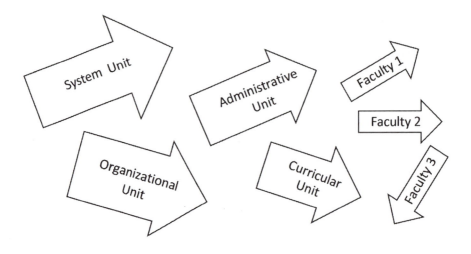

Figure 8.5 Plans, Efforts, and Resources Lack Unity of Purpose—Faculty Act as Free Agents

in different directions (i.e., the organization will lack unity of purpose). Under these circumstances, alignment of curriculum and resources will be very difficult and results will likely be sub-optimal.

In contrast to Figure 8.5, an ideal strategic planning process will be competently executed at each level of the organization and coordinated with organizational levels above and below. Strategic plans at all levels will be explicit and purposeful in their consideration of curricula as tools for achieving the mission of the institution. The individuals involved will be knowledgeable about developing missions and strategies and have the leadership skills necessary to develop buy-in from those impacted by their plans. When this level of coordination and curricular planning occurs, the organization is more likely to be unified in its purpose and more successful at moving in the desired direction; see Figure 8.6.

To summarize, colleges and universities face the following challenges when undertaking strategic planning in general and strategic curriculum planning in particular:

- Educational institutions often lack a history and tradition of strategic planning.
- Educational administrators may have weak strategic planning knowledge and skills.
- Strategic plans often lack a purposeful curriculum component.
- Strategic plans at the SU, OU, AU, and CU levels may be absent, weak, or inconsistent.
- At any level of the organization, buy-in by those affected by a strategic plan may be lacking. Without faculty buy-in, faculty are likely to act as free agents with regard to what and how they teach.

An awareness of these challenges is the first step to addressing them. Training and professional guidance from experts are important. Once the challenges are addressed, the institution will be in a position to consider and specify the strategic role(s) of each of its programs and curricula.

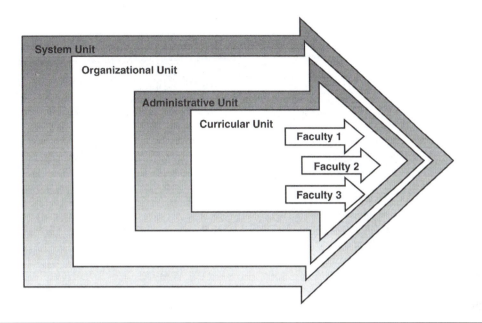

System Unit

Organizational Unit

Administrative Unit

Curricular Unit

Faculty 1

Faculty 2

Faculty 3

Figure 8.6 Coordinated Planning at Each Level Leads to Unity in Purpose and Direction

Strategic Roles of Curricula

With regard to strategic curriculum planning, one of the most important decisions that any educational institution must make is to determine what academic programs it will offer and what strategic role each will play. As summarized in Table 8.1, the reasons for offering various programs, and the courses that support them, are myriad.

The first programs referenced in Table 8.1 are those designated strategically as *medallion programs* (i.e., programs of priority and strong repute for which the institution is to be known). Typically, the prominent reputation of a medallion program will attract students, faculty, resources, and employers from outside the normal calling population of the institution. There are profound resource implications for assigning this designation to a program. Specialized facilities and equipment will need to be updated and maintained on a regular basis. Courses will need to be staffed by individuals that have a strong reputation in their field. Course offerings may need to be extensive and include a high degree of specialization. It may be crucial to obtain and maintain program accreditation and to devote the resources required to meet accreditation standards. Accreditation standards are likely to limit class sizes and adjunct staffing as well as require a substantive assessment initiative. Even if they do not, it may be difficult to maintain program reputation if class sizes are too large or the use of adjunct faculty is too pervasive.

To maintain program reputation, student entrance requirements are likely to be competitive, resulting in a high-parameter student body. While high-parameter students are unlikely to need remedial courses (which saves resources), they may require specialized placement support or other types of support (e.g., visa and specialized housing support for international students).

Table 8.1 Strategic Aspects of Various Program Types

Program Type	Strategic Role of Program	Resource Implications
Medallion	Program of high repute, used to attract local and non-local students to the institution (OU).	Program is heavily resourced in terms of Ph.D. faculty, specialized (depth) course offerings, support staff, program marketing, etc. Program accreditation likely to be maintained. Enrollments may be carefully managed.
High-Demand	Responds to popular demand and bolsters institutional enrollments. Strong cash flows help pay for smaller, more esoteric programs.	Program is structured to efficiently manage large numbers of students (e.g., larger sections, mass advisement, increased use of adjunct faculty to ensure sufficient staffing).
Niche	Responds to niche presented by local environment, e.g., a Southern California school offers specialized degrees in seaport management and container logistics.	Program may receive support from local business partners. Program may be practice focused and include strong experiential learning component.
Complementary	Program is a logical complement to existing programs and used to convey a sense of "completeness" of program offerings.	Program is likely to share foundation and core courses with existing programs, with incremental resources required to staff specialization courses.
Mission-Obligated	Program is almost necessitated by mission of institution, e.g., a liberal arts school will have a general education program.	Resources required will vary with the scope and purpose of program and how it is intended to support the mission of the institution.
Inertial	No strategic role. Program exists because it has always existed.	Institution should decide whether this program can be incorporated into its strategic goals or whether resources might be better applied elsewhere.

Another reason that an institution might choose to offer a program is perceived *high demand* (i.e., the program is popular among the calling population). Demand for a program can be inferred from a number of sources, including inquiries of potential students and their parents, search terms entered by visitors to the institution's website, or the student career interest survey published annually by the National Research Center for College & University Admissions, a not-for-profit organization.

High-demand programs are strategically important as they can bolster institutional enrollments and generate strong, steady cash flows (thereby supporting smaller, esoteric programs). According to the College Board, between 50% and 70% of college students will change their major at least once. It is likely, therefore, that a strategy of attracting students to high-demand programs will serve a secondary purpose of providing enrollments for less popular or less visible programs, as some of the students drawn to high-demand programs will probably change their course of study.

Running large (popular) programs has obvious resource consequences. The program and curriculum must be structured to efficiently manage large numbers of students. This might include running large course sections or, alternatively, many smaller sections. If many sections of a course are offered, reliance on adjunct faculty resources may increase, as will the need to coordinate course content and assessment protocols. Support services, such as academic advisement, must also be conducted in an efficient manner (e.g., in a web-based or mass advisement format). More time and thought may need to be devoted to course, room, and facilities scheduling. Depending on institution and program entrance requirements, large programs are likely to contain a broad spectrum of students, with a substantial number needing tutorial or remedial support. The institution will have to work purposely to develop a sense of community so that students do not feel "lost in the crowd."

Resources applied to large programs can vary drastically. Consider that an institution may choose to designate one of its large programs as a medallion program; this will demand a serious commitment of resources. At the opposite end of the spectrum is a large program that acts as a cash cow for the university. A cash cow is the term applied to one of the four categories (quadrants) in the Boston Consulting Group (BCG) market growth/market share matrix (Stern & Stalk, 1998). Cash cows generate substantial revenue while consuming minimal resources.

Another strategic role is the *niche program*. A niche program, as the name suggests, is an institutional response to a specialized educational need, often pertaining to localized circumstances or stakeholder(s) that have unique needs. For example, a school near Las Vegas may provide specialized education opportunities for casino workers or managers. A school near Los Angeles (and its seaport) might offer programs focused on international trade and maritime logistics or associated with some aspect of the music or film industry. A niche program may emphasize practice over theory and may include significant experiential learning opportunities for students.

Niche programs offer a (strategic) opportunity for the educational institution to set itself apart and may provide development opportunities if the school is effective at developing strong relationships with key stakeholders. Stakeholders may be willing to provide external funding support for the program, donate specialized equipment, arrange for guest speakers for classes, support experiential learning opportunities for students, and offer placement opportunities for program graduates.

While niche programs provide certain strategic opportunities, they can be unique in their resource requirements. The liaison function, for the purpose of maintaining strong relationships between the niche program and key stakeholders, is critical. Experiential learning opportunities need to be identified on an ongoing basis, and practicum experiences must be supervised. Specialized equipment or facilities may be required. The applied nature of many niche programs suggests the need to staff courses with (or provide other exposure to) practitioners and not just theorists.

Complementary programs provide an opportunity for the institution to convey an air of completeness, focus, or "one-stop shopping." By sharing a common foundation and core component with other programs, a complementary program will allow the institution to offer a broader curriculum with minimal incremental resources. For example, it may be relatively easy for a university with several traditional engineering programs (electrical, mechanical, and civil) to add programs in materials engineering, nano-engineering, and environmental engineering with very few incremental resources (assuming the programs share the same foundation courses). As a result, the school's "brand" will appear to have more of an engineering focus. The breadth of offerings at this institution may attract students that want to go into engineering but are unsure of what type.

The resource implications, however, are important to understand. A complementary program will generate enrollments in both shared and specialized courses. If, for example, the shared courses are slightly under-enrolled in their current state, the addition of a few students in a complementary program may increase enrollments in core courses to an optimal size. However, the institution will also need to be willing to allocate resources to staff a few specialty seminars with potentially low enrollments. Worse yet, if core courses are already full, the few extra students generated by the complementary program may require more sections of core courses *and* tolerance of small enrollments for specialty seminars. Enrollment and section planning become very important in this context.

Mission-obligated programs and courses are those that are arguably required given the mission of the institution. A liberal arts college must have a general education program that ensures that each student gets a broad exposure to the liberal arts. A denominational school is almost obliged to have a program called "religious studies" (or its equivalent).

However, an institution has many degrees of freedom in determining the scope and nature of a mission-obligated program and the resources to be expended. In the case of general education, schools vary greatly with regard to use of large vs. small lecture, adjunct vs. full-time faculty, required course structure, and breadth of course offerings. An institution that has many liberal arts programs may be able to compose its general education program entirely from the foundation courses required by the various liberal arts degrees. In contrast, an institution with a technical focus may have to develop general education courses for the sole purpose of providing a general education core for its students.

In contrast to the program types described above, an *inertial program* exists for no other reason than that it has always existed. Unfortunately, inertial programs are often more the rule than the exception. An inertial program may be a strong program by some metric or it may be a weak program, but its status and existence are happenstance rather than purposeful and planned.

A number of factors can contribute to the existence of inertial programs. For example, tenure and union contracts may make it difficult for institutions to shut down certain programs and shift resources to emerging needs. However, the reason that inertial programs exist can always be summarized as lack of strategic curriculum planning. In an environment that embraces such planning, inertial programs do not exist; all programs contribute (in a planned way) to the mission and/or the competitive strategy of the institution. An optimal allocation of resources to the delivery of curriculum cannot occur without thoughtful inclusion of curriculum in the strategic planning process.

THE CHALLENGE OF CURRICULUM ALIGNMENT

Specifying the strategic role of a curriculum is an important step in managing academic program resources. However, resources assigned to a curriculum will not achieve their full potential if the curriculum is not well aligned. *Curriculum alignment* is the process of making sure that students are taught that which they are expected to learn. This requires that (1) learning goals are identified, (2) corresponding curricula are developed and specified with some detail, and (3) competent instruction (consistent with the curriculum design) takes place. Assessment is the process that determines the degree

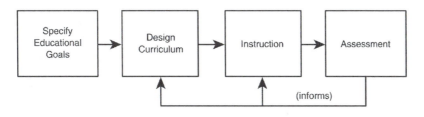

Figure 8.7 Alignment Requires Goals, Design, Instruction, and Assessment to Be Consistent

to which learning goals have been achieved (see Figure 8.7). As Figure 8.7 illustrates, curriculum alignment, similarly to assessment, is never "done"; rather, it is an iterative process informed by assessment outcomes.

It is easy to espouse that curricula should be well aligned in order for resources to be applied with maximal benefit. Attaining alignment, however, can be challenging and requires administrative direction and oversight. This section considers various challenges to curriculum alignment in the higher education context and how these challenges can be addressed. The section concludes with thoughts on how the aforementioned issues relate to the alignment of resources and curriculum.

The traditional alignment paradigm begins with the establishment of educational goals relating to both knowledge and skills. These goals should reflect the requirements of various stakeholders and may reflect national and state curriculum standards, educational traditions, and/or mandates by state legislatures, boards of regents or their equivalents, and accrediting bodies. Goals may also result from benchmark comparisons with other institutions or recognized educational best practices.

Once goals are established, a curricular response can be devised and an assessment protocol developed. Alignment is easiest to achieve when educational goals are clear and well articulated.

Given the management focus of this text, it is not our purpose here to provide a prescriptive narrative describing the process for articulating and measuring learning goals and outcomes. The assessment literature has now matured sufficiently to provide many guides for those who develop and assess curricula (e.g., Bresciani, Zelna, & Anderson, 2004 and Suskie, 2009). Additionally, various associations and universities offer guidance through their websites.

While guidance abounds, administrators must be mindful that aligning learning goals, curricula, and assessment protocols is not a trivial task and is unlikely to be done well if the individuals responsible for accomplishing it are not well trained and if it is not incorporated in a meaningful way into the organization's roles and rewards system. Further, the development of so-called "soft skills," such as writing skills, presentation skills, teamwork skills, and research skills, is likely to span several points in a curriculum, and collaboration on curriculum design and execution is critical. Administrators must ensure that said collaboration takes place and is productive.

It is also important to understand that how a learning goal is defined, and the portion(s) of a curriculum to which it is attached, can have a significant impact on resources required. Consider a course that is designed, in part, to focus on development of writing skills and presentation skills. Suppose also that the instructional design requires students to give three impromptu presentations and complete a series of significant written assignments on which they will receive detailed constructive feedback. Suppose further that this feedback is iterative and accompanied by several opportunities for students to revise and resubmit work. Unless significant additional instructional resources were assigned to this course, it is unlikely that this curriculum design could be well executed in a 500-student, large lecture format. Any instructor assigned to the course would need to be skilled at coaching both oral presentations and writing.

Thus, the outcome of the curriculum alignment process will place constraints on how a curriculum is delivered and how resources are best applied to individual courses within that curriculum; curriculum alignment is a necessary companion to resource alignment. Given that a particular curricular solution may exceed the resources made available to a program via the strategic planning process, it is likely that alignment of curriculum and resources will need to occur concurrently as suggested in Figure 8.2 and iteratively as suggested in Figure 8.7. It is a waste of time to specify a set of learning objectives, a corresponding curriculum, and an assessment protocol only to find out that the necessary resources are not available.

While a well-aligned curriculum design is a necessary condition for effective resource alignment, it is not the only one. Faculty buy-in and ownership of the curriculum design (including assessment) must occur for the design to be successful. Sufficient resources must be made available to support the assessment process, and assessment measures and results must be actionable if the curriculum design and instruction are to evolve to address gaps suggested by assessment results. Administrators must not insist that faculty undertake assessment processes only to then suggest that there have been no resources allocated to support remediation of problems thereby identified. While not all assessment responses require additional resources, it is reasonable to expect that some may.

Obstacles to Curriculum Alignment

The underlying tenets of curriculum alignment have been embraced for some time by the K-12 community; this is not the case in higher education institutions. Some of challenges that postsecondary organizations face with regard to curriculum alignment are as follows:

- *Novel nature of the task:* Many tertiary CUs have never undergone a comprehensive curriculum review and alignment process.
- *Faculty expertise:* In higher education, curricula are often devised by faculty whose training and background are unlikely to encompass the intricacies of education theory. In most university disciplines, faculty training and expertise are generally associated with topical knowledge and/or researching a very narrow subject matter. Ph.D. faculty are unlikely to have significant training in issues of curriculum design, and it is doubtful that they would be hired for their expertise in these areas. The discord between faculty expertise and the expertise required for broad curriculum planning is likely to be exacerbated as higher education relies increasingly on part-time staffing to meet budget constraints. Adjunct staffing relationships are apt to be ephemeral, and adjuncts are presumably hired for their expertise in a subject area, not for their stewardship of curricula and expertise in curriculum design.

- *Faculty roles and rewards:* The traditional faculty roles and rewards system is liable to undervalue curriculum development and program stewardship efforts. Recognition and incentive systems are much more likely to reward stellar teaching evaluations, strong publication records, and successful procurement of grants.
- *Ownership of curriculum:* In K-12 education, curricula are often devised or dictated by a board of regents or other body of authority. A parallel structure may be seen in higher education when licensure is involved (e.g., nursing programs). Organizations that grant professional accreditation may also dictate certain broad curriculum content.

   In the absence of discipline-specific standards, curriculum is generally developed at the CU level. In environments where faculty expertise is narrowly focused, individual courses, their content, and the pedagogy applied are often proposed and "owned" by specific faculty. Courses may be developed as stand-alone silos, with little consideration given to integration between courses and with limited thought expended on broader curricular goals, such as developing the capacity of students to plan and manage their own learning.
- *A tradition of reactive oversight:* In many academic settings, curriculum oversight is assigned to a committee. However, traditional curriculum committees are often reactive bodies (i.e., they respond to a proposal, perhaps for a new course or perhaps for a program change). The committee considers the proposal then approves it, rejects it, or makes a recommendation to a higher authority.

In contrast, curriculum alignment is prescriptive, requiring faculty to cooperate and coordinate amongst themselves and to relinquish ownership of courses and their content. For many institutions and faculty, this represents a major shift in how they view curriculum development, ownership, and oversight. Without proper training, education, and buy-in, resistance to change is probable. Concerns over academic freedom are likely to develop.

Overcoming Obstacles

It is the responsibility of higher education administrators to anticipate and overcome the above-mentioned impediments to curriculum alignment. Where curriculum alignment is novel or where existing processes are weak, an institution is unlikely to achieve alignment without first educating participants (faculty, staff, and administrators) and then formalizing and communicating a process. Education and training will need to occur at three levels.

- *Education leading to buy-in (Why?):* Help faculty, staff, and administrators understand why curriculum alignment is necessary and important. Those involved will embrace curriculum alignment only when they understand the nature and necessity of the process. Therefore, it is important to educate faculty, staff, and administrators about the process and potential benefits of curriculum alignment and to contrast the alignment paradigm with the status quo.
- *Process training (How?):* Teach individuals how curriculum alignment is done. Curriculum alignment is a non-trivial exercise. For many participants, the process is outside the scope of their experience and training. It may be appropriate to invest in consultative training and prescriptive guidance at this time.

Teams should be led by trusted individuals who buy into the curriculum alignment process. Since this process is ongoing, it should be codified and become part of the governance structure of the CU. The parameters should include, among other things, scope, frequency, inputs, outputs, required activities, timelines, and roles. This codified process will serve as a "contract" between those directly involved in carrying it out, the broader faculty, and those that administer the CU. It will also serve to convey standard operating procedures to future teams of faculty that periodically undertake the review and alignment process.

- *Training Related to Expanded Learning Outcomes (What?):* Various stakeholder groups are asking that tertiary education evolve beyond the transfer of discipline-related knowledge and skills. There are educational outcomes that (1) transcend subject matter, and (2) have been argued to be important in the literature (e.g., Baxter Magolda, King, & Drobney, 2010). Some of these are delineated in Table 8.2. A well-aligned curriculum will explicitly consider priorities for these outcomes based on their importance to a particular discipline.

Regardless of where these learning goals are addressed in the curriculum design, it will be the responsibility of the faculty to ensure that they are attained. Unfortunately, even if faculty members accept that a particular goal is important, they may lack skill in helping students achieve it. Making students give presentations is not teaching them to do so. Making students work in teams is not teaching them how to work in teams. Curriculum alignment is unlikely to have the desired outcomes if faculty are not appropriately trained.

While the importance of training is self-evident, the literature offers very little prescriptive guidance in this regard, and a successful track record by tertiary institutions has yet to be documented therein. To the contrary, Munter and Reckers (2010) report, for example, that of 500 accounting educators surveyed, the vast majority (91%) said that it was either important or very important that accounting graduates have a strong grounding in ethics and 98% believed that accounting graduates should have strong critical thinking skills. Yet of those respondents who said they would be directly responsible for teaching ethics ($n = 387$), 64% said that they had received no financial or release-time support for training in ethics. The challenge is to ensure that faculty are equipped to help students achieve the desired outcomes; it is the responsibility of administrators to help identify the need and to provide the required resources.

Table 8.2 Skills and Traits that Transcend Curricular Subject Matter

• Moral reasoning skills	• Ability to identify and use sources of data
• Ability to think critically	• Ability to determine cause-and-effect relationships
• Ability to resolve conflicts	• Ability to compare and contrast competing solutions
• Oral communication skills	• Socially responsible leadership
• Written communication skills	• Personal health and psychological well-being
• Love of learning	• Willingness to give back to society
• Self-direction as a learner	• Political and social involvement
• Ability to argue persuasively	• Ethical behavior and interactions with others
• Ability to work in teams	• Diversity awareness and openness to diversity

Depending on the nature of the institution and the current state of curriculum alignment, the scope of attempts to provide faculty and staff with the types of education and training suggested above might be institution-wide (all programs) or sequential, based on some metric of program priority. Priorities may reflect the strategic importance of the curriculum in question (most important programs first), the value of the resources at risk (larger programs first), or the perceived size of the gap between what currently exists and the desired state (most egregious offenders first).

A review of Figure 8.2 will remind us that resource alignment depends on an understanding of the strategic role of a particular program, and coincides with the development of curricular goals and designs. As not all programs will have the same resource base (consistent with strategic plans), the pursuit of broader curricular goals will necessarily be more modest in some programs than in others. Similarly, resources devoted to assessment may be substantially different in various programs depending on each program's strategic role.

COST CONSIDERATIONS

Costs are an important consideration when aligning resources with strategy and programs. The aspirations of even a well-aligned organization will often exceed the budget available. One solution is to aspire less; another is to reduce costs. There are any number of cost-analysis and cost-cutting strategies that can be borrowed from the private sector and applied to the management of educational costs. These strategies include automation, substitution of part-time labor for full-time labor, and outsourcing. Virtually any activity can be reduced, eliminated, or consolidated. Campuses, like factories, can be closed. However, it is important to realize that for-profit organizations have been developing these strategies for many years, making many mistakes and learning many lessons along the way. If misapplied, these approaches will deliver poor results, just as they sometimes do in the private sector.

In the case of automation, for example, there have already been profound developments in how educational content is packaged and delivered. Emerging technologies make it possible to deliver educational content in ways that contrast starkly with the traditional lecture-centric approach, which is bound by time and location. Lectures can now be broadcast and/or recorded and delivered to remote locations either synchronously or asynchronously. Notes and instructional resources can be compiled and made available via instructional portals. Assessments can be automatically graded and grade books updated in real time.

As complex as the college or university budget setting can be, it is possible to simplify the task at hand. Figure 8.8 depicts resource alignment as a machine with four levers that must be adjusted in order to achieve balance between revenues and costs. The first lever alters the funds available to support all campus programs and activities. On a good day, the lever can be adjusted to bring in more funds, perhaps as a result of a tuition increase or the generosity of a donor. On a bad day, however, the state budget process might adjust the lever in the opposite direction, leaving fewer funds available.

The second lever (moving left to right) reallocates funds between activities; an adjustment could mean less spending on campus grounds maintenance and more spending on computer laboratories.

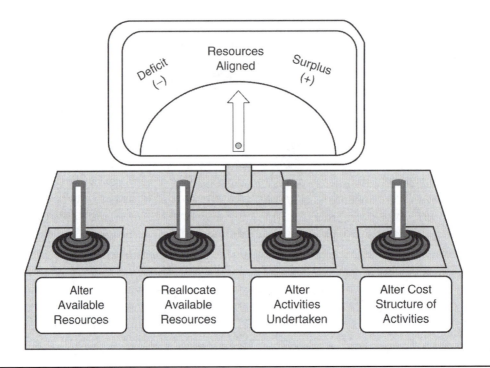

Figure 8.8 Determinants of Resource Alignment

The third lever can be adjusted to change the activities that the institution undertakes. The school might phase out two undergraduate programs, which may allow it to decrease costs (but perhaps decrease revenue as well), or perhaps replace those programs with a new graduate program.

The fourth lever changes the cost of some activity. The institution might, for example, choose to staff a course with part-time faculty rather than full-time faculty.

Without loss of generality, it is possible to limit the use of this machine to issues of curriculum. The institution can increase or decrease the funds available to support curricula (lever 1), reallocate resources between curricula (lever 2), choose to add or delete curricula (lever 3), or change the cost structure of its curricula (lever 4). All of the issues addressed in the remainder of the chapter can be associated with one of the levers depicted in Figure 8.8.

In a general sense, higher education institutions face the same cost-volume-profit relationships as a typical business enterprise. The more that any business sells, the more revenue it generates. However, there is typically a variable cost that accompanies each unit of sales, i.e., the more items sell, the more costs accumulate. In a successful business, the profit on each unit (unit revenue minus unit cost) will be large enough so that the sum of the profits on all sales will exceed the total fixed costs.

Similarly, the number of credit hours "sold" by a college or university will increase with the number of students and the number of courses each student takes. More students mean more revenues; however, more students also mean more costs. Thus, for higher education institutions, the number of students and the number of credit hours taught are primary drivers of both revenues and costs.

Unfortunately, beyond these basics, the numbers get muddled by some of the unique characteristics of university economics. These include the following:

- Some students pay less (or pay zero) because of scholarships.
- Adding one student to a class does not necessarily increase costs. Sometimes more students require more sections of classes; other times they fit nicely into the classes already being offered.
- At many schools, students are not charged for additional courses once a certain threshold is achieved, e.g., the tuition charged for five courses may be the same as that charged for four.

Whatever the revenue is, costs must be managed to align revenues and costs. In its simplest form, unit curricular cost can be envisioned as:

$$\text{Cost per Student} = \frac{\text{Cost of Curriculum}}{\text{Number of Students}}$$

Expression 8.1 Determinants of Cost per Student

This equation suggests that cost management can be approached from two related perspectives. The first is to determine whether the same curriculum can be offered for a reduced cost, i.e., driving down the numerator will decrease the cost per student. The second approach would be to find a way to offer the same curriculum to a larger number of students, i.e., driving up the denominator will decrease the cost per student. Both of these perspectives are examined throughout the remainder of this chapter.

The Basic Economics of Curriculum

The cost of delivering a particular curriculum has many components, including the cost of providing the component courses and any supporting supplies and equipment, administrative costs, and facilities costs. We focus here on the interplay between staffing costs and section size.

For purposes of illustration, consider a single section of a single course. Let NS_j be the number of students enrolled in course j. Let CF_j be the cost of the faculty resource assigned to the course (faculty and assistants) and CO_j be the sum of other course-related costs (e.g., copying, visual aids, laboratory materials, guest speakers). The cost per student (CPS) enrolled in course j is defined as:

$$CPS_j = \frac{CF_j + CO_j}{NS_j}$$

Expression 8.2 Determinants of Cost per Section

The economics are fairly straightforward. To reduce CPS, the institution may:

1. Decrease the staffing costs (CF) associated with course j.
2. Decrease other course-related costs (CO).
3. Increase the number of students (NS) enrolled in course j.
4. Eliminate the course and channel students into less expensive venues.

Each option is discussed below.

Decrease Faculty Cost

Having faced budget pressures for some time now, many educational institutions have already pursued substitution of lower cost teaching resources for traditional full-time, tenure-track faculty resources. Today's caricature of teaching at large state universities often involves an inexperienced graduate student, possibly with poor English language skills, staffing undergraduate courses. In fact, the practice of staffing undergraduate courses with graduate students was already pervasive at four-year public institutions by 1995, with 32% of course sections staffed by graduate students (Benjamin, 2002). While certainly less expensive, this approach to staffing is generally perceived as offering an inferior educational experience.

Time has witnessed a decrease in the proportion of classes staffed by full-time, tenure-track faculty, while the number of classes staffed by adjunct or contingent faculty (other than graduate students) continues to grow. As reported in Umbach (2007), between 1970 and 2003, the number of part-time faculty increased by 422%, while full-time faculty increased by only 71%. This shift can be traced directly to the growing financial pressures faced by public and private higher education institutions discussed elsewhere in this text and in the literature (e.g., Ehrenberg & Zhang, 2005).

While many contingent faculty are gifted instructors, there are some indications that over-reliance on them has hurt the quality of education (Jaeger & Eagan, 2009; Jaeger & Hinz, 2008). Full-time faculty spend substantially (and proportionately) more out-of-class time on activities that support student learning than do part-time faculty. Over 50% of part-time faculty at two-year colleges and 31% of part-time faculty at four-year colleges report holding no office hours, while only 2% and 7% of their full-time counterparts (respectively) made the same assertion (Benjamin, 1998). A study by Ehrenberg and Zhang (2005) found that an increase in the proportion of contingent faculty had an adverse effect on graduation rates. Umbach (2007) found that part-time faculty tend to be less effective in their instruction and are less committed to teaching than their full-time peers.

Despite the problems with contingent staffing, the economics are fairly compelling. Consider a section of 35 students staffed by a full-time faculty member paid $90,000 per year. Taking fringe benefits and salary devoted to professional obligations such as scholarship and research out of the equation, if said professor teaches four courses per year (as is common at many research-oriented schools), one-fourth of his or her salary may be attributed to this course. Compare this structure with that of a class of 35 students taught by a part-time instructor who receives $4,000 per section taught.

For the moment, assume that other course-related costs (CO), such as copying, are $20 per student plus $500 of fixed expenses in both cases. The two cost structures are compared as shown below:

$$CPS_{FT} = \frac{22500+1200}{35} \qquad\qquad CPS_{PT} = \frac{4000 + 1200}{35}$$

$$CPS_{FT} = \$677 \qquad\qquad CPS_{PT} = \$149$$

Expressions 8.3a and 8.3b Full-Time (FT) Staffing is 450% More than Part-Time (PT)

The 450% differential does not take into account the other expenses associated with full-time staffing, such as travel, research support, and sabbatical. If, in the example above, the part-time faculty member were to be replaced with a full-time lecturer paid $60,000 per year to teach eight courses, the CPS would be $249; tenure-track staffing under the stated assumptions is still about 270% more expensive.

Because the economics are so compelling, institutions will continue to rely on adjunct staffing. While proper direction, supervision, training, and incentives can address many of the associated challenges, adjunct faculty assignments should be consistent with strategic and curricular goals (as discussed earlier in the chapter). Table 8.3 lists factors to consider when making adjunct staffing arrangements.

Another strategy to reduce faculty costs is to increase the revenue-generating activity base across which faculty salaries are distributed. For example, suppose that the institution has traditionally hired non-tenure-track full-time faculty (henceforth "lecturers") for $55,000 per year with an obligation to teach four courses in the fall semester and four courses in the spring. Salary per course would be $6,875. In the future, an alternative contractual arrangement for newly hired lecturers might be $60,000 per calendar year with an obligation to teach ten courses per year: four in the fall, four in the spring, and (assuming the institution runs sessions in winter and/or summer) two courses in the special sessions. Salary per course would be $6,000, a modest saving of about 13%. However, revenue generated in the special sessions would also be retained by the institution.

Given that the proportion of available tenure-track positions is shrinking, these positions are becoming (comparatively) harder to obtain and, therefore, comparatively more attractive to faculty seeking employment. As a result, colleges and universities may have an opportunity to negotiate a more favorable activity level compared to historical practices. For example, instead of negotiating a three-year contract requiring six courses (3/3 load) per year (18 courses total), the contract might specify a total of 19 or even 20 courses, with the faculty member having significant control over when the additional courses would be taught. This would allow the faculty member to arrange and manage his or her other obligations (service and research) as required. The same contract might allow the faculty member to trade teaching a large section for one or both of the additional courses. These changes would, of course, be subject to union and other workload rules and competitive forces. The institution might have to maintain traditional contract terms for medallion programs (consistent with market practices), programs of high strategic importance, and in disciplines where Ph.D. faculty are in short supply.

Table 8.3 Factors to Consider When Assigning Contingent Faculty

Factor	Outcome Favoring Adjunct Staffing	Comments
Class size	Small	• Isolate problems to a small number of students • CPS is high when full-time tenured faculty staff small courses
Supervision	Supervision available	• Need to ensure coverage of specified learning outcomes, participation in assessment protocols, and rigor in course content and grading consistent with traditional faculty
Program size	Large	• Multiple sections require flexibility in staffing • Students have option of choosing to take course from traditional faculty • Supervision and guidance of adjunct faculty should be available from full-time faculty teaching same course • Large programs are likely to have some strategic importance and therefore well-defined and documented learning outcomes and assessment protocols, providing maximum guidance
Strategic role	Niche program	• Specialized, practitioner knowledge often required
Strategic role	Inertial, low-priority, or terminated program	• Minimize cost by using adjunct faculty while program being phased out or until future direction determined
Strategic role	Medallion program	• Use adjunct faculty within accreditation guidelines • Learning outcomes and assessment protocols are more likely to be well-defined and documented, providing maximum guidance on course content • Enhanced administrative support associated with medallion status fosters direction and supervision • Specialized expertise may be required
Learning outcomes	See below	• Left side of continuum generally more appropriate for contingent faculty

Nature of Learning Outcomes

Dissemination of Knowledge	Discipline-Based Skills, Methods	Skills that Transcend Discipline	Development of the Person

⟵——————————————————————————————⟶

Larger Classes

Large lectures are generally perceived to offer an impersonal and inferior educational experience (especially when staffed by graduate students). The economics, however, are compelling. Consider a large section of 400 students staffed by a full-time professor paid $90,000 per year. Taking fringe benefits and salary devoted to other professional obligations such as scholarship and research out of the equation, if said faculty member teaches four courses per year, one-fourth of his or her salary may be attributed to this course. Assume also that the professor of the large section is assigned two teaching assistants at a per-course cost of $4,800. Compare this structure with that of a class taught in a (rather large) seminar format of 35 students, with no grading support. For the moment, assume that other course-related costs (CO), such as copying, are $20 per student and $1,000 fixed in both cases. Expressions 8.4a and 8.4b illustrate the two cost structures.

$$CPS_{400} = \frac{27300+9000}{400} \qquad CPS_{35} = \frac{22500 + 1700}{35}$$

$$CPS_{400} = \$90.75 \qquad CPS_{PT} = \$691.43$$

Expressions 8.4a and 8.4b Cost per Student—400 Students vs. 35 Students

The economics are hard to ignore. While large-section classes have, over time, become associated with lower quality education, a number of technology developments that have occurred over the last ten to 15 years may change public and student perception. Technology-based enhancements that enable larger class sizes while enhancing effectiveness include the following:

- Campus portal and cloud-based repositories for class notes and other course-related materials, including videos of lectures.
- Smart-board systems integrated with texting apps that allow students to text questions during lectures and professors (or a teaching assistant) to then post written or diagramed responses visible in real time to the whole class or post to the cloud or campus portal.
- Fourth-generation HD-quality LCD projectors that render large, sharp images even under bright ambient lighting conditions.
- Large supplementary LED monitor displays that help ensure that all students (e.g., those seated at the sides and rear or a facility) can see the material being presented.
- Wireless audience response systems (WARS), more commonly known as "clickers," that make large classes more interactive while at the same time providing immediate feedback on learning. Authors have found positive benefits to WARS across a wide range of courses, in terms of either student attitudes and/or improved learning. Relevant studies include Guthrie and Carlin (2004); Barnett (2006); Graham, Tripp, Seawright, and Joeckel (2007); Hunsinger, Poirier, and Feldman (2008); and Milner-Bolotin, Antimirova, and Petrov (2010).
- Automated grading systems: While grading can represent a "cost" for a course of any size, grading costs can be significant for large courses. Historically, in the absence of substantial (and talented) grading support, the assignment of significant graded homework as a learning aid has been impractical in a large lecture format. However, textbook publishers now provide sophisticated automated evaluation and grading systems for homework and assessment. Grading systems have evolved beyond simple "right/wrong" grading responses. Students' responses to practice problems are used to generate directives as to what material they should review to improve their performance on the final assessment. Students receive immediate feedback, including a grade, and instructors receive formative feedback concerning topics where students are struggling.

- Large classes can benefit from supplemental tutoring resources, and online tutoring systems are now a reality for many subjects. As described in Carey (2009), a service called Smarthinking provides 24/7, on-demand, one-on-one tutoring in a range of introductory college courses. The tutors have bachelor's and master's degrees in their fields and communicate with students via computer, using an onscreen, interactive "whiteboard." Writing tutors give feedback on essays within 24 hours. By pooling demand from many institutions and locating tutoring resources in lower wage environments, this approach can provide high-quality 24/7 tutoring in a wide variety of subjects, at a cost lower than what many colleges afford.

In summary, these are not your parents' large lectures anymore. Of course, the use of technology may add costs that need to be considered within the costing model shown in Expression 8.2. Further, there are a host of other factors that should be contemplated before pursuing large lecture formats, as shown in Table 8.4.

Channeling Students into Less Expensive Venues

Depending on the work and compensation rules in place at the institution, it is not unusual for salary discrepancies to exist between disciplines. Hypothetically, there are courses staffed by faculty in one discipline that might be staffed (with less expense) by faculty in another. Courses in statistics that support psychology, mathematics,

Table 8.4 Factors Favoring the Use of Large Sections

Factor	Outcome Favoring Large Sections	Comments
Strategic brand	Large comprehensive university	Not consistent with a brand image of a small, intimate college
Strength of student body	More capable	Not appropriate for students that need significant coaching and individual attention
Program size	Large	Efficient delivery of curriculum to large numbers of students
Strategic role	Cash cow	Generate maximum revenue at lowest cost and at an acceptable level of quality
Facilities	Large-lecture-oriented	Lecture halls Media support, including ARS Recitation support if required
Faculty skills	Strong teaching skills, experienced	It takes a special instructor to do this well
Assessment protocols	Well-established, highly efficient	Assessment data should be easy to collect, code, and analyze
Learning outcomes	See below	Left side of continuum most appropriate for large lectures

Nature of Learning Outcomes

Dissemination of Knowledge	Discipline-Based Skills, Methods	Skills that Transcend Discipline	Development of the Person

←——————————————————————→

economics, business, teacher education, and so on come to mind. As another way to manipulate the cost of faculty (CF) factor in Expression 8.2, the common component of the various course curricula could be defined and staffed by the least expensive program in terms of average faculty cost. Similarly, certain general education courses (e.g., ethics courses) are potentially staffed by several disciplines. It may be worthwhile to have instructors from the low-cost discipline teach the course, assuming that they are willing and able to satisfy the learning outcomes required by the other programs.

The Problem of Small Classes

Large classes can have a significant impact on costs. It is equally important, though, to consider the cost implications of small classes. The discussion of strategic curriculum planning that took place earlier in the chapter should serve as a lens through which to examine small class sizes.

Class size is the most sensitive factor in determining the cost per student. Given the scale of full-time faculty salaries, the per-student cost of running a small class will normally exceed the revenue that small class enrollments generate unless the organization can charge a significant price per credit hour or the course can be staffed with a less expensive resource. If these conditions do not exist, the course must be "subsidized." This provides a convenient definition of a small class, i.e., a class that has not generated sufficient revenues to cover its cost. Frankly, there are relatively few instances when subsidization can be justified; these include the following:

- The small class size is a temporary development based on unforeseen circumstances.
- The small class size is a temporary development resulting from planned circumstances such as a new program startup.
- The small class size is planned and deemed necessary, and the course supports a curriculum that is of primary strategic significance to the institution.
- The course supports a faculty research agenda or project that is monetarily or strategically important to the institution.
- There are critical learning outcomes for (an important) program that can only be achieved by running a small class.
- The enrollment cannot be deferred, for example by running the course every two semesters instead of every semester.

If the justification is strategic in nature, then the strategic curriculum plan should have identified the source of funds to support the cost. For example, the instructor of the small class might also teach a large lecture. Otherwise, if the shortfall in enrollment is perennial and unplanned, it is indicative of an enrollment management model that needs to be revised or a program for which a critical level of demand is not being met by enrollment management processes. If the enrollment management process cannot resolve the issue, then a less expensive curricular solution should be sought. If none exists, the program that the course supports may not be viable.

BUSINESS PROCESS REENGINEERING

Administrators are frequently asked to reduce costs, and that is the essence of lever number four in Figure 8.8. Common approaches include across-the-board budget reductions, targeted budget reductions applied to specific activities, and elimination of budget for certain activities. The common mindset underlying all these approaches to budget reductions is to question the budget applied to existing activities rather than to consider the nature of the activity itself. In contrast, Business Process Reengineering (BPR) is the practice of studying and deconstructing current organizational activities, programs, processes, and practices with a goal of improving quality, efficiency (cost), and/or effectiveness. Under BPR, the organization examines virtually everything it does and questions the reason(s) for performing each activity in order to determine if the activity is really necessary. If the activity is deemed necessary, the next step is to question the way it is done currently in order to determine whether it could be done better. Figure 8.9 illustrates these steps.

BPR can be applied to either manufacturing or service processes. The practice gained much attention in the management literature during the 1970s and 1980s as business began to automate more and more processes in response to the increasing capabilities and decreased costs of technology. However, many companies discovered that they were automating "bad processes" and came to realize that, prior to investing in automation, they should first scrutinize each process to make sure that it was actually required. If a process was indeed required, they needed to determine how to perform it in the best way possible.

Companies have been shedding all but their "core business" for some time now, allowing business partners to fill parts of the supply chain that they can do either better and/or at a lower cost. Colleges and universities have pursued this strategy to a much lesser extent, if at all. As a fundamental component of any BPR investigation, educational institutions should always ask the question "Can we share the costs?" For example, The Boston Conservatory has arranged for its students to use Northeastern University's dining and athletic facilities. It is not difficult to envision two competing educational institutions sharing the cost of remote classroom space rather than renting separate facilities. While much attention has been given to distance education, less has been given

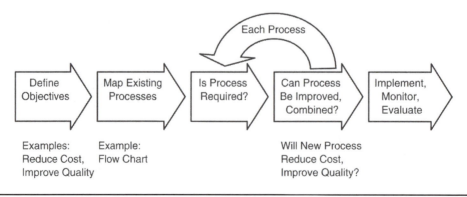

Figure 8.9 Business Process Reengineering

to "distance administration," where two or more organizations share administrative staff such as financial aid counselors or purchasing staff. More broadly, embracing BPR with regard to administrative processes could potentially liberate resources that could be shifted to the core mission of education.

BPR has the potential to encourage "out of the box" thinking with solutions that can significantly improve efficiency and reduce costs. Given that the lecture-centric approach to college education is well over 100 years old, the case can be made that the collegiate environment provides fertile grounds for BPR.

As an example, consider an institution with only two large lecture facilities. Further, suppose that there are no appropriate facilities nearby that can be shared or leased. The compelling economics of large lectures notwithstanding, the school is able to offer very few classes in large lecture format because it simply does not have the space. The obvious solution, building new lecture halls, is expensive and may not be economically feasible for the institution; the payback period would be measured in decades.

A BPR-like process might reveal the following solution. Suppose that traditional class times and/or inter-class times were to be shortened by 10 to 15 minutes per class meeting. For example, class periods for courses that meet Monday, Wednesday, and Friday might be revised downward to 50 minutes long rather than the traditional 60-minute standard. This change (which is consistent with practices at other colleges and universities) could make one more scheduling time-slot per day available and permit each large lecture facility to be used one more time per day. This would allow for approximately four additional sections per semester in the larger format.

An alternative solution to the problem might be to design a course that meets once a week in a large-capacity venue while also providing students with self-directed learning opportunities supported by on-demand video, interactive homework sites, and so on. This self-directed component of the course would be completed in lieu of a second (large-format) weekly meeting, freeing up the lecture hall for a second course of the same type. While some might object to the loss of contact hours, the growing body of data on online learning suggests that contact hours are not always the key to effective instruction.

Thinking Outside the Box: A Final BPR Example

Our overview of BPR has been purposefully short; interested readers can see numerous sources, e.g., Vakola and Rezgui (2000), for a deeper treatment of the subject. We end our BPR discussion with a rather ambitious and detailed example related to enhancing curriculum capacity while lowering costs. Our goal is to emphasize the point that even the most fundamental assumptions should be challenged in a BPR exercise.

The essence of BPR is to question everything that an organization assumes and everything it does, and to understand the reasons and premises behind each activity. One of the most fundamental assumptions and basic building blocks of tertiary education is the student credit-hour system and the three-credit-hour college course. Credit hours (contact hours) are supposed to represent the amount of learning undertaken, and grades are supposed to reflect the degree of subject mastery. Many would argue that neither is true. The use of student hours has a long history and many critics; see Shedd (2003). However, until another system is devised, credit hours will remain important in terms of financial aid, student billing, course transfer, and financial analysis of educational institutions.

While it is possible to argue the need for a measuring system, it is not possible to argue that the current system is precise or comparable across institutions. At some institutions, a credit hour means 50 minutes of contact; at others, it means 60. Some colleges have 13-week semesters; others have 15-week semesters. Some colleges count two hours of lab time as one credit; others, as two. Students can receive credit for experience or credit by exam—with no hours of contact in a classroom. The online revolution has brought the notion of contact hours as a measure of learning very much into question.

Consider also that stakeholders are demanding that educators do more and that education be more comprehensive. In response, textbooks have grown to include chapters on, among others, ethics, diversity, sustainability, and technology. Educators are being asked to cover more information, to do a better job of teaching so-called soft skills, and to incorporate service learning into their courses. If the knowledge content and rigor associated with a particular course remain constant and these other learning outcomes are to be added, then how can a course still be awarded only three credit hours?

Juxtaposing this discussion of credit hours with the earlier discussion of costs, revenues, and the budget environment raises an interesting question: What if there were a new generation of four- (or more) credit-hour courses? In this new generation of courses, students would actually learn more (beyond basic knowledge transfer), including the skills and traits listed in Table 8.2; technology would enable professors to have significant contact with students outside of the classroom. To complete the fantasy, suppose that assessment results actually indicated that students were learning more and developing critical thinking skills, communication skills, etc.

Simulation can be used to explore the economics of this switch from three to four credit hours. To simplify the example, consider two undergraduate-only public institutions, each with 4,000 students, all of whom pay in-state tuition rates. At one school, all courses are three credit hours; at the other, they are four. The institutions fund no scholarships. Assume that the definition of full-time attendance (for financial aid purposes) is 12 credit hours at both schools. Assume also that students need to take one course above the full-time rate each semester in order to graduate in four years. Said another way, students at one school take 40 three-credit courses (five per semester) and graduate in four years with 120 credits, while students at the other school take 32 four-credit courses (four per semester) and graduate in four years with 128 credits.

Assume also that the commonly used "flat fee" rule applies, i.e., after paying for full-time tuition (12 hours), students do not incur additional tuition charges for taking additional courses. Suppose that, at both schools, 50% of the students take a sufficient number of courses to graduate in four years, and 10% take an additional course beyond this level. Another 20% are full-time for financial aid purposes (12 hours). Finally, assume that students who take just one course per semester constitute 5% of the population, as do students taking two courses. See Figure 8.10 for the remaining assumptions.

Under these assumptions, in a single semester, the four-credit model generates approximately $1,398,000 more revenue in excess of costs versus the three-credit model. This reflects, in part, a lower proportion of students taking "free" courses above the

Tuition Per credit	$210.00
Course-Related Fees Per Credit	$50.00
Revenue Per Credit	$260.00

	Salary	Teaches Courses/yr	Percent Of Classes Staffed
Average Salary FT Tenure-Track Faculty	$85,000	6	50%
Average Salary Full-time Lecturer	$60,000	8	20%
Average Part Time Salary	$3,500	4	30%

Average Course Size	25	students

Average Course Cost Per Student		
Salary Cost Per Student	$385.33	(weighted avg from above)
Incidentals per student	$50.00	
Total Per Student	$435.33	

Courses Per Semester	Enrollment Patterns	
	School 1 (3cr)	School 2 (4cr)
1	5%	5%
2	5%	5%
3	9%	20%
4	20%	50%
5	50%	10%
6	9%	9%
7	2%	1%
	100%	100%

Figure 8.10 Assumptions Underlying the Simulation

12-hour (full-time) threshold. Part-time students are also paying more per course; price sensitivity could be built into the model to reflect a reduction in part-time students, but the results would still favor the four-credit model.

Obviously, the parameters specified for this model are arbitrary, but these can be challenged. For example, based on a 1,000-trial Monte Carlo simulation, if the enrollment patterns associated with the number of courses taken per semester are randomly varied ±5% in all categories, the four-credit model generates average savings of approximately $1,116,000 each semester, with a minimum savings of $703,000 and a maximum savings of $1,610,000. Savings are directly proportionate to the number of students assumed; double the students and double the savings. Altering the class-size assumption yields the pattern of savings shown in Figure 8.11.

From the faculty's point of view, there is little to dislike. Faculty teaching loads, in terms of number of courses per semester, remain unchanged. Faculty are being asked to do more in terms of active learning and soft-skill development, but these pressures will exist regardless of the credit-hour structure. The four-hour structure at least acknowledges the evolution away from the traditional lecture.

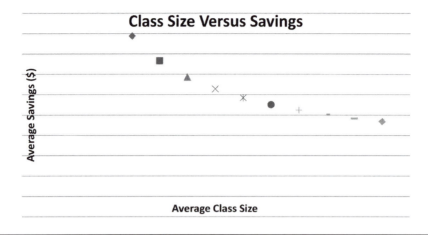

Figure 8.11 For Classes Size <70, Four-Credit Savings Increase as Class Size Decreases

As for the students, those graduating in four years need to take only four courses per semester instead of five. Class scheduling becomes easier, and there are fewer textbooks to purchase. Given that more students are now working more hours to pay for their education, this may be a more realistic definition of full-time.

Obviously, an institution would have to consider such a radical change with great care. For example, how would the school handle transfer of (primarily) three-credit courses? While these challenges are significant, it is worth noting that Binghamton University, which is part of the State University of New York system, has adopted this model and is consistently ranked as one of the best public universities in the nation.

CONCLUSION

This chapter examined some alignments that are key to the proper allocation of resources to academic programs and important to improving organizational performance. More specifically, the chapter examined the interplay between various aspects of strategic planning, curriculum planning, and the allocation of resources. The basic premises of the chapter are that (1) resources cannot be optimally allocated to curricula until the strategic role of each component of the curriculum is defined (strategic alignment), and (2) allocation of resources to curriculum that are not aligned in terms of learning goals, course content/pedagogy, and assessment (curriculum alignment) is inefficient. It is unlikely that learning goals will be achieved (as measured by assessments) unless the curriculum is aligned. Hence, neither the institution nor its students will derive maximum benefit from the resources applied.

The importance of strategic curriculum planning and the nature and outcome of curriculum alignment were emphasized. The curriculum alignment process must occur after the strategic role of a program has been defined. The scope and intensity of the curriculum alignment process must reflect the program's strategic role and the resources made available to support the program. Curriculum planning in general and curriculum alignment in particular are necessary for the proper allocation of resources. Resources cannot be thoughtfully allocated to curriculum unless there is a clear understanding of how various educational goals will be achieved in the curriculum design. Broader curricular goals that transcend specific courses, such as the development of learning skills and communication skills, can be a challenging aspect of curriculum design.

A number of challenges to achieving alignment between strategy, resources, and curriculum were discussed. These included the nature of faculty expertise, traditional faculty roles and rewards systems, and traditional concepts of curriculum ownership. The importance of education and training as a tool for overcoming these challenges was developed in some detail. Both faculty and administrators must be educated on how to pursue strategic alignments, achieve broad buy-in of the alignment process, and review and align the curriculum. Roles and rewards systems must be adjusted to recognize the important contribution made by stewards of the curriculum.

We then examined the economics of course staffing, considering the implications of both large and small lecture formats. Contingencies associated with using large lecture formats and contingent staffing were specified. The chapter concluded with a discussion of business process reengineering (BPR) as a tool to question not only the resource use and costs associated with various activities, but also the very essence of the activities, processes, and programs undertaken by the institution.

DISCUSSION PROMPTS

1. Identify a medallion program and niche program at your university. Compare and contrast the resources applied to each.

2. Consider the process(es) at your university by which students select and register for courses. In the spirit of BPR, break the process down into fundamental activities and make suggestions for eliminating, improving, or reducing the cost of these activities.

3. Which category or categories in Table 8.1 best describe the program in which you are currently enrolled? Defend your answer.

4. Ask your instructor whether any of the traits listed in Table 8.2 are points of emphasis in the program in which you are enrolled. Are these traits explicitly considered in the curriculum design and, if so, how and where are they emphasized? Were resources devoted to helping faculty learn how to develop these traits in their students?

5. Pay a visit to the largest lecture facility at your university. What technology or other resources have been employed to facilitate effective instruction in this facility. If possible, visit someone who teaches in this facility. What resources do they wish were available to support instruction?

6. Ask your instructor to describe strategic planning at the program level (if any) for the program in which you are enrolled. Do they perceive any discord between the strategic direction/goals of the program and the strategic direction/goals of the institution or is alignment evident?

7. Use the Internet to locate the strategic plans of two colleges or universities. To what degree are various curricula, or curriculum in general, considered in the plans (or their supporting documents)? Do the plans suggest, in any way, what curricula the institution will emphasize?

8. Either as an individual or as a group, schedule a brief meeting with a program head (e.g., Department Chair, Director, etc.) for the purpose of understanding their perceptions of the strategic planning process at your university and their own role within that process. Some questions you might ask include:

   a. Does the program unit have its own strategic plan and, if so, how was it developed?

   b. Was your program provided an opportunity to provide input to the university's strategic plan and, if so, how was that accomplished?

   c. Does the university's plan have a curricular component and, if so, is their program mentioned explicitly in the plan? What is the role of their program within the plan?

9. Either as an individual or as a group, schedule a brief meeting with a program head (e.g., Department Chair, Director, etc.) for the purpose of understanding their perceptions of the strategic role that their program plays within the broader university curriculum. Specifically, how do they view their program versus the categories defined in Table 8.2? Has the role that their program plays changed over time? Are there categories in Table 8.2 that they would like to move towards or away from and, if so, what are the barriers to this evolution?

10. Either as an individual or as a group, schedule a brief meeting with a member of the faculty in an academic program or unit on your campus for the purpose of understanding their perceptions of the strategic role that their program plays within the broader university curriculum. Specifically, how do they view their program versus the categories defined in Table 8.2? Are there categories in Table 8.2 that they would like to move towards or away from and, if so, what are the barriers to this evolution?

REFERENCES

Barnett, J. (2006). Implementation of personal response units in very large lecture classes: Student perceptions. *Australasian Journal of Educational Technology, 22*, 474–494.

Baxter Magolda, M. B., King, P. M., & Drobney, K. L. (2010). Practices that provide effective academic challenge for first-year students. *Journal on Excellence in College Teaching, 21*(2), 45–65.

Benjamin, E. (1998). Declining faculty availability to students is the problem—but tenure is not the explanation. *American Behavioral Scientist, 41*(5), 716–735.

Benjamin, E. (2002). How over-reliance on contingent appointments diminishes faculty involvement in student learning. *Peer Review, 5*(1), 4–10.

Bresciani, M. J., Zelna, C. L., & Anderson, J. A. (2004). *Assessing student learning and development: A handbook for practitioners.* Washington, DC.: National Association of Student Personnel Administrators.

Carey, K. (2009). *College for $99 a month.* Washington Monthly.com, September/October. Retrieved March 20, 2011 from http://www.washingtonmonthly.com/college_guide/feature/college_for_99_a_month.php?page=1

Dingman, S. W. (2010). Curriculum alignment in an era of standards and high-stakes testing. *Yearbook of the National Council of Teachers of Mathematics, 72*, 103–114.

Ehrenberg, R. G., & Zhang, L. (2005). Do tenured and tenure-track faculty matter? *Journal of Human Resources, 40*(3), 647–659.

English, F. W. (1992) *Deciding what to teach and test: Developing, aligning, and auditing the curriculum.* Newbury Park, California: Corwin Press.

Glatthorn, A. A. (1999). Curriculum alignment revisited. *Journal of Curriculum and Supervision, 15*(1), 26–34.

Graham, C. R., Tripp, T. R., Seawright, L., & Joeckel, G. L. (2007). Empowering or compelling reluctant participators using audience response systems. *Active Learning in Higher Education, 8*, 233–258.

Guthrie, R. W., & Carlin, A. (2004). Waking the dead: Using interactive technology to engage passive listeners in the classroom. In *Proceedings of the Tenth Americas Conference on Information Systems*, New York, August.

Hunsinger, M., Poirier, C. R., & Feldman, R. S. (2008). The roles of personality and class size in student attitudes toward individual response technology. *Computers in Human Behavior, 24*, 2792–2798.

Jaeger, A. J., & Eagan, M. K. (2009). Effects of exposure to part-time faculty on associate's degree completion. *Community College Review, 36*(3), 167–194.

Jaeger, A. J., & Hinz, D. (2008). The effects of part-time faculty on first-year freshman retention: A predictive model using logistic regression. *Journal of College Student Retention: Research, Theory & Practice, 10*(3), 265–286.

Kaplan, R., & Norton, D. (1996). Using the balanced scorecard as a strategic management system. *Harvard Business Review*, January–February, 75–85.

Lowe, K. R. (2001). Resource alignment: Providing curriculum support in the school library media center. *Knowledge Quest, 30*(2), 27–32.

Miller, S. (1997). Implementing strategic decisions: Four key success factors. *Organization Studies, 18*(4), 577–602.

Milner-Bolotin, M., Antimirova, T., & Petrov, A. (2010). Clickers beyond the first-year science classroom. *Journal of College Science Teaching, 40*(2), 14–18.

Munter, P., & Reckers, P. M. (2010). Uncertainties and budget shortfalls hamper curriculum progress on IFRS. *Issues in Accounting Education, 25*(2), 189–198.

Shedd, J. M. (2003). The history of the student credit hour. *New Directions for Higher Education, 122*, 5–12.

Sinofsky, S., & Iansiti, M. (2009). *One Strategy: Organization, planning, and decision making*. New York: John Wiley & Sons.

Stern, C. W., & Stalk, G. (1998). *Perspectives on strategy from the Boston Consulting Group*. New York: John Wiley & Sons.

Suskie, L. A. (2009). *Assessing student learning: A common sense guide* (2nd ed.). San Francisco: Jossey-Bass.

Umbach, P. D. (2007). How effective are they? Exploring the impact of contingent faculty on undergraduate education. *Review of Higher Education, 30*(2), 91–123.

Vakola, M., & Rezgui, Y. (2000). Critique of existing business process re-engineering methodologies: The development and implementation of a new methodology. *Business Process Management Journal, 6*(3), 238–250.

Wraga, W. G. (1999). The educational and political implications of curriculum alignment and standards-based reform. *Journal of Curriculum and Supervision, 13*, Fall, 4–25.

9

OVERVIEW OF ACCREDITATION

Kristina Powers and Angela E. Henderson

INTRODUCTION

Moving is both exciting and stressful. A simple move in the same town and a cross-country relocation alike require a well-organized and clearly defined plan with specific deadlines for a successful outcome. When one's personal items finally arrive (hopefully all in one piece) at one's new home, the daunting task of opening boxes, unpacking, and getting organized in an unfamiliar space can feel like it will never end. Finally, after hours of work, those items begin to fit into place and context at the new location.

Accreditation is much like the process of moving, requiring a highly organized effort and a review of all items in house. The process resembles unpacking in that one needs to review existing information in the context of a changed environment to determine not only how items at hand fit into the new place but also what new items are needed to create the best conditions possible given the available means.

This chapter begins with a general overview of accreditation at the regional and programmatic levels before moving on to a comparison of the regional accrediting bodies. As it takes multiple people working in sync to accomplish accreditation tasks, the key roles and responsibilities of those who should be involved are described, along with financial considerations. Recent and major changes in higher education that have had—or ultimately will have—an impact on institutions are also discussed.

UNDERSTANDING ACCREDITATION

As defined by the Council for Higher Education Accreditation (CHEA), accreditation is a form of review designed to evaluate the quality of higher education institutions and programs (Eaton, 2015). Accreditation status is often perceived as an indicator of an institution's quality and considered as a deciding factor in college choice. Accredited institutions are eligible to award federal financial aid and are generally more favorably viewed by employers and professional organizations. They enjoy benefits that their non-accredited counterparts do not. For example, regionally accredited institutions are eligible to distribute federal financial aid to their students, while their counterparts cannot. Programmatic accreditors allow programs that have met their standards to use the programmatic accrediting agency's name in their marketing materials, thereby suggesting that the program is superior to those that have not met the standards.

Postsecondary accreditation is conducted by a number of private organizations whose sole purposes are to review and evaluate the quality of institutions and programs within defined regions or areas.

TYPES OF ACCREDITATION

Accrediting agencies have ensured the quality of higher education institutions and programs for more than 100 years (Eaton, 2015). While the benefits of regional accreditation have a significant financial impact on institutional budgets, "receiving accreditation does not send a strong signal of high quality so much as the lack of accreditation by a well-known accreditor sends a signal of poor quality" (Weisbrod, Ballou, & Asch, 2008, p. 186). Establishing standards of quality are evident across all accreditation agencies, of which there are four types:

1. Regional accreditors—accredit public and private, mainly non-profit and degree-granting, two- and four-year institutions.
2. Faith-based accreditors—accredit religiously affiliated and doctrinally based institutions, mainly non-profit and degree-granting.
3. Private career accreditors—accredit for-profit, career-based, single purpose institutions, both degree-granting and non-degree.
4. Programmatic accreditors—accredit specific programs, professions and freestanding schools, e.g., law, medicine, engineering and health professions (Eaton, 2015, p. 4).

This section focuses on regional accrediting agencies, with emphasis on the scopes of these types of accreditation. As defined by the Department of Education's Office of Postsecondary Education, regional accreditation assesses whether "each of an institution's parts is contributing to the achievement of the institution's objectives," while programmatic accreditation evaluates specific programs, departments, or schools within an institution (U.S. Department of Education, Office of Postsecondary Education, n.d.).

REGIONAL ACCREDITING AGENCIES

Regional accreditation affords significant benefits to an institution by authenticating quality, providing access to federal and state funds, creating employer confidence, and facilitating the student transfer process (Eaton, 2015). Regional accreditors require higher education institutions to demonstrate accountability and evidence of effectiveness on a regular basis, generally every 5 to 10 years. As demands on colleges and universities have intensified from all stakeholders (i.e., federal, state, and local), so too has the emphasis on accreditation and the role of the administrator in ensuring that the institution is reaffirmed (Burke & Associates, 2005; Kramer & Swing, 2010).

Table 9.1 profiles the six regional agencies that accredit institutions throughout the United States. As shown, the North Central Association of Colleges and Schools, Higher

Table 9.1 Overview of the Six Regional Accrediting Organizations

Accrediting Body	Middle States Commission on Higher Education (MSCHE)	New England Association of Schools and Colleges, Commission on Institutions of Higher Education (NEASC-CIHE)	North Central Association of Colleges and Schools, The Higher Learning Commission (NCA-HLC)	Northwest Commission on Colleges and Universities (NWCCU)	Southern Association of Colleges and Schools, Commission on Colleges (SACSCOC)	Western Association of Schools and Colleges (WASC)
Year Established	1919	1885	1895	1917	1895	1962
Duration of Accreditation (up to X years)	10	10	10	7	10	10 (Colleges/Universities) 7 (Community/Junior Colleges)
Number of States/Areas Included	8	6	19	7	12	8
States/Areas Included	Delaware, the District of Columbia, Maryland, New Jersey, New York, Pennsylvania, Puerto Rico, and the U.S. Virgin Islands	Connecticut, Maine, Massachusetts, New Hampshire, Rhode Island, Vermont, and American/international schools in more than 60 nations	Arizona, Arkansas, Colorado, Illinois, Indiana, Iowa, Kansas, Michigan, Minnesota, Missouri, Nebraska, New Mexico, North Dakota, Ohio, Oklahoma, South Dakota, West Virginia, Wisconsin, and Wyoming	Alaska, Idaho, Montana, Nevada, Oregon, Utah, and Washington	Alabama, Florida, Georgia, Kentucky, Louisiana, Mississippi, North Carolina, South Carolina, Tennessee, Texas, Virginia, and Latin America	California, Hawaii, Guam, Asia, the Pacific Region, the Middle East, Africa, and Europe
Number of Standards	7	9	5	5	4	4
Number of Institutions	525	241	1,038	162	827	188 Colleges/Universities 145 Community/Junior Colleges
Number of Students	3,025,461	990,927	5,867,385	1,133,326	5,491,411	2,612,126
Website	www.msche.org	https://cihe.neasc.org/	www.hlcommission.org/	www.nwccu.org	www.sacscoc.org	www.wascsenior.org/ www.acjc.org/

Sources: Database of Accredited Postsecondary Institutions and Programs, Retrieved from http://ope.ed.gov/accreditation/ Accessed 4/21/16 IPEDS Data Center, http://nces.ed.gov/ipeds/datacenter/Data.aspx Accessed 2/29/16.

Learning Commission (NCA-HLC) accredits more institutions than any other agency, while the Southern Association of Colleges and Schools Commission on Colleges (SACS-COC) is responsible for the greatest number of students.

OVERVIEW OF THE INSTITUTIONAL ACCREDITATION PROCESS

All six regional accrediting agencies have the same overarching goals and responsibilities for ensuring institutional quality. Despite variation in criteria across regional accrediting agencies, all require institutions seeking accreditation to follow a similar five-step process:

> 1) Self-study: … a written summary of performance, based on accrediting organizations' standards; 2) Peer review: by faculty and administrative peers in the profession; 3) Site visit: by faculty and administrative peers in the profession; 4) Judgment by accrediting organizations; and 5) Periodic external review: commissions decide on accreditation status.
>
> (Eaton, 2015, p. 6)

One of the most obvious differences between the reaffirmation processes of the six regional accrediting agencies is SACS-COC's requirement of a Quality Enhancement Plan (QEP). Required of all institutions seeking reaffirmation since 2004, the QEP is intended to engage the entire campus in continuous improvement that enhances student learning. Whether it is a new plan or an enhancement of an existing plan, the QEP needs to provide: (1) depth of intended activities demonstrating substantial goals and learning outcomes as a result of the plan; (2) sufficient funding to support the plan; (3) a detailed five-year timeline for accomplishing all facets of the plan; and (4) a thorough assessment and evaluation process to determine if the goals and desired learning outcomes have been accomplished.

Decisions, Outcomes and Sharing the Results of the Accreditation Visit

Following the completion and submission of the on-site review team's written report to the regional accreditor, the regional accreditor commission reviews the materials to determine the final outcome for the institution. Decisions can range from reaffirmation for a specified number of years (depending upon the issues identified in the report) or other, negative actions such as warning, probation, sanction, denial of reaffirmation, revocation of membership, show cause, etc. The results of the Commission's decision are then publically displayed on each regional accreditor's website and the institution must provide appropriate notification to the public, including, faculty, staff, and current and prospective students.

As of July 2016, the WASC Senior College and University Commission is the only regional accreditor who also publically posts on its website the on-site review team's full report, which provides detailed information from the on-site review team's findings, recommendations, and commendations (when applicable). Posting the on-site review team's report was an attempt to create greater transparency throughout the accreditation process, institutional findings, and commission decisions.

ROLES AND RESPONSIBILITIES OF THE ACCREDITATION PROCESS

Accreditation is a complex process that requires participation from all arenas of the institution: administration, faculty, staff, students, and other stakeholders. The following section outlines key roles and responsibilities for the accreditation process. Given that all regional accreditors have moved to a process requiring more frequent interaction between accreditor and institution (e.g., from once every 10 years to at least once every 5 to 7 years), the roles and responsibilities associated with accreditation require ongoing institutional effort.

The Accreditation Liaison

For regional accreditors and many programmatic accreditors, the accreditation liaison serves as the primary contact and organizer for the accreditation process. The scope of this role can range considerably, depending on an institution's organizational structure and approach to accreditation. At smaller institutions, the liaison may have complete authority over the accreditation process and be responsible for initial preparations, writing responses to standards, and overseeing the site visit. The liaison role is typically awarded to an individual who is in a position of some administrative authority at the institution but has time and flexibility to devote to accreditation. Many accreditation liaisons come from areas associated with reporting and compliance, such as institutional effectiveness or institutional research. Typical responsibilities of accreditation liaisons are shown in Figure 9.1.

As might be expected, the workload associated with the role of the accreditation liaison fluctuates with an institution's accreditation cycle. As reaffirmation deadlines approach, the liaison's time is devoted nearly exclusively to collecting and preparing necessary documentation and planning the site visit.

- Remaining informed on standards, policies, and procedures related to accreditation.
- Serving as the primary contact person for the accrediting organization.
- Familiarizing campus constituents with accrediting policies, procedures, and standards.
- Serving as an institutional source of information related to accreditation.
- Ensuring broad-based institutional understanding of and involvement in institutional compliance with standards, policies, and procedures.
- Ensuring accreditation requirements are appropriately integrated into the institution's planning and evaluation processes.
- Ensuring data submitted to the accrediting organization is accurate and timely.
- Informing accreditor prior to implementation of any substantive institutional changes.
- Serving as a key resource person for preparation of documents related to accreditation.
- Assisting with planning, preparations, and coordination of reaffirmations and site visits.
- Maintaining an institutional archive of documents related to accreditation.

(MSCHE, 2012, n.d.; NCA-HLC, 2016; NEASC-CIHE, 2001, n.d.; NWCCU, 2013, 2015; SACSCOC, 2012, 2015; WASC-SCUS, 2013; WASC-SCUC, n.d.; WASC, 2015)

Figure 9.1 Typical Responsibilities of Accreditation Liaisons

The President

The president of the institution bears ultimate responsibility for the accreditation process and must be kept apprised of progress from the beginning to the end. Therefore, the selection of the accreditation liaison is an important decision for the president. An informed and involved president can be a crucial advocate for inspiring campus buy-in for compliance-related undertakings such as assessment and strategic planning. Although a president may not wish to be intimately involved in the minutiae of the accreditation process, he or she should meet with the liaison at regular intervals throughout the accreditation process to keep well informed.

The Provost

It is no surprise that accreditors examine and evaluate the degree to which an institution is meeting its mission of promoting student learning and success. Thus, the provost's role as the chief academic officer is critical in the accreditation process. As many accreditation standards focus on academic elements of the institution, academic leaders such as deans and department chairs, as well as faculty, will be called upon to provide information, documentation, evidence, and support that the institution is compliant with all relevant standards. The relationship between the provost and the accreditation liaison is key, as the liaison needs the support of the provost to attain buy-in from academic leadership. Conversely, the provost must rely on the accreditation liaison to organize the process in such a way that the institution, including academics, will be successful in their accreditation review.

The Faculty

As an extension of the provost's office, faculty involvement is critical. The visiting team performing the review on behalf of the accreditor will speak directly with faculty to determine consistency of policies, procedures, and processes throughout the institution. Additionally, accreditors will want to ensure that the faculty, who are subject matter experts, are directly involved in curriculum decisions and that a process for faculty review and feedback exists for decisions that impact faculty.

Given the importance of faculty involvement in accreditation review, institutions typically appoint respected faculty members with institutional longevity to chair specific aspects of the process. For example, a past president of the faculty senate may be asked to take the lead on sections of the report that focus on program review or curriculum development/changes as they can write from experience and know faculty members from a variety of colleges and departments within the institution, thereby ensuring that the response will comprehensively reflect multiple faculty perspectives.

Institutional Research

Accreditation reports require data to demonstrate institutional changes and student learning. Providing data in an easy to understand way that utilizes traditional higher education reporting standards is critical. It is important to include individuals who understand both the detailed data and the context of the data in the accreditation process. Given that institutional researchers study all aspects of the institution (e.g., faculty, staff, admissions, financial resources, enrollment, grades, retention, graduation, policies), they are well suited to serve as report reviewers. In reading the document in its entirety, including appendices, they can leverage their institutional knowledge to identify any inconsistencies therein. As valuable as their perspective may be, however, institutional researchers should not be the only ones to review the report.

The Staff

With the exception of employees who provide direct support for accreditation activities, staff members may be largely unaware of the process and its importance to the institution as a whole. Therefore, it is important to hold town hall meetings and to distribute informational emails or flyers to increase awareness of the accreditation process as well as the individuals involved with institutional accreditation efforts. Clear and frequent communication with all faculty and staff provides the community with progress updates and gives constituent groups an opportunity to ask questions. As part of these updates, the institution may announce the composition of committees supporting the accreditation liaison and provide guidance on how others might become involved in the accreditation process.

The Students

As students should be represented throughout the accreditation process, the specifics of their involvement should be determined at the outset. Student government association officers are often ideal candidates, as they have been elected by their peers to represent student interests. Additionally, student government officers typically draw on multiple students' experiences rather than just their own when providing examples. Given that students' primary responsibility is to their studies, it is best not to assign them to write any portions of the report, but instead to offer a variety of opportunities for them to provide comments and feedback.

External Stakeholders

Feedback from external stakeholders can provide strong evidence in support of accreditation. For example, alumni associations can demonstrate the extended impact of the institution on graduates. This information can be supplemented with evidence from alumni surveys. Additionally, employers of alumni can attest to the quality and success of graduates in the field. This information can be gathered through a survey of employers that collects both quantitative and qualitative data so sample quotes from employers can be showcased within the accreditation report.

Local community relationships are critical to institutional success. Colleges and universities spend considerable time building relationships with local officials, leaders, and business persons, as well as giving back to the community. Given the importance of the town–gown relationship, institutions should make efforts to include community relations and impacts in their accreditation materials. Community members may be invited to serve on accreditation committees, thus providing an appropriate outlet for their input and feedback. As with students, the primary responsibility of external stakeholders should not be to formally develop the accreditation report, but rather to provide a unique perspective on the actions and impacts of the institution.

ADMINISTERING AND FUNDING A SUCCESSFUL REAFFIRMATION

With limited financial and personnel resources available at many institutions, preparing for accreditation can be a daunting task. As accreditation is a constantly evolving process, many administrators have yet to experience reaffirmation under the most recent principles of their regional accreditor. Many institutions experience significant institutional changes during the lengthy span between on-site visits, which can contribute to the challenges of a successful reaffirmation.

An analysis of the requirements of the six regional accrediting agencies, particularly those that require substantial attention from administrators in terms of time and careful resource allocation, provides a broader understanding of accreditation across regions. There are 12 common categories of accreditation standards: administration, admissions, curriculum, faculty, institutional effectiveness, integrity, planning, professional development, public disclosures, resources, student support services, and timely reporting. For each category, relevant accreditation standards are identified by specific regional accrediting standard numbers.

FINANCIAL IMPLICATIONS

Regional accreditation is optional for institutions; each institution must choose whether to undergo the rigorous application process. While participation is not mandatory, the financial gains associated with recognition by a regional accreditor far outweigh any cost. One of the most significant benefits of accreditation is that the federal government offers federal financial aid only to students attending an institution that is regionally accredited by one of the six agencies.

Simply applying for regional accreditation does not automatically guarantee that an institution will be accredited. Regional accrediting agencies are required by CHEA to publicly disclose the names of all institutions' status (e.g., candidacy, accredited through X date, show cause, probation, etc.). In the event that an accreditor finds an institution in non-compliance in one or more areas, the institution is given the opportunity to resolve the issues internally before the final decision of the accrediting body is made public. There is a financial cost involved in correcting any item judged to be non-compliant, regardless of its severity. These costs can be avoided by maintaining compliance on all items in between reaffirmation periods, which also reduces the amount of work required prior to reaffirmation.

CONCLUSION

Former U.S. Secretary of Education Margaret Spellings was most compelling when she stated in 2006:

> We have noted a remarkable shortage of clear, accessible information about crucial aspects of American colleges and universities. ... Our complex, decentralized postsecondary education system has no comprehensive strategy, particularly for undergraduate programs, to provide either adequate internal accountability systems or effective public information.
>
> (U.S. Department of Education, 2006, pp. 4, 13)

Since the release of the Spellings Commission report in 2006, there has been more emphasis nationally on accountability in higher education and thus greater pressure on institutions to demonstrate actual learning outcomes.

The federal government has a long history of adding and/or increasing institutional requirements. For example, institutions that receive and distribute Title IV financial aid are required to submit accurate and timely Integrated Postsecondary Education Data System (IPEDS) data as part of their agreement and ability to offer financial aid. The amount and type of information that must be submitted to IPEDS has grown substantially over time.

Historically, it has been incumbent on institutions to demonstrate compliance with federal requirements. Recently, however, the federal government has been calling on regional accreditors to bear greater responsibility for institutional success. Higher education leaders can expect to see this trend continue, which will likely lead to a more in-depth accreditation process in the future.

DISCUSSION PROMPTS

1. What is the purpose of accreditation? What does an institution gain from being accredited? Are there benefits specific to faculty, staff, students, and administrators?
2. Select a specific administrator role. What role does this position play in the accreditation process? What challenges would you anticipate this role to face, and how would you mitigate them?
3. In what ways are the processes of the regional accreditors similar and different? Which process is most attractive to you as an administrator and why?
4. Given the roles and responsibilities of an accreditation liaison, what are three primary skillsets that you would look for in selecting an accreditation liaison?
5. Identify and describe three financial considerations and implications involved in obtaining reaffirmation of accreditation.
6. Building relationships within and outside of the institution is critical for a successful reaffirmation. Name two institution positions that were not identified which you feel could or should play a critical part in the accreditation process. Why?
7. How do you think the role of accreditors will change in the next five years? What impact will that have on higher education administrators?
8. Which bodies have accredited your institution? Where would students find this information on the institution's website?

9. In what ways can you creatively engage faculty, staff, students, and community members in the accreditation process?

10. Obtain the standards document for your institution's regional accrediting body (see websites in Table 9.1). After reviewing it, discuss how you would begin organizing institutional resources in your division to prepare for the written report and the on-site visit.

REFERENCES

Burke, J. C., & Associates. (Ed.). (2005). *Achieving accountability in higher education: Balancing public, academic, and market demands*. San Francisco: Jossey-Bass.

Eaton, J. (2015). *An overview of U.S. accreditation (revised)*. Washington, DC: Council for Higher Education Accreditation. Retrieved from http://www.chea.org/pdf/Overview%20of%20US%20Accreditation%202015.pdf

Kramer, G. L., & Swing, R. L. (Eds.). (2010). *Higher education assessments: Leadership matters*. Lanham, Maryland: Rowman & Littlefield.

MSCHE. (2012). *Self study: Creating a useful process and report* (2nd ed.). Retrieved from https://www.msche.org/publications/SelfStudy2012FINAL.pdf

MSCHE. (n.d.). *The accreditation liaison officer: Role and responsibilities*. Retrieved May 12, 2016, from http://www.msche.org/documents/6B---5-ALO-guidelines-122109.pdf

NCA-HLC. (2016). *Comprehensive evaluation*. HLC Institutions. Retrieved June 7, 2016, from https://www.hlcommission.org/Accreditation-Processes/comprehensive-evaluation.html

NEASC-CIHE. (2001). *Accreditation liaison officer*. Retrieved May 12, 2016, from https://cihe.neasc.org/downloads/POLICIES/Pp01_Accreditation_Liaison_Officer.pdf

NEASC-CIHE. (n.d.). *Comprehensive evaluation*. Retrieved June 7, 2016, from https://cihe.neasc.org/institutional-reports-resources/reporting-guidelines/comprehensive-evaluation

NWCCU. (2013). *Accreditation liaison officer policy*. Retrieved May 12, 2016, from http://www.nwccu.org/Standards%20and%20Policies/Policies/PolicyDocs/Accreditation%20Liaison%20Officer%20Policy.pdf

NWCCU. (2015). *Accreditation handbook*. Retrieved June 7, 2016, from http://www.nwccu.org/Pubs%20Forms%20and%20Updates/Publications/Accreditation%20Handbook,%202015%20Edition.pdf

SACSCOC. (2012). *The accreditation liaison*. Retrieved May 12, 2016, from http://www.sacscoc.org/pdf/081705/accreditation%20liaison.pdf

SACSCOC. (2015). *General information on the reaffirmation process*. Retrieved June 7, 2016, from http://www.sacscoc.org/genaccproc.asp

U.S. Department of Education. (2006). *A test of leadership: Charting the future of U.S. higher education* (ED-06-C0-0013). Washington, DC: Education Publication Center.

U.S. Department of Education, Office of Postsecondary Education. (n.d.). *FAQs about accreditation*. Retrieved February 2016, from http://ope.ed.gov/accreditation/FAQAccr.aspx

WASC Accrediting Commission for Community and Junior Colleges. (2015). *Guide to evaluating and improving institutions*. Retrieved June 7, 2016, from http://www.accjc.org/wpcontent/uploads/2015/10/Guide_to_Evaluating_and_Improving_Institutions_July_2015_REVISED.pdf

WASC Senior College and University Commission. (2013). *Overview of the institutional review process*. Retrieved June 7, 2016, from https://www.wascsenior.org/resources/handbook-accreditation-2013/part-iii-wasc-quality-assurance/overview-institutional-review-process

WASC Senior College and University Commission. (n.d.). *Accreditation liaison officer policy*. Retrieved May 12, 2016, from, https://www.wascsenior.org/content/accreditation-liaison-officer-policy

Weisbrod, B. A., Ballou, J. P., & Asch, E. D. (2008). *Mission and money: Understanding the university*. New York: Cambridge University Press.

Part III

Events and Issues Today That Shape
Higher Education

10

KEY LEGAL ASPECTS FOR HIGHER EDUCATION ADMINISTRATORS

Janet Park Balanoff and Monoka Venters

INTRODUCTION

The laws governing higher education are like a blanket: multidimensional and flexible. Although a blanket appears to be one cohesive color or texture, in reality it consists of numerous interwoven threads. The threads in the blanket of higher education law consist of statutes passed by Congress, laws passed by state legislatures, and policies adopted by colleges and universities. Each thread may have a different purpose, but they all combine to serve a common goal: to provide a shield that is flexible enough to protect student and institution, employee and employer.

Although control of educational issues is reserved to the states under the 10th Amendment of the U.S. Constitution, the federal government has imposed numerous statutory restraints on higher education through "valid exercises of congressional power, such as the authority to regulate matters that affect interstate commerce and the national economy" (Hutchens, 2011, p. 35). In addition, the federal government has encouraged postsecondary institutions to conform to various practices by utilizing the spending clause of the U.S. Constitution to condition receipt of federal funding, in particular federal student financial aid, on adherence to certain standards. For instance, institutions must agree to protect student educational records in accordance with the Family Educational Rights and Privacy Act (FERPA) in exchange for receiving federal funding (Hutchens, 2011).

Among the most important federal laws that institutions of higher education must be aware of are FERPA, the Higher Education Opportunity Act of 2008, the Copyright Act of 1976, the Technology Education and Copyright Harmonization Act of 2002 (TEACH Act), the Civil Rights Act of 1964, the Americans with Disabilities Act of 1990, the Family and Medical Leave Act of 1993, and the Age Discrimination in Employment Act of 1967. This chapter discusses how each of these federal laws applies to institutions of higher education.

FAMILY EDUCATIONAL RIGHTS AND PRIVACY ACT

The Family Educational Rights and Privacy Act (FERPA) was enacted by Congress and signed into law in 1974 to serve the dual purpose of protecting rights and preserving privacy (Education Amendments of 1974, Pub. Law No. 93-380, 88 Stat. 484). FERPA has been amended numerous times, but current law still balances protection of rights and privacy.

On the rights side, FERPA ensures access to educational records by appropriate parties; on the privacy side, FERPA protects unwarranted access to educational records by others. To protect those rights, federal law provides that no funds will be made available to an institution that has a policy or practice of denying or effectively preventing a student who is or has been in attendance at the institution the right to review and inspect educational records. To preserve privacy, federal law provides that no funds will be made available to an institution that has a policy or practice of permitting the release of educational records of students unless the institution has written permission to release such information or federal law provides a specific exception for the release. Both public and private postsecondary institutions typically receive federal funding and are therefore subject to FERPA (Family Educational Rights and Privacy Act [FERPA], 20 U.S.C. §1232g, 2016).

Rights of Eligible Students Under FERPA

In the postsecondary context, the rights of access to and privacy for educational records belong to the student. Federal regulations refer to postsecondary students as eligible students (Family Educational Rights and Privacy Rule [FERPR], 2015). Institutions must notify eligible students about FERPA rights on an annual basis. An eligible student has the right to inspect and review his or her educational records. Such access must be granted within a reasonable period not to exceed 45 days from the date of the request. If an eligible student would like to obtain copies of educational records, the institution may charge a reasonable fee for the copies unless doing so would effectively prevent the student from inspecting and reviewing the records.

If the eligible student finds information in an educational record that he or she feels is inaccurate or misleading, the student has the right to request that the institution correct the record. The institution is not required to make the requested correction to the educational record, but must permit the student to request a formal hearing in cases where it decides not to do so. If the institution does not make the requested correction after the formal hearing, it must allow the student to place a statement outlining his or her position in the educational record (FERPA, 2016; FERPR, 2015). None of these rights may be used to challenge a grade, an opinion, or a substantive decision made by an institution.

When an institution receives a request for information about a student, the first question to address is whether the request is being made by an eligible student. Even eligible students do not have access to all records. For instance, students do not have access to their parents' financial records. Students also do not have access to letters of recommendation for admission, employment, or honorary recognition if the student signed a voluntary waiver of such rights (FERPA, 2016).

Rights of Others Under FERPA

Regardless of the postsecondary student's age (even if he or she is under the age of 18), the right to access educational records does not extend to the student's parents except in limited circumstances. For instance, an institution may disclose educational records to parents if the student is a dependent for federal income tax purposes. An institution may also inform parents or legal guardians about any violation of a law, rule, or policy if the institution determines that a student under the age of 21 committed a disciplinary violation related to the use or possession of alcohol or a controlled substance. Finally, an institution may disclose educational records to parents in connection with an emergency if such knowledge is necessary to protect the health or safety of the student or other persons. The institution may share information only during the time of the emergency; moreover, the institution must note in the student's educational record the articulable and significant threat that formed the basis of the disclosure (FERPA, 2016; FERPR, 2015).

In addition, an eligible student may provide written consent to the institution to allow third parties, including his or her parents, access to educational records (FERPR, 2015). Higher education institutions routinely receive requests from parents for information contained in a protected educational record. Parents who pay tuition and fees to a college or university often feel that the institution has no right to refuse to provide requested information. Unless the parents fall into one of the specified exceptions, FERPA prohibits the institution from disclosing educational records. It is essential that institutions establish policies for responding to requests from parents and train relevant employees accordingly. During orientation or at the beginning of each academic year, some institutions ask eligible students to sign a written authorization allowing the institution to provide educational records to the students' parents. Even if the institution has a signed authorization, it should confirm that the student still wants the institution to release his or her educational records to the parent at the time of any request because the student has the right to withdraw consent at will.

Education Records Under FERPA

If the request comes from an eligible student, the first question to address is whether the document is an educational record. Educational records are defined as materials that contain information directly related to a student and are maintained by the educational institution (FERPA, 2016). Once a document has been defined as an educational record, an institution must provide appropriate parties access to the record while protecting the record from being disclosed to others unless a specific exception applies. Federal law provides certain exclusions from the definition of educational records. For instance, educational records do not include documents made by an employee for the employee's use that are not accessible or revealed to any other person (FERPA, 2016). Personal notes that an instructor maintains about a student would fall under this exclusion and would not be considered an educational record; therefore, a student cannot review and inspect such notes.

Records created and maintained by a law enforcement unit of the institution for law enforcement purposes are also not considered educational records (FERPA, 2016). Therefore, law enforcement units may choose whether to disclose their records to eligible students and others (even without consent of the eligible student). If a law enforcement unit receives educational records from other campus representatives, those records are protected under FERPA. The best course of action for law enforcement units is to keep records created for law enforcement purposes separate from educational records received from other campus representatives.

Records relating to the treatment of a postsecondary student by a physician, psychiatrist, psychologist, or other recognized professional are excluded from educational records if the records are made, maintained, and used only in connection with the student's treatment and are disclosed only to treatment providers (FERPA, 2016). To be classified as a treatment record, the record must be shared only with health professionals and cannot be provided to the student or anyone else. If an institution chooses to provide the record to the student, the record is then classified as an educational record rather than as a treatment record, meaning that the protections of FERPA apply. The records may be shared with others if the student consents in writing or the situation falls into one of the exceptions outlined in FERPA. For instance, the records may be shared with the parents if the parents claim the student as a dependent for federal income tax purposes.

Directory Information Under FERPA

If the institution receives a request from someone other than an eligible student, the first question to consider is whether the information is an educational record or directory information. Directory information is not considered an educational record; therefore, such information is not protected under FERPA and may be made public. Directory information is not generally considered harmful or an invasion of privacy if disclosed (FERPR, 2015). Specifically, directory information includes the student's name, address, telephone number, email address, photograph, date and place of birth, major field of study, enrollment status, dates of attendance, and degrees and awards received; the most recent previous educational agency or institution attended by the student; the student's participation in officially recognized activities and sports; and, for members of athletic teams, weight and height. Directory information includes unique personal identifiers such as student ID numbers if the identifier cannot be used to gain access to educational records except in combination with another authentication source such as a password. Directory information does not include the student's Social Security number (FERPA, 2016; FERPR, 2015).

The institution must provide public notice to the eligible student if it intends to make directory information public and allow the student to opt out of public disclosures. The public notice must inform the eligible student of the deadline by which the student must notify the institution in writing that the student does not want such information released as directory information. Such notification does not have to be directed to the eligible student individually and may be made in numerous ways, such as in a student handbook or a newsletter. Institutions may also adopt limited directory information policies that allow disclosure of directory information only for specific purposes (such as publishing a graduation program or yearbook), to specific parties, or both (FERPA, 2016; FERPR, 2015). Such policies allow institutions to restrict disclosure of directory information to protect students from becoming targets of marketing campaigns or criminal activity.

Exclusions From FERPA

If the information is an educational record but is being requested by someone other than the eligible student, the second question is whether an applicable exclusion exists. FERPA provides numerous exclusions that allow disclosure of otherwise protected educational records. The first permitted exclusion from the privacy protections of FERPA is via the written consent of an eligible student (FERPA, 2016; FERPR, 2015).

Additional permitted exclusions relate to specific educational reasons and include the following exceptions:

- School officials who have legitimate educational interests;
- Officials from other schools in which the student seeks or intends to enroll;
- Accrediting organizations to the extent necessary to carry out accrediting functions; and
- Appropriate persons in connection with an emergency if such knowledge is necessary to protect the health or safety of the student or other persons (FERPA, 2016; FERPR, 2015).

There is also an exclusion relating to the student's application for or receipt of financial aid. Disclosure of such information is allowed to determine eligibility for or the amount of the financial aid as well as to enforce the terms and conditions of the aid (FERPR, 2015).

As mentioned earlier, two specific exceptions to the protections of FERPA apply to the parents of eligible students. Institutions may share protected information with parents in cases where the student is defined as a dependent in the Internal Revenue Code of 1982. The second exception allows parents or legal guardians of students under the age of 21 to receive information regarding the violation of a law, rule, or policy if the institution determines that the student committed a disciplinary violation with respect to the use or possession of alcohol or a controlled substance (FERPA, 2016; FERPR, 2015).

Another group of permitted exceptions to the protections of FERPA applies in various circumstances related to the judicial system. Institutions may release information without the consent of the eligible student in the following cases:

- Upon request by authorized representatives of the Attorney General for law enforcement purposes, provided that personally identifiable data will be destroyed when no longer needed;
- Upon request by State or local officials pursuant to state statute if disclosure relates to the juvenile justice system;
- As information provided under the Violent Crime Control and Law Enforcement Act of 1994 concerning registered sex offenders;
- Upon request by designated federal representatives of the Attorney General who are investigating and prosecuting acts of domestic or international terrorism and who have obtained a court order (FERPA, 2016; FERPR, 2015);
- In response to a judicial order or lawfully issued subpoena provided the eligible student is notified in advance unless the judicial order is in a proceeding involving child abuse and neglect or dependency matters (FERPA, 2016; Uninterrupted Scholars Act, 2013); and
- Upon request by caseworkers or other designated representatives who have the right to access the case plan of a student in foster care (FERPA, 2016; Uninterrupted Scholars Act, 2013).

Two exclusions to the protections of FERPA relate to disciplinary proceedings. First, alleged victims of any crime of violence or non-forcible sex offense may be provided the final results of any disciplinary proceeding conducted by the institution against the alleged perpetrator with respect to such offense. Second, the final results of any disciplinary proceeding in which a student is found to have committed a violation of the institution's policy for any crime of violence or non-forcible sex offense may be provided to anyone (FERPA, 2016; FERPR, 2015).

The final three exclusions relate to evaluation or research. First, authorized persons conducting program monitoring, evaluations, and performance measurements of agencies and institutions receiving or providing benefits under the Richard B. Russell National School Lunch Act or the Child Nutrition Act of 1966 may access educational records provided that such aggregate de-identified data will be destroyed when no longer needed (FERPA, 2016; FERPR, 2015).

Second, educational records may be released to authorized representatives of the Comptroller General, the Secretary of the U.S. Department of Education, or State educational authorities for audit, evaluation, or required enforcement activities provided there is a written agreement that:

- designates an individual or entity as an authorized representative;
- specifies the personally identifiable information to be disclosed;
- specifies the purpose as being in furtherance of an audit, evaluation, or enforcement activity;
- describes the activity;
- specifies that personally identifiable data will be destroyed when no longer needed;
- specifies the time period in which the personally identifiable information must be destroyed; and
- protects the education records from further disclosure (FERPA, 2016; FERPR, 2015).

Third, organizations conducting studies for, or on behalf of educational agencies may receive educational records or the institutions themselves may receive educational records for the purpose of developing, validating, or administering predictive tests, administering student aid programs, and improving instruction. In both cases, the organization must enter into an agreement that:

- specifies the purpose, scope, and duration of the study;
- specifies the information to be disclosed;
- requires the organization to use the information only for the purposes identified in the agreement;
- requires the organization to conduct the study without identifying students or parents;
- requires the organization to destroy personally identifiable data when it is no longer needed for the purpose of the study; and
- specifies the time period in which the information must be destroyed (FERPA, 2016; FERPR, 2015).

It is important to remember that the exclusions discussed in this section are permitted but not required. Institutions should develop policies to guide the circumstances under which information will be released as allowed under the exclusions.

Records Under FERPA

Institutions must maintain a record of all individuals (other than school officials with a legitimate educational interest) who have requested and obtained access to educational records. The record must indicate the legitimate interest of each person or organization in requesting or obtaining access to educational records (FERPA, 2016). If personally identifiable information is released during a health or safety emergency, this record must also include "the articulable and significant threat to the health or safety of a student or other individuals that formed the basis for the disclosure" (FERPR, 2015, §99.32). This record must be maintained with the student's educational record and is accessible only by the eligible student, officials responsible for the custody of educational records, and authorized representatives of the Comptroller General, the Secretary of the U.S. Department of Education, or State educational authorities auditing the system (FERPA, 2016).

Complaints Under FERPA

An eligible student may file a complaint with the U.S. Department of Education Family Policy Compliance Office (FPCO) if the student feels that a violation of his or her rights under FERPA has occurred. Such complaints must be submitted within 180 days of the alleged violation or within 180 days of the date that the student knew or reasonably should have known about the alleged violation. FCPO may extend the filing deadline for good cause. FCPO notifies institutions if it institutes an investigation and may direct the institution to submit a written response within a specified period of time. FCPO must provide written notice of its findings and the basis for the findings to the eligible student and the institution. If FCPO finds that an institution has not complied with FERPA, FCPO must provide a statement of the specific steps that the institution must take to comply and a reasonable time period within which the institution may comply voluntarily. If the institution does not comply during the established time period, the Secretary of Education may withhold or terminate federal funding (FERPR, 2015). To date, the Secretary has not terminated federal funding for any institution based on failure to comply with FERPA.

HIGHER EDUCATION OPPORTUNITY ACT OF 2008

In 2008, Congress reauthorized the Higher Education Act of 1965 by passing the Higher Education Opportunity Act ([HEOA], Pub. L. No.110-315, 122 Stat. 3078). The text of HEOA is more than 400 pages long and contains hundreds of amendments to the Higher Education Act. Of necessity, our summary will cover only select changes.

Transparency in College Tuition for Consumers in HEOA

Many of the changes contained in HEOA are intended to assist students and parents in determining the costs of college by increasing the availability of information. For instance, the Transparency in College Tuition for Consumers section of HEOA requires the U.S. Department of Education (U.S. DOE) to publish information on the College Navigator website such as college affordability lists and consumer information including, among other things, descriptions of institutional mission, admissions statistics, and demographic composition of the student body (HEOA, 2008, §111). The college affordability lists must be published annually for public, private non-profit, and private for-profit institutions at the four-year, two-year, and less than two-year levels and must include the following categories: (1) institutions with the highest tuition and fees, (2) institutions with the lowest tuition and fees, (3) institutions with the highest net price (tuition and fees minus grant aid), (4) institutions with the lowest net price, (5) institutions with the largest increase in tuition and fees, and (6) institutions with the largest increase in net price.

In addition, the Transparency in College Tuition for Consumers section of HEOA requires the U.S. DOE to publish a net price calculator showing the cost of tuition and fees minus grant aid for each institution of higher education. Moreover, each institution of higher education that receives federal financial aid funds must publish its own net price calculator showing the cost of tuition and fees minus grant aid using institutional data and allowing students to base the calculation on their family circumstances. HEOA allowed institutions to link to the net price calculator on College Navigator (HEOA, 2008, §111).

Textbook Information in HEOA

The Textbook Information section of HEOA requires institutions of higher education receiving federal financial aid to ensure that students have timely access to affordable course materials (HEOA, 2008, §112). Institutions must provide students with information about the costs of availability of required textbooks, recommended textbooks, and supplemental materials. Each institution must include on its online course schedule either (1) the International Standard Book Number (ISBN) and retail price of required textbooks, recommended textbooks, and supplemental material; (2) the author, title, publisher, and copyright date of the material; or (3) a statement that the information is "To Be Determined." Institutions are encouraged to provide information about renting textbooks, purchasing used textbooks, textbook buy-back programs, and alternative content delivery programs. In addition, the Textbook Information section of HEOA requires textbook publishers to provide faculty with the following information about textbooks and supplemental materials: (1) the price of the textbook, (2) the copyright dates of the three previous editions of the textbook, (3) a description of substantial revisions from the prior edition, (4) the availability and price of other formats, and (5) the price of the textbook without supplemental materials (HEOA, 2008, §112).

Copyrighted Material in HEOA

HEOA also amended the Copyrighted Material section of the Program Participation Agreement. Each institution of higher education must certify that it has policies in place addressing the unauthorized distribution of copyrighted material, including unauthorized peer-to-peer file sharing. Such policies must be made available to prospective and enrolled students and must list not only institutional sanctions but also civil and criminal penalties for unauthorized distribution of copyrighted material (HEOA, 2008, §488). In addition, each institution must, to the extent practicable, offer alternatives to illegal downloading or unauthorized peer-to-peer file sharing (HEOA, 2008, §493).

COPYRIGHT ACT OF 1976

The Copyright Act of 1976 protects original works of authorship fixed in any tangible medium of expression including literary works, musical works, dramatic works, motion pictures, and sound recordings. The Act does not protect ideas, procedures, processes, systems, methods of operation, concepts, or principles (Copyright Act, 2016).

The owner of a copyright has the exclusive right to reproduce the work; to prepare derivative works; to distribute copies for sale, rental, lease, or lending; to perform or display literary, musical, dramatic, choreographic, or cinematographic works publicly; and to transmit sound recordings digitally. The author or authors of a work own the copyright unless the work is considered a work made for hire. The employer or the person for whom the work was prepared owns the copyright of a work made for hire (Copyright Act, 2016).

The protections provided by the Copyright Act exist from the moment that the work is fixed in tangible form. Neither publication of the work nor registration of the work is necessary to secure protection under the Copyright Act. Although notice of the copyright was originally required under the Copyright Act of 1976, notice has not been required to achieve protection since March 1, 1989. However, providing notice of copyright is important because it alerts the public to the protections and eliminates the use of the innocent infringement defense in a copyright infringement lawsuit. Notice of copyright should contain three elements: (1) the © symbol or the word "copyright," (2) the year of first publication, and (3) the name of the owner of the copyright (Copyright Act, 2016).

Typically, a person who wishes to make use of copyrighted material must obtain permission from the owner. If a person uses copyrighted material without permission from the owner, he or she may be sued for copyright infringement. Relief for copyright infringement may include an injunction to prevent or restrain further use of the copyrighted work, a judgment for damages and profits made by the infringer, and costs and attorney's fees. In addition, a person who willfully infringes a copyright for commercial advantage or private financial gain may be found guilty of criminal infringement (Copyright Act, 2016).

However, a number of exceptions exist that allow someone other than the owner of a copyright to use copyrighted material without obtaining permission. Perhaps the most common exception is fair use, which allows reproduction for purposes such as criticism, comment, news reporting, teaching (including multiple copies for classroom use), scholarship, or research. To determine whether a particular use falls within the fair use exception, a four-factor test is used. First, the purpose and character of the use, including whether the use is commercial or educational, is assessed. Second, the nature of the copyrighted work is evaluated. Third, the amount and substantiality of the portion used in relationship to the entire copyrighted work is determined. Fourth, the effect of the use upon the potential market for or value of the copyrighted work is considered (Copyright Act, 2016).

Another exception to copyright protection that is particularly relevant in the higher education context is for face-to-face teaching activities. This exception allows a faculty member or a student to display or perform copyrighted materials during a face-to-face class. If the faculty member or student is using a copy of a motion picture or other audiovisual work, the copy must have been obtained within the parameters of the Copyright Act (Copyright Act, 2016).

TECHNOLOGY EDUCATION AND COPYRIGHT HARMONIZATION ACT OF 2002

Because instruction is no longer limited to face-to-face courses, Congress in 2002 passed the Technology Education and Copyright Harmonization Act ([TEACH Act], Pub. L. No. 107-273, §13301, 116 Stat. 1910). The TEACH Act allows faculty and students in distance learning or online classes to perform or display non-dramatic literary works, musical works, and reasonable and limited portions of other works in an amount comparable to what is typically displayed in a live classroom under the circumstances specified in the following paragraph.

To qualify under the TEACH Act, the performance or display must be made by, at the direction of, or under the actual supervision of the instructor as an integral part of a class session at an accredited non-profit educational institution. In addition, the performance or display must be directly related and of material assistance to the teaching content. The transmission must be made solely for and, to the extent technologically feasible, limited to students officially enrolled in the course. The institution must take the following additional steps:

- adopt policies related to copyright;
- provide information to students, faculty, and other relevant staff that describe and promote compliance with copyright laws;
- provide notice to students that materials used in connection with the course may be subject to copyright protection; and
- apply technological measures that reasonably prevent the retention of the work for longer than the class session or unauthorized further dissemination of the work.

The institution also must not engage in conduct that could reasonably be expected to interfere with technological measures used by copyright owners to prevent retention or unauthorized further dissemination (TEACH Act, 2002).

The TEACH Act does not cover certain materials. For instance, copyrighted materials produced or marketed primarily for distance learning or online courses are not covered (TEACH Act, 2002). Students must still obtain these materials in compliance with copyright laws.

Institutions and faculty should not confuse the TEACH Act with the fair use exception to the copyright laws. The TEACH Act does not replace the fair use exception; instead, both provisions are exceptions to the copyright protections. Therefore, faculty members teaching distance learning courses should analyze whether either provision allows distribution of otherwise protected material. If material is not allowed to be distributed to students in a distance learning course under the TEACH Act, the faculty member should evaluate whether the material could be distributed to students under the fair use exception.

When considering whether to utilize the benefits provided by the TEACH Act, an institution must evaluate the costs of compliance with the law. Ashley (2004) recommends that the analysis address three questions:

(1) What is the role of distance or online learning in the overall delivery of instruction?
(2) What is the likelihood of successfully coordinating faculty, administration, and IT staff to ensure that procedures are in the place to meet the requirements?
(3) What is the feasibility of implementing the necessary technological controls?

Ashley (2004) suggests that institutions that are replacing face-to-face instruction with distance or online learning should invest time and resources into complying with the provisions of the TEACH Act.

CIVIL RIGHTS ACT OF 1964: TITLE VI AND VII

In 1964, Congress passed the Civil Rights Act (Pub. L. No. 88-52, 78 Stat. 241), covering several types of employers in its prohibition of unlawful discrimination. Title VI of the Civil Rights Act pertains only to programs receiving federal financial assistance, while Title VII pertains to all employers with a workforce of 15 or more. The Civil Rights Act of 1991 (Pub. L. No. 102-166, 105 Stat. 1071) amended this law to change the legal remedies available to plaintiffs. It added jury trials and punitive as well as compensatory damages as options.

Title VI

Congress limited Title VI to prohibiting discrimination on the bases of race, color, and national origin in federally funded programs (Civil Rights Act, 1964). Only in 1972 did they address sex discrimination in federally funded programs, passing Title IX of the Education Amendments (Pub. L. No. 92-318, 86 Stat. 373). The ultimate penalty for employers violating Title VI (or Title IX) is termination of federal funds to the program (following extensive administrative processing). To support this law, various federal agencies have issued rules, regulations, or orders. Those same agencies also may issue guidance documents, which do not have the force of law.

The law prohibits an employer from preferring candidates of one race over another or advertising such hints as a preference for U.S. born applicants. Each of those practices represents disparate treatment—basic discrimination. The regulations for the U.S. Department of Education (one agency offering federal funding) also prohibit the recipient employer from practices that create disparate impact—patterns and practices that have the effect of discriminating based on race, color, or national origin. The U.S. Department of Justice investigates complaints of discrimination under Title VI.

The U.S. Department of Education would ask an employer responding to a complaint involving a hiring decision to identify the steps taken to make the decision. In the following example, Candidate is an external applicant alleging that the employer's interview practices discriminated based on race. Candidate is African American (race) and Hispanic (ethnicity). Race and ethnicity are separate identifiers chosen voluntarily by applicants.

By chance, Candidate's acquaintance (Caucasian, non-Hispanic) also participated in an interview and shared all details with him. Their experiences were unalike in many ways:

- Candidate was required to provide a transcript as a condition of interview. Acquaintance was not.
- Interview questions for Candidate were cursory, requiring Yes/No answers, with no follow-up on "No" answers. When Acquaintance had little experience in an area, the interviewer asked about related experience and transferable skills.
- Candidate was told that his grades in college (20 years ago) did not seem to support his application for the level of the open position. The interviewer made no mention of Acquaintance's college experience.

The employer selected Acquaintance for the position. As the Respondent to the complaint, the employer (a small public institution of higher education) first outlined the criteria for employment and identified them as neutral. They included filing an application by the posted deadline, possessing the required degree, documenting the required years of experience, and successfully completing an interview. Candidate met the first three criteria and alleged disparate treatment based on race in disputing the negative result within the fourth criterion.

Specifically, he alleged that the employer sought information after "No" answers from Acquaintance, who was thus able to showcase transferable skills acceptable to the employer. However, the employer simply noted "No" answers from Candidate and ended the interview. In addition, Candidate's college grades from 20 years ago were used as a factor in non-selection. Acquaintance's grades were unknown to the employer; therefore, Candidate alleged that the selection criterion of a transcript with grades at a certain level was discriminatory.

If this were the complete set of facts, Candidate likely would win this charge of discrimination. The employer used selection criteria against Candidate without applying them to a candidate of another race, making the criteria appear irrelevant and thus invalid. In addition, the employer did not apply the same standards within the interview. The employer accepted "No" answers at face value for one candidate, but sought (and valued) related skills and experience from another of a difference race.

Originally, the federal agencies bound by Title VI interpreted regulations supporting Title VI quite broadly, especially in the area of a federally funded program or activity. They used the term to mean that acceptance of federal assistance resulted in coverage of the entity. After 20 years of such interpretations, a Supreme Court case sharply narrowed the definition. While the case actually addressed Title IX, the companion language that prohibited sex discrimination in federally funded programs, it also applied to Title VI and two other statutes that used Title VI as a model: the Age Discrimination Act and Section 504 of the Rehabilitation Act, focused on individuals with disabilities.

Grove City College v. Bell (1984) restricted coverage of Title IX to the actual office receiving federal funds: the student financial aid office. The *Grove City* decision (1984) held that applicants or employees could challenge the employment practices within the financial aid office, but in no other area of the university.

For four years, employers who were recipients of federal funds functioned as if the only requirement for accepting all those dollars was to maintain non-discriminatory practices in the financial aid workforce. By 1988, Congress asserted its original intent, passing the Civil Rights Restoration Act (Pub. L. No. 100-259, 102 Stat. 28). Agencies returned to interpreting enforcement regulations as covering all programs and activities of the recipient.

Title VII

Title VII prohibits an employer from taking an adverse employment action based on race, color, religion, sex, or national origin (Civil Rights Act, 1964). Congress amended the law in 1978 to add pregnancy as a protected class and a basis for discrimination, as part of the definition of sex discrimination (Pregnancy Discrimination Act of 1978, Pub. L. No. 95-555, 92 Stat. 2076). Within each basis, employers also are liable if their representatives take adverse action against participants in the process to resolve discrimination.

Retaliation against a party who complains of discrimination or files a charge is prohibited. Witnesses are also protected; the language covers individuals who participate in an employment discrimination investigation, complaint, or lawsuit and then experience an adverse action based on that participation. The Equal Employment Opportunity Commission investigates complaints of discrimination under all areas of Title VII.

This prohibition of retaliation accompanied the Pregnancy Discrimination Act in 1978. Three decades later, retaliation had become the most frequent basis for all the civil rights complaints filed with the agency responsible for investigation. The Equal Employment Opportunity Commission (EEOC) reported that, in 2010, retaliation topped race for the first time in the 50-year history of the agency. It remains the leading basis for EEOC complaints at this time (FY2014).

Title VII covers two types of actions. The first includes negative actions in terms or conditions of employment (hiring, compensation, or promotion, for example). The second is when an employer limits or classifies employees to deprive them of opportunities. A Title VII claim requires a showing that the employer took the adverse action based on race, color, religion, sex, or national origin.

Congress spoke to such practices by employment agencies, labor organizations, and training programs, as well: they must avoid the same actions that an employer must avoid (Civil Rights Act, 1964). Therefore, the use of an agency that discriminates in its practices to avoid hiring certain groups of applicants will not insulate an employer from a discrimination charge.

The case records of the EEOC contain many examples of each type of prohibited action. Since Congress passed the Civil Rights Act of 1964, the EEOC has issued regulations, guidelines, and Memos of Understanding. Prohibited actions include printing employment notices that specify or indicate a refusal to hire or a preference, such as advertising for a "girl Friday" or a "Christian trainee." Another prohibited action is stereotyping opportunities with more arduous or time-consuming roles in contrast to those with less structure, such as "both Partner- and Mommy-track opportunities available."

The EEOC will consider an employer's argument that a posting specification was a bona fide occupational qualification (BFOQ). Employers must be aware that BFOQs must be defined very narrowly, by specific circumstance, and in functional terms rather than by sex or other protected class. A requirement for a female or male actor is considered a BFOQ when the face and/or body must convey the role without artifice. It is far more difficult to impose "sex" as a BFOQ for costumed, cosmetically made-up, and masked characters.

Title VII—Race

Until 2010, the EEOC most frequently received complaints of discrimination based on race. Race discrimination includes adverse employment actions based on the identification of an individual as belonging to a particular race. The person taking the discriminatory action does not have to be correct in identifying the race. Even if the perception was mistaken, a hiring official's refusal to hire an applicant perceived to be African American would constitute race discrimination.

One of the leading race discrimination cases, *Griggs v. Duke Power Company* (1971), forever changed employers' understanding of the term "job-related criterion." Prior to the Civil Rights Act, Duke Power hired African Americans only in the Labor division. Thirteen African American employees challenged the company's new criteria of possessing a high school diploma and passing two general aptitude tests for transfer from Labor to other divisions. The employees cited a disparate impact on African Americans with a claim that the diploma and the two tests were unrelated to the jobs in the inside divisions with starting salaries above the highest salary in Labor. As evidence, they cited the continued successful performance of white colleagues who transferred among other divisions without having a high school diploma or taking either test. Those colleagues continued to be promoted within the company. The Supreme Court ruled that tests producing an adverse impact by race must be job-related. Employers also must document whether instruments with lower adverse impact are available and reasonable (*Griggs v. Duke Power Company*, 1971).

Adverse actions extend beyond failure to hire and include demotions, failure to promote, layoffs, or other negative terms or conditions of employment. An employee may bring a viable charge if discriminated against because of affiliation with an individual who brought a charge based on race. As an example, if an employer feels prejudice against employees involved in biracial relationships or marriage, it would be unlawful for the employer to terminate employees on that basis. Adverse action based on affiliation with an individual of another race can support a charge of race discrimination.

Title VII—Color

This section within Title VII addresses the pigmentation or skin tone of an individual. This element was intended to halt the onerous "paper bag test" employed with African Americans: only if their skin tone was lighter than a paper bag would they be employed in front-desk or customer service positions. The skin tone of the alleged discriminating official may be the same as or similar to that of the target of discrimination; a complaint would still be viable. Harassment based on color might include the display of racially offensive symbols such as a noose, practices such as the paper bag test, or slurs, if they create a hostile or offensive work environment or result in an adverse employment action (Civil Rights Act, 1964).

Title VII—Religion

Incorporating religious practices into the workplace starts with a good-faith statement by the employee regarding the needs that might require accommodation. Even if a small or relatively unknown sect or group of individuals might follow these practices, the EEOC has held that the popularity of the beliefs is irrelevant (Civil Rights Act, 1964). The employer may challenge the nature of the beliefs in highly limited circumstances. If the religious beliefs are sincerely held, the employer must provide reasonable accommodation, unless doing so would impose an undue hardship on the operation of the employer's business. When the employer considers the applicant's or employee's religious observance or practice, it is important to solicit specific information from the individual. The requestor is responsible for explaining the functional impact on the employer, but has no requirement to explain or defend the tenets of the faith.

As an example, an employee may request authorization to pray at noon for 10 minutes each workday. She may cite her sincerely held religious belief without identifying the name of the religion. In order to make an informed decision, an employer faced with that vague request may open a dialogue that pinpoints the request in business terms. That inquiry might include when the employee will need to leave the workplace, when she will return to the workplace, and on what pay status she will take this time.

After receiving those specifics, the employer also will consider the employee's assigned position. Is she in charge of small children who require adult supervision at the time she requests? Is her unpaid 30-minute lunch break normally at noon? If the absence coincides with her scheduled midday meal break, which she may use in any way she sees fit, this solution represents coordination and communication. It involves no accommodation to religious observance. Religious accommodation occurs when the employer changes her regular 1 p.m. lunch break to noon.

In more complex cases, an employee's responsibilities might place him or her in a singular situation. An example might be a police officer, who must continue responding to a crisis no matter what the time of day. These cases call for the employer to discuss options with the employee. It is critical to ensure the employee's participation in developing the list of options. The employer then chooses which accommodation(s) to offer.

Title VII—Sex

Sex discrimination involves adverse actions taken because of a person's sex. These could include discriminatory practices in hiring, compensation, shift scheduling, assignments, and training opportunities.

Basic sex discrimination: Based on being male or female

In early cases resolved in this area, the hiring decisions in question favored the sex that had historically predominated in the role. These included cases involving the first male applicants for flight attendant positions. Respondent airlines defended the non-selection based on the image they were trying to create: male business travelers served in a home-like atmosphere by attractive, ostensibly single females. However, customer preference fails as a defense to claims of discrimination.

In the education arena, cases relating to tenure or continuing contract status consistently failed when the educational institution included stereotypes in its processes. One such stereotype involved the perceived likelihood of continuation in the position when assessing a female who had children or appeared of an age to have children. Because discrimination rests on a theory of comparability, an essential element of those cases was the frequent promotion and relative success of males who had children. The speculation of how children might affect the career of females (only) was held to be an invalid criterion for tenure.

More recently, and more importantly for higher education, cases highlighting class actions have become a higher priority for enforcement. Disparities in pay have been ruled unlawful when an institution asserts that males simply command a higher salary to join the teaching profession or to accept the specific position. Courts have taken a dim view of salary disparities based on sex when an employer stated only that applicants of one sex proved to be better negotiators than the applicants of the other sex.

Sex discrimination: Gender identity and sexual orientation

The EEOC also has published interpretations of sex discrimination that protect individuals based on gender identity and sexual orientation. The agency set an enforcement priority through at least the end of 2016 relating to efforts covering lesbian, gay, bisexual and transgender individuals under Title VII's sex discrimination provisions.

As with other areas, the alleged discriminating individual may have misidentified the gender of the complainant. If a biologically male applicant consistently expresses female gender in appearance and presentation during the application period, the hiring official may perceive the individual as female. If the hiring official refuses to hire the individual, stating that the position was better suited for men, that refusal would support a claim of discrimination based on sex.

Gender identity/expression differs from sexual orientation, although enforcement announcements collapse the descriptive term to LGBT.

- An applicant or employee has a sexual orientation: the person(s) to whom they are attracted (mainly described with terms such as heterosexual, homosexual, gay, lesbian, bisexual, pansexual, and asexual).
- An applicant or employee has a gender identity, a personal perception of being male, female, or some combination of the two that might be a gender or reflect a decision not to identify in the binary description (mainly known as genderfluid).
- An applicant or employee who identifies as a gender different from their biological sex at birth is known as transgender. This is accurate even without sex reassignment surgery: it refers to identity and expression.

Employers can avoid charges of sex discrimination from transitioning employees (male to female or female to male, for instance) by creating a transition plan that neutralizes all working conditions and terms of employment based on sex. Steps in such a plan might include changing ID badges to the employee's newly selected name; meeting with work contacts (without the employee present) to inform them of the transition and the use of a new name, identifying pronouns, and other indicators; and settling restroom questions.

In most states, a person of either biological sex can legally use any restroom regardless of posted sign. For reasons of safety, transgender individuals should use the restroom with the posted sign that reflects their gender identity and expression; this will reduce the likelihood of workplace hate crimes directed at individuals perceived to be using the "wrong" restroom. They may use that restroom regardless of whether they have completed gender-reassignment surgery.

Employers may provide single-user facilities but may not require a transgender employee to use them. Employees may indicate that they do not wish to use the multi-user restroom used by a transgender employee. Their preference may not be used to urge or require the transgender employee to use the single-user restroom. Those employees may choose to use the single-user restroom.

Sex discrimination: Sexual harassment

Sexual harassment is a type of sex discrimination that generally follows the same case law as that for harassment based on race or national origin, as an example. This similarity stems from the definition of harassment as offensive conduct that unreasonably interferes with employment terms or conditions, including performance. Sexual harassment has specific definitions: unwelcome sexual advances, requests for sexual favors, and other verbal or physical conduct of a sexual nature constitute sexual harassment when this conduct explicitly or implicitly affects an individual's employment, unreasonably interferes with performance, or creates a hostile, intimidating, or offensive environment.

Sexual harassment may include quid pro quo: the exchange of an employee's sexual favors for a positive action or the prevention of a negative action. Sexual harassment also is identified in patterns of behavior unrelated to any specific employment action but which create a hostile environment. It can include unwanted touching; subjecting the employee to sexually themed jokes or conversation; discussion of sexual topics with or near the employee; repeated requests for dates following a negative response; placement of sexual items where the employee will encounter them; and many other examples up to and including sexual assault.

Employers should ensure that such environments are corrected immediately when observed or reported, through emphasis on policy, discipline of those whose conduct is in question; or other strategies effective in eliminating the actions. This should preclude forced transfers of the targeted employee or any changes that might be perceived as adverse.

Employers may defeat the presumption that a supervisor acted for the institution when engaged in sexual harassment by providing supervisor training regarding the prohibition of sexual harassment, creating an effective policy statement and publicizing it well, and investigating promptly through an established procedure upon receiving a complaint.

Title VII: Sex discrimination—Pregnancy

Pregnancy is defined more broadly than the physical status of currently carrying a fetus (Pregnancy Discrimination Act, 1978). The Pregnancy Discrimination Act (1978) includes pregnancy, childbirth, or a medical condition related to pregnancy or childbirth in its definition. Females experiencing these conditions must be treated the same as other employees for all purposes related to employment.

This includes work that requires travel, as an example. An employer should assign travel as usual. A pregnant employee whose physician advises against travel, or who cannot meet the requirements of the common carrier, should be provided with an alternate strategy for accomplishing the responsibilities of the position. Similarly, an employer should continue consideration for leadership assignments, training opportunities, and promotions for the eligible employee who is pregnant.

If an employer considers males in staff positions for unpaid leaves of absence following exhaustion of all sick, annual, and compensatory time, the employer must consider females for such leaves of absence related to pregnancy. Parental leave, if offered by an employer, must be available to both male and female parents.

Each provision in the Pregnancy Discrimination Act (1978) addresses the right of the employee to continue working when she is able or to be treated similarly to any other employee when she is unable to work. This involves sick leave authorizations based on inability to work, without regard to the cause, and continuation of benefits during authorized leave, to the extent provided to other individuals on authorized leave.

Title VII—National Origin

National origin discrimination received heightened enforcement attention in 2015, and leaders in higher education are involved in many prevention strategies. In the wake of tragic events in the United States and internationally, federal agencies urged employers and educational leaders to renew efforts to prevent and correct harassment, intimidation, or discrimination based on national origin.

The EEOC issued a statement that referenced religion and national origin as factors that might lead to targeting of employees. It restated the Title VII prohibition of actions that compromise the safety and productivity of employees. The EEOC issued guidelines for employers who choose to be proactive in preventing and correcting harassment or discrimination, with an emphasis on individuals who are, or are perceived to be, Muslim or Middle Eastern.

The U.S. Department of Education issued a similar statement, listing its Office for Civil Rights (OCR) as the resource provider. The "Dear Colleague Letter", known as a DCL and often used to convey guidance without force of law, focused on the need to create and maintain safe spaces for students. It noted that discrimination and harassment of refugees are not new concepts and encouraged educational leaders to ensure that students face no discrimination or harassment based on race, religion, or national origin (real or perceived). The OCR also listed resources to guide leaders in this task. Table 10.1 provides a summary.

National origin differs from race. National origin refers to the country of birth, the part of the world from which an individual comes to the United States' jurisdiction, ethnicity from within a country, or even accents that suggest heritage. As with other types of discrimination, the alleged discriminating official could be wrong about the national origin of the complainant, but his or her perception can nonetheless be the basis for a successful charge if it led to an adverse action. As with race, sex, and other

Table 10.1 Strategies to Prevent Harassment and Discrimination Based on National Origin

Student Enrollment	Employment
• Refresh and publish reminders to students regarding existing consequences for name-calling, graffiti, or physical violence. • Encourage classroom discussions and other activities that examine issues faced by Syrian, Muslim, Middle Eastern, Arab, Sikh, Jewish, or students of color. Model learning styles that reflect respect and inquiry, rather than harassment or blame. • Foster free speech in settings that do not infringe on students' rights to pursue their education in a safe environment. • Help students feel comfortable in reporting concerns to instructors or other leaders. • Remind instructors, coaches, and club sponsors that misconduct is prohibited on campus and off when students participate in extra-curricular activities.	• Refresh and publish non-discrimination, anti-bullying, or civility policies, procedures, and institutional guidelines. • Encourage employees to report concerns to supervisors, Human Resources, or the equity representative. Early reports and resolutions may prevent teasing from escalating to harassment. • Utilize policies, procedures, and departmental guidelines regarding personal conversations on work time to minimize employees' questioning of a colleague's cultural or religious practices or beliefs. • Review dress codes and grooming codes to clearly define "business necessity." Facial hair may be prohibited on employees whose safety depends on a mask that seals tightly to the facial skin. A male whose religion calls for him to be bearded may be able to confirm alternate safety measures, or he may request a transfer to an equivalent position without the requirement. • Apply requirements for background checks impartially, regardless of applicants' national origin. • Remember that "customer preference" is not a valid criterion for adverse action, such as failure to hire.

categories, the national origin of the alleged discriminating party is irrelevant; it might be the same as that of the person claiming discrimination. Title VII covers terms and conditions of employment (Civil Rights Act, 1964). Title VI covers actions of federally funded programs, including education.

One of the most common violations of Title VII relating to national origin is the requirement to speak only English in the workplace. A broad statement to that effect, if not job-related and necessary to the operation of the business, is unlawful. Broad, unlawful statements would include language such as, "When this office is open, all employees will speak only English."

An employer may require employees executing work functions to speak only English if doing so promotes the safety and well-being of all employees (a non-discriminatory reason). This may be needed when the unit's mission is health care, and each member of the team must communicate clearly to all other members in the shortest possible time.

However, it is not job related to regulate an individual's conversation in a language other than English while that person is on a meal break or otherwise using personal time. Disciplining an employee for such an infraction could be considered discriminatory.

A related area of discrimination occurs when an individual's accent is used as the basis for an adverse action. This relates only to national origin: a Southern United States accent considered by some to represent a slow cadence or a New York accent considered by some to be fast paced would not qualify. The employer may take an action based on the employee's ability to communicate in English in situations experienced on the job, but not on an accent itself.

Table 10.2 Title VII Remedies and Avenues

Administrative	Judicial
• EEOC complaint substantiated	• Federal district court, regardless of EEOC finding
• EEOC negotiation with employer	• Declaratory relief
• EEOC notification that conciliation has been filed, with time for recipient to reply	• Injunctive relief
	• Attorney's fees and costs
• Civil action by U.S. Department of Justice, if recommended by EEOC	• Reinstatement with back pay up to two years (if discrimination was intentional)

The third most common area of complaint under this section is citizenship discrimination. An individual is eligible to work in the United States with appropriate documentation. Employers may not tell an applicant that he or she must present a driver's license and U.S. passport just because they are familiar with such documents. An employer may require such documentation if the job calls for U.S. citizenship as a qualification, such as in certain jobs requiring security clearances.

Title VII—Remedies

Table 10.2 presents the administrative and judicial components of Title VII.

AMERICANS WITH DISABILITIES ACT OF 1990

Disability discrimination by non-governmental employers was only loosely constrained prior to the Americans with Disabilities Act of 1990 (ADA). This Act (Pub. L. No. 101-336, 104 Stat. 327) was a landmark, including for the first time a large segment of private-sector employers. Prior to the ADA, employers such as schools and postsecondary institutions that accepted federal contracts responded to Sections 503 and 504 of the Rehabilitation Act of 1973 (Pub. L. No. 93-112, 87 Stat. 355) protecting against discrimination on the basis of disability. The Equal Employment Opportunity Commission investigates complaints of employment discrimination under all areas of the ADA. The U.S. Department of Education, OCR, investigates complaints from students.

The ADA prohibits employers from discriminating against qualified individuals with a disability (Pub. L. No. 101-336, 104 Stat. 327, 1990). Table 10.3 summarizes the components of the Americans with Disabilities Act of 1990.

There are many aspects to determining if an individual is covered by the ADA. The basic definition speaks to a physical or mental impairment that substantially limits a major life activity. After the status determination, the employer proceeds to identify a reasonable accommodation.

The status determination assumed a much lower threshold in 2008, when Congress passed the ADA Amendments Act (Pub. L. No. 110-325, 122 Stat. 3553). Now, an employer may assume that any substantial limitation of a major life activity or major bodily function will trigger the ADA coverage. The life activity may be unrelated to the job. Examples of major life activities include sleeping and lifting; examples of newly covered "major bodily functions" include circulatory or reproductive functions. It is irrelevant that the job does not require the employee to lift, or to reproduce. The status

Table 10.3 Components of the Americans with Disabilities Act of 1990

Section Description	Implementation Tips
Title I Employment—prohibits discrimination against qualified employees in the private sector and in state and local government; prohibits retaliation	Plan to offer reasonable accommodation to the known physical or mental limitations of an otherwise qualified applicant or employee with a disability.
Title II Public Entities and Transportation—programs, activities, services of public entities	Ensure both physical access and program access. The educational program includes such learning strategies as readers, interpreters, technological assistance, extended time on tests, among others.
Title III Public Accommodations (commercial facilities)	Consider accessibility of the institution's public retail outlets, lodging, recreation, transportation, dining, places of public display. If the public can access a location without an institutional ID or registration, Title III covers it. Institutions must remove architectural barriers and observe barrier-free building standards.
Title IV Telecommunications	Led to wide use of Telecommunications Device for the Deaf (TDD) installations. Established foundation for dual-party relay systems in all 50 states, where deaf individuals call an operator on a TDD and the operator voices information over a telephone and vice versa.
Title V Miscellaneous provisions	Specifies the non-retaliation provisions.

of a substantial limitation in lifting or reproducing makes the employee an individual with a disability (ADA Amendments Act, 2008).

An employer also may trigger coverage with an action that implies belief that the individual has a disability, even if that is not the case (ADA Amendments Act, 2008). If the employer does not promote the employee to a position involving public presentations because of a fear that clients will not respond well to an individual with a prominent scar, the employer has discriminated based on the belief that the individual has a substantial limitation.

In addition, if an employer refuses to hire applicants because they attended a school known for addressing a particular health condition or status, such as deafness, the employer has regarded the applicant as an individual with a disability. That refusal to hire, regardless of whether the applicants actually are deaf or hard of hearing, is unlawful.

There are transitory and minor conditions that do not trigger ADA protection. Generally, transitory conditions are those that a physician expects to heal or resolve within six months (ADA Amendments Act, 2008). The ADA required no accommodation. Recent interpretations caution that the severity of the condition (no matter the projected duration) may require the employer to treat the condition as a disability. For example, an individual treated for a wound might submit a request for extended leave. The wound is expected to heal or resolve, but at this time the individual is severely impaired. The leave time may call for an accommodation, such as an extension of leave without pay following any Family and Medical Leave Act (FMLA) benefits.

The employer is responsible for screening against the definition of "an otherwise qualified individual." A qualified individual can perform the essential functions of the position with or without reasonable accommodation (ADA Amendments Act, 2008). Examples of individuals not qualified would include employees terminated for violating conduct rules or applicants who do not possess the minimum posted qualifications. In those cases, the individual is not otherwise qualified no matter what his or her physical or mental condition. Employers who define essential functions prior to filling the job present a defensible rationale for applying those decisions later, because they made the decisions without knowing the applicants in the pool.

If pre-employment skill tests are essential elements of the hiring process, they must be required of all applicants. Employers must offer applicants accommodations such as speech-to-text or text-to-speech versions of tests, adjustments in time, or use of specific equipment when that is reasonable. On the job, reasonable accommodations might include readers, sign language interpreters, speech-to-text or text-to-speech technology, or modified work schedules.

An employer must offer a reasonable accommodation unless doing so would pose an undue hardship on the operation of that employer's business (ADA Amendments Act, 2008). The EEOC regards employers in large systems (public universities, state or community colleges, school districts) as single employers with access to substantial resources. The EEOC is likely to compare the cost of an accommodation with the total institutional budget to test the assertion that the cost was an unreasonable burden.

The ADA Amendments Act (2008) clarified several definitions left vague in competing federal district court cases. Most pertinent to educational leaders, the ADA Amendments Act (2008) specified that employers must consider applicants and employees without mitigating measures such as medicine or technological support. If their physical or mental condition produces a disability without medication, therapy, or accommodation, they are individuals with disabilities (ADA Amendments Act, 2008).

Examples include individuals who control diabetes with insulin, regulating their blood sugar to acceptable levels each day, and individuals with multiple sclerosis, who may have intermittent days on which they experience mobility impairments. Substantially limiting conditions (even when helped with medication) or conditions that produce substantial limitations only intermittently are disabilities.

The definitions of discrimination within the ADA include two types: limiting or classifying employees to deprive them of opportunities, or a failure to accommodate (ADA, 1990). There are specific exemptions to the ADA, such as current illegal use of drugs, status as an individual with a communicable disease when no reasonable accommodation will achieve safety for the food supply, near-sightedness corrected with corrective lenses, and compulsive gambling.

FAMILY AND MEDICAL LEAVE ACT OF 1993

The Family and Medical Leave Act of 1993 ([FMLA], Pub. L. No. 103-3, 107 Stat. 6) provides a safety net for parents, caregivers, and employees who experience a serious illness. This law protects the individual's job during his or her absence, without guaranteeing paid leave status. The U.S. Department of Labor investigates FMLA claims. The employer must consider whether the employee is eligible, whether the purpose meets the definition in the law, and how the employee must document the authorized leave.

After all these steps are taken, what does the employee actually receive? The employee's absence is authorized, and he or she returns to the same or a similar position. The leave is limited to 12 workweeks in any 12-month period (FMLA, 1993). Some employers fix that period, starting the calculation over on July 1 or January 1 of each year. Others follow the definition of the 12-month period, floating the period from the current date to 12 months ago to determine the remaining authorization for leave.

The authorization under the law relates to unpaid leave, but employers may grant paid leave in accordance with their policies. Common types of paid leave include sick, annual, and accrued compensatory time. Employers determine eligibility first by considering the size of their workforce; smaller employers may be exempt from this law. They then look to the employee's work history to confirm that the employee has worked there for at least 1,250 hours in the 12 months prior to the leave. Military service and collective bargaining agreements impact these calculations as well.

FMLA leave is provided for specific purposes, which have been enhanced since the 1993 passage of the law. These purposes are as follows:

- birth and care of a newborn child of the employee; bonding time;
- placement with the employee of a child for adoption or foster care; bonding time;
- care for a one-degree relative (spouse, parent, or child) with a serious health condition—in-laws are not covered in this definition;
- inability of the employee to work due to a serious health condition;
- circumstances relating to the employee's spouse, child, or parent who is on active military duty or called to active duty from Reserve, National Guard status, or Regular Armed Forces. An employee may care for a covered service member with a serious injury or illness for up to 26 weeks.

The employer may collect documentation to support the use of leave under the FMLA. Certain illnesses might occur suddenly, providing no opportunity to notify the employer at that time. Notice must follow in a reasonable time. In situations where notice is possible, the employee is required to provide it. When medical treatments are pre-scheduled, the employee must show reasonable care to avoid disrupting the business functions.

The employee may utilize intermittent leave for medical care, such as chemotherapy or physical therapy. This may involve reducing the normal work schedule and taking FMLA leave for part of a day or a week. The employer may choose whether to approve intermittent leave related to the birth and care of a child, or the placement of a child for adoption or foster care.

The definitions of a serious health condition differ from medical concepts within the Americans with Disabilities Act, which deals with "substantial limitations to a major life activity or major bodily function" (ADA Amendments, 2008). For the FMLA, there are several definitions of a serious health condition. They include a physical or mental condition that calls for inpatient care (an overnight stay) in a treatment facility; conditions causing incapacity for more than three days; chronic conditions causing incapacity more than twice a year; and pregnancy (including prenatal medical appointments and incapacity due to "morning sickness").

As an example, an employee reports that he experienced suicidal behaviors, was admitted by a psychiatrist to a residential care facility for two days, and then was prescribed strong drugs to regulate his mood and behaviors. During the drugs' adjustment period, he was unable to work or perform other daily activities. The physician cleared him for return to work on the seventh workday following the admission date. The employer checks the employment record: the date of hire was two years ago, and the employee has taken no leaves of absence or other significant interruptions, just vacations. The employee meets the tests of 12 months of employment with that employer as well as 1,250 working hours in the past 12 months. He meets the test of a serious health condition: it required inpatient care. He meets the test of incapacity: the physician documented that he could not work while the drugs were taking effect and the dosage was regulated. In this example, all seven workdays of absence (date of admission plus six more) would be authorized under the FMLA.

To take this example a step further, it may be assumed that this employer offers sick and annual leave accrual to employees. The employee has 17 hours of sick leave and 3 hours of annual leave accrued. The employee may choose to use all 20 leave hours to place him in pay status within the 56 hours of leave. The employer may withhold pay for the balance, 36 hours of absence. However, the employer may not take any adverse action because of that 36-hour leave without pay status.

The FMLA also protects employees requiring intermittent leave. The provisions related to intermittent care are extensive, and the summary in Table 10.4 is general in nature.

Educational leaders may authorize leave in complex situations involving two or more laws. The following example illustrates a balance of the Family and Medical Leave Act and the Americans with Disabilities Act. The employee has developed a serious health condition (cancer). Over the past two years of employment, she has taken extensive periods of leave without pay. The employer measures FMLA entitlement by fiscal year starting July 1. The employee provided a physician's statement containing all the elements the employer needed: her name, treating physician's full contact information, duration

Table 10.4 Summary of Eligible Leave Circumstances for Continuing Care

FMLA Provision	Guidelines and Strategies
Incapacity lasting more than three days, including certain treatment schedules	The employer may require documentation related to the specific definitions involving dates of treatment and continuing treatment regimens.
Prenatal care or incapacity related to pregnancy	The employee is not required to visit a health care provider for each episode.
Treatment for or incapacity based on a chronic serious health condition which continues over an extended period of time	The employee is not required to visit a health care provider for each episode.
Permanent or long-term incapacity for a condition for which treatment may not be effective	The employer may require documentation of supervision of a health care provider, but active treatment is not required.
Multiple treatments for restorative surgery or a condition that would result in more than three days' incapacity if not treated	The employer may require documentation related to the specific definitions involving the condition and the dates of treatment.

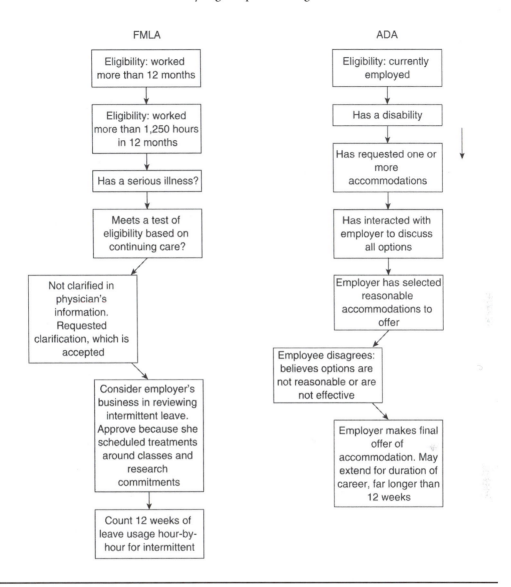

Figure 10.1 Flow Chart for FMLA and ADA

of the condition, prognosis, functional limitations, ability to perform certain job tasks, and expected date of recovery or return to work. She requests intermittent leave and preservation of the same job. She is a faculty member with an active research program involving live cell cultures and experiments.

To determine her FMLA eligibility, conduct the following analysis using the flow chart in Figure 10.1: Has the employee worked for this employer for at least one year? Did the employee work 1,250 hours this eligibility year? Is the illness serious? If the employee meets at least one test of eligibility based on continuing care, then proceed. The employee is eligible for FMLA if she provides clarification for intermittent leave.

For ADA eligibility, conduct the following analysis using the flow chart in Figure 10.1: Is the employee currently employed for the period foreseen by the leave? Is the employee an individual with a disability? What other options are possible in addition to intermittent leave (discuss with employee)? The options must be reasonable. It would not be reasonable to eliminate research from her assignments or to pay her full time for research and eliminate all her teaching duties. If intermittent leave is not approvable, the employer has to offer something equivalent. The employer and employee must negotiate over the offered accommodation.

AGE DISCRIMINATION IN EMPLOYMENT ACT OF 1967

Under the Age Discrimination in Employment Act ([ADEA], Pub. L. No. 90-202, 81 Stat. 602, 1967), the protected class starts at age 40 and continues without limit. No employer may take an adverse employment action based on age. This law echoes other civil rights laws in prohibiting retaliation for having complained or participated in a complaint. Congress intended the ADEA to prohibit artificial barriers to employment, such as arbitrary age limits or requirements for retirement. The law encourages employers to base decisions on the potential for full job performance. Similar to Title VII, it prohibits two types of actions by employers: actions within terms and conditions of employment, and harassment based on age.

The ADEA covers hiring, compensation, promotion, training, and other employment factors. Employers also should be mindful of the work environment: if the employer tolerates an atmosphere in which an older worker is referred to as "Gramps," his parking space is decorated with a "Dinosaur Parking" sign, and canes or mobility aids appear at his desk, that employer may be tolerating a hostile environment based on age. The Equal Employment Opportunity Commission investigates complaints of discrimination under all areas of the ADEA.

Congress recognized that age may be a BFOQ, but the EEOC has limited the application of this possibility. Employers may set a minimum age for employment consistent with state and federal labor restrictions. Congress also authorized the payment of pension benefits that differ according to the age of the recipient as well as the decision of an employer to offer an early retirement incentive plan if based on employer needs.

One of the most common complaints results from a reduction in force (RIF) following economic trends. Employers may select the smallest number of higher paid employees necessary to balance the budget in an RIF, unintentionally selecting the oldest employees in the workforce. When they are the only individuals laid off, it creates an adverse impact for those in the protected age category of 40 and older.

The EEOC recommends that employers use analyses that determine which employees are "similarly situated." That term refers to individuals who are similar in terms of compensation, position, date of hire, work history, and other relevant factors, such as performance appraisals and lead-worker status. Use of those factors in layoffs can be documented as neutral in regard to age.

The ADEA contains a specific requirement for ample notice and time to consider all settlements. This notice provision differs from other civil rights laws and should be strictly observed.

CONCLUSION

This chapter discussed how the Family Educational Rights and Privacy Act, the Higher Education Opportunity Act of 2008, the Copyright Act of 1976, the Technology Education and Copyright Harmonization Act of 2002, the Civil Rights Act of 1964, the Americans with Disabilities Act of 1990, the Family and Medical Leave Act of 1993, and the Age Discrimination in Employment Act of 1967 apply to institutions of higher education. Each of these laws has complexities and provisions outside the limits of this chapter, whose purpose was to acquaint higher education administrators with important points to consider when implementing policies. This information should also be useful when administrators inevitably encounter issues; however, administrators should seek legal counsel. Each law may have a different purpose, but, like the threads of a blanket, they all combine to provide a flexible yet protective shield.

DISCUSSION PROMPTS

1. What are the circumstances under which a postsecondary institution is permitted to share information with a student's parent?
2. Are there circumstances under which a postsecondary institution may share information about student A with student B?
3. What are the mandatory provisions for written agreements under the studies exception to the protections of FERPA? How do these mandatory provisions differ for the audit and evaluation exception? What are some additional best practices that institutions may want to consider before sharing information under either exception?
4. How can higher education leaders avoid disparate treatment and disparate impact in employment policies? Which areas of a university's programs are subject to federal discrimination charges?
5. What are the considerations in setting a BFOQ in a hiring action?
6. What additional information would you need to assess the liability of an employer when the complainant, African American, names an African American supervisor as the alleged discriminating official?
7. What is the difference between gender identity/expression and sexual orientation? Discrimination on either basis is prohibited by Title VII as types of sex discrimination.
8. What are examples of sexual harassment other than an unwelcome sexual advance or touch, such as a hostile environment? An intimidating environment? An offensive environment?
9. When do colleagues' interested questions about an employee's culture, heritage, or religion become harassment based on national origin?
10. Briefly, how does the FMLA differ from the ADA? What should a higher education leader do when receiving a request for religious accommodation? How does an employer review a request for accommodation to a disability?

REFERENCES

ADA Amendments Act of 2008, Pub. L. No. 110-325, 122 Stat. 3553 (2008).

Age Discrimination in Employment Act, Pub. L. No. 90-202, 81 Stat. 602 (1967).

Americans with Disabilities Act of 1990, Pub. L. No. 101-336, 104 Stat. 327 (1990).

Ashley, C. L. (2004). The TEACH Act: Higher education challenges for compliance. *Educause Center for Applied Research—Research Bulletin, 2004*(13), 1–11. Retrieved December 10, 2011, from http://net.educause.edu/ir/library/pdf/ERB0413.pdf

Civil Rights Act of 1964, Pub. L. No. 88-52, 78 Stat. 241 (1964).

Civil Rights Act of 1991, Pub. L. No. 102-166, 105 Stat. 1071 (1991).

Civil Rights Restoration Act of 1987, Pub. L. No. 100-259, 102 Stat. 28 (1988).

Copyright Act, 17 U.S.C. §101 *et seq.* (2016).

Education Amendments of 1974, Pub. L. No. 93-380, 88 Stat. 484 (1974).

Family and Medical Leave Act of 1993, Pub. L. No. 103-3, 107 Stat. 6 (1993).

Family Educational Rights and Privacy Act, 20 U.S.C. §1232g (2016).

Family Educational Rights and Privacy Rule, 34 C.F.R. §99 (2015).

Griggs v. Duke Power Company, 401 U.S. 424 (1971).

Grove City College v. Bell, 465 U.S. 555 (1984).

Higher Education Opportunity Act of 2008, Pub. L. No. 110-315, 122 Stat. 3078 (2008).

Hutchens, N. H. (2011). Systems governance. In R. Fossey, K. B. Melear, & J. B. Beckham (Eds.), *Contemporary issues in higher education law* (2nd ed.) (pp. 19–36). Dayton, Ohio: Education Law Association.

Pregnancy Discrimination Act of 1978, Pub. L. No. 95-555, 92 Stat. 2076 (1978).

Rehabilitation Act of 1973, Pub. L. No. 93-112, 87 Stat. 355 (1973).

Technology Education and Copyright Harmonization Act, Pub. L. No. 112-278, §13301, 116 Stat. 1910 (2002).

Uninterrupted Scholars Act, Pub. L. No. 112-278, 126 Stat. 2480 (2013).

11

TITLE IX AND THE IMPACT ON COLLEGES AND UNIVERSITIES TODAY AND OVER THE NEXT DECADE

Amelia Parnell and Andrew Morse

INTRODUCTION

Minnie Kovitch, the vice president for student affairs at a large public institution in the southeast United States, has just returned from a three-day workshop on Title IX compliance. Minnie, who has been in her role for three years, previously held the same role at a small, private institution. She knows that her current institution has taken primary steps to comply with Title IX but realizes more can be done to prepare for the possible challenges that lie ahead. As Minnie stays attuned to the national discourse around gender-based violence, sexual assault, and gender equity on college campuses, she has determined that her institution needs a more holistic approach to addressing Title IX. She decides to form a campus workgroup composed of administrators from several divisions to discuss the relevance of Title IX to all major functions on the campus and to identify key areas and considerations for effectively managing compliance over the next decade.

Minnie invites the Title IX coordinator, director of campus activities, chair of the faculty senate, chief of police, director of the counseling center, and general counsel to participate in the group. She is aware that the members' respective roles in helping the institution comply with Title IX may at times create difficult conversations regarding the process for handling issues that arise. In her invitation to the group, Minnie explains that the primary purpose of their convening will be to engage in thoughtful dialogue and careful review of how the institution's existing resources, policies, and procedures are used to create and sustain safe learning environments for all students. She wants the group to stay connected to student perspectives of the institution, so she also invites the president of the student government association to periodically confer with the workgroup on certain topics.

Minnie starts the first group meeting by asking each member to answer one question: How can we work together to effectively comply with Title IX in ways that help our students feel supported, our administrators feel prepared to make good decisions, and our external communities feel welcome to engage?

Since its enactment more than four decades ago, Title IX of the Education Amendments of 1972, 20 U.S.C. §1681 (Title IX) has made important steps toward defining campus' responsibilities to prevent and address discrimination based on sex in education programs or activities that receive financial assistance from the United States Department of Education. Although decades old, the effort to create and maintain compliance with the legislation's scope and intent has remained an imperative element of the responsibilities of college and university leaders. To that end, the enforcement agency for Title IX, the Department of Education's Office for Civil Rights (OCR), has published numerous documents offering guidance and technical assistance with the law (United States Department of Education, 2015). Three overarching policy domains have captured the interest of federal officials: equal opportunity in athletics, sexual harassment, and gender-based violence. The OCR has published comprehensive technical assistance to support institutional efforts to comply with the scope and intent of the law (United States Department of Education, 2015). With an understanding of recent action related to Title IX, administrators can leverage leadership and knowledge to create equitable institutions that deliver on the intent of this broad federal law.

With regard to the impact of Title IX on colleges and universities in the coming years, a discussion of future implications must first acknowledge a significant shift that has occurred over the past decade. Although Title IX has laid the foundation for multiple successes in colleges' approaches to providing equal opportunities for men and women who participate in athletics, the law has also illuminated serious concerns about how institutions prevent and address sexual harassment and gender-based violence. Title IX compliance in the next decade will still have important connections to colleges' allocation and use of athletic and academic resources, but these connections will likely be overshadowed by the issues of gender-based violence and sexual harassment until more institutions have sufficiently addressed what some have described as an epidemic. This chapter will begin with a discussion of the evolving application of Title IX in higher education settings with a focus on athletics, followed by considerations for academic and co-curricular resources, gender-based violence, and sexual harassment. Woven into the discussion will be explanations of the components of Title IX and related laws, the impact of these laws on the management of colleges and universities, campus applications of regulatory guidance, and state and federal policy implications.

LEGAL AND REGULATORY COMPONENTS OF TITLE IX

As college administrators determine strategies for effectively managing the requirements of Title IX for today and the next decade, they must have a clear understanding of what the law requires. Title IX of the Education Amendments of 1972, 20 U.S.C. has eight sections, enumerated below:

1681. Sex.

  (a) Prohibition against discrimination; exceptions.
  (b) Preferential or disparate treatment because of imbalance in participation or receipt of Federal benefits; statistical evidence of imbalance.
  (c) "Educational institution" defined.

1682. Federal administrative enforcement; report to Congressional committees.
1683. Judicial review.
1684. Blindness or visual impairment; prohibition against discrimination.
1685. Authority under other laws unaffected.
1686. Interpretation with respect to living facilities.
1687. Interpretation of "program or activity".
1688. Neutrality with respect to abortion.

Much of the focus on Title IX in college settings relates to section 1681, which addresses discrimination based on sex in subsection (a) with the following statement:

> No person in the United States shall, on the basis of sex, be excluded from participation in, be denied the benefits of, or be subjected to discrimination under any education program or activity receiving Federal financial assistance.

Title IX further defines "educational institution" as:

> any public or private preschool, elementary, or secondary school, or any institution of vocational, professional, or higher education, except that in the case of an educational institution composed of more than one school, college, or department which are administratively separate units, such term means each such school, college, or department.

With regard to an "education program or activity", Title IX refers to operations of state and local governments, as well as those of a college, university, or other postsecondary institution, or a public system of higher education.

Equal Opportunity in Athletics

In 1979, the Department of Education articulates the Title IX obligations of postsecondary institutions that offer athletics programs and outlines the guidelines by which the Department's enforcement authority, the OCR, will determine compliance with equal opportunity to participation in athletics (United States Department of Education, 1979). This decades-old document has framed the contours of federal non-discrimination policy undergirding college athletics and is still in effect today. Embedded throughout it are comprehensive provisions that administrators should take due care to understand and apply to their campus settings to ensure that institutional policies and practices related to athletics are non-discriminatory in language and effect. Two key elements of compliance with Title IX in athletics programs are the amount of financial support (i.e., scholarship aid) that is distributed between men's and women's intercollegiate athletics programs and the selection of sports in an institution's athletics program. The Department stated that compliance with Title IX in athletics will be determined primarily by comparing the distribution of scholarship aid to examine whether proportionately equal amounts of such assistance are made available to men's and women's athletic programs (United States Department of Education, 1979, Section VII(A)). If the amounts are substantially equal, an institution is found to be in compliance with the law (United States Department of Education, 1979, Section VII(A)).

This language has been grounds for confusion throughout the decades. Following an inquiry by Bowling Green State University, for example, OCR published a Dear College letter (DCL) to clarify the levers by which it determined non-compliance with the proportionately equal clauses of aid distributions of athletics scholarship (Cantú, 1998). In particular, the guidance articulated that OCR does not mandate institutions to award the same number of scholarships to men and women who are engaged in intercollegiate athletics programs (Cantú, 1998). The law does require that individual scholarships maintain equal value and that the total amount of scholarship aid be substantially proportionate to the overall participation rates at a particular postsecondary institution. In the DCL, Cantú (1998) articulated:

> Thus, for example, if men are 60% of the athletes, OCR would expect that the men's athletic scholarship budget would be within 59%–61% of the total budget for athletic scholarships for all athletes, after accounting for legitimate nondiscriminatory reasons for any larger disparity.

Further, in articulating the elements of compliance, the Department has published two examples through which disproportionality in scholarship aid may not result in a determination of non-compliance. First, at public institutions out-of-state tuition and fees may result in uneven distributions of scholarship aid in a particular year or set of years (United States Department of Education, 1979). In these cases, the institution must take precautions to avoid policies or practices that lead to the disproportionate award of out-of-state scholarships for men or women. Such precautions may include an audit of the procedures by which athletics departments recruit and award scholarships to athletes from out of state to ensure consistency and collaboration across athletics units to avoid inadvertent missteps with the law. Second, when most appropriate for program development, institutions may reasonably make award decisions that enable an athletics department to build a particular team by spreading scholarships across the four years of an athlete's participation in a team sport. This could possibly lead to disproportions in aid (United States Department of Education, 1979). In such cases, where program development may contribute to the disproportionate awards of scholarship aid, the institution should take precautions to provide clear documentation to support the rationale for such a decision, providing a detailed record of the amount and term of the awards.

When it comes to selecting athletics programs, it is important to note that Title IX does not require institutions to offer the same sports to both men and women (United States Department of Education, 1979, 1997, 2010; Reynolds, 2003; Spellings, 2008). The spirit of the law is to affirm that the institution effectively accommodates the interests and abilities of both male and female athletes and that the participation by sex is proportionate to the respective numbers of male and female students. Additionally, institutions that operate or sponsor a team in a particular sport for members of only one sex must allow the excluded sex to try out for the team (34 C.F.R. §106.41). However, current law exempts sports in which bodily contact is the purpose or a major activity—including, but not necessarily limited to, boxing, wrestling, rugby, ice hockey, football, and basketball (34 C.F.R. §106.41(b)).

To evaluate institutional accommodation of student interests and abilities in a manner consistent with the non-discrimination policies articulated in Title IX, OCR established a three-part test and requires institutions to demonstrate compliance with only one of the parts (United States Department of Education, 1979, 1997). This test was first released in the Department of Education's 1979 Policy Interpretation letter and has remained intact throughout the decades. It is outlined below:

OCR Three-Part Test to Determine Non-Discrimination in Athletics Programs

1. Whether intercollegiate level participation opportunities for male and female students are provided in numbers substantially proportionate to their respective enrollments; or
2. Where the members of one sex have been and are underrepresented among inter-collegiate athletes, whether the institution can show a history and continuing practice of program expansion which is demonstrably responsive to the developing interests and abilities of the members of that sex; or
3. Where the members of one sex are underrepresented among intercollegiate athletes, and the institution cannot show a history and continuing practice of program expansion, as described above, whether it can be demonstrated that the interests and abilities of the members of that sex have been fully and effectively accommodated by the present program.

Situating institutions for compliance and the effective management of college athletics involves at least two consonant streams of thought and action. First is the precedent set by a raft of implementing regulation and interpretive guidance which has bolstered the legal architecture of Title IX's provisions as they relate to non-discrimination based on sex in college athletics. In a 2008 letter to petitioners, for instance, then-Secretary of Education Margaret Spellings articulated that nearly 20 years of case law have conferred substantial deference on the legal defensibility of the Three-Part Test as an enforcement mechanism for non-discrimination in athletics programs. Second is the recognition that our nation continues to widen its evolving definition of acceptance and inclusion in both social and legal settings, giving rise to new expectations that may not explicitly be covered under existing law. In the spirit of progress, these should be addressed from a perspective of broad inclusiveness. Reflecting a tipping point in the visibility and acceptance of transgender individuals in sport, for example, Harvard University became the first institution to allow a transgender athlete to make the transition from the women's to the men's swimming and diving teams. These consonant streams require us to hold closely to our legal past, but keep our sights firmly set on the future and call upon us to define and refine strategies that empower our campus communities to deliver compliance and excellence in tandem. The effective management of athletics in a manner that accords with Title IX and encompasses our nation's evolving definition of inclusion need not be done in silos.

Title IX is not a mandate for all that campuses can and should do to affirm equal opportunity for student athletes. Embedded in the provisions and technical assistance of the law are areas of latitude to create and maintain student experiences that bolster holistic student learning and development. Though designated officials may hold authority for compliance with law and regulation, these individuals can work to anticipate the facets of the student athlete experience that are not addressed in the law, how their experiences may differ along demographic lines, and the ways in which campus partners can provide attention and leadership to affirm inclusive policy actions and support systems where needed. It may be helpful, for instance, to work within existing assessment teams to examine points of difference that fall along demographic lines in the use of and experiences with academic and student support services on campus. Coordinating with heads of the various functional areas can yield strategies to anticipate and address inequities that may occur among student athletes.

Further, our nation's growing acceptance of transgender individuals will continue to extend across and within our nation's social and economic structures. Indeed, this is a trend that will continue to gain resonance within college and university athletics programs as transitioning athletes look toward their destination institutions and teams for the acceptance and inclusion they deserve. Such momentum will increasingly require institutional leaders to proactively engage in efforts to build support and policy structures that ensure equal opportunity to participation while affirming positive and welcoming campus experiences. Leadership strategies like these enable institutions to hold hands with the legal past of Title IX within athletics while looking toward the future of higher education as one of our nation's most integral social and economic structures.

Resources on Anticipating and Addressing Compliance Responsibilities for Title IX and Athletics

- Code of Federal Regulations 34 C.F.R. § 106.41 Athletics: The full list of current Title IX regulations related to intercollegiate athletics programs. Accessible at http://www2.ed.gov/policy/rights/reg/ocr/edlite-34cfr106.html#S41
- Policy Interpretation of Title IX and Intercollegiate Athletics: Originally published in 1979, this document offers a comprehensive overview of the criteria by which institutions are examined for compliance with each element of Title IX as it relates to intercollegiate athletics. Accessible at http://www2.ed.gov/about/offices/list/ocr/docs/t9interp.html
- 2007 DCL on the application of Title IX regulatory requirements in the context of non-discriminatory treatment of pregnant students in the issuance of athletic scholarships. This letter offers technical guidance on the appropriate handling of scholarship awards to pregnant student athletes under Title IX. Accessible at http://www2.ed.gov/about/offices/list/ocr/letters/colleague-20070625.html
- 2003 DCL further clarifying the use of the three-prong test for Title IX non-discrimination in Athletics programs. This letter offers a reaffirmation of the 1996 Dear Colleague Letter on the use of the Three-Part Test to determine compliance with athletics non-discrimination regulations under Title IX. Accessible at http://www2.ed.gov/about/offices/list/ocr/title9guidanceFinal.html

- 1998 DCL articulating guidance on the funding of athletics scholarships under Title IX non-discrimination regulations. This letter offers technical assistance on the criteria that the Department of Education's OCR uses to evaluate compliance with the appropriate distribution of scholarship funds to athletes. Accessible at http://www2.ed.gov/about/offices/list/ocr/docs/bowlgrn.html
- 1996 DCL clarifying the Three-Part Test to determine non-discrimination in athletics participation under Title IX. This letter offers technical guidance on institutional compliance with the Three-Part Test to determine compliance with athletics non-discrimination regulation under Title IX. Accessible at http://www2.ed.gov/about/offices/list/ocr/docs/clarific.html#one

Gender-Based Harassment and Sexual Violence

Although Title IX broadly applies to a number of academic and co-curricular settings, programs, and activities, one area of increased attention is its application to incidents of sexual harassment and sexual violence. Research suggests that although one in five college students will be a victim of sexual violence, these incidents are largely under-reported. Sexual violence can create a disruptive learning environment that places an institution in violation of Title IX requirements; thus, administrators are keenly focused on guidance from OCR regarding compliance with Title IX. The Jeanne Clery Disclosure of Campus Security and Campus Crime Statistics Act (Clery Act) is also an area that commands close attention.

Office for Civil Rights Guidance

In 1997, OCR issued *Sexual Harassment Guidance: Harassment of Students by School Employees, Other Students, or Third Parties*, which included guidance on the applicability of Title IX to public and private higher education institutions (United States Department of Education, 1997). Following the release of the 1997 Guidance, the United States Supreme Court issued several important decisions related to sexual harassment cases under Title IX. As a result, OCR issued revised guidance in 2001 (United States Department of Education, 2001). This guidance further established a foundation for applying Title IX to incidents of sexual harassment and violence on college campuses by stating that "when a student sexually harasses another student, the harassing conduct creates a hostile environment if the conduct is sufficiently serious that it interferes with or limits a student's ability to participate in or benefit from the school's program".

The 2001 Guidance includes six elements that colleges should use to determine whether their grievance procedures provide for prompt and equitable resolution of sexual harassment and sexual violence complaints:

1. Notice to students and employees of the grievance procedures, including where complaints may be filed;
2. Application of the procedures to complaints alleging harassment carried out by employees, other students, or third parties;
3. Adequate, reliable, and impartial investigation of complaints, including the opportunity for both parties to present witnesses and other evidence;
4. Designated and reasonably prompt time frames for the major stages of the complaint process;

5. Notice to parties of the outcome of the complaint; and
6. An assurance that the institution will take steps to prevent recurrence of any harassment and to correct its discriminatory effects on the complainant and others, if appropriate.

In 2011, to supplement the 2001 Guidance and help colleges effectively comply with Title IX requirements, OCR released a DCL. The DCL includes effective steps for addressing and preventing sexual harassment and violence, including proactive approaches for addressing recurrence. Title IX implementing regulations specifically require institutions to complete three procedures: disseminate a notice of non-discrimination; designate at least one employee to coordinate its efforts to comply with and carry out its responsibilities under Title IX; and adopt and publish grievance procedures for prompt and equitable resolution of student and employee sex discrimination complaints.

Some administrators, particularly those who have higher levels of personal interaction with students, are concerned that focusing too narrowly on compliance could result in unintended, and possibly harmful, consequences. As administrators consider how to respond to sexual violence with approaches that are both nurturing and compliant with the law, for instance, it is imperative that careful attention be placed on the methods by which students, both victims and accused, are treated throughout the entire process following a report of sexual violence. For example, institutions that are informed by a student that they have been a victim of sexual violence are required by Title IX to notify the student of their right to file a complaint with local law enforcement and any available resources such as counseling or health services. This could present a difficult challenge for administrators to achieve a balance of being sensitive to the student's needs and complying with the law, as certain types of communication could, if handled inappropriately, threaten confidentiality. For example, if an institution sends a letter to a student's home address detailing the reporting options, that letter may expose details of the encounter to the student's parent or guardian.

In recent years, OCR guidance has sought to articulate the strategies by which institutions can comply with the provisions and spirit of Title IX by embedding trauma-informed practices while managing our constant expectation to uphold fairness for all parties involved in a report of sexual violence. For example, additional DCL released between 2010 and 2015 provide guidance pertaining to college and university Title IX coordinators, allegations of sexual violence, proactive efforts to prevent sexual violence and educate employees and students, bullying, and discriminatory harassment (Lhamon, 2015; Ali, 2011; United States Department of Education, 2014; Ali, 2010).

Key Leadership Strategies on Campus Sexual Violence Prevention and Handling

Coordinated Community Response Teams (CCRTs): CCRTs operate as cross-functional networks of staff, faculty, institutional leaders, and community stakeholders such as law enforcement and victim advocates to leverage existing prevention, handling, and responses processes on campus to encompass sexual violence, domestic violence, sexual harassment, and other forms of gender-based violence as it may occur on campus. These individuals connect to assess areas of improvement in campus' efforts to prevent and address sexual misconduct and harassment and to lead efforts to bolster campus policy and practice where it may be needed. Because these teams comprise a network of stakeholders, CCRTs act as an efficient way to share knowledge with their offices and divisions across campus or within the broader community.

Campus Climate Surveys: One key purpose of these surveys is to capture actual incidents of sexual misconduct that may or may not have been reported through campus law enforcement or student conduct channels, or through local law enforcement. Another is to capture the perceived climate on campus as it relates to campus safety in the context of the prevention and handling of sexual misconduct. Administered with the protection of respondent anonymity, these instruments seek to yield insights about students' experiences with and perceptions of sexual misconduct that may not be captured through conduct and law enforcement channels. Such insights may provide a richer depiction of the landscape of actual and perceived campus safety issues and provide added layers of knowledge to support efforts to bolster safe, inclusive, and welcoming environments for all students.

Prevention and Intervention Programming: Educating the campus community—including staff, faculty, and students—about what sexual assault, domestic violence, sexual harassment, and other forms of gender-based violence look like and providing safe and effective ways to intervene is an important strategy to prevent such incidents from occurring. Educating students about safe, healthy, and consensual relationships, and dispelling common societal narratives that perpetuate victim-blaming, can benefit students during and after their time on campus.

Survivor Support Training: Following an incident of sexual violence, survivors may turn to trusted individuals for support. Regardless of whether such violence was initiated by another student or occurred on campus property, the individuals to whom survivors turn may be institutional personnel, faculty, or students. Training the community about trauma-informed practices that can affirm and empower survivors is an important approach to promoting an inclusive campus environment. Training can reinforce communications strategies that avoid placing the blame for the incident on the victim. Rather, such training can educate the campus community about campus and community resources available to survivors and teach listening and communications skills that help survivors feel nurtured and empowered.

Community Partnerships: Many communities have organizations and offices that support survivors of sexual violence, domestic abuse, stalking, sexual harassment, or other forms of gender-based violence. Such organizations may provide connections to individuals who are able to support and affirm survivors following an incident. These organizations may also have free sexual offense evidence collection kits for survivors who may choose to have such evidence stored to pursue legal action when she or he is ready. Developing relationships and partnerships to connect their mission within the campus support infrastructure where possible and appropriate can bolster institutional strategies to prevent and address sexual assault.

Clery Act

The Clery Act was passed in 1990 and requires all colleges and universities receiving federal student financial aid funding to share information about crime on their campus in an annual report (20 U.S.C. §1092(f)). One area of consideration is the influence of publicly available data on institutions' recruitment and admissions. For example, the Clery Act requires that institutions provide statistics concerning the occurrence of criminal offenses, including forcible or non-forcible sex offenses. It is reasonable for administrators to be concerned that poor statistics would negatively affect the reputation of the institution. However, given the seriousness of both sexual violence and the implications of non-compliance with Title IX, colleges must establish a safe and inclusive campus environment.

In 2013, President Obama signed the reauthorization of the Violence Against Women Act (VAWA) into law. VAWA's broad intent of providing continued legal protection for survivors of violence encompassed a set of new provisions to the Clery Act. The new provisions articulated new action that colleges and universities must take to affirm the rights of students who experience campus violence. To deliver the statutory intent of the law, then Secretary of Education Arne Duncan established a Negotiated Rulemaking Committee comprised of a cross-section of stakeholders and constituents to promulgate the implementing regulations of the amendments to the Clery Act. Published in 2014 with an effective date of July 1, 2015, the final regulations (34 C.F.R. § 668.46) undergirding the VAWA amendments to the Clery Act brought change to five major areas of campus' efforts to prevent and address violence:

1. Prevention—the VAWA amendments to Clery mandate the provision of prevention programming that promotes awareness and education about safe strategies to stop incidents of violence before they occur.
2. Gender-based violence—Colleges and universities are required to document their policies and procedures following incidents and make clear the options that are available to survivors.
3. Protecting confidentiality and affirming the rights of survivors—In assembling their annual security reports, institutions are required to document their steps for ensuring the confidentiality of survivors in both crime statistics reporting and protective measures. Further, institutions must allow students the right to decline a report of violence, including sexual violence or domestic abuse, to local law enforcement.
4. Defining or refining the relationship with local law enforcement—Institutions are expected to have and clearly articulate a policy undergirding the jurisdiction of campus and local law enforcement related to the investigation of alleged crime.
5. Broader definition of hate crimes—VAWA broadened the Clery Act's reporting guidelines to encompass gender identity and national origin as two demographic characteristics that must now be reported in crime statistics.

These new provisions follow a national conversation surrounding campus' efforts to prevent violence and address safety that has built to a crescendo in recent years, illuminating the closely tethered strands of the prevention of campus violence and the promotion of equal opportunity on the basis of sex. Knowing through recent national surveys that one in four college women is victimized by sexual violence, and recognizing the impediments that such violence poses to safe and inclusive educational opportunity when left unaddressed, campuses will increasingly be expected to take proactive steps to ensure that survivors are provided with adequate support and campuses have preventive measures in place (Cantor, Fisher, Chibnall, Townsend, Lee, Bruce, & Thomas, 2015; DiJulio, Norton, Craighill, Clemens, & Brodie, 2015).

With regard to prevention, however, these expectations are coming at a time when campuses have little evidence of what is working to prevent campus violence. According to the Centers for Disease Control, for instance, only three sexual violence prevention programs across all levels and sectors of education have been shown, through rigorous evaluation methodology, to significantly reduce incidents of such violence in educational settings. The common elements are that raising awareness about sexual abuse and harassment in the environments where students live, learn, and work is an important strategy, as is the promotion of positive, healthy attitudes toward dating and sexual activity. These programs further emphasize bystander intervention training to help members of the higher education community dispel rape myths and non-violently intervene in a moment of potential sexual violence (United States Department of Health and Human Services, Centers for Disease Control, 2016). Although individual programs have been established as effective in their individual settings, this does not necessarily imply that the replication of one particular program across different institutional contexts will achieve a similar outcome. The implication for practice here is that assessment and evaluation on the efficacy of strategies to prevent and address violence are a predominant leadership imperative in the coming years.

Not only will campus leaders continue to be tasked with delivering institutional policies and procedures that align with the intent and provisions of recently enacted law and regulation, but this effort will coincide with a policy conversation still unfolding among lawmakers from the states to the White House. Though framed under a common theme that campuses have the public expectation to provide safe, inclusive, and fair violence prevention and response strategies for all students, the proposals that have emerged do raise the prospect that institutional leaders may face the challenge of complying with conflicting state and federal laws. Such conflicts may create compliance challenges that prompt partnership and dialogue with lawmakers.

Forming a partnership to illuminate this very line of policy dialogue, NASPA—Student Affairs Administrators in Higher Education and Education Commission of the States (2015) released a report titled *State Legislative Developments on Campus Sexual Violence: Issues in the Context of Safety*. Morse, Sponsler, and Fulton (2015) examined state legislative activity from the 2013 to 2015 legislative sessions to examine policies and provisions that, if enacted, would bring change to how colleges and universities prevent and address sexual violence on campus. At least two strands of policy activity across the states—namely the expanded role of counsel and mandatory reporting—raise concern that institutions were being asked to comply with laws that create conflicts with statutory responsibilities under state law and Title IX. The April 4, 2011, DCL articulated the following:

> While OCR does not require schools to permit parties to have lawyers at any stage of the proceedings, if a school chooses to allow the parties to have their lawyers participate in the proceedings, it must do so equally for both parties. Additionally, any school-imposed restrictions on the ability of lawyers to speak or otherwise participate in the proceedings should apply equally.
>
> (Ali, 2011, p. 12)

In three states—North Carolina, North Dakota, and Arkansas—legal counsel have been granted authority to fully participate on behalf of student clients involved in campus conduct proceedings and processes, including campus adjudications of alleged incidents of sexual assault. As an added point of consideration, North Carolina's law, which applies to public institutions in the state, extends such rights to representation solely to the accused (Morse et al., 2015).

Federal law has long allowed for students to have lawyers present in conduct proceedings insofar as institutions are provided the discretion to define the boundaries of their participation and utilize this latitude to ascertain that such provisions apply equally to all parties involved (Ali, 2011). Laws that override these expectations by mandating the participation of counsel on full behalf of the student without providing funds to ensure that all students have equal access to such representation will lead to incidents in which one party can afford an attorney and the other cannot. In these cases, the campus will be forced into non-compliance with superseding federal law where a student can document how such a system impeded their equal access rights to postsecondary education afforded under Title IX.

Policy developments on the issue of defining the relationship between institutional and local police forces have also added layers of complexity and conflict as campus administrators work to navigate toward compliance with state and federal law. In recent years, policymakers in California and Virginia have enacted statutes that articulate requirements for institutions to mandatorily report incidents of campus sexual violence (Morse et al., 2015). Though the policy architecture differs in both states, both laws insert the likely possibility of conflicting with students' rights to deny that a report of violence be handed over to local law enforcement as articulated under 668.46(b)(11)(iii) of the Clery Act regulations, which state:

> (11) A statement of policy regarding the institution's campus sexual assault programs to prevent sex offenses, and procedures to follow when a sex offense occurs. The statement must include—... **(iii)** Information on a student's **option** [emphasis added] to notify appropriate law enforcement authorities, including on-campus and local police, and a statement that institutional personnel will assist the student in notifying these authorities, if the student requests the assistance of these personnel.

It is important to note that the power to choose was afforded to survivors of such violence not only as a matter of self-affirmation, but also out of the recognition that the justice system has, by and large, not been able to deliver positive outcomes for survivors of violent crimes, namely rape.

Though such action may be done with the best of intent, the emergence of separate streams of lawmaking at the state and federal levels has created challenges of both practice and leadership as campus administrators look not only to comply with the spirit of the law, but to deliver excellence in supporting the safety and well-being of all students. This emergent area of policy development, in turn, signals an important responsibility on the part of administrators to promote equal opportunity on the basis of sex not just by sound decision-making at the campus levels, but also by keeping a pulse of the policy context and being thoughtfully engaged about the extent to which policy proposals deliver on their intent or create negative, unintended consequences.

But the wide interest in campus prevention and handling of violence has spurred another line of practical consideration, one in which stakeholders are raising questions about how campuses can take action to anticipate areas of need and focus related to promoting safety. Policy experts are continuing to inquire, for instance, why federal law—whether the Clery Act or other campus safety law—does not require institutions to collect, utilize, and report campus climate data. While retrospective reports of criminal offenses are certainly valuable to members of the campus community and potential students, one critique of the annual security report is that it provides a limited perspective of the campus environment. A more comprehensive picture of a campus' current environment would include information on interactions that, if not handled appropriately, could also create a somewhat hostile environment. For example, a climate survey examines not only the actual prevalence or incidences of sexual violence, but also the degree to which an atmosphere of sexual violence is perceived to exist. While faculty, staff, and student perceptions would not likely lead to criminal reporting, those views do shape the climate of the institution. As administrators consider the ways in which a non-hostile environment can be sustained, it is critical for them to continuously assess and monitor their campus climate.

Prevention

The Clery Act requires that institutions' annual security reports include a policy to address primary education and awareness programs for all incoming students and employees and ongoing prevention strategies. With regard to addressing sexual violence, as mentioned earlier, the 2001 Guidance from OCR states that one procedural element for providing prompt and equitable resolution of sexual harassment and sexual violence complaints is an assurance that the institution will take steps to prevent recurrence. One approach is to establish educational programs and resources for students and staff. Prevention strategies help colleges be more proactive in promoting a positive campus environment. Many colleges provide students with educational resources on sexual assault and misconduct during their orientation program but some institutions are expanding their prevention strategies even farther. For example, the Indiana University (IU) System requires that students complete an online module on sexual assault and misconduct prior to their arrival at the campus. The IU also provides educational resources to parents. Prevention strategies should also include education and training efforts for personnel across the institution.

IMPACT OF TITLE IX ON MANAGING HIGHER EDUCATION INSTITUTIONS

Administrators are particularly aware of the financial implications of non-compliance with Title IX requirements. Section 1682 states that institutions that receive Federal funding are required to adhere to the provisions of section 1681 and that non-compliance can result in termination of funding. The DCL specifically states that OCR seeks to obtain voluntary compliance from institutions; however, when voluntary compliance does not occur, OCR may initiate proceedings to withdraw Federal funds.

Though all colleges are focused on Title IX compliance, there are some important considerations for community colleges and online institutions. For example, community colleges often enroll non-traditional students, many of whom are typically older and may attend part time. These institutions may also have fewer resources to respond to sexual violence and, as a result, could rely more on community resources and establish partnerships with local agencies and organizations. Although online institutions may have a lower focus on Title IX as it connects to bathrooms, athletic teams, and sexual violence, the legal expectations for maintaining a safe inclusive learning environment are still very relevant. There are varying interpretations of the law with regard to requirements for public institutions versus private institutions. One area for debate is related to due process for an accused student, which has led some scholars to question whether public institutions have greater requirements to provide due process than private institutions. For example, Cantalupo (2010) suggests that private institutions are mainly bound by their own policies and procedures related to disciplinary actions, which could result in court interpretations that relations between a student and private university are a matter of contract.

As in the opening story, senior leaders who are tasked with developing sound institutional practices for Title IX compliance are charged with examining the entire campus environment and effective practice in both academic and co-curricular settings. A holistic approach is necessary, one that explores everything from how to help victims of sexual violence navigate their class schedule to how to modify campus restrooms to better serve transgender students.

Academic and co-curricular programs

To examine the impact of Title IX on academic programs, colleges will need to examine the proportion of men and women in certain courses of study, especially in relation to science, technology, engineering, or mathematics (STEM) fields. For the majority of these fields, a smaller percentage of women than men earn a bachelor's degree (Rodriguez, Kirshstein, Amos, Jones, Espinosa, & Watnick, 2012). Administrators may want to review their process for supporting women who enroll in STEM programs. Strong procedures for helping women get acclimated to the program and connect to resources could positively affect the rates at which women complete STEM degrees. This outcome would reflect the spirit of Title IX, which is intended to ensure inclusive educational opportunities to all students.

As administrators address Title IX compliance with a focus on inclusive programming, it will also be important for them to examine how such programming influences certain student populations. For example, Title IX prohibits discrimination on the basis of sex, which means that institutions must provide pregnant students the same educational resources that are available to other students. Title IX also requires that pregnant students be given any special services available to students with a temporary disability.

Administrators should consider the impact of Title IX on the delivery of resources to transgender students. In 2016, the U.S. Departments of Education and Justice issued joint guidance on transgender students and civil rights which addresses how colleges should approach four key areas: safe and non-discriminatory environments; identification documents, names, and pronouns; sex-segregated activities and facilities; and privacy and education records (United States Department of Education, 2016). For example, registrars will need to establish the processes by which a transgender student can have their educational record amended to reflect a name change. Student affairs professionals will also need to support transgender students who live in a single-gender residence hall and ensure the availability of all-gender or gender-neutral restrooms on the campus, especially in frequently used public spaces.

Admissions and transfer

Though the majority of the attention on Title IX compliance often relates to athletics, gender-based violence, and sexual harassment, there are also considerations for college admissions and transfer policies. Two emerging practices that college administrators should consider in relation to Title IX compliance are to include criminal history information on the application for admission and notating a student's academic record. These practices relate to Title IX because both are approaches that some colleges are using to prevent a hostile learning environment.

A possible unintended consequence of using criminal history in admission decisions is that it could lead to inequity in student admissions on the basis of sex, which has major implications for Title IX compliance. The Center for American Progress reports that due to disparities in arrests and sentencing, students of color are disproportionately affected (Vallas & Dietrich, 2014). Considering the demographic background of many Americans who have a criminal record, the statistics are disproportionately high for men, particularly men of color. It is imperative that administrators be careful in their review of students' admission materials, especially in reference to criminal history information, and it appears that there is room for more formal procedures. The Center for Community Alternatives (CCA) surveyed institutions and found that less than half of those that collect and use criminal justice information have written policies in place and only 40% train staff on how to interpret the information (Weissman, Rosenthal, Warth, Wolf, Messina-Yauchzy, & Siegel, 2009, p. i). However, CCA also found that most schools that collect and use criminal justice information have adopted additional steps in their admissions decision process, the most common of which is consulting with academic deans and campus security personnel (Weissman et al., 2009). Such additional steps will help colleges move toward a more consistent process for making admissions decisions, thus lowering the risk of disparity on the basis of sex.

Section 99.31(a)(2) of the Family Educational Rights Privacy Act (FERPA) states that an educational agency or institution may disclose personally identifiable information from an education record without consent if the disclosure is, subject to the requirements of section 99.34, to officials of another school, school system, or institution of postsecondary education where the student seeks or intends to enroll, or where the student is already enrolled so long as the disclosure is for purposes related to the student's enrollment or transfer. There has been increased discussion of whether institutions should notate an accused student's record. For example, in relation to transfer, if an institution finds that a student has committed a violation of the code of conduct and decides to add a notation to the educational record, that student may still depart the institution and apply to another.

While FERPA allows such notation, the majority of colleges are not doing so. The American Association of Collegiate Registrars and Admissions Officers (AACRAO) surveyed its member institutions about their recording of disciplinary violations on a student's record and found that, for 85% of the institutions, the academic transcript did not reflect students' ineligibility to re-enroll due to major disciplinary violations (AACRAO, 2015, Table 2, p. 3). As we continue to grapple with the challenges of combatting sexual violence, more institutions that receive transfer students may decide to request additional information from the sending institution in order to proactively mitigate the risk of creating a hostile environment. Such practice does make the assumption that a student found to have violated a conduct code at one institution would do so at another. However, considering the high stakes of non-compliance with Title IX, more institutions may consider transcript notation in the years ahead.

CONCLUSION

Focusing on the legal and regulatory components as well as managing Title IX at a higher education institution are two critical elements for any college or university administrator. This chapter has aimed to address both of those elements. Additionally, this chapter emphasized that, while many regard Title IX as being sports-related, it is much more broad and complex than that. This chapter highlighted the impact of Title IX on key areas such as athletics, gender-based harassment, academics and co-curricular activities, and admissions and transfer. Strategies for maintaining Title IX compliance were also offered. Finally, it is important to note that while Title IX is not new, it is important to higher education administrators to be in compliance with all federal regulations—including Title IX. Therefore, leaders should review this chapter and the federal regulations on Title IX in the context of their institution to identify and remedy any Title IX non-compliance risks.

DISCUSSION PROMPTS

1. Who holds responsibility for ensuring compliance with Title IX and its regulations on campus, and, given the many facets of Title IX that intersect with campus management, are there opportunities to strengthen coordination among all who hold such responsibility on campus? Further, are there opportunities to engage new personnel and/or faculty to bolster your campus' efforts to comply with Title IX?
2. How does the institution utilize assessment to monitor and measure the level of inclusiveness for its programs, services, and activities? In addition to looking at differences between male and female students, can the institution incorporate new layers of analysis in existing or forthcoming instruments by looking at other demographic characteristics such as race/ethnicity, gender identity, sexual orientation, or others to broaden insight into the student experience on campus?
3. How often does the institution audit its policies and procedures related to Title IX within the administration of its men's and women's athletics programs? For public institutions, have audits examined out-of-state scholarship distributions across men's and women's programs to ensure against policy and procedure that create disproportionate allocations to one program over another?

4. Across men's and women's athletics programs at the institution, to what extent does policy and procedure related to the recruitment and participation of student athletes encompass transgender student athletes? Are there opportunities to revisit policy and practice to protect against discrimination based on gender identity within athletics programs at the institution?

5. How can administrators and staff partner to increase students' awareness of institutional resources to prevent gender-based violence and to support survivors of sexual violence? Further, what is the institution doing to strengthen students' knowledge of the grievance process and the designated personnel on campus to whom students can turn following an incident of such violence?

6. When and where should ongoing sexual violence prevention strategies be employed during the academic year? Considering the strategies described in this chapter, are there ways that prevention strategies can be strengthened?

7. What resources are in place on campus to assess climate as it relates to actual and perceived gender-based violence and discrimination among students? Are there opportunities to build on campus' efforts to embed climate assessment into its existing efforts to promote safety and inclusion on campus?

8. With regard to transgender students, what approaches can the institution use to find a balance between notifying the appropriate faculty, staff, and administrators of a student's change in gender identity and the student's right to privacy?

9. What are the institution's primary considerations for determining whether a conduct code violation will be noted on a student's transcript?

10. When forming and facilitating a campus workgroup to address Title IX compliance, what strategies can senior leaders use to address institution-wide issues in the context of each member's functional area?

REFERENCES

Ali, R. (2010). Dear Colleague Letter: Office of the Assistant Secretary. United States Department of Education, Office for Civil Rights, Washington, DC. Retrieved from http://www2.ed.gov/about/offices/list/ocr/letters/colleague-201010.html

Ali, R. (2011). Dear Colleague Letter: Office of the Assistant Secretary. United States Department of Education, Office for Civil Rights, Washington, DC. Retrieved from http://www2.ed.gov/about/offices/list/ocr/letters/colleague-201104.html

American Association of Collegiate Registrars and Admissions Officers (AACRAO). (2015). *2015 U.S. Higher Education Transcript Practices and Best Practice Opinions—Results of the AACRAO 2015 Academic Record and Transcript Survey*. Washington, DC. Retrieved from http://www.aacrao.org/docs/default-source/PDF-Files/2015-transcript-practices-at-u-s-institutions-%281%29.pdf?sfvrsn=4

Cantalupo, N.C. (2010). *How should colleges and universities respond to peer sexual violence on campus? What the current legal environment tells us*. Washington, DC: Georgetown University Law Center. Retrieved from http://scholarship.law.georgetown.edu/cgi/viewcontent.cgi?article=1430&context=facpub

Cantor, D., Fisher, B., Chibnall, S., Townsend, R., Lee, H., Bruce, C., & Thomas, G. (2015). *Report on the AAU Campus Climate Survey on Sexual Assault and Sexual Misconduct*. Rockville, Maryland: Westat. Retrieved from https://www.aau.edu/uploadedFiles/AAU_Publications/AAU_Reports/Sexual_Assault_Campus_Survey/AAU_Campus_Climate_Survey_12_14_15.pdf

Cantú, N. (1998). Dear Colleague Letter: Bowling Green State University. United States Department of Education, Office for Civil Rights, Washington, DC. Retrieved from http://www2.ed.gov/about/offices/list/ocr/docs/bowlgrn.html

DiJulio, B., Norton, M., Craighill, P., Clemens, S., & Brodie, M. (2015). *Survey of current and recent college students on sexual assault*. Washington, DC: Kaiser Family Foundation. Retrieved from http://kff.org/other/poll-finding/survey-of-current-and-recent-college-students-on-sexual-assault

Institutional and Financial Information for Students, 20 U.S.C. §1092(f) (1990).

Institutional Security Policies and Crime Statistics, 34 C.F.R. §668.46 (2013).

Lhamon, C. E. (2015). Dear Colleague Letter: Office of the Assistant Secretary. United States Department of Education, Office for Civil Rights, Washington, DC. Retrieved from http://www2.ed.gov/policy/rights/guid/ocr/title-ix-coordinators.html

Morse, A., Sponsler, B., & Fulton, M. (2015). *State legislative developments on campus sexual violence: Issues in the context of safety*. Washington, DC: NASPA—Student Affairs Administrators in Higher Education. Retrieved from http://www.naspa.org/rpi/reports/state-legislative-developments-on-campus-sexual-violence-issues-in-the-cont

Nondiscrimination on the basis of sex in education programs or activities receiving federal financial assistance, 34 C.F.R. §106 (2000).

Nondiscrimination on the basis of sex in education programs or activities receiving federal financial assistance, 34 C.F.R. §106.41 Athletics (2000).

Reynolds, G. (2003). *Further clarification of intercollegiate athletics policy guidance regarding Title IX compliance*. United States Department of Education, Office for Civil Rights, Washington, DC. Retrieved from http://www2.ed.gov/about/offices/list/ocr/title9guidanceFinal.html

Rodriguez, C., Kirshstein, R., Banks Amos, L., Jones, W., Espinosa, L., & Watnick, D. (2012). *Broadening participation in STEM: A call to action*. Retrieved from http://www.air.org/sites/default/files/downloads/report/Broadening_Participation_in_STEM_Feb_14_2013_0.pdf

Spellings, M. (2008). *Title IX Athletics Three-Part Test*. United States Department of Education, Washington, DC. Retrieved from http://www2.ed.gov/about/offices/list/ocr/letters/title-ix-2008-0327.pdf

Title IX of the Education Amendments of 1972, 20 U.S.C. §1681 (2016).

United States Department of Education, Office for Civil Rights. (1979). *A Policy Interpretation: Title IX and Intercollegiate Athletics*. Washington, DC. Retrieved from http://www2.ed.gov/about/offices/list/ocr/docs/t9interp.html

United States Department of Education, Office of Civil Rights. (1997). *Sexual harassment guidance: Harassment of students by school employees, other students, or third parties*. Washington, DC. Retrieved from http://www2.ed.gov/about/offices/list/ocr/docs/sexhar01.html

United States Department of Education, Office of Civil Rights. (2001). *Revised sexual harassment guidance: Harassment of students by school employees, other students, or third parties*. Washington, DC. Retrieved from http://www2.ed.gov/about/offices/list/ocr/docs/shguide.html

United States Department of Education, Office for Civil Rights. (2010). Dear Colleague Letter. Washington, DC. Retrieved from http://www2.ed.gov/about/offices/list/ocr/letters/colleague-20100420.html

United States Department of Education, Office for Civil Rights. (2014). Dear Colleague Letter. Washington, DC. Retrieved from http://www2.ed.gov/about/offices/list/ocr/docs/qa-201404-title-ix.pdf

United States Department of Education, Office for Civil Rights. (2015). *Laws and Guidance: Title IX and Sex Discrimination*. Washington, DC. Retrieved from http://www2.ed.gov/about/offices/list/oCr/docs/tix_dis.html

United States Department of Education, Office for Civil Rights. (2016). Dear Colleague Letter. Washington, DC. Retrieved from http://www2.ed.gov/about/offices/list/ocr/letters/colleague-201605-title-ix-transgender.pdf

United States Department of Health and Human Services, Centers for Disease Control. (2016). *Injury prevention & control: Division of violence prevention: Sexual violence prevention strategies*. Washington, DC. Retrieved from http://www.cdc.gov/violenceprevention/sexualviolence/prevention.html

Vallas, R., & Dietrich, S. (2014). *One strike and you're out: How we can eliminate barrier to economic security and mobility for people with criminal records*. Retrieved March 2016 from https://cdn.americanprogress.org/wp-content/uploads/2014/12/VallasCriminalRecordsReport.pdf

Violence Against Women Reauthorization Act of 2013, 42 U.S.C. §13701-14040 (2013).

Weissman, M., Rosenthal, A., Warth, P., Wolf, E., Messina-Yauchzy, M. & Siegel, L. (2009). *The use of criminal history records in college admissions reconsidered*. Center for Community Alternatives: Brooklyn, New York. Retrieved http://www.communityalternatives.org/pdf/Reconsidered-criminal-hist-recs-in-college-admissions.pdf

12

PURPOSE, VALUE, AND UNINTENDED CONSEQUENCES OF SOCIAL MEDIA IN HIGHER EDUCATION

Regina Luttrell, Karen McGrath, and Christopher A. Medjesky

INTRODUCTION

What would happen if a student approached you at the end of class and presented you with a screen capture of more than one hundred demeaning Yik Yak posts, including sexually charged comments, threatening remarks, and personal insults related to your appearance and teaching style (Schmidt, 2015, p. 13)? What might you do? Who would you reach out to? If you put yourself in the shoes of the college or university administration, where does your support align—with the faculty member or with the students responsible for the postings? Is this free speech or hate speech? Whose rights, if any, have been violated?

This exact scenario unfolded in March of 2015 on the campus of Eastern Michigan University. Three female faculty members teaching a mandatory interdisciplinary studies course to 230 freshmen were harassed via Yik Yak, a smartphone application that allows users to anonymously post brief remarks on virtual bulletin boards. The app has been wreaking havoc on campuses across the nation, as students readily post threats of harm, racial slurs, and slanderous gossip (Schmidt, 2015, p. 13).

Does a former student's extensive online commentary about a professor's teaching style amount to defamation? Dr. Sally Vogl-Bauer, a tenured professor of communications, formerly with the University of Wisconsin at Whitewater, sued a student for carrying out a malicious campaign to besmirch her reputation. The lawsuit alleged that Anthony Llewellyn "engaged in an intentional, malicious and unprivileged campaign" to defame Dr. Vogl-Bauer, resulting in "substantial economic, reputational and emotional injuries" (Flaherty, 2016a, para. 2). In contrast, the student saw it as his right to share his experiences with the online community. In a 2014 interview with *GazetteXtra*, Llewellyn said it "was important for the videos and comments to stay online to keep the public informed" (para. 14).

The University of Wisconsin at Whitewater and Eastern Michigan University are certainly not alone in their experiences. The University of North Carolina, Penn State University, Michigan State University, Clemson University, Emory University, Colgate University, the University of Texas, and Kenyon College are all among the growing list of educational establishments that have dealt with issues ranging from homophobic and/or misogynistic comments to threats of violence, including gang rape (Mahler, 2015). These are not easy scenarios to manage in today's technologically connected, 24/7 world. However, knowing their rights and the rights of others in these situations will assist administrators in making more informed decisions. At a minimum, a case-by-case evaluation of the evidence and related policies is in order. Understanding the rules and regulations of the various social media forums is equally important.

The prevalence of social media has led to people of all ages experiencing a phenomenon known as FOMO (Fear of Missing Out) should they go a week, day, or even hour without keeping up with the social media worlds. Yet, while marketing and public relations departments at educational institutions are capitalizing on social media outlets to recruit and retain students, "faculty are much more willing to embrace social media in their personal lives than they are to use it for professional or teaching purposes." Additionally, "faculty professional use of social media has lagged somewhat behind their personal use, but has increased each year" (Seaman & Tinti-Kane, 2013, p. 3). As a result, the timing is appropriate to explore ways for faculty and others at educational institutions to engage in productive social media use.

Before moving forward, it is necessary to recognize that the role of social media as a tool within education is still highly debated. Fears of distraction and fads run rampant on the "dangers" side of the debate, while ease of access to current, real-time information and a media-rich landscape often lead the "benefits" side (Guy, 2013). Whatever the preference, numerous colleges and universities have been quite successful at integrating social media into their curricula (Foulger, 2014; Stansbury, 2015).

WHAT QUALIFIES AS SOCIAL MEDIA?

Technically, social media refer to those media outlets or apps that allow users to interface with each other for social purposes. Many people use the phrase "social media" in reference to any connections they have with others via the Internet or email. Some groups further distinguish email as a method of communication that is not so much a social medium, but rather a private or professional way to connect with others; emails are sent directly to individual users, even if they are part of a much larger distribution group. By contrast, social media platforms like Facebook, Instagram, and Twitter often use messages that are meant to be shared with others, hence the "social" aspect of the phrase. Yet, on many of these platforms, private messaging is also an option, and email allows users to create large group messages to include many known and unknown people. The same can be said about electronic mailing lists; while they provide an outlet for multiple people at one time, the focus is clearly on one item, organization, topic, etc.

Luttrell (2015) suggests that social media be considered this way: "how a company or brand effectively utilizes each of the aforementioned technologies to connect, interact, and cultivate trusting relationships with *people* [sic]," and her definition guides the rest of this chapter (p. 23).

STRATEGICALLY CREATING CONTENT

The goal of any institution of higher education resides in its ability to teach and learn from others with a particular set of stakeholders—students. These individuals not only graduate from a college or university with a degree, but also maintain a relationship with that institution for the rest of their lives. Therefore, one primary responsibility of an institution and its other stakeholders (faculty, staff, and administrators) is to "connect, interact, and cultivate trusting relationships" with enrolled students, potential students, alumni, and each other (Luttrell, 2015, p. 23).

Social media use is one prominent and useful approach to connecting with others; after all, most stakeholders are embracing and using some form of social media on a daily basis. That said, connecting with a large number of stakeholders *exclusively* through social media is not only overwhelming, but also ill advised. The content manager of various social media sites should instead understand which platforms are preferred by the targeted stakeholders and monitor that usage accordingly. For example, while 77% of female Internet users visit Facebook each day, only 44% visit Pinterest and even fewer visit Instagram (31%); age is another determining factor for usage (Duggan, 2015). Strategic outreach with purpose and audience in mind is paramount to building and maintaining successful relationships.

University and Departmental Social Media Use

Colleges and universities typically rely on their brand to guide all internal and external communications. This brand is both created and monitored by the marketing and/or public relations offices (Hanover Research, 2014). Therefore, the focus must be the institution as a whole. Each institution must decide who should create, use, and monitor social media content. In an email interview, Ted Coutilish, Associate Vice President for University Marketing and Communications at Eastern Michigan University, said:

> EMU's social media goal is engagement. It's about shares and comments rather than likes or retweets. We found it's critical to be authentic, relevant, a trusted information source with good and bad news (don't filter out bad news, rather learn from it and engage to stop rumors and innuendos) and trust is everything. It takes a long time to build trust, but just a few seconds to lose it. We also found it's important to customize a strategy for each social media platform. Twitter is water cooler and Facebook is lunch. We learned the sweet spot is posting relevant content three-to-five times per day to engage audiences. Any more and you are risking annoying followers. We also found posting text is good, pictures are better and videos are best. Videos often receive more engagement and attention. Other tips: Remove irrelevant content or offensive comments/photos, don't fool the audience, if someone is paid to blog, self-identify, people love to feel special so ask them questions, quickly respond to posted questions and take social media threats seriously.

Knowing the rationale for using social media to reach specific audiences is the first step. Understanding how this strategy will be interpreted by the stakeholders and setting clear objectives for individual social media outlets is the second step. For example, does the institution want to post images of students simply to capture the essence of a moment, or will it accompany the photos with emotionally charged or informative content? The answer may be both, but the choice of social media platform makes a difference. If the goal is to share images of current students with little context, then Instagram, Snapchat, or Flickr are good choices. These platforms can also be connected to the institution's Facebook or Twitter accounts using a social media dashboard such as Hootsuite. On the other hand, if the objective is to provide an image and some information, then Facebook or Twitter may be more appropriate.

Users readily check social media sites based on what they want to derive from their visit; they have limited time and want to be efficient. Institutional websites are great tools for reaching potential students and updating alumni or the community. However, most websites tend to focus on what the institution can do for visitors personally, assuming they decide to attend. This means that currently enrolled students, faculty, and staff may only visit the website if they have a specific inquiry that can be answered using the search tool. Many stakeholders do not regularly visit the site for updates or connect to RSS feeds because other social media sites may be more current and useful.

If an institution can create a mobile app and encourage stakeholders to use it daily, then trending news and events can be increasingly focused and managed through that single medium. Some useful mobile apps calculate GPAs or deliver weather, transit, and emergency push notifications (Lynch, 2012; SUNY Albany, 2016). Ultimately, social media sites connected to mobile apps can benefit all potential or current stakeholders. The number of colleges and universities incorporating mobile apps grew by 23% to a total of 83% over the two-year period from 2012 to 2014 (Geiger, 2015).

Individual departments, on the other hand, have a slightly different social media strategy to employ. First, departments must fully understand the social media policies enforced by their institutions. Once they have established that the policy allows for independent social media use at the departmental level, personnel can begin to form strategies for content and outlet. For example, the Communications Department at the College of Saint Rose in Albany, New York, decided to create its own brand by using "COMmunity" as its moniker. In 2009, it created a private Facebook group to directly engage with current students and alumni. The department uses this platform to post job opportunities and events, network with members, provide alumni updates, encourage members to share their ideas, and even discuss issues relevant to the discipline.

As the resulting social media engagement grew, more sites were incorporated into the strategy. Today, in addition to the original Facebook page, the department now manages Twitter, YouTube, Instagram, and LinkedIn accounts, all monitored continuously via Hootsuite. Twitter chats, trending stories, photos, events, and news are easily shared across platforms using this tool.

A departmental email account was created to receive all questions for the administrators of the social media platforms. This enabled the department to connect with current students throughout the year. Moreover, potential students, alumni, and community members can correspond with the department using this outlet, which thus sets the tone for building and maintaining relationships with a broader, connected audience.

Social Media Functions and Responsibilities

What are the functions and responsibilities of educational institutions and departments when operating multiple social media sites simultaneously? One primary purpose of social media is to keep those with whom an institution shares a connection (e.g., stakeholders or shareholders) "in the loop" and engaged. As an example, alumni may want to inquire about other graduates, retired faculty, current students and faculty, program initiatives, and upcoming events. Of particular importance, and something that institutions must consider, is who the administrator(s) will be and who will have permission(s) to post original content on the site(s).

In a small academic or marketing department, the input of all colleagues may be required to keep the site(s) active and updated. It is important to use a dashboard to ensure that all social media platforms are active, especially if analytics are involved and the sites are updated daily. When one department member takes on this responsibility, he or she can easily become overwhelmed by the amount of time and information needed to increase and/or maintain followers. In the case of a small department, setting up a rotation of responsibilities can make it easier to promote a consistent message. No matter who is assigned with the administrative permissions, the institution or department should be consistent when promoting its brand over multiple social outlets. The Management of Social Media section below provides additional details and suggestions for how to divide the work and incorporate others, such as graduate assistants, academic administrators, as well as non-academic administrators, into the social media landscape.

It should be obvious that the successful implementation of a social media strategy depends on ensuring that the lines of communication are open to current students and that these students are engaged with relevant, professional posts. Some institutions create "social media business cards" with the college, university, or even individual department Facebook, Instagram, LinkedIn, and Twitter account information. The cards can be given to all students or specifically to those within a specific major, allowing them to keep current with the latest events, professional tips, and job and internship opportunities, as well as view photos capturing poignant moments from a particular event. Students can post, respond, critique, and inquire, while the administrator monitors the interaction in the background. Developing themed days, such as Meme Monday or Words of Wisdom Wednesday, can encourage dialogue with an intended audience.

It is imperative that whoever assumes the responsibility for content management know how to communicate effectively in the social media sphere. Knowing simple persuasion concepts like Aristotle's ethos, pathos, and logos can assist a content provider in making informed decisions. Ethos (ethics of an intended message) needs to be thought about on all levels. Which messages or images lend credibility to this post? Is humor appropriate? Slang? Derision? For example, memes are a popular social media tool in Facebook communications. Often, they are simply created or borrowed using a free meme generator. While they can be funny in and of themselves, some memes may have a negative effect when posted on a university or departmental page; this is especially true of those related to race, sex, sexuality, and politics. Anyone using a department member's image to create new memes should be sure to receive the appropriate permissions beforehand to avoid the apologia that may follow when making a decision to post the meme in the first place.

As for pathos (evoking a feeling), feelings often rule social media sites as followers "like" a page and add emoticons. While some followers dislike seeing emoticons in posts, the plethora of options now available allows some insight into feelings that the content provider may have. It is wise not to overuse emoticons in a post, however, as they can often detract from the message itself.

Lastly, logos (logicalness of messages) is just as complex. Institutions want to provide clear messaging but must also remember that social media posts are generally meant to be clear and concise, may use texting lingo (e.g., LOL, GTG), and may not follow the rules of formal English. Followers are interested in being engaged quickly and don't want to devote a lot of time to reading posts written like an essay. Long, expository writing, reminiscent of a thesis or final paper, is ill suited to social media sites, except for blogging purposes. Incorporating hyperlinks or bit.ly addresses to direct and connect interested readers elsewhere is more effective.

Management of Social Media

Social media is prevalent in our culture, not only in our personal and professional lives, but also in our educational lives. While the primary goal of business is to make money by promoting services and products, education is a bit different. As not-for-profit institutions, universities or colleges should also expect to grow and change with the times, yet, far too frequently, faculty, staff, and the broader administration fall behind in their use of social media to engage students. Research indicates that in the past ten to 15 years there has been a significant increase in the use of social and networking media among those 18 to 29 years old (Millennials) and that within the educational setting, faculty between the ages of 34 and 64 have increased their social media use for personal and professional reasons (Lenhart, 2015; Seaman & Tinti-Kane, 2013). The debate about whether social media and integrated technology devices are useful in the classroom rages on; however, the use of social media for college and university marketing and branding has continued to increase as there is more demand than ever for communications professionals in educational settings. On job sites like indeed.com and HigherEdJobs.com, there are new listings each day for people with the requisite technological skills and vision for such positions.

Potential students naturally visit institutional websites and use social media sites like Facebook and Twitter to learn about the schools they are interested in attending. Current students also use websites and mobile apps like RateMyProfessors.com and Yik Yak, which encourage student and "customer" participation and sharing, whether accurate or not. Alumni of higher education institutions have an increasingly large virtual presence and connectivity to platforms like Facebook, Twitter, Instagram, or even LinkedIn to find a potential employee from an institution's social media pages. These pages prove useful in facilitating and establishing connections. What we now know is that educational institutions, departments, and individual faculty would be best served by strategically planning their use of social media to recruit, retain, and promote themselves and, where possible, each other.

Faculty must also stay current on research related to incorporating social media and other technologies into the classroom. They need to acknowledge that the use of social media in the curriculum is still being debated, discover how they are most comfortable reaching students inside and outside of the classroom, and ensure that their institution can provide the appropriate resources for implementing and sustaining social media use for educational endeavors. While some faculty may not wish to allow smartphones in the classroom, fearing distraction, others embrace them and incorporate them into their lessons (Coffin & Fournier, 2015; O'Brien, 2012).

Other avenues that assist in reaching this new learning cohort of Millennials and Neo-Millennials include flipped classrooms, gamification, and in-class survey apps (e.g., i>clicker). If an educational institution expects faculty to adopt technology in their classrooms, then there must be an abundant and easily accessible support network for both students and faculty; institutions must put resources into their IT areas and hire the appropriate experts, who are on call when technological problems emerge (Chen, Seilhamer, Bennett, & Bauer, 2015). Using a learning app may be a great idea, but if no one is able to address an app glitch at 2:00 a.m., when students are working, the app will fall short and negatively impact learning. Learning happens 24/7 for most students (faculty need only check the time stamps on their learning management system—e.g., Blackboard or Canvas—to see just how much work students complete between the hours of midnight and 5:00 a.m.), and resources are needed to support round-the-clock education.

Senior-Level Administrators: Presidents, Vice Presidents, and Deans

Should presidents, vice presidents, and deans have a Twitter and/or Instagram account? Should they be on LinkedIn or friend students on Facebook? Not unlike CEOs of a corporation, senior-level administrators are extremely busy; however, even one direct post a day on multiple social media channels will allow students, faculty, and staff to directly engage with them. From something as simple as posting a photo from lunch in a common area with students to making a formal announcement about the college, each opportunity sets the administrator on a course toward greater interaction and engagement. In fact, followers may even be journalists looking to form relationships or potential donors who like the ideas coming out of the university.

Either way, social media can and should be used, but caution should always prevail. Administrators should keep in mind that any type of post can generate both favorable and unfavorable responses that can't always be controlled. It is important to fact-check posts and provide queries to active followers or participants to ensure appropriate interaction and avoid associations with undesirables. No administrator wants an inappropriate tweet or photo to set his or her institution on the wrong path and then have to implement a crisis plan. Instead, using an assistant to the dean, VP, or president to capture and share moments and conduct social media research can be quite beneficial, and is often recommended.

Imagine an office hour held by an upper-level administrator that is open to all campus constituents via Twitter chat or Skype. This could be a dynamic way to encourage students, faculty, and staff to engage with the administration and with one other. As a word of caution, administrators should avoid allowing others to post on their behalf, as they would not want to find themselves in the unenviable situation of being unable to recall information in social and professional settings.

Academic Administrators

Chairs, coordinators, and directors of programs can easily adapt to social media opportunities and should do so with an eye toward open and honest communication and exchange. Among other things, social media channels provide department and program leaders with avenues for communicating announcements, events, and schedule changes, as well as introducing faculty and staff to the social media audience. Posting a reminder about advisement or applying for graduation is just the beginning. Imagine a world where faculty, staff, and students are portrayed in academic and professional settings such that they can Tweet, Facebook, Instagram, etc. to update a status and demonstrate an atmosphere of collegiality and collaboration. Current and future students alike may find this practice to be an open invitation to join the program. Who knows, the resulting engagement could assist with recruitment and retention, both of which are major buzzwords on college campuses worldwide. It is helpful to have a weekly theme, such as profiles of adjunct faculty, current faculty research and professional work, and, of course, current students' and alumni's academic and professional work.

This type of outreach can certainly bolster enrollment and keep alumni and current students interested and engaged. However, let's be clear: "having an account in the first place, for example, is important only if you intend to use it, as a lackluster presence is often worse than no presence at all" (Mathewson, 2015, para. 1). For social media efforts to have any chance of success, each platform must be closely monitored and its use regulated by clear guidelines.

Non-academic Administrators

Any individual that is highly involved in a department and other campus activities can also be an important adopter of social media in higher education. Oftentimes, non-academic professionals engage with students, faculty, and other administrators in ways in that most professors do not. They develop relationships with all types of stakeholders and frequently handle crises that emerge on a daily basis. These individuals may also supervise work-study students and engage faculty on research projects and professional documents. Keenly aware of the culture of the campus and programs, they are vital to the development and integration of social media. An administrative assistant is in an excellent position to conduct or oversee news- or program-related social media searches. Responsibilities for these individuals may include retweeting positive stories and managing small crises using these platforms.

All academic and non-academic administrators must be well-versed in social media and digital formats, feel comfortable being "on" social media in all of its forms, and be aware of the institutional and departmental brand and reputation of which they are a part. Of course, the tried and true method of building rapport in person should never be neglected. Just because we are active on social media doesn't mean that we should forego human interaction in real time.

Faculty

Many faculty members have proven to be hesitant to adopt social media within their professional and teaching lives (Seaman & Tinti-Kane, 2013). However, there are specific ways in which faculty can incorporate social media in both areas. One way is to use social media to market their professional work. A professional website can inform visitors of research, publications, career advances and more. With institutions struggling to maintain enrollment and recruit new students, the time is now for faculty to do some of this legwork themselves. Beyond a professional website, faculty can also use LinkedIn to connect with peers in their field and network with others for grant and research opportunities. Some successfully use Facebook and Twitter to maintain connections with alumni or create a page or group to encourage classroom participation rather than using other content management systems. Others hold Twitter chats for review sessions, classroom discussion and debate, or hosting a professional to answer questions relevant to course foci. Some connect with guest speakers via Skype (Blankenship, 2015). Instructors' office hours can even be held via Skype or Twitter, making faculty more accessible, regardless of whether students still "visit" them during those scheduled hours.

Other Groups

Graduate assistants should also be considered as empowered social media managers and content providers. These individuals can be tasked with posting newsletters to Facebook, sending mass emails via MailChimp, organizing Twitter events, holding Twitter chats, monitoring social media outlets for program-related news, engaging constituents on multiple levels, and becoming part of the general conversation. However, they may need time to develop acuity if they are not accustomed to being a content creator and manager. Additionally, a graduate assistant's supervisor would want to ensure that clear rules and policies are in place, review the posts on a weekly or biweekly basis, and edit or retract as necessary. Graduate assistants who are teaching classes or supporting other instructors can also engage students via social media. They can hold review sessions on Twitter, hold Skype office hours, scan Yik Yak and other sites for comments about the class, and, in essence, be a crisis manager should the need arise.

RISE OF THE DARK SIDE OF SOCIAL MEDIA

University administrators and affiliated communicators have tapped into both the obvious and the hidden potentials of social media. One longitudinal study reported that 100% of colleges and universities surveyed had adopted social media as a communication tool (Barnes & Lescault, 2011). Social media has provided top-level administrators with a public-facing, relatable voice (Barnes & Lescault, 2013), created new ways to recruit and retain students (Barnes & Jacobsen, 2012; Ghosh, Chawla, & Mallott, 2012), extended education beyond the traditional brick-and-mortar classroom (Taylor, 2015), and expanded the geographical reach of institutions (Kelleher & Sweetser, 2012). In addition, Ghosh et al. (2012) highlight that social media has been shown to open doors for increased alumni engagement, provide new fundraising channels, and allow for accessible early alert communication across the institutional community.

However, it is also important to point out that social media can have an opposite, negative effect on institutions that is either obvious in nature or dangerously veiled. Research confirms the prevalence of cyberbullying among college students, with social media providing a multitude of anonymous choices for those engaging in these hurtful attacks (Rivituso, 2014). Legaree (2015) further emphasizes the need for higher education officials to be concerned about cyberbullying along with other serious issues including sexual harassment via social media.

Institutions must be wary of issues of defamation that may occur on institutionally related social media channels. Barnes (2012) notes that current laws may protect organizations from accountability with regard to third-party communication; however, any communication from employees may leave the institution vulnerable to legal action. Obviously, threats of legal consequences should be concerning for any organization.

> The very design of "Web 2.0" is about user contributions and conversation, yet sometimes users say things that are troubling, if not downright offensive. Some commentators theorize that the anonymity of the Internet, combined with an audience, brings out the worst in people.
>
> (Barnes, 2012, p. 56)

Integrating social media into the college experience, whether anonymous or not, opens up the community to "online security threats like account, hacking, stalking, harassment, and reputation damage" (Taylor, 2015, p. 43).

Such threats may be legal issues, but the potential for other forms of damage to the individuals as well as the institution is further disconcerting.

While it may be a stretch to suggest that the Internet brings out the worst in people, one can see how the lines between the private and professional use of social media can become blurred, raising privacy concerns. Taylor (2015) asks some important questions on the matter:

> If faculty invite themselves into [social media], currently one of students' most intimate social spaces, could they be invading students' personal developmental spaces? Faculty who are active on social media may also have concerns about students accessing their personal and private details and posts.
>
> (p. 43)

Social media, with its lack of nonverbal communication, creates a space of slippery meaning and interpretation. When combined with the possibility of private interactions, this builds fears of social media stoking questionable relationships, particularly between students and faculty. At the moment, such fears seem to be impacting the high school environment more frequently than higher education, yet the potential remains.

Of course, the blending of private and professional utilization of social media in the academic world has proven problematic on many occasions. A clear example of this is the revocation of Steven Salaita's tenure-track position offer from the University of Illinois. Salaita, whose anti-Israel Twitter comments led to Illinois's decision to revoke the position, received nearly $900,000 in a settlement with the university (Cohen, 2015). Illinois admitted no wrongdoing in the settlement, but it is clear their response to Salaita's social media communication left faculty across the country concerned over the supervision of their social media use. As a result of this episode, academics have published on ways to protect themselves on social media, suggesting a fear of administrative retaliation (see, for example, Owen, 2015). This type of wedge between faculty and administration reveals how social media can have a long-lasting negative impact on an institution and on higher education as a whole.

However, not all academics react in fear while communicating using social media. Many faculty members, for example, make use of social media outlets such as Twitter to reveal details related to some of the darker moments of the profession. Twitter affords a platform for members of a higher education institution to comment on the conditions of their lives and build community across campuses (Flaherty, 2016a). Administrators and marketing professionals should be wary of how such communication may impact the institutional brand. Casey & Llewellyn (2012) warn of the challenges of maintaining brand consistency and the role that social media holds in potentially fragmenting institutional brands.

Faculty members are not the only individuals who take to social media to discuss their lives on campus. Taylor (2015) warns that social media, when integrated into the college experience, provides an opportunity for students to deliver unfiltered and unsupervised critiques that may play against the brand of the institution. Particularly worrisome are anonymous outlets such as Yik Yak and Yeti, where conversations and postings trend toward rumor and debauchery.

Concerns over communication from members of the institutional community also draw attention to the topic of censorship. Research suggests that institutions would be wise to invest in social media policies, a concept that will be discussed momentarily (Barnes & Jacobsen, 2012). Barnes (2012) argues for justification of censorship related to specific types of communication, including hate speeches or a violation of terms of service. Ultimately, however, directly engaging with problematic communication is more effective than outright censorship (Barnes, 2012; Ghosh et al., 2012). Constructive engagement requires an institutional investment in training and resources, and the knowledge that using social media, in any capacity, can be difficult and time-consuming for institutional employees (Ghosh et al, 2012; Kelleher & Sweetser, 2012; Legaree, 2015). This can certainly lead one to wonder how prepared colleges and universities are to address social media crises.

Furthermore, the ability to actually predict a social media crisis is difficult in and of itself. Harassment, bullying, censorship, legal issues, and reputation damage are all ways social media may throw an institution into crisis. While administration may expect such problems to originate with students or faculty (e.g., Salaita), crises can also arise from unexpected sources affiliated with the institution. Mount Saint Mary College saw the resignation of Trustee Andrew Bournos after his controversial use of social media criticizing Jews and Muslims (Flaherty, 2016b). California State University, Los Angeles President William Covino also faced a complicated situation regarding social media when Ben Shapiro, a controversial conservative speaker, was set to speak at the university regarding social media concerns. Some took to social media to protest the event. When Covino cancelled the speaking engagement altogether, citing the need to balance the presentation with an additional speaker, many again took to social media to criticize his decision (Logue, 2016). This incident highlights how social media opens up institutional administrators to attacks from any party expressing interest. Kelly (2016) aptly reminds us that, in a crisis, social media poses both a benefit and a risk.

Each of these examples presents different elements for consideration when using social media. But social media can also pose other noteworthy concerns for administrators, many of which are hiding behind a seeming benefit. A Kaplan Testing study suggested that 40% of college and university admissions officers use social media to research applicants. However, a number of anecdotal reports of "admissions sabotage" have been noted wherein individuals have called out potential applicants to influence or hurt their chances of admission (Jaschik, 2016). Even the exercise of attending a departmental or function-related meeting has fallen victim to the guiles of social media. Kim (2016) argues that social media may be changing how meetings actually work. It has been noted that the increased use of social media may actually improve listening during meetings, particularly among the Millennial generation as they are accustomed to a deeper level of multi-tasking. However, but may also limit how much meeting participants are willing to communicate. Additionally, social media may increase the number of channels for communicating, but this increase in communication may lead to the loss of control of content (Ghosh et al., 2012, Kelleher & Sweetser, 2012). For example, social media may allow for better interactions with students, but sharing of student posts may violate the Family Educational Rights Privacy Act (FERPA) by revealing geolocation information (Barnes, 2012).

Forms of the Dark Social Media

Cyberbullying or other forms of harassment have become a prevalent problem for many individuals and workplaces. In an academic environment, where free speech is typically valued, social media outlets are often the go-to place for opinions, misinterpretations, verbal assaults, and stalking. Cyberbullying has had an impact on the reputations both of institutions and of their individual employees. With this in mind, the current social media policies may be inadequate and need to be revamped. Oftentimes, harassment occurs between groups with differing points of view; thus, the careful monitoring of social media sites needs to be a primary focus. When interactions occur via university or college websites, oversight responsibilities fall to the administrators of the pages, who must "listen to" (read and understand) posts made by visitors. Cyberbullying may not be intentional on the part of the posting author, but intent is difficult to measure in a media form that relies on text.

This is may be the reason why the social media sphere is often seen as the "Wild West" by many university legal departments. Social media sites seem to work outside normal social laws and rules; thus, the overarching liability element is generally a top priority for lawyers when considering social media use. Defamation, liability, privacy, copyright, and data protection are all modern legal issues universities must contend with in the social media sphere. Understanding what to do when an online conversation crosses the proverbial line should be clear to all social media participants. A social media guideline statement in the information section of a Facebook page, Twitter feed, university blog, or other social media channel can allay fears and concerns and set the tone for those who wish to follow, comment, and/or create new posts.

By now, it should be evident how critical social media policies are within a college or university setting. Institutions must determine how to use social media outlets and what use is appropriate for their employees. Some questions to consider: Can a department set up a page independently, or must the page be approved by the marketing, public relations, or human resources department? What language must be avoided? What about personal information? Is there such a thing as TMI (too much information) in a post? Who determines that line? Who administers and monitors the social media presence? More questions than answers emerge, but it would behoove institutional administrators, faculty, and staff to read the policy, and, if one doesn't exist, then demand that one be created ... NOW! The National Labor Relations Board (NLRB) provides more than 30 examples of acceptable policies (NLRB, 2015). In general, the NLRB includes the following recommendations (Berkowitz, n.d.):

- Avoid broad, blanket prohibitions on any employee actions with respect to social media. This includes banning employees from talking about their job, complaining about their department head or co-workers, or disparaging university policies.
- Be specific about what employees may not reveal about the university. NLRB has found that employees could have the right to discuss certain aspects of their confidential employment situation (such as salaries or bonuses) via social media.
- Give employees specific examples of inappropriate postings. Suggested acceptable limits include prohibitions on bullying, discrimination, and retaliation. It is best to talk to a lawyer before disciplining an employee for defaming or otherwise lying about the university via social media.
- Do not restrict employees' ability to "friend" co-workers or even students on their personal social media pages.
- Unless you have a legitimate and defensible business purpose as part of your social media guidelines, do not ask employees or applicants for their social media account information or passwords.
- Be consistent in how and when the university reviews the social media accounts for prospective employees and document these policies.

Table 12.1 provides social media policies from some higher education institutions.

Managing "weird," uninvited, or malicious followers can also be a necessary part of safeguarding the online reputation of the institution. An appropriate exercise to conduct would be to develop a list of, say, students, alumni, and relevant professional organizations and then search for them on Facebook, Twitter, and other social media platforms. Based on the search results, any of the following strategies may be appropriate to implement:

- *Blocking:* Un-invite those who appear to disrupt the flow of information on the sites in question, or those who write offensive posts or comments. Another option is to "Hide" certain followers from feeds while allowing others to read those feeds, thus preserving the desired level of free speech.
- *Security:* Check the security on computers and social media outlets to ensure that adequate virus protection exists and that it is possible to secure the sites as updates are made. Try to be cognizant of new viruses or hacking attempts so as not to infect others. For example, many quizzes posted on Facebook allow complete strangers access to participants' personal information and increase the risk of identity theft or viruses. It is therefore wise to avoid those quizzes that ask, "Which Disney character are you?" or "Which Harry Potter character is your Mom most like?"

- *Privacy:* Always check the privacy settings on every social media outlet, but do not assume that clicking a button prevents others from accessing or sharing information on the institution's page. Ask the information technology department for tips on how to secure privacy for all content creators and followers. Also, know the social media rules and regulations as well as the institution's policies on posting. Preserving privacy and keeping others from sharing is difficult in many outlets, but there are ways to control the flow and sharing of information.

Table 12.1 Social Media Policies from Selected Institutions

Institution	Openly Available Policy	Policy Given Via Email	URL
Bowling Green	x		http://scholarworks.bgsu.edu/cgi/viewcontent.cgi?article=1194&context=honorsprojects
Concordia College	x		https://www.concordiacollege.edu/directories/offices-services/communication-marketing/communications-guide/resources/social-media-best-practices/
Eastern Michigan U	x		http://www.emich.edu/communications/documents/guidelines_social_media.pdf
Heidelberg U	x		http://www.heidelberg.edu/offices/mcs/guides/social
Indiana Tech	x – student athlete policy	x	http://indianatechwarriors.com/documents/2014/8/9/Social_Media_Policy.pdf
Ivy Tech CC	x		http://wwwqa.ivytech.edu/humanresources/handbook/ft/personnel-policies-and-procedures/general-college-operations/
Marygrove College	x		http://research.marygrove.edu/about-the-library/policies/10-about-the-library/policies.html
Michigan State U	x		http://cabs.msu.edu/web/msu-social-media-guidelines.html
Oaklund U	x		http://wwwp.oakland.edu/Assets/Oakland/ucm/files-and-documents/social/Oakland-University-Social-Media-Guidelines2015.docx
Ohio Northern U	x		https://www.onu.edu/files/administrative_handbook_-_2013.pdf
Owens CC	x		http://wwwqa.ivytech.edu/humanresources/handbook/ft/personnel-policies-and-procedures/general-college-operations/
Schoolcraft College	x		http://schoolcraft.edu/connect/social-media/social-media-comments#.VtXwcdDqV1F
Tiffin U	x		http://www.tiffin.edu/privacy/Tiffin_University_Social_Media_Policy.pdf
U of Detroit Mercy	x		https://www.udmercy.edu/governance/proposals/adopted-proposals/pdf/UDM_Social_media_policy_May%202012.pdf
U of Michigan	x		http://www.crlt.umich.edu/gsis/p4_3_5_5
U of Toledo	x – several policies		https://www.utoledo.edu/csjhs/coun/Policies/PDFs/Social_Media_Policy.pdf; https://www.utoledo.edu/policies/utmc/administrative/pdfs/3364-100-90-19.pdf
Wayne State U	x		http://www.asp.med.wayne.edu/socialmedia.php

THE ROI OF SOCIAL MEDIA

One of the most prevalent buzzwords in academe today is "return on investment," or ROI. With concerns about sagging enrollment, fewer endowments, and increased tuition costs, many academic institutions are embracing assessments and program cuts to ensure that the appropriate programs are available to students. One way to stress the importance of ROI is to engage stakeholders with outcomes, but not those that are financially related to ROI directly. The use of social media to argue financial ROI is not usually in the best interests of the stakeholders. However, it may be appropriate to discuss outcomes such as alumni news, current students' internship success stories, or grants received from external agencies. For example, if an institution or department wants to inform enrolled students about the current assessment initiative, setting up an event while also sending a mass email about the time, place, and topic may not the best option. Creating an event on Facebook and asking for RSVPs would be more beneficial than mass emailing all students with the specific details of the initiative. In addition to an in-person event, try Livestreaming the event so that those interested can "participate." Keep in mind that too many messages on one specific topic may lead to fewer followers.

There are also arguments for and against measuring social media ROI when it comes to marketing. In educational settings where financial and human resources are shrinking, social media use has proven helpful for branding without a great deal of additional budget. If roughly 75% of students visit a college's social media sites, then appropriately leveraging each site to communicate a brand is paramount to ROI. With dwindling economic resources, higher education institutions would be remiss if they didn't engage in a strategic social media plan that focuses on how visitors use social media and not that they simply visit a site (Fisher, 2009, p. 191). Are they creating a buzz about "people-centric" (not sales-centric or donation-centric) information because "people" is the key term and relies on buzzwords like "community, conversation, dialog, sharing" (Fisher, 2009, p. 193).

A PATH FORWARD AND CONCLUSIONS

Social media can fit naturally into a college or university's broader public relations, marketing, and communications strategies. Integrating social media allows institutions to share what makes them unique, spread the word about specific departments or units, focus on conversations that bond an audience together, and, most important, build a community. Social media platforms are built to maintain a sense of unity among people who share similar interests or backgrounds. Some are ephemeral and are used simply to organize events, while others have long lives and are meant to encourage lasting bonds.

While social media has opened up new doors and avenues of communication, college and university administrators should also consider the associated dangers it presents. By setting clear goals, instituting social media policies, and monitoring what happens in the social media sphere, institutions can ensure that their efforts in this area are successful.

RECOMMENDED RESOURES

- NYC Department of Education. (2013, Spring). *NYC department of education social media guidelines*. Retrieved from http://schools. nyc.gov/NR/rdonlyres/ BCF47CED-604B-4FDD-B752-DC2D81504478/0/DOESocialMediaGuidelines 20120430.pdf
- Pew Research Center. (2015). *Social media usage: 2005–2015*. Pew Internet. Retrieved from http://www.pewinternet.org/2015/10/08/social-networking-usage-2005-2015/
- Reuben, R. (2008). *The use of social media in higher education for marketing and communications: A Guide for Professionals in Higher Education*. Retrieved from http://www.fullerton.edu/technologyservices/_resources/pdfs/social-media-in-higher-education.pdf
- *The future of teaching and learning in higher education*. (Version 13). RIT. Retrieved from https://www.rit.edu/provost/sites/rit.edu.provost/files/future_of_teaching_ and_learning_reportv13.pdf
- *Rowan University's social media policy*. Retrieved from http://www.rowan.edu/web/ social-media-policy

DISCUSSION PROMPTS

1. What does the phrase "social media" mean?
2. What are the functions of social media?
3. What are the responsibilities of content providers when using social media?
4. Why are institutional and departmental branding important to social media use in academic settings?
5. Who should manage the social media sites for the following:
   a. Upper-level administrators?
   b. Department and program heads?
   c. Students?
6. What can be done to protect students when they are harassed online by other students? What can be done to protect faculty or staff if they are being attacked online?
7. Is posting anonymous comments online freedom of speech or defamation of character?
8. How can a college or university best equip faculty and staff and empower them to be institutional advocates and ambassadors on the social Web?
9. Some institutions have one universal social media policy. Others have policies developed by specific programs or for specific audiences (e.g., student athletes). How might a single policy impact an institution differently than varying policies? Which, do you believe, would work best for your institution?
10. Compare the social media policies linked at the end of this chapter. Are there noticeable differences between large universities and small colleges? How might the size of an institution shape its social media needs? How often should a policy be updated?

REFERENCES

Barnes, N. (2012). Potential liability of social media in higher education marketing. *Journal of Higher Education Theory and Practice, 12*(5), 54–59.

Barnes, N. G., & Jacobsen, S. L. (2012). Fish where the fish are: Higher-ed embraces new communications tools to recruit the wired generation. *Journal of Higher Education Theory and Practice, 12*(1), 108-118. doi: 10.1177/0047239515570575

Barnes, N. G., & Lescault, A. V. (2011). *Social media adoption soars as higher-ed experiments and reevaluates its use of new communications tools.* Society for New Communications Research. Retrieved from http://sncr.org/sites/default/files/higherEd.pdf

Barnes, N. G., & Lescault, A. V. (2013). College presidents out-blog and out-Tweet corporate CEOs as higher ed delves deeper into social media to recruit students. *Journal of New Communications Research, 5*(2), 91–105.

Berkowitz, M., Esq. (n.d.). *New NLRB Guidelines for social media in the workplace.* Monster.com. Retrieved March 13, 2016, from http://hiring.monster.com/hr/hr-best-practices/small-business/news/NLRB.aspx

Blankenship, M. (2015). How social media can and should impact higher education. *Hispanic Outlook in Higher Education, 21,* Nov. 29, 2010, 11–12. Retrieved from http://www.hispanicoutlook.com/mark-blankenship/

Casey, R., & Llewellyn, L. P. (2012). Brand consistency in social media: WVU's Eberly works toward a conceptual framework of integrated marketing communications. *International Journal of Integrated Marketing Communications, 4*(2), 17–26.

Chen, B., Seilhamer, R., Bennett, L., & Bauer, S. (2015, June 22). Students' mobile learning practices in higher education: A multi-year study. *Educause.* Retrieved from goo.gl/pCYV3D

Coffin, T., & Fournier, J. (2015, June). *Social media in the learning setting: Opportunities and challenges.* University of Washington: Information Technology. Retrieved from https://itconnect.uw.edu/wp-content/uploads/2013/10/Social-Media-in-the-Learning-Setting.pdf

Cohen, J. S. (2015, November 12). University of Illinois OKs $875,000 settlement to end Steven Salaita dispute. *The Chicago Tribune.* Retrieved from http://www.chicagotribune.com/news/local/breaking/ct-steven-salaita-settlement-met-20151112-story.html

Coutilish, T. (2016). Personal communication with author, Feb. 26.

Duggan, M. (2015). *The demographics of social media users.* Pew Research Center. Retrieved from http://www.pewinternet.org/2015/08/19/the-demographics

Fisher, T. (2009). ROI in social media: A look at the arguments. *Database Marketing & Customer Strategy Management, 16*(3), 189–195. doi: 10.1057/dbm.2009.16. Retrieved from http://www.palgrave-journals.com/dbm/journal/v16/n3/full/dbm200916a.html

Flaherty, C. (2016a). Academics get real. *Inside Higher Ed.* Retrieved from https://www.insidehighered.com/news/2016/01/28/hashtag-unites-adjuncts-and-tenure-line-professors-over-work-life-balance-and-other

Flaherty, C. (2016b). Controversial trustee quits at N.Y.'s Mount Saint Mary. *Inside Higher Ed.* Retrieved from https://www.insidehighered.com/quicktakes/2016/02/17/controversial-trustee-quits-nys-mount-saint-mary

Foulger, M. (2014, June 25). *Higher education success stories: How 3 leading universities use social media.* Retrieved from https://blog.hootsuite.com/higher-education-success-stories-3-leading-universities/

Geiger, M. (2015, September 14). Why colleges should have their own apps. *The App Maker Blog.* Retrieved from https://www.appmakr.com/blog/how-schools-can-utilize-apps/

Ghosh, K., Chawla, S., & Mallott, K. (2012). Use of social media by U.S. colleges: Potentials and pitfalls. *Journal of Higher Education Theory and Practice, 12*(2), 105–118.

Guy, M. (2013). Benefits and dangers of social media in education. *Elearning for all: Principles, best practices and potential of technology in education.* Retrieved from http://elearningtransforms.com/benefits-and-dangers-of-social-media-in-education/

Hanover Research. (2014). Trends in higher education, marketing, recruitment, and technology. Washington, DC: Hanover Research. Retrieved from http://www.hanoverresearch.com/media/Trends-in-Higher-Education-Marketing-Recruitment-and-Technology-2.pdf

Jaschik, J. (2016). Admissions officers check applicants on social media. *Inside Higher Ed.* Retrieved from https://www.insidehighered.com/quicktakes/2016/01/14/admissions-officers-check-applicants-social-media

Kelleher, T., & Sweetser, K. (2012). Social media adoption among university communicators. *Journal of Public Relations Research, 24,* 105–122. doi: 10.1080/1062726X.2012.626130

Kelly, J. (2016). The calm before the crisis. *Inside Higher Ed.* Retrieved from https://www.insidehighered.com/blogs/call-action-marketing-and-communications-higher-education/calm-crisis

Kim, J. (2016). Social media, talking, and meetings. *Inside Higher Ed*. Retrieved from https://www.insidehighered.com/blogs/technology-and-learning/social-media-talking-and-meetings

Legaree, B. A. (2015). Considering the changing face of social media in higher education. *FEMS Microbiology Letters, 362*(15), 1–3. doi: http://dx.doi.org/10.1093/femsle/fnv128

Lenhart, A. (2015). Teens, social media & technology overview 2015. *Pew Research Center, 9.*

Logue, J. (2016). Another speaker blocked. *Inside Higher Ed*. Retrieved from https://www.insidehighered.com/news/2016/02/24/cal-state-los-angeles-cancels-conservative-speakers-appearance

Luttrell, R. (2015). *Social media: How to engage, share, and connect*. Lanham, Maryland: Rowman & Littlefield.

Lynch, L. (2012). Five colleges with great mobile apps. *USA Today*. Retrieved from http://college.usatoday.com/2012/08/15/5-colleges-with-great-mobile-apps/

Mahler, J. (2015). Who spewed that abuse? Anonymous Yik Yak app isn't telling. *New York Times*. Retrieved from http://www.nytimes.com/2015/03/09/technology/popular-yik-yak-app-confers-anonymity-and-delivers-abuse.html?_r=0

Mathewson, T. G. (2015). 5 keys to social media success for higher education administrators. *Education Dive*. Retrieved from http://www.educationdive.com/news/5-keys-to-social-media-success-for-higher-administrators/

National Labor Relations Board (NLRB). (2015). *NLRB's Do's and Don'ts of Employer Handbooks*. Retrieved from https://www.mcguirewoods.com/Client-Resources/Alerts/2015/3/NLRBS-Dos-Donts-Employer-Handbooks-Part-I.aspx

O'Brien, L. (2012). *Six ways to use social media in education*. Duke Center for Instructional Technology. Retrieved from https://cit.duke.edu/blog/2012/04/six-ways-to-use-social-media-in-education/

Owen, L. (2015). Protecting yourself on social media, Part 1. *Inside Higher Ed*. Retrieved from https://www.insidehighered.com/blogs/gradhacker/protecting-yourself-social-media-part-1

Rivituso, J. (2014). Cyberbullying victimization among college students: An interpretive phenomenological analysis. *Journal of Information Systems Education, 21*(5), 71–75.

Schmidt, P. (2015). A new faculty challenge: Fending off abuse on Yik Yak. *Chronicle of Higher Education, 61*(21), 13. Retrieved from http://chronicle.com/article/A-New-Faculty-Challenge-/151463/

Seaman, J., & Tinti-Kane, H. (2013). *Social media for teaching and learning*. Boston: Pearson Learning Solutions and Babson Survey Research Group. Retrieved from http://www.pearsonlearningsolutions.com/higher-education/social-media-survey.php

Stansbury, M. (2015). 5 major trends in higher education's use of social media. *eCampus News*. Retrieved from http://www.ecampusnews.com/top-news/trends-social-media-620/print/

SUNY Albany. (2016). *University releases UAlbany App, Version 2.0*. Retrieved from http://www.albany.edu/news/66436.php

Taylor, M. (2015). Leveraging social media for instructional goals: Status, possibilities, and concerns. *New Directions for Teaching and Learning, 144*, 37–46. doi: 10.1002/tl.20161

13

DEVELOPING CRISIS MANAGEMENT AND EMERGENCY PLANS

Cyndy Caravelis and Thomas C. Johnson

INTRODUCTION

In 2015 alone, there were 23 shootings on college campuses, which resulted in 18 deaths and 27 injuries. Oftentimes, such events are over within ten to 15 minutes, before law enforcement has even had a chance to arrive and assess the situation. This means that the initial responsibility for reacting to a crisis event, such as an active shooter, often falls squarely on the staff and administration. This chapter contains strategies that will help an institution of higher education formulate and implement a successful crisis management plan. Crises come in all shapes and sizes. From active shooter scenarios to hurricanes, these events have the potential to affect thousands of students, faculty, staff, and visitors. Crisis management may be one of the most important elements of institutional planning, since well-formulated plans for various types of emergencies may mean the difference between life and death.

This chapter is written to address general crises management. Many factors influence the size and dynamics of the crisis response structure, including the institution's size, location, budget, and place within the greater community. The following sections are meant to encourage higher education administrators to think about the various factors involved in creating a crisis management response team and implementing an action plan for the different types of emergencies that could potentially threaten their campus.

TYPES OF EMERGENCIES AND LEVELS OF SERIOUSNESS

Table 13.1 lists natural and technological (man-made) disasters that could affect an institution. Depending on the institution's geographic location, only a small percentage of the natural disasters may apply. Unfortunately, a larger percentage of the technological

Table 13.1 Examples of Natural and Technological Disasters

Natural Disasters	Technological Disasters
• Earthquake	• Fire
• Sinkhole/land subsidence	• Hazardous materials, e.g., chemicals
• Flood	• Nuclear accidents
• Hurricane/tropical storm	• Terrorism
• Storm surge	• Active shooter
• Tornado	• Hostage situation
• Wildfire	• Crashes (motor vehicle, aircraft, boat/ship)
• Landslide	• Escaped prisoner
• Tsunami	• Major crime (e.g., armed robbery)
• Volcano	• Riot/crowd control
• Severe storm/thunderstorm	• Bomb threat
• Straight-line wind	• Explosion
• Blizzard/ice storm	• Computer hacker/IT failure
• Drought	• Pandemic flu/mass illness
• Extreme heat	• Power failure
• Hail storm	• Employee strike/unrest
• Avalanche	• Structural collapse
	• Traffic control
	• Dam failure

hazards may be applicable to almost every institution, regardless of size and location. A crisis management team should create a list of disasters that could affect their area and plan for each one accordingly.

In formulating an "all hazards" plan, administrators must not only anticipate the types of disasters that may commonly occur, but also understand that no catastrophic event has boundaries. Even the most unlikely disaster scenario has the potential to materialize, and administrators must be prepared. For example, in 2004, Western Carolina University, the University of North Carolina—Asheville, and the surrounding mountainous area of western North Carolina and eastern Tennessee experienced massive flooding and strong wind gusts caused by the remnants of Hurricanes Frances and Ivan, which occurred within a week of one another. While the mountains of western North Carolina hardly seem a location where university officials should be concerned about hurricanes, the area nonetheless experienced up to 23 inches of rainfall and strong, gusty winds of between 40 and 60 miles per hour (National Weather Service, 2004; Roth, 2004). These two systems produced flooding, landslides, and road/bridge washouts. Additionally, the water supply, electricity, and transportation were adversely affected and several deaths were recorded.

It is important to rank the relative seriousness of each potential disaster. Different seriousness levels will require different response levels from the crisis management team. Seriousness scales are readily available for a number of natural disasters (see Table 13.2). For example, a thunderstorm is classified as severe if its winds reach or exceed 58 miles per hour, it drops surface hail at least 0.75 inches in diameter, or it produces a tornado (Haddow, Bullock, & Coppola, 2011). Pre-establishing various actions plans based on

Table 13.2 Examples of Seriousness Scales

Tornadoes	Enhanced Fujita–Pearson Scale
Hurricanes	Saffir–Simpson Scale
Earthquakes	Richter Scale and Modified Mercalli Intensity (MMI)
Severe winter storms	Northeast Snowfall Impact Scale (NESIS)

the seriousness level will enable the crisis management team to respond to a disaster immediately upon recognition of the event.

Without a mitigation plan in place, smaller institutions may be unable to successfully recover from a major disaster. Institutions with a comprehensive plan in place can resume regular operations more quickly, which helps them reduce the effects on students, faculty, and staff (Brown, 2008). Additional mitigation activities that a number of institutions have adopted include obtaining flood insurance and improving building practices. One study reported that each dollar spent on mitigation activities saved society an average of $4 in return (MMC, 2005).

LOCAL COMMUNITY

Before establishing a crisis management planning committee, an institution must consider its position in the surrounding community. Based on that relationship, the institution may play an instrumental role in handling larger community disasters. For example, when a deadly F5 tornado struck Tuscaloosa, Alabama, on April 27, 2011, the University of Alabama assisted in recovery efforts. The university provided shelter during and after the tornado (Jones & Grayson, 2011) and coordinated a disaster relief fund entitled Acts of Kindness (Kausler, 2011). Moreover, faculty, staff, and students focused their service learning projects on helping the community to rebuild (Dialog, 2011; Pow, 2011). By assuming a helping role to their local community, institutions in rural areas may provide shelter or other services during certain disasters. By identifying whether the community at large considers campus buildings to be shelter points, the crisis management team can anticipate the number of evacuees they may be taking in during subsequent disasters.

Institutions may have access to community resources and capabilities that can be utilized in emergency situations (Chachkes, Nelson, Portelli, Woodrow, Bloch, & Goldfrank, 2007). They should work with their local government partners to include mutual aid agreements in critical incident response and emergency management areas. While many colleges and universities may be prepared to respond to minor emergencies, large-scale disasters often overwhelm an institution's response capability. Their first responders frequently require assistance from the surrounding community's first responders to restore order, protect property, and save lives.

In its basic form, a mutual aid agreement is a compact among emergency responders across jurisdictional boundaries to assist one another during certain events. When the institution is a state entity, the agreement must be made between the institution's chief executive officer and the agency head in the adjoining community. Many states have laws that establish requirements for mutual aid agreements, including identifying who may enter into such compacts. The mutual aid agreement should specify information such as the type of events for which assistance may be requested, who may initiate the request on behalf of an agency, who may approve the response for the other agency, the duration for which the aid may be provided, and indemnification provisions (Commission on Accreditation for Law Enforcement Agencies, 2006). After the mutual aid agreement is written, it should be signed by representatives of the involved parties.

For any event that involves multiple government entities, command structures can be confusing. It is important that written agreements clarifying command structure and coordination be in place before a crisis occurs. By establishing intergovernmental agreements, public agencies will work together to develop operational plans and share resources, such as radio systems, information technologies, and facilities. Intergovernmental agreements may be particularly important for institutions without sworn police officers. These agreements differ from mutual aid agreements in that they tend to define long-term relationships between organizations, while mutual aid agreements define the short-term provision of aid. Intergovernmental agreements are typically used for the sharing of resources, authority, or services.

The complexity and expense of specialized equipment, coupled with budget restraints, makes it appropriate for organizations to share resources. For example, after the September 11 terrorist attacks, it became apparent that radio interoperability was a major issue. The State of North Carolina invested heavily in developing the Voice Interoperability Plan for Emergency Responders system, which provides an 800-megahertz infrastructure for public safety agencies. Currently, 314 agencies have signed intergovernmental agreements to share this system (North Carolina Department of Crime Control & Public Safety, 2016).

Many institutions are private and therefore not covered by state laws that grant police authority to state institutions. An intergovernmental agreement may allow for a private institution to create its own police department. For example, the University of Miami has such an agreement with the Coral Gables (FL) Police Department. The agreement conveys authority to the university police officers and provides them with citywide jurisdiction. It further holds the City of Coral Gables harmless for the actions of the university police officers. Finally, it also serves as a mutual aid agreement between the university and city (Chief David Rivero, personal communication, March 11, 2011).

While many institutions may desire to have a police force on campus, they may have neither the authority nor the resources to establish such a force. In this situation, the institution may enter into an intergovernmental agreement with a local law enforcement agency. Perhaps the largest arrangement of this type exists between the Los Angeles County Sheriff's Department and the Los Angeles Community College District, with the sheriff's department serving nine campuses and over 130,000 students (Los Angeles County Sheriff's Department, 2014). Such agreements can be tailored to fit the institution's needs. For example, Pensacola State College in Florida has its own police officers on duty from 7:00 a.m. to 11:00 p.m. during the week, while the Pensacola Police Department responds to crime calls on campus outside those times (Coreen Goben, personal communication, March 11, 2011). This agreement saves the college the expense of providing 24-hour law enforcement coverage.

Institutions that have intergovernmental agreements with community first responders generally have close working relationships and understandings with these responders.

These agreements ensure that the necessary rules are in place with regard to responsibilities, liability, accountability, authority, training, and cost (Burdick, 2006). Additionally, institutions that have pre-existing arrangements for food, fuel, water, buses, and IT functions generally have a faster response time and experience smoother recovery operations (U.S. Department of Homeland Security, 2006).

STATE AND FEDERAL AGENCIES

In addition to coordinating with public agencies on the city or county level, institutions must also coordinate with state and federal agencies that assist with funding planning, preparedness, response, and recovery initiatives (Brown, 2008). Based on the Disaster Mitigation Act of 2000, all communities are required to develop hazard mitigation plans to be eligible for funding related to disasters. Institutions should make certain that they are included in any Federal Emergency Management Agency (FEMA) grant proposals, which can assist with the development of mitigation plans and programs to increase disaster awareness. Also, academic institutions should ensure that their buildings and property are included in the damage assessments conducted by FEMA after a disaster.

CRISIS MANAGEMENT PLANNING COMMITTEE

Depending on the institution's size, there are numerous functions that may be handled by a single committee or divided among multiple committees. Regardless of the committee type and size, certain crisis management elements must be discussed: emergency preparedness, threat assessment, and crisis response. The purpose of each is discussed below, as are the recommended representatives from various departments who may serve key roles on the committee.

Emergency Preparedness Committee

The emergency preparedness committee's role is twofold. First, the committee must anticipate the numerous crises that could impact the campus community. Second, they must then formulate an appropriate plan of action. Research findings consistently point to inadequate safety planning, ineffective management, poor crisis manager training, and uncoordinated communication methods as primary concerns (Mak, Mallard, Bui, & Au, 1999; Piotrowski, Armstrong, & Stopp, 1997; Reilly, 2008; Smith, Kress, Fenstemaker, & Hyder, 2001; Wang, 2008). These areas of concern can be anticipated and alleviated with proper planning.

Members

1. *Emergency manager:* 70% of larger institutions (15,000 students or more) have a dedicated emergency manager with sole responsibility for disaster planning, preparation, and response (National Association of College and University Business Officers, 2009).
2. *Campus police or security director:* Many institutions that do not have an emergency manager do have a safety, security, or police director, who generally assumes many of the same responsibilities. Further, campus safety, security, or police officers are typically present on campus 24 hours a day and are the first responders to any event.

The officers' response is typically dictated by policies, procedures, and training developed or mandated by the campus safety, security, or police director. The campus safety, security, or police director is the individual to whom these officers first report the incident; therefore, the director must collect the initial emergency or disaster information and make the appropriate notifications to the institution's management team. The director is frequently the individual charged with ensuring that the campus community is notified of the emergency and that mutual aid is requested from adjacent jurisdictions.

3. *Provost/chancellor/president:* By virtue of their position, senior officials are the parties ultimately accountable for how the institution copes with the incident. They also have the latitude to commit resources, make policy decisions, and obtain any additional resources necessary to avert or respond to a crisis. While they will delegate authority to the individual in charge of managing the incident, they serve a vital role in planning and preparing for emergencies (FEMA, 2008).

4. *Business office representative:* The business office is typically responsible for implementing the institution's continuity-of-operations plan in the event of an emergency or disaster. The representative generally partners with other senior campus administrators to ensure that the institution's business continues as normally as possible. Additionally, he or she plays a key role in helping to make emergency purchases that aid in the response to a crisis.

5. *IT representative:* Information technology is critical to business continuity and disseminating information to the campus community. The IT representative is a key partner with the business office representative in implementing the institution's continuity-of-operations plan. Further, the IT representative is responsible for ensuring that sensitive data remain protected and that the institution continues to comply with privacy and data protection laws.

6. *Faculty representative:* Faculty partner with university administrators to support the institution in its response to and recovery from an emergency or disaster. Faculty can provide much-needed staffing for critical functions such as communications and transportation. Further, they play a key role in continuity of operations to ensure that classes continue and students complete the semester.

7. *Student representative:* This individual is key to representing student interests in the institution's response to and recovery from an emergency or disaster. The student representative can further work with administrators to determine how students can assist the institution during and after the crisis. Finally, the student representative can keep the student body informed of the institution's response and recovery plans.

Threat Assessment Team

One challenge with many crises is that critical decisions with long-term impacts need to be made with limited, unofficial information in a relatively short period of time (Piotrowski & Guyette, 2009). The threat assessment team's purposes are to analyze the threat potential of any given situation and recommend de-escalation strategies (Jaeger, Deisinger, Houghton, & Cychosz, 2003). For smaller institutions, the emergency preparedness committee and threat assessment team may consist of the same members and have overlapping responsibilities.

Members

1. *Campus police or security director:* The campus police or security director is responsible for providing a first response to an active threat. When the potential threat is a person who is jeopardizing others with threats of violence, it may be necessary to remove the person from the campus or even arrest the person. The campus police or security director coordinates these activities.

2. *Human resources representative:* When the person posing the threat is an employee, the human resources representative is responsible for interpreting institutional personnel policies and state and federal workplace violence laws as they relate to personnel actions. The human resources representative provides guidance for supervisors and other employees.

3. *Student and academic affairs representatives:* When the person posing the threat is a student, student affairs and academic affairs representatives are important in helping to assess the individual and suggest a course of action. Student affairs representatives generally provide information regarding the student's out-of-classroom activities and behavior and enforce the student code of conduct. The academic affairs representatives provide information regarding the student's academic progress, classroom demeanor, and relationships with faculty and other students, along with options for addressing the student's academic performance.

4. *Legal counsel:* The legal counsel assists with interpreting institutional policies and procedures, as well as state and federal laws. Further, the legal counsel assists in determining a lawful course of action for the institution's officials in addressing the threat.

5. *Mental health services representatives:* The mental health services representative is helpful in assessing the person of concern's behavior. Frequently, a mental health services representative can meet with the individual, conduct an assessment, and recommend a course of action to assist the individual. In extreme cases, the mental health services representative may recommend that a student be withdrawn from courses or an employee placed on leave due to an imminent threat.

Crisis Response Team

The crisis response team is a group of individuals that can be brought quickly together to initiate an incident response. On some campuses, the threat assessment team and the crisis response team serve the same role. The crisis response team's role may include managing potentially violent or dangerous situations, advising administrators and other appropriate personnel on critical incidents, facilitating the delivery of post-incident recovery needs, and disseminating information about the crisis (Jaeger et al., 2003).

Members

1. *Campus police or security director:* The campus police or security director generally is responsible for coordinating the initial emergency response to an event. Additionally, the campus police or security director frequently serves as a liaison to local community first-responder agencies and is responsible for making mutual aid requests. Further, the campus police or security director keeps other team members and senior administrators informed of conditions or activities related to the incident.

2. *Provost's office representative:* The provost's office representative is responsible for assessing the event's impact upon the institution's academic mission and determining how academic resources can support the institution's response and recovery. In the absence of the institution's president or chancellor, the provost is often the senior administrator and assumes responsibility for directing institutional activities.

3. *Human resources representative:* The human resources representative is responsible for assessing the event's impact upon the institution's employees and identifying resources that are available to support employees during and after the crisis. The representative is also helpful in interpreting institutional policies and procedures, as well as state and federal laws that affect employees and their presence during or after an event.

4. *Dean of students' office (student affairs) representative:* The dean of students' representative is responsible for determining the event's impact upon students, and for coordinating or directing activities designed to enhance student safety. Further, the representative is responsible for identifying and implementing resources to help students recover from the event.

5. *Parent liaison:* The parent liaison is responsible for keeping fellow parents informed about an event, the event's effect upon students, and the students' welfare. This liaison provides timely updates to parents and helps them communicate with their children. Generally, the liaison is a member of the student affairs division.

6. *Mental health services representative:* The use of a mental health services representative frequently depends upon the nature of the event. In situations where the threat results from an individual, the mental health services representative may be helpful in assessing that person's behavior. However, in all events, the mental health services representative can provide assistance to individuals who may be traumatized and identify ways in which the institution can help the campus community emotionally recover from an event.

Once the committee(s) have been established, it is important to determine a succession order for each member, particularly with regard to the crisis response team. Generally, the members appointed to the crisis response team serve a critical function that must be addressed during any event. A succession order defines the roles that must be staffed and who will staff them in the absence of the incumbent members (Perry & Lindell, 2007). The crisis response team will be discussed in greater detail later in the chapter.

PLACEMENT OF THE PLANNING COMMITTEES

Timely response to a crisis of any magnitude is of paramount importance. Virtually all crisis responses require the mobilization of resources. Therefore, the office of emergency and disaster management should be closely aligned to the institution's senior operations officer with decision-making authority (Thrower, Healy, Margolis, Lynch, Stafford, & Taylor, 2008). At larger institutions, the emergency management function may be its own department and report directly to a vice president or vice chancellor for administration or business operations. At smaller institutions, the emergency management function may be placed under the police or security department, or the facilities management department, as these departments often have resources that can be quickly mobilized to respond to an emergency or disaster. It is important that the relationship between the campus public safety executive and the senior decision-makers be established in advance so that the emergency response team has direct access to an individual who can grant them the authority to mobilize resources for an emergency event.

BUDGET AND FUNDING

Mobilization of resources (such as personnel, equipment, and supplies) is critical to the successful implementation of the crisis management plan (FEMA, 2008). Regardless of the crisis management budget size, it is important to have a flexible plan that is adaptable to various situations. The ability to manage resources to adjust to changing conditions is particularly vital in light of increasing budget constraints.

Campus police, security, and safety officials are charged with protecting sensitive research projects and facilities (such as nuclear, biological, and chemical projects and areas), large-venue events (such as football games), and a vulnerable population consisting primarily of 18- to 22-year-old students, yet they are frequently denied access to external grant and funding sources that are available to traditional law enforcement and public safety agencies (Greenberg, 2007). For example, when the Department of Homeland Security was created and began issuing grants for emergency preparedness, higher education institutions were all but excluded. Grants were made available only to governmental entities, leaving private institutions ineligible to receive these funds (Greenberg, 2005). State-supported institutions had to compete with state highway patrols, police, and bureaus of investigation and frequently were denied access to funding. While many law enforcement and public safety agencies in communities that were home to colleges and universities used the presence of these institutions to justify, at least in part, their need for these grants, very little, if any, grant funds actually made their way into the budgets of campus police, security, and safety departments. Although there have been calls for increased grant funding for higher education institutions (Greenberg, 2005), this money has not substantially materialized.

Even when grants are available, campus police, safety, and security agencies are confronted with the challenge that many such grants require some level of matching funding. Additionally, many grants have use restrictions or require a continuing obligation that must be met within an agency's resources. For example, the Emergency Management Performance Grants Program, that can help institutions develop emergency and mitigation plans, conduct preparedness exercises, or develop continuity-of-operations plans, requires a 50% funding match (Hodges, 2016). The inability to provide the matching funding or otherwise comply with the conditions of a grant is a primary reason why many agencies do not avail themselves of these opportunities (Haddow et al., 2011).

THE CRISIS MANAGEMENT RESPONSE STRUCTURE

Once the crisis management team is in place and an "all hazards plan" has been formulated, the next crucial steps are to implement the plan through pre-disaster preparation and to provide proper training. Part of pre-disaster preparedness is creating a Crisis Response

Box (Williams, 2009), which contains directions that will facilitate a streamlined response to the crisis. A number of other elements are also included in the Crisis Response Box; below is a list of some common components:

1. *Map of campus and the surrounding areas:* Crisis planners should review traffic patterns and create an emergency traffic plan that will both accommodate traffic and allow emergency personnel direct access to the crisis location.
2. *Aerial photos of the campus:* Providing all critical response agencies (including police, paramedics, and fire personnel) with an aerial perspective of both the campus and its surrounding areas is very helpful in expediting their response to a disaster.
3. *Campus layout:* Beyond current and accurate blueprints of all campus buildings, this includes information about water lines, gas lines, electric, cable, telephone, sprinkler systems, alarm systems, elevators, and hazardous material locations.
4. *Keys:* A master key and an extra set of keys when the master key cannot be used should be made readily available.
5. *Fire alarm turn-off procedures:* The fire alarm can make it difficult for responders to communicate with each other and potential victims in a crisis.
6. *Sprinkler system turn-off procedures:* Water may make evacuations more difficult and could lead to a secondary hazardous situation if it comes into contact with electrical outlets.
7. *Utility shut-off valves:* There should be clear identification of the access points and shut-off points for all utilities (water, electricity, and gas) so that they can be quickly shut off.
8. *Layout of gas and utility lines:* A diagram that shows all of the utility lines on campus should be readily available.
9. *Telephone numbers for the key crisis response team members:* Include the names and telephone numbers of key individuals responsible for coordinating with the local emergency responders. Other helpful numbers to have available would include those of the public information officer, student affairs, grounds and maintenance (facilities management), and the coordinator for food, water, and supplies.
10. *Designated command post and staging areas:* Three distinct staging areas should be predetermined, one for each of the following groups: (1) emergency personnel and law enforcement, (2) media, and (3) parents and students.
11. *Emergency resource list:* A list of organizations and individuals who may be called on to assist in an emergency should be compiled and readily available. This list might include the following, with complete contact information:

    - American Red Cross;
    - Federal Aviation Authority (FAA) local office;
    - National Organization for Victim Assistance (NOVA);
    - Local emergency radio channels;
    - County District Attorney's Victim/Witness Assistance;
    - Parent representatives (trained to help parents receive information and answer questions);
    - Trained crisis intervention counselors.

12. *Evacuation sites:* Several predetermined evacuation sites should be included based on the type and nature of the disaster. For example, the evacuation site designated for a school shooter may be different from the one designated for a large chemical spill.

13. *First-aid supplies location:* First-aid supplies should be located throughout the campus. The locations can be noted on the building blueprints and layouts.

Once all of the requisite plans and documents are in place, the necessary personnel must be trained to respond appropriately during an emergency. Institutions must do more than just plan for all hazards; they must train on their plans. Plans without training are almost worthless. The rapid and fluid nature of emergencies and disasters does not allow time for campus officials to pull a plan off of a shelf and read it. The time to read, understand, and prepare to implement a crisis management plan is *before* the crisis occurs. It is recommended that plans be assessed annually in some form, such as a seminar, tabletop, functional, or full-scale exercise (Drake, 2014).

The most comprehensive and well-developed crisis management plan is only as good as the ability of campus officials to implement it. Therefore, campus officials should conduct regular training on the plan with all those who share responsibility for its implementation. Training exercises not only prepare campus officials for implementing the plan, they also expose flaws in the plan before an emergency or disaster occurs and allow campus officials the opportunity to correct or compensate for these flaws. Further, training enables campus officials to practice skills or use equipment and tools that do not figure into their everyday duties, promoting a greater level of proficiency that will reduce their stress and anxiety during a crisis.

Even though campus administrators are generally not considered first responders, they should participate in crisis management plan training. This participation provides administrators with direct knowledge of the various components of the plan, the response capability of campus employees, and the level of cooperation that exists with community public safety officials. Such knowledge is important for campus administrators, who in times of crisis must frequently make critical decisions under time pressures and with limited information (Hale, Hale, & Dulek, 2006; Moats, Chermak, & Dooley, 2008).

The campus community must be informed of the crisis management plan so its members understand how campus officials and public safety officials will respond. Additionally, the campus community shares responsibility for its own safety and should understand how its members may contribute to the effectiveness of the plan. Many institutions have posted this information online (http://www-bfs.ucsd.edu/emerg/ ucsdemp.htm) or have developed presentations (http://www.police.vt.edu/VTPD_v2.1/ emergencytraining.html) for training their campus community.

INCIDENT COMMAND GROUP FUNCTION
AND RESPONSIBILITY

The Incident Command System (ICS) is a standardized, all-hazard, on-scene management approach that allows community responders and campus personnel to adopt an organizational structure that matches the demands of the crisis without being hindered by jurisdictional boundaries (FEMA, 2008). Based on the overlap between higher education institutions and the greater community that was discussed earlier in the chapter, the ICS model allows all parties to know their assigned roles and work together in an effective manner. The flexibility of ICS makes it a cost-effective approach, as it can readily grow or shrink to meet the various institutional crises that may arise.

ICS is based on proven best practices and consists of procedures for managing personnel, equipment, facilities, and communications. Its three primary purposes are (1) the safety of responders and others, (2) the achievement of tactical objectives, and (3) the efficient use of resources. Standard management and command features of ICS provide for the efficient direction of the operations, planning, logistics, and finance/administration functions. Other features include a common terminology, modular organization, use of position titles, unified command structure, incident action plans, manageable span of control, organizational facilities, integrated communications, accountability, and an emergency operations center.

While the features of ICS are consistent regardless of the application, FEMA recognizes the uniqueness of applying ICS within the higher education environment. To help campus administrators and first responders understand and implement ICS, FEMA has developed an ICS for Higher Education training course (https://training.fema.gov/hiedu/aemrc/eplanning/l363.aspx).

Just as they need to train on their crisis management plans, campus administrators and first responders must also train in the use of ICS. While ICS is flexible and can expand or contract to meet the size of the crisis, campus officials and first responders must practice this expansion and contraction. Further, campus employees who are seldom used in a crisis response except in the most serious situations must still be trained on how they would fit into an expanded ICS. To ensure familiarity with ICS, many campuses use it to manage major non-emergency events. For example, Appalachian State University uses ICS to manage its home football games (Norris, 2011).

It is critical to establish command before the onset of a crisis for a variety of reasons. First, decision-making is impossible without a command structure. Second, lack of command can become a safety hazard in and of itself for first responders, students, and staff. Events such as Hurricane Katrina and the Platte Canyon school shooting illustrate that failure to establish command hampers a coordinated response and further threatens life safety when multiple agencies and organizations respond to a major event, Therefore, a designated Incident Commander is responsible for all management functions until he or she delegates the function to another party. The Incident Commander is, essentially, in charge of managing the scene and performing of the following functions:

- Establishing a command post;
- Mobilizing personnel;
- Requesting outside assistance;
- Preparing a staging area;
- Maintaining media relations.

Besides the Incident Command function, there are other essential roles that need to be filled during a crisis situation, the first of which is the Operations function. The Operations Section director is responsible for all activities related to the tactical response to the event (FEMA, 2008). The Operations Section director is usually the person with the greatest experience and/or training in addressing the tactical response. He or she is responsible for organizing, supervising, and assigning resources for the tactical response.

The Operations Section is usually one of the first staff functions created and involves a bottom-up development starting with the first units on the scene (FEMA, 2008). As additional units become available for the tactical response, such as police, firefighters, or air units, these resources are fed into the Operations Section. If resources are available for a tactical response but are not immediately deployed, they are frequently assigned to a staging area, where the Operations Section director appoints a liaison (FEMA, 2008). The liaison organizes the units when they report to the staging area, assigns them to teams, if necessary, and then dispatches them as instructed by the Operations Section director.

The individual appointed to direct the Planning Section is responsible for collecting and disseminating useful information to the responders (FEMA, 2008). For example, in an active shooter response in a class building, it may be helpful for responders to know how many classes are currently being conducted in the target building and how many students are enrolled in those classes. Additionally, the Planning Section can obtain campus maps, building floor plans, incident action plans, and other documents. Therefore, the Planning Section director should be a person who knows how to access resources that will provide useful information to the Incident Commander and other section directors.

In an expanded response, the Planning Section may be subdivided into four units: the Resources Unit, the Situation Unit, the Documentation Unit, and the Demobilization Unit (FEMA, 2008). The Resources Unit manages check-in activities, monitors the status of all event resources, and plays a significant role in writing the crisis management plan. The Situation Unit collects and analyzes data on the situation; prepares situation reports, displays, and summaries; and develops maps and overviews. The Documentation Unit provides duplication services, maintains the crisis management plan, and records and archives data relevant to the event. The Demobilization Unit works with the Incident Commander and section directors to ensure that resources are released from the event in an orderly manner and also documents expenditure of resources to assist with resource replenishment.

The Logistics Section supports the response by managing service and support needs (FEMA, 2008). According to FEMA (2008), the duties of the Logistics Support function include:

- Ordering, obtaining, maintaining, and accounting for essential personnel, equipment, and supplies;
- Providing communication planning and resources;
- Setting up food services for responders;
- Setting up and maintaining incident facilities;
- Providing support transportation;
- Providing medical services to incident personnel (pp. 5–33).

In an expanded incident, the Logistics Section director has to work closely with the Finance/Administration Section (see below) director to purchase or otherwise acquire the services and supplies needed.

Depending upon the size of the event, the Logistics Section can be expanded to include a number of different units to support the response. The communications, medical, food, supplies, facilities, and ground support units are those most commonly included in the Logistics Section. The director of the Logistics Section must be someone who is adept at acquiring and coordinating the necessary resources to support the first responders.

The Finance/Administration Section addresses the primary issue of paying for the response. For minor events, agencies typically fund their response from their operating budgets. However, for major events, such as when a formal disaster declaration is made, the Finance/Administration Section director must ensure meticulous record-keeping to apply for disaster funding or grants to pay for the response. Personnel administration is also part of the Finance/Administration Section function. Employees must be tracked so that they can be paid for their services. Further, the Finance/Administration Section administers workers' compensation and insurance claims for employees who are injured or killed in the response. Given the overlapping responsibilities of the Finance/Administration Section, it is not uncommon to find administrators from different campus business functions involved in the section's operations.

Declaring a State of Emergency

Declaring a state of emergency allows for the suspension of some or all normal activities in response to or anticipation of a threat to personal safety, property, or both. This suspension of activities permits first responders and critical employees to respond to or prepare for the threatening event. An institution can be affected by a declaration of emergency issued at the institutional, local, state, or federal level.

The president, chancellor, or board of trustees is usually allowed to declare an institutional state of emergency by virtue of legislative or other official action. As chief executive officers, these officials are responsible for the campus community and facilities, and are expected to take reasonable and prudent actions to protect them. Institutions may also use declarations of emergency to raise public awareness of the risks associated with the crisis and let people know what safety measures need to be taken. When conditions dictate, administrators may suspend normal operations and mobilize campus resources to respond to an actual or anticipated threat. When the institution has mutual aid agreements or memoranda of understanding with local public safety agencies, officials may request assistance from these agencies even when there is no local declaration of emergency.

A local declaration of emergency is generally issued by the city or county emergency manager. An institution situated within the jurisdiction of the declaring official is covered by this local declaration of emergency. State law, mutual aid agreements, and memoranda of understanding dictate how resources will be mobilized and shared between the institution and the local government. Communities with an institution in their jurisdiction have a valuable asset, given that these institutions often have resources and capabilities that can be shared in emergency situations (Chachkes et al., 2007). Many communities avail themselves of these resources and capabilities and have incorporated them into their crisis management plan. For example, many local governments include their local institution's facilities as shelter locations in their crisis management plan.

When the scope of the emergency or disaster is beyond the capabilities of local government, the emergency manager may request assistance or mutual aid from other municipalities and/or counties, or appeal to the state for aid. However, institutions are generally excluded from state laws allowing for the requesting of state aid due to their status as either private or state-supported institutions rather than local governmental entities. Therefore, when an on-campus emergency or disaster exceeds the response capability of the institution and local government, it is the local emergency manager, rather than the institution's chief executive officer, who must request aid from the state (Oliver, 2011).

Generally, when a local emergency manager requests aid from the state, that request is made to the state emergency management office, which forwards the request to the governor's office (Oliver, 2011). If the request is approved, the governor's office may activate the state emergency plan and provide state resources to assist in response and recovery. Additionally, governors frequently have the authority to suspend state laws or local ordinances if doing so will aid in the response to and recovery from the emergency (Oliver, 2011).

Major disasters, such as tornadoes or hurricanes, may affect a substantial portion of a state, prompting the governor to declare a state of emergency in the affected areas; this includes local institutions. A state declaration of emergency allows the governor to suspend laws, establish economic controls over resources such as food and gasoline, issue emergency orders, and mobilize the National Guard (Oliver, 2011). Further, governors generally work with state legislators to release emergency funds and reallocate state agency budgets to benefit state-supported institutions that expend resources in emergency response and need assistance in repairing or replacing facilities and equipment (Oliver, 2011).

When the scope of the emergency or disaster is beyond the capabilities of the state, the governor may request that the President of the United States declare a state emergency as allowed by the Robert T. Stafford Act (2007). A presidential declaration allows FEMA to coordinate the mobilization of federal resources to respond to the event. Depending upon the event, the President may issue either an emergency or disaster declaration (FEMA, 2010). The President may appoint officials and agencies to address the emergency and to use resources and override processes for the response effort.

COMMUNICATION NETWORK

Incident responders rely heavily upon effective communications and information systems to coordinate disaster efforts. The National Incident Management System (NIMS) describes the requirements necessary to create a standardized communications framework (FEMA, 2008). Those requirements include the following:

1. *Interoperability:* Interoperable communications systems are those that allow for multiple agencies to exchange information directly, even if they are using disparate communication systems (Thrower et al., 2008).
2. *Reliability:* The communication means and equipment must be resilient and capable of allowing for the continuous sharing of information for the duration of the emergency or disaster. Institutions should have a contingency plan in the event that their normal communications network fails.

3. *Scalability:* This refers to the ability of a communications system to expand or contract as needed for an emergency or disaster response (DHS, 2008). Scalability does not simply refer to the number of radios, cellular telephones, or other communications devices that are available; it also refers to the capability of a system to accommodate a large number of these devices.
4. *Portability:* This refers to the capability of communications equipment and protocols to be carried, available, or otherwise used by first responders and officials involved in an emergency or disaster (DHS, 2008). It also refers to the capability of communications systems to allow for the assignment of radio frequencies across jurisdictions so that mutual aid responders can communicate with primary first responders (DHS, 2008).
5. *Redundancy:* This refers to the capability to accomplish a task using alternative means and/or equipment. In communications, it refers to the ability of first responders and officials to sustain communications in the event that the primary communications system breaks down (DHS, 2008).

EMERGENCY NOTIFICATION

Depending on the nature and size of the crisis, the Incident Commander may designate personnel to disseminate information about the event and provide safety information and liaison services (FEMA, 2008). Campus public safety officials should have the authority to send emergency messages both from campus and off of campus grounds. Before sending an emergency message, officials should consider its timeliness and accuracy, and only relay information that is useful to recipients (Thrower et al., 2008). The Public Information Officer (PIO), or an individual in a similar role, typically serves as the conduit of information to the media, parents, and other interested parties. While the Incident Commander ultimately approves information released by the PIO, the PIO advises the Incident Commander about media relations and the necessary dissemination of information.

Institutions should employ a variety of methods to disseminate emergency information. The campus mass-notification system should include both high-technology (i.e., cellphone texts, email communications, etc.) and low-technology solutions (i.e., flyers, loudspeakers, etc.) (Thrower et al., 2008). The criticism surrounding Virginia Tech's failure to issue timely information about the campus shooting in 2007, coupled with the Clery Act, which requires institutions to disclose information about campus crime, has led many institutions to avail themselves of both high- and low-technology emergency communications solutions. The use of high and low technology provides redundancy to ensure that information is disseminated through multiple channels. Institutions should use the following criteria when selecting their emergency notification systems:

1. *Multi-point communication:* The system should have the capability of notifying the entire campus through multiple channels and points of contact, such as text messaging, voice messages, and email.
2. *Capacity:* The system should be proficient in delivering all messages reliably and quickly.

3. *Security:* In the event that a third-party vendor is used, access to private data should be limited to authorized personnel.
4. *24/7 service:* Training, customer support, and technical support should be included in services provided by a third-party vendor.
5. *Experience:* A third-party vendor should have considerable experience in providing this service to institutions of all sizes.
6. *Assessment:* The service should generate reports that allow institutions to monitor, measure, and manage the effectiveness of the system.

Although a large number of institutions report the use of multiple means of emergency notification, a number of these notification systems are based on an "opt-in for participation" approach where faculty, staff, and students must sign up to be included (Piotrowski & Guyette, 2009). A major problem with opt-in systems is that many students choose not to subscribe, thus depriving themselves of critical and timely notification and information in the event of an emergency. An alternative to the opt-in feature is an opt-out feature whereby students are automatically included in the emergency notification system and must choose to remove themselves from it. Research suggests that less than 8% of students remove themselves from opt-out systems, while less than 40% register when the system provides an opt-in feature (Staman, Katsouros, & Hach, 2009).

LEGAL IMPLICATIONS

When planning for campus disasters and emergencies, certain legal requirements set forth by federal, state, and local entities may need to be considered in the formulation and implementation of a crisis management plan. While virtually all businesses and organizations can benefit from the creation of such plans, colleges and universities are among the few higher education institutions that are federally mandated to create and assess management plans for dangerous and emergency situations (Healy, 2010). For example, as mentioned earlier in the chapter, institutions of higher education must comply with the Clery Act. Also, federal law requires that colleges and universities include an emergency response and evacuation policy statement in their annual security report.

Another relevant federal law that could potentially impact crisis management plans is the Superfund Amendments and Reauthorization Act (SARA) of 1986, which established federal regulations for handling hazardous materials. Under this law, institutions that store large quantities of certain chemicals must provide regular reports to the Occupational Safety and Health Administration (OSHA) regarding the storage of these chemicals. One reason for this requirement is so that first responders will have rapid access to information regarding these chemicals and plan their response accordingly. However, what may be of greater importance is that, on campuses where these chemicals are stored, OSHA requires campus first responders to use the Incident Command System for their response protocol (FEMA, 2008).

In addition to federal laws, there are also state laws to consider. For example, in North Carolina, state law gives a county or municipal health director jurisdiction over an institution in the event of an infectious or pandemic disease outbreak (North Carolina General Statutes §130A-41, 1999). State laws also address the use, maintenance, and care of state-supported institutions' property. For example, Florida state statute mandates that state-supported universities shall make their facilities available to a local emergency manager upon request as a public hurricane evacuation shelter (Florida State Statute §252.385, 2006).

ACTIVE SHOOTER SCENARIOS

Law enforcement uses the term "active shooter" to describe a crisis that is in progress. Implicit in this definition is that crisis responders have the ability to affect the outcomes based on their responses. Of the 160 active shooter incidents in the United States between 2000 and 2013, 7.5% occurred at institutions of higher education. Based on the FBI's report, shooters ranged from 18 to 62 years of age, and the vast majority of them were former or current students. In 2008, the Department of Homeland Security created a booklet entitled *Active Shooter: How to Respond* (https://www.dhs.gov/xlibrary/assets/active_shooter_booklet.pdf). This document stresses the importance of creating an emergency action plan and conducting staff training exercises. As is recommended for other types of scenarios, the best training comes in the form of mock exercises so that staff can:

- Recognize the sound of gunshots;
- Learn reaction techniques based on different scenarios;
- Know how to react when law enforcement arrives on scene.

Over the past few years, the debate over whether firearms should be allowed on college campuses has intensified. Supporters of guns on campus argue that if students and staff are allowed to carry a firearm, they could potentially end the active shooter threat more quickly with defensive gun use. Those against allowing guns on college campuses argue that risk of collateral injury is high if individuals are returning gunfire in crowded buildings. Plus, when law enforcement arrives on scene, it would be difficult for the officers to ascertain who is the active shooter and who is the defensive shooter.

While all 50 states allow citizens who meet certain requirements to carry concealed weapons, college campuses were traditionally gun-free zones. This is no longer the case (see Table 13.3). Legislation is evolving annually, so it is important for staff and administrators to know the specific legislation that applies to their campus.

Table 13.3 Concealed Weapons on College Campuses by State

States that ban carrying a concealed weapon on a college campus	California, Florida, Georgia, Illinois, Louisiana, Massachusetts, Michigan, Missouri, Nebraska, Nevada, New Jersey, New Mexico, New York, North Carolina, North Dakota, Ohio, South Carolina, Tennessee, Wyoming
States that permit each college campus to decide whether to allow concealed weapons on campus	Alabama, Alaska, Arizona, Arkansas, Connecticut, Delaware, Hawaii, Indiana, Iowa, Kentucky, Maine, Maryland, Minnesota, Montana, New Hampshire, Oklahoma, Pennsylvania, Rhode Island, South Dakota, Vermont, Virginia, Washington, West Virginia
States that allow concealed weapons on public postsecondary campuses	Colorado, Idaho, Kansas, Mississippi, Oregon, Texas, Utah, Wisconsin

STUDENT UNREST

Student unrest on campus, such as that which began at the University of Missouri in 2015 and spread to other campuses, is not new. In the early 19th century, Harvard students blew up inhabited buildings on campus and Yale students celebrated Christmas by vandalizing campus buildings (Bledstein, 1976). The 1960s and early 1970s were a particularly active time for student unrest over issues such as civil rights, the Vietnam War, and other emerging social issues, such as conservation. Campus unrest and violence were so prevalent during this era that President Nixon convened the Scranton Commission to investigate dissent, disorder, and violence on campuses (Sorey & Gregory, 2010). Institutional commitment to making students world citizens (Lilley, Barker, & Harris, 2015) and students' access to diverse and conflicting viewpoints, free time to engage in socially conscious activities, and who are only on campus for a short time and want quick changes all but ensure that student activism and unrest will continue (Broadhurst, 2014).

While techniques for responding to student unrest, particularly incidents that are spiraling out of control and may become violent, may be similar to those for general crowd and riot control, campus officials would prefer to prevent such events. There are strategies that campus officials can consider to help avoid campus unrest. First, research suggests the campus culture does much to influence student activism (Van Dyke, 1998); therefore, institutions should develop cultures that support positive student activism. Holding frequent forums to allow administrators, students, and other stakeholders to address issues together contributes greatly to an open culture. Communicating social norms and modeling appropriate behavior that includes respecting all positions and discussing issues non-defensively helps students learn how to express concerns and address problems responsibly. Making these behaviors part of the campus culture can be helpful, since these behaviors can affect student behavior (Haines & Spear, 1996; Reilly & Wood, 2008).

Second, institutions can increase activism opportunities that provide students with university-sanctioned forums for addressing concerns, expressing ideas, and engaging in behaviors. This suggestion is important for a couple of reasons. Research suggests that many students tend to be apathetic about social issues (Wattenberg, 2007; U.S. Census Bureau, 2010) and are more aware of them than actively engaged with them, a behavior referred to as "slactivism" (Marichal, 2013) However, when a catalyzing event makes students feel that they should immediately respond to a cause, they are frequently unaware of how to do so appropriately. Rather, they tend to blindly follow the actions of others, known as the bandwagon effect (Xu et al., 2012). Moreover, by providing frequent structured activities related to social issues, such as resident hall floor meetings, campus forums, guest speakers, and service learning projects, institutions teach students constructive methods for addressing issues (Taha, Hastings, & Minei, 2015).

Finally, institutions should work to dissuade improper, illegal, and unsafe behavior associated with student demonstrations. Strong relationships between student groups and student affairs administrators, institutional security or police, and other safety officials can help educate students about laws and institutional rules and policies so that they can frame their activities. These strong relations can also provide communication avenues to help address rumors and misperceptions (Weinberg & Eich, 1978).

MEDICAL AID

The most important planning with regard to medical aid is developing relationships with the local emergency medical services (EMS) and with local hospitals. Whether it takes the form of a mutual aid agreement or a memorandum of understanding, a contract should be in place to specify how the local EMS will be used in the crisis management plan. Additionally, disaster drills should be held on an annual basis and should include the Incident Command Team, the EMS, local hospitals, and other appropriate public safety and state agencies. These training drills should be followed by a formal post-incident evaluation to assess the success of the drill and any problems that may have arisen.

Institutions take a variety of approaches to providing EMS. The many small and private institutions that exist in the United States generally rely upon local community EMS. In areas where there are well-equipped, well-staffed, and well-trained EMS units, high-quality treatment and care of pre-hospital injuries and reliable transport are reasonably assured. However, in rural areas, particularly those that may be staffed by volunteer EMS units, the service can be problematic.

A study conducted by the North Carolina Rural Health & Research Policy Centers highlighted two major problems with volunteer EMS units: recruitment/retention and training (Freeman, Rutledge, Hamon, & Slifkin, 2010). According to the study, most volunteer EMS organizations only offer basic life support services. Additionally, most of these organizations have difficulty recruiting and retaining trained volunteers, with approximately half of EMS organizations reporting that these problems are not improving or are worsening. Institutions located in areas that are serviced by volunteer EMS organizations will do well to partner with these organizations and support their training and recruitment/retention efforts.

More than 100 institutions have their own EMS unit. Many of these organizations are partnered with an EMS training/degree program and provide students with supervised practical experience. Other institutions have EMS units with a paid staff. The paid staff may work on their own, in conjunction with student employees or volunteers, or as a hybrid organization with police officers or firefighters cross-trained as emergency medical technicians or paramedics.

The level of service provided by these units also varies. Given that many are staffed by students who are in training, most offer only basic emergency services. Because of this, the institution must still have a relationship with community EMS units that are capable of providing advance emergency services and rapid emergency transport, such as by helicopter. Institutions with medical schools, medical centers, or hospitals may have EMS units that are capable of providing comprehensive services.

FIRE SUPPRESSION

While building codes have been steadily improving since the 1970s, the level of fire safety in older buildings is not equal to that of newer facilities. In older buildings, fires often result in a total loss due to a variety of factors including delay of discovery and alarm, lack of firewalls and/or compartmentalization, lack of automated sprinkler systems, lack of draft stopping and combustible attacks, and inadequate water supplies for manual fire suppression (FEMA, 2004).

The level of fire safety of older buildings must be evaluated and solutions must be developed to protect both life and property. According to FEMA (2004), the evaluation comprises three categories: fire safety, means of egress, and general safety. The evaluation of fire safety includes automatic fire detection, structural fire safety, and fire alarm and fire suppression systems. The means of egress portion of the evaluation includes the configuration, characteristics, and support features of the means of egress. Finally, the general safety section includes an evaluation of various fire safety and means of egress parameters.

When institutions consider upgrading existing facilities, the most effective method of providing fire protection is to install automatic fire sprinklers, but more cost-effective methods might include installing automatic fire alarms and detection, draft stopping in combustible attic spaces, and smoke and fire compartmentalization walls in occupied spaces.

Generally, the cost of fire suppression equipment and employing firefighters makes it cost prohibitive for institutions to have their own fire departments. However, many institutions have partnered with their local community fire department to enhance their capability to respond to fires and other emergencies on campus. For example, the University of New Hampshire has partnered with the City of Durham to jointly fund the area's paid fire department. In some areas, high-rise residence halls are the tallest structures, and institutions with these buildings have helped their local fire department acquire ladder or aerial platform trucks (Longwood University, 2005). Other institutions have partnered with fire departments to either contract or reimburse the fire department for calls to the campus.

Institutions can help decrease the response time for fire emergencies by having a fast-response vehicle on campus. A fast-response vehicle need not be a fully equipped pumper or ladder truck, but may consist simply of a pick-up truck with a small water tank, pump, and hose. Indeed, some manufacturers are producing miniature fire engines that are built on frames not much bigger than an oversized golf cart, but capable of carrying a foam container and firefighting equipment. In areas where the campus is served by a volunteer fire department, a fast-response vehicle can make up for some of the time it takes, after the alarm first sounds, for the first volunteers to arrive at the fire station, procure trucks, and respond to the scene. In situations where institution employees are volunteer firefighters, their access to a fast-response vehicle can save precious minutes in knocking down a fire in its infancy.

SEARCH AND RESCUE

The search-and-rescue function of a crisis management plan serves most frequently to ensure that the disaster areas have been successfully evacuated. In many jurisdictions, responsibility for search and rescue falls to the local fire department, although multiple public safety agencies may partner to ensure this function is addressed. In areas where there are actual search-and-rescue units, these teams may specialize in urban, mountain, ground, water, or vertical search and rescues.

Urban search and rescue frequently occurs in populated areas where there is a danger of people being trapped in collapsed buildings. These teams tend to be multi-jurisdictional and consist of personnel from different public safety organizations. Mountain search and rescue occurs in mountainous or rugged terrain where accessibility is difficult, often requiring specialized equipment and techniques. Ground search-and-rescue operations assist people who are lost or in distress on land or certain inland waterways. Although traditionally associated with woods, forests, and wilderness areas, ground search-and-rescue units can be used to locate lost children or elderly individuals suffering from Alzheimer's disease.

Water rescue is used to search for lost individuals on lakes or other large bodies of water. For institutions located on or near the coast of an ocean, this type of search and rescue may be referred to as air-sea rescue. Aircraft and boats are frequently used to search for lost individuals or rescue those in distress. Vertical rescue involves the use of ropes to rescue individuals who may be in distress in a location accessible only by rappelling or climbing. Vertical rescues can occur on cliffs, in elevator shafts, in silos, in wells, on towers, and in a variety of industrial settings.

CONTINGENCY PLANS

An integral part of crisis management is the development of a continuity-of-operations plan, which is designed to return the campus to normal operations after a disaster. While many institutions have plans that provide for three days of self-sufficiency, the U.S. Department of Homeland Security (2006) recommends developing a seven- to ten-day provision plan. Having access to stored provisions is particularly important during natural disasters, such as hurricanes and earthquakes, when the surrounding community has also been heavily impacted. With regard to the acquisition of food and supplies, campuses with national or regional food service contractors fare better than those who rely on local resources.

Other considerations in the formation of contingency plans include anticipating equipment needs. In many cases, backup generators are designed to provide power only for short periods of time. Additional generators may be needed in the event of a sustained and prolonged power outage. All generators should be located well above ground level to account for the potential of rising water levels. Likewise, patrol vehicles should be located out of flood zones during weather incidents so that they do not become inoperable.

Institutions rely heavily on wireless and online environments. Careful consideration should be given to the preservation of information technology functionality. One method of dealing with the potential loss of IT systems is to establish a "cold site" that is equipped with backup systems and where the IT personnel could relocate if the institutional site became inoperable. Alternatively, servers can be permanently located at an off-campus location to ensure the preservation of payroll operations, Web pages that can serve as sources of information, and other vital materials.

In the event of an evacuation, key personnel and administrators should account for their whereabouts to be reachable when decisions need to be made regarding post-incident operations.

CONCLUSION

This chapter discussed strategies to help institutions of higher education formulate and implement a successful crisis management plan. While every institution hopes that it will never have need of such a plan, this chapter sought to highlight important considerations that must be taken into account before disaster strikes to help those institutions that do face crises respond to these events effectively and resume normal operations in a timely manner.

DISCUSSION PROMPTS

1. How do you feel about the protests and civil disobedience that occur on campuses and the safety challenges that these events pose for higher educator administrators? What suggestions do you have for protecting students' First Amendment rights while ensuring everyone's safety during these events?

2. What are some of the most serious natural and technological threats to your higher education institution? How prepared do you feel your higher education institution is to respond to these threats?

3. What do you feel are the advantages and disadvantages for including off-campus officials on campus teams that address threats? What type of search-and-rescue team would best serve your higher education institution in an emergency and why? How do you feel the lack of grant funding for public safety on higher education institutions should be addressed?

4. What type of training on your higher education institution's emergency plan will best prepare your campus officials to respond to an emergency?

5. What do you feel is the best way for your higher education institution's administrators to provide emergency notifications and information to your institution's community?

6. What are the advantages and disadvantages to opt-in and opt-out emergency notification systems?

7. How important do you think the Clery Act statistics are to a student's choice of which higher education institution to attend?

8. What are the problems that rural higher education institutions face in ensuring quality emergency medical care for their community? How may these problems be addressed?

9. What are the advantages and disadvantages of having a fast-response fire vehicle at your higher education institution?

10. How frequently should higher education institutions practice building evacuations? What recommendations do you have for your higher education institution regarding the practice of building evacuation?

REFERENCES

Bledstein, B. (1976). *The culture of professionalism: The middle class and the development of higher education in America*. New York: Norton. doi: 10.2307/1979015

Broadhurst, C. (2014). Campus activism in the 21st century: A historical framing. *New Directions for Higher Education, 2014*(167), 3–15. doi:10.1002/he.20101

Brown, V. (2008). A campus plan for natural and man-made disasters. *The Police Chief, 75*(2), 66–71.

Burdick, C. (2006). The impact of governance, operations, and technology on critical emergency response: Lessons learned from Columbine. *Campus Law Enforcement Journal, 36*(6), 11–13.

Chachkes, E., Nelson, L., Portelli, I., Woodrow, R., Bloch, R., & Goldfrank, L. (2007). An organisational safety net in an academic setting: An evaluation. *Journal of Business Continuity & Emergency Planning, 2*(4), 403–415.

Commission on Accreditation for Law Enforcement Agencies. (2006). *Standards for law enforcement agencies: The standards manual of the Law Enforcement Agency Accreditation Program*. Fairfax, Virginia: CALEA.

Department of Homeland Security (DHS). (2008). *National incident management system.* Washington, DC: Department of Homeland Security.

Dialog. (2011). APR professor recognized for post-tornado volunteer service, August 29. Retrieved from http://dialog.ua.edu/2011/08/accolades-for-aug-29-2011/

Drake, K. (2014). *How often should I test my disaster recovery plan?* Retrieved from http://ongoingoperations.com/blog/2012/10/how-often-should-test-disaster-recovery-plan/

Federal Emergency Management Agency (FEMA). (2004). *Design guide for improving school safety in earthquakes, floods, and high winds.* Retrieved February 8, 2011 from http://www.fema.gov/library/view Record. do?id=1986

Federal Emergency Management Agency. (2008). *IS-100.HE: Introduction to the Incident Command System, ICS-100 for higher education instructor guide.* Retrieved February 8, 2011 from http://training.fema.gov/EMIWeb/IS/IS100HE/IG_PDF /ICS100 HigherEd_IG.pdf

Freeman, V., Rutledge, S., Hamon, M., & Slifkin, R. (2010). *Rural volunteer EMS: Reports from the field.* Chapel Hill: North Carolina Rural Health Research & Policy Centers.

Greenberg, S. (2005). *National summit on campus public safety: Strategies for colleges and universities in a homeland security environment.* Washington, DC: Office of Community Oriented Policing Services, U.S. Department of Justice.

Greenberg, S. (2007). State of security at US colleges and universities: A national stakeholder assessment and recommendations. *Disaster Medicine and Public Health Preparedness, 1*(1), S47–S50.

Haddow, G., Bullock, J., & Coppola, D. (2011). *Introduction to Emergency Management* (4th ed.). Boston: Elsevier.

Haines, M., & Spear, S. (1996). Changing the perception of the norm: A strategy to decrease binge drinking among college students. *Journal of American College Health, 45,* 134–140. PMID: 8952206.

Hale, J., Hale, D., & Dulek, R. (2006). Decision processes during crisis response: An exploratory investigation. *Journal of Managerial Issues, 18,* 301–320.

Healy, P. (2010). Sacred Heart University's online emergency plan boosts interagency cooperation. *Campus Law Enforcement Journal, 40*(1), 21–22.

Hodges, R. (2016). A primer on federal and state disaster funds and funding. In Alessandra Jerolleman & John J. Kiefer (Eds.), *Leveraging the private sector in emergency management* (pp. 51–80). Boca Raton, Florida: Taylor & Francis.

Jaeger, L., Deisinger, E., Houghton, D., & Cychosz, C. (2003). *A coordinated response to critical incidents.* Ames: Iowa State University.

Jones, A., & Grayson, W. (2011). Survivors emerge, fill up local shelters quickly. *Tuscaloosa News,* April 28. Retrieved from http://www.tuscaloosanews.com/article/20110428 /NEWS/110429648

Kausler Jr., D. (2011). UA Acts of Kindness fund gets $1 million donation from Alabama athletics department, May 6. Retrieved from http://www.al.com/sports/index.ssf/2011 /05/ua_acts_of_kindness_fun_gets_1.html

Lilley, K., Barker, M., & Harris, N. (2015). Exploring the process of global citizen learning and the student mindset. *Journal of Studies in International Education, 19*(3), 225–245. doi: 10.1177/1028315314547822

Longwood University (2005). Longwood University donates $100,000 to Town of Farmville for new ladder truck for Farmville Fire Department, August 5. Retrieved March 21, 2011 from http://www.longwood.edu/news/releases/laddertruck.html

Los Angeles County Sheriff's Department. (2014). *Community College Bureau Patrol Area.* Retrieved from shq. lasdnews.net/crimestats/yir9600/yir2014/maps/ccs.html

Mak, H., Mallard, A., Bui, T., & Au, G. (1999). Building online crisis management support using work flow systems. *Decision Support Systems, 25,* 209–224.

Marichal, J. (2013). Political Facebook groups: Micro-activism and the digital front stage. *First Monday, 18*(12). doi:10.5210/fm.v18i12.4653

Moats, J., Chermack, T., & Dooley, L. (2008). Using scenarios to develop crisis managers. *Advances in Developing Human Resources, 10,* 397–424.

Multihazard Mitigation Council (MMC). (2005). *Natural hazard mitigation saves: An independent study to assess the future savings from mitigation activities.* Washington, DC: National Institute of Building Sciences.

National Association of College and University Business Officers. (2009). *Results of the National Campus Safety and Security Project Survey.* Retrieved February 8, 2011 from http://www.nacubo.org/Documents/Initiatives/CSSPSurveyResults.pdf

National Weather Service (2004). *Hurricane Frances.* Retrieved March 11, 2011 from http://www4.ncsu.edu/~nwsfo/storage/cases/20040908/

Norris, S. (2011). *University emergency operations plan—Basic plan.* Retrieved March 15, 2011 from http://epo. appstate.edu/emergency-operations-plan-basic-plan

North Carolina Department of Crime Control & Public Safety. (2016). *Quick Facts.* Retrieved from https://www. ncdps.gov/Index2.cfm?a=000001,001148,001664

North Carolina General Statutes. (1999). Powers and duties of local health director. §130A-41.

Oliver, C. (2011). *Catastrophic disaster planning and response.* Boca Raton, Florida: CRC Press.

Perry, R., & Lindell, M. (2007). *Emergency planning.* Hoboken, New Jersey: Wiley.

Piotrowski, C., Armstrong, T., & Stopp, H. (1997). Stress factors in the aftermath of Hurricanes Erin and Opal: Data from small business owners. *Psychological Reports, 80,* 1387–1391.

Piotrowski, C., & Guyette, R. (2009). Lockdown: Reactions of university faculty and staff. *Organizational Development Journal, 27*(4), 93–99.

Pow, C. (2011). UA service projects to involve students in rebuilding Tuscaloosa, August 22. Retrieved from http:// blog.al.com/tuscaloosa/2011/08/ua_service_projects_to _involve.html

Reilly, A. (2008). The role of human resource development competencies in facilitating effective crisis communication. *Advances in Developing Human Resources, 10,* 331–351.

Reilly, D., & Wood, M. (2008). A randomized test of a small-group interactive social norms intervention. *Journal of American College Health, 57*(1), 53–60. doi: 10.3200/JACH.57.1.53-60

Roth, D. (2004). *Hurricane Frances rainfall.* Retrieved March 11, 2011 from http://www.hpc.ncep.noaa.gov/ tropical/ rain/frances2004.html

Smith, S., Kress, T., Fenstemaker, M., & Hyder, G. (2001). Crisis management preparedness of school districts in three southern states in the USA. *Safety Science, 39,* 83–92.

Sorey, K., & Gregory, D. (2010). Protests in the sixties. *College Student Affairs Journal, 28*(2), 184–206.

Staman, E., Katsouros, M., & Hach, R. (2009). The multi-dimension nature of emergency communications management. *EDUCAUSE Review, 44*(1), 48–62.

Taha, D., Hastings, S., & Minei, E. (2015). Shaping student activists: Discursive-sensemaking of activism and participation research. *Journal of the Scholarship of Teaching and Learning, 15*(6), 1–15. doi: 10.14434/josotl. v15i6.13820

Thrower, R., Healy, S., Margolis, G., Lynch, M., Stafford, D., & Taylor, W. (2008). *Overview of the Virginia Tech tragedy and implications for campus safety: The IACLEA blueprint for safer campuses.* Retrieved February 8, 2011 from http://www.iaclea.org/visitors /PDFs/VT-taskforce-report_ Virginia-Tech.pdf

U.S. Census Bureau. (2010). *The statistical abstract of the United States: 2012.* Retrieved from http://www.census. gov/library/publications/2011/compendia/statab/131ed.html

United States Department of Homeland Security, the Federal Bureau of Investigation, and the International Association of Chiefs of Police. (2006). *Campus public safety preparedness for catastrophic events: Lessons learned from hurricanes and explosives,* June. Retrieved February 8, 2011 from http://www.iaclea.org/visitors / PDFs /Hurricane2.pdf

Van Dyke, N. (1998). Hotbeds of activism: Locations of student protest. *Social Problems, 45*(1), 205–220.

Wang, J. (2008). Developing organizational learning capacity in crisis management. *Advances in Developing Human Resources, 10,* 425–445.

Wattenberg, M. (2007). *Is voting for young people?* New York: Pearson-Longman.

Weinberg, S., & Eich, R. (1978). Fighting fire with fire: Establishment of a rumor control center. *Communications Quarterly, 26*(3), 26–31.

Williams, J. (2009). *Active shooter: School safety considerations.* Retrieved February 8, 2011 from http://info. publicintelligence.net/laactive shootertactics.pdf

Xu, Q., Schmierbach, M., Bellur, S., Ash, E., Oeldorf-Hirsch, A., & Kegerise, A. (2012). The effects of "friend" characteristics on evaluations of an activist group in a social networking context. *Mass Communication & Society, 15*(3), 432–453. doi: 10.1080/15205436.2011.583862

ABOUT THE EDITORS

Kristina Powers serves as Associate Vice President of Institutional Research Services at Bridgepoint Education, the parent company of Ashford University (San Diego), a national IPEDS trainer, a Research Fellow on Student Achievement with the WASC Senior College and University Commission, and the 2016 President of the California Association for Institutional Research (CAIR). Prior to working at Bridgepoint, Kristina was Assistant to the President for Strategic Research & Analysis at Valdosta State University (Georgia), where she served as the head of institutional research. Other higher education roles have included, lead author for the *Statements of Aspirational Practice for Institutional Research* with the Association for Institutional Research (AIR), teaching and developing institutional research and higher education administration courses at three institutions, conducting policy education research at the Florida Legislature, consulting services at MGT of America, and an admissions advisor at the State University of New York, College at Brockport. Dr. Powers earned her doctorate in Educational Leadership and Policy Studies with a concentration in Higher Education Policy and a Master's in Higher Education Administration from Florida State University, and a Bachelor's from the State University of New York, College at Brockport. She publishes and presents in the areas of higher education administration and organization, institutional research, as well as student success with a focus on retention and graduation rates using national databases and institutional data.

Patrick J. Schloss served as the eighth president of Valdosta State University from 2008 to 2011. He was born in Harvey, Illinois on October 1, 1953. President Schloss' academic career includes appointments as a tenured professor and chair at Penn State and the University of Missouri. He is among the most prolific and influential scholars in special education, having authored 20 books and over 100 research publications. Prior to serving at VSU, Dr. Schloss was provost at Bloomsburg University of Pennsylvania from 1994 to 2004, and president at Northern State University in Aberdeen, South Dakota from 2004 to 2008.

ABOUT THE CONTRIBUTORS

Danielle Morgan Acosta serves as the Director of the Department of Student Government and is a doctoral student in the higher education student affairs program at Florida State University. Professionally she is actively involved in ACPA-College Student Educators, International. Her ten years of work experience focuses on advising student organizations, student advocacy, and inclusive leadership.

Janet Park Balanoff is the Associate Vice President for Equity and Diversity/Title IX, Seminole State College of Florida. She leads programs promoting equity measures to ensure a climate of achievement for students and employees, including the College's actions to prevent and correct sexual violence under Title IX. Since Ms. Balanoff arrived two years ago, the College has received national and regional diversity awards including Corporate Champion of Change, Multicultural Leadership, and the Higher Education Excellence in Diversity award (twice). Ms. Balanoff holds an M.S. in Public Administration from Florida State University and a B.S. in journalism from the University of Florida.

Steven T. Breslawski is Associate Professor of Management and MIS and former Head of the Business Degree Programs at the College at Brockport, State University of New York. He is perennially immersed in the strategic planning, curriculum development, accreditation, and assessment activities of the school. Recipient of the SUNY Chancellor's Award for Excellence in Teaching, Dr. Breslawski's research pursuits include topical research in business as well as business education research in the areas of student motivation, student quality metrics, and analysis of assessment outcomes.

Cyndy Caravelis is an Associate Professor of Criminology and Criminal Justice at Western Carolina University. She received her doctorate from Florida State University. Her research interests include the relationship between social threat and social control, the effect of inequality on crime, social justice and the death penalty. She is the lead author of the book *Social Justice, Criminal Justice* and her research has appeared in journals such as *Justice Quarterly* and the *Journal of Quantitative Criminology*. Additionally, her field experience includes working as a legislative analyst for Florida's Commission on Capital Cases, as a crime intelligence analyst for the Florida Department of Law Enforcement, and as an academic instructor in both male and female correctional institutions.

Julie Carpenter-Hubin is Assistant Vice President for Institutional Research and Planning at The Ohio State University. Julie represents Ohio State to the Association of American Universities Data Exchange, and is a past chair of the Exchange's governing council. She is a past President of the Association for Institutional Research, and she served on the National Research Council's Data Panel, which advised the NRC's Committee on an Assessment of Research-Doctorate Programs on the questionnaires used in the assessment. Julie's research interests include higher education performance measurement and its use in developing improvement strategies.

Christopher Ferland is the Assistant Vice President for Institutional Research and Effectiveness at Georgia College. He serves as co-facilitator of the strategic plan and a member of the enrollment management team. He is the current president of the University System of Georgia Institutional Research and Planning advisory committee. He was previously a senior research associate for the University System of Georgia. He has also held the position of associate director of enrollment management at the University of Georgia. Ferland received his Ph.D. in higher education at the University of Georgia; a Master of Science in applied economics and a Master of Science in applied sociology from Clemson University; and his Bachelor of Arts in sociology from the University of Rhode Island.

Angela E. Henderson is Associate Director of Institutional Research & Effectiveness at Stetson University. Her areas of expertise and interest include data-driven analyses, data visualization, and development of tools to facilitate institutional research and accreditation processes. She has served as issue co-editor and author for *New Directions of Institutional Research* and presented sessions on organizing assessment and compliance processes at conferences including the Association for Institutional Research, the Southern Association of Colleges and Schools, and the Southern Association for Institutional Research. She is currently pursuing a Ph.D. in Education and Human Resource Studies, with a specialization in Higher Education Leadership at Colorado State University.

Carrie E. Henderson is the Interim Vice President for Institutional Advancement at Florida State College at Jacksonville. In this role, Carrie provides leadership over strategic planning, resource development, marketing and communications, service learning and civic engagement, institutional analytics and research, state and federal reporting, and accreditation and outcomes assessment. Carrie holds a Ph.D. in higher education administration and graduate certificate in institutional research from Florida State University.

Shouping Hu is the Louis W. & Elizabeth N. Bender Endowed Professor and the director of the Center for Postsecondary Success at Florida State University. His research interests examine issues related to college access and success, student engagement, and higher education policy. Dr. Hu currently serves as an editorial/advisory board member of *Journal of Higher Education, Educational Researcher, Research in Higher Education*, and *Journal of College Student Development*.

Jennifer Iacino serves as Advising Specialist and Coordinator of the Golden Guarantee Programs at Tallahassee Community College. She previously served the Student Affairs divisions of Berkeley College, Florida State University, and Johnson & Wales University. Her professional experiences include areas of Title IX and ADA compliance, policy and program development, student organization and academic advising, campus event and facilities planning, women in STEM programs, program assessment and evaluation, and promoting student access and transfer opportunities. Additionally, her research interests include issues related to faculty development, student engagement via online technologies and social media, institutional culture, and the application of various qualitative methodologies. Dr. Iacino recently developed a model, Faculty Development for Interdisciplinary Team-Teaching, to support collaborative innovations in sustainability curriculum.

Thomas C. Johnson is an Assistant Professor in the Emergency and Disaster Management Program in the Criminology and Criminal Justice Department at Western Carolina University. Dr. Johnson previously served for 35 years in the municipal and campus law enforcement profession including 15 years as a police chief for the Marshall University, Mississippi State University, and Western Carolina University police departments. Dr. Johnson's research interests are in emergency management technology and emergency management issues for special populations.

Regina Luttrell is an Associate Professor at Eastern Michigan University where she researches, publishes, and discusses public relations, social media, and the Millennial generation. Prior to entering the educational field, Luttrell spent the first half of her career in corporate public relations and marketing. Her extensive background includes strategic development and implementation of public relations and social media, advertising, marketing and corporate communications. She has led multiple re-branding campaigns, designed numerous websites, managed high-level crisis situations, and garnered media coverage that included hits with the New York Times, the CBS Evening News, and the Associated Press. She is the author of *Social Media: How to Engage, Share, and Connect* and co-author of *The Millennial Mindset: Unraveling Fact from Fiction.* Twitter: @ginaluttrell

Valerie Martin Conley is Dean of the College of Education and Professor of Leadership, Research, and Foundations at the University of Colorado, Colorado Springs. She previously served as Department Chair of Counseling and Higher Education, Director of the Center for Higher Education, and Professor of Higher Education and Student Affairs at Ohio University. Dr. Conley has served as principal investigator for two National Science Foundation funded research projects: "Academic Career Success in Science and Engineering-Related Fields for Female Faculty at Public Two-Year Institutions" and "Collaborative Research: Increasing Minority Presence within Academia through Continuous Training (IMPACT)". She is a TIAA-CREF Institute Research Fellow, received the Ohio University Outstanding Graduate Faculty Award in 2007, and served on the Association for Institutional Research Board of Directors. Dr. Conley has published widely on faculty issues and is nationally recognized for her expertise on faculty retirement.

Charles Mathies is the Senior Expert (adviser) in the Division of Strategic Planning and Development at the University of Jyväskylä, Finland. He has held multiple university management positions in Europe and the United States. Dr. Mathies has published, taught, and facilitated workshops globally on topics ranging from strategic planning and institutional data management to university rankings and performance evaluations of student, staff, and research. In 2015 he was named a Global Ambassador for the Association for Institutional Research (AIR) Forum. He is also a co-founder and partner in an international higher education consulting firm specializing in data management and assisting universities in linking data to strategic decision making.

Karen McGrath is Professor of Communication at the College of Saint Rose in Albany, NY for 19 years. She co-authored *The Millennial Mindset: Unraveling Fact from Fiction* (2016) with Dr. Regina Luttrell and is currently working on a new co-authored book about the craft beer industry to be released in late 2017. Her areas of expertise include media representations of diverse audiences including her most recent academic journal publication, "Communication Deficiencies Provide Incongruities for Humor: The Asperger's-like Case of *The Big Bang Theory*'s Sheldon Cooper." She has also been the social media manager of her department's online presence and is currently creating an App specific to her department's and students' needs. Twitter: @karenmcgrath

Christopher A. Medjesky is an Assistant Professor of Communication at the University of Findlay. His research focuses on the relationship between rhetoric and media. This scholarship often focuses on the significance of humor, intertextuality, and interactivity in rhetoric. Twitter: @medjesky.

Kerry Brian Melear is Professor of Higher Education at the University of Mississippi, and his areas of expertise include college and university legal, financial, and public policy concerns. He was a member of the Board of Directors of the Education Law Association, and is currently a member of the Author's Committee of *West's Education Law Reporter*, the editorial board of the *Journal of Cases in Educational Leadership*, and serves as the Book Review Editor for the *Journal of Law and Education*. He was selected as the University of Mississippi School of Education's Researcher of the Year in 2007, 2010, 2013, and Teacher of the Year in 2015.

Andrew Morse is director for policy research and advocacy with NASPA – Student Affairs Administrators in Higher Education's Research and Policy Institute. Prior to joining NASPA, Morse served state higher education agencies in Tennessee and Florida where he worked to inform key stakeholders on issues related to access, completion, and the post-college outcomes of baccalaureate graduates. At NASPA, Morse manages a portfolio of policy and research projects to advance the postsecondary success of students and to elevate the student affairs perspective in national policy conversations.

Amelia Parnell is Vice President for Research and Policy at NASPA – Student Affairs Administrators in Higher Education, where she directs the Research and Policy Institute (RPI), which links research, policy, and effective student affairs practice in support of student success. Prior to her arrival at NASPA, Amelia was Director of Research Initiatives at the Association for Institutional Research (AIR), where she conducted two national studies related to future directions of the institutional research function. Amelia's current research portfolio includes studies on the leadership attributes of college presidents and vice presidents, documenting and assessing co-curricular learning, and assessment and evaluation in student affairs. She has taught graduate courses in the higher education department at Florida State University.

Kent J. Smith, Jr. currently serves as President and full Professor with tenure at Langston University. Dr. Smith has co-authored multiple publications. The topics of his most recent publications include cyberbullying in higher education, and managing human resources at colleges and universities. Dr. Smith received his Bachelor of Science and Master of Education from Southern University. His Doctor of Philosophy degree was conferred from Colorado State University in Education and Human Resource Studies. Dr. Smith resides in Langston, OK with his five children: Morgan, Trey, Tyler, Trent and Tanner.

Lydia Snover has been with MIT since 1971 and is currently the Director of Institutional Research at MIT. She received a BA in Philosophy and an MBA, both from Boston University. The first part of her career at MIT was spent in departmental and research administration in several academic departments. Lydia established the first institutional research office at MIT in 1986. The MIT Office of Institutional Research has a broad range of responsibilities, including maintenance of institutional databases on faculty, graduate admissions, honors and awards, and faculty productivity; survey research, responding to external requests for institutional data, distribution of MITx data, preparation of briefing documents for external review committees and support for ABET and NEASC reaccreditation. The office provides analytical support for senior administrators, the Office of the Dean for Graduate Education, the deans of undergraduate education and student life as well as academic departments and programs, research laboratories and centers. Lydia is a member of MIT's Institution Review Board on Animal Care. Lydia represents MIT in the Association of American Universities Data Exchange (AAUDE) and the Consortium on the Financing of Higher Education (COFHE) Institutional Research Group.

Monoka Venters is an educational consultant working to enable the use of actionable research to increase postsecondary student success for low-income students. She received her Ph.D. in higher education administration from Florida State University, a J.D. from Washington and Lee University School of Law, and a B.A. in English from Furman University. Prior to becoming a consultant, she worked at the State University System of Florida Board of Governors as a senior policy advisor to the chancellor and the Board, a policy analyst in the academic and student affairs unit, and a research associate for the general counsel. Her research interests include understanding the factors behind the development of education policy and the legal aspects of higher education, including federal policies designed to assist low-income students prepare for and enroll in college.

INDEX

Note: Page numbers in **bold** refer to figures, page numbers in *italic* refer to tables.